WARM
& SNUG

WARM & SNUG

THE HISTORY OF THE BED

LAWRENCE WRIGHT

SUTTON PUBLISHING

This book was first published in 1962 by
Routledge & Kegan Paul Limited. This edition published by
arrangement with Taylor & Francis Books Ltd.

This edition first published in 2004 by
Sutton Publishing Limited · Phoenix Mill
Thrupp · Stroud · Gloucestershire · GL5 2BU

British Library Cataloguing in Publication Data
A catalogue record for this book is available from the British Library

ISBN 0 7509 3728 9

Printed and bound in Great Britain by
J.H. Haynes & Co. Ltd, Sparkford.

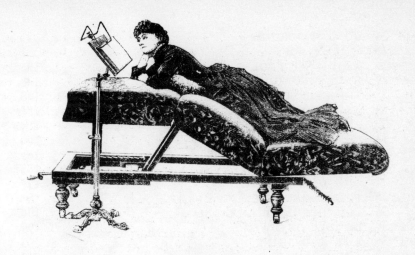

Contents

Author's Preface

FROM nearly all social history and biography, one third of the story is missing. This book sets out to fill the gap—a gap of about eight hours in every day, hours which need by no means be uneventful or without significance. Keen observers like Boswell or Creevey note the minutiae of human behaviour right up to the moment of saying good night, but we do not meet their subjects again until breakfast-time. Pepys, Aubrey, Saint-Simon, Casanova and Mayhew are exceptional in that they often do take us into the bedroom; Horace Walpole and Fanny Burney seldom; most others, never. It is as if man ceased to exist overnight. But to venture upstairs is to satisfy more than mere keyhole curiosity. No human subject can be seen steadily and seen whole, if we are denied a glimpse of the room where he is conceived, is born, makes love, and dies. One line from Pepys such as

I had the boy up tonight for his sister to teach him to put me to bed

is worth a page describing his daily duties at the Admiralty. Thackeray portrayed *Le Roi Soleil* in two parallel drawings, firstly in his robes and trappings of state, and then in his underwear; a salutary debunking such as will often recur here, as when we find Louis XIII winding his alarm-clock and complaining testily that somebody has been fiddling with it; the Dauphin falling out of bed; Mr. Gladstone drinking from his hot-water bottle, before rising, the tea kept in it overnight. The very attitude in which man lies abed can reflect his attitude to life—compare the monarch propped up stiffly in his *lit de parade* with the beatnik flopping prone on his 'pad'. The valet in his little wheeled truckle-bed underneath his master's four-poster demonstrates that he knows his place (and literally truckles to his master). The royal cocotte is attended at her ceremonial *coucher* by a circle of adoring gallants, while the nun furtively disrobes by a process designed to deny her one glimpse of her own person. The *chaise longue* in the perfumed alcove, and the great brass double bed of the nineteenth century, likewise illustrate two quite different attitudes to sex. The purpose, then, is to take a new slant on human behaviour; the subject is people rather than furniture. Although the carpenter, the joiner, the cabinet-maker and the industrial designer will come in, the shape of the bed itself will be interesting chiefly in what it reveals of manners. So with the shape of the surrounding bedroom, from which the bed cannot be considered apart. This room, in its turn, must be seen as part of a house, and thus we must touch on the history of domestic planning. The plan grows around daily habits and relationships, and adapts itself as these change: the Saxons huddle together in the fug of the common hall; the Elizabethans circulate unconcerned through each other's bedchambers; we demand isolated boxes for our rest. The digging up of old foundations would be a dull game if it revealed only the facts of building construction. A house plan is human behaviour in diagrammatic form. The history of the bed is thus interwoven with the histories of social, sexual and sanitary attitudes, of architecture and building, of interior decoration and furniture.

At the near end of the row of beds of all shapes and sizes that runs down towards the dark end of the long dormitory of history, not much space can be allotted to those of our century. They are too close, and must not be allowed to spoil the perspective. There is no future in writing the history of the present before it is past.

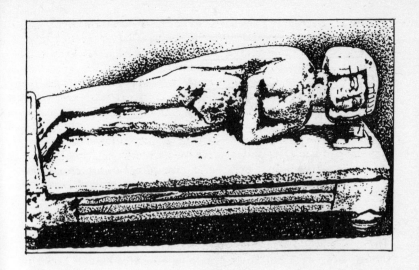

1

The Bed of Cleopatra

IT would be easier to discuss the typical bedroom of ancient Egypt if there were such a thing as a typical house plan, but the excavated houses vary widely, and their interior details have to be deduced from paintings. The house of Meryre the High Priest, at Tel-el-Amarna, has an outer court, a vestibule, a large hall used for dining, and eight other rooms; but it seems to have only one bedroom, suggesting that most of the household slept in the hall. This bedroom is entered through a small ante-chamber, and it has a large couch-bed piled high with bolsters. There are no women's apartments, nor should there be in a High Priest's house. The larger house of Ey, in the same town, is better bedded. Ey was an important man at court, and although he too was a priest, his religious rank was not so high as to deny him a wife and a harem too. His big 'master bedroom' has a huge four-poster bed, and three small beds which may be for children. There are four sets of women's apartments, each with two bedrooms, and two small bedrooms adjoin the servants' hall. In the house of the Vizier Nekht, the best bedroom has its walls specially thickened around the raised platform where the bed stands, to insulate it from the midnight cold and midday heat.

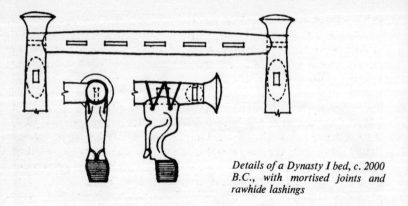

Details of a Dynasty I bed, c. 2000 B.C., with mortised joints and rawhide lashings

We know much more about the furniture than about its setting. The native wood was poor stuff. Ancient Egypt had no forests, though trees were not so rare as now—the tree-feeding camel is much to blame. But the granaries held vast surplus stocks, available as capital to finance imports of fine hardwoods and metals, especially copper. This capital also allowed the support of full-time luxury craftsmen who need not grow their own food. The court, the priesthood and the all-too-prosperous official class provided the necessary wealthy customers. Their furniture shows a standard of craftsmanship unequalled in Europe until the Renaissance.

The earliest known Egyptian beds are made of palm-sticks, or of wicker formed with the mid-ribs of palm leaves. To us they would be light couches; they resemble the Indian *charpoy*. The basic needs of man do not change: this primitive bed survived into World War II, when thousands on the accepted local pattern were hastily put together for the use of British troops reposing by the Suez Canal, and should have proved comfortable, had they not become so quickly bug-ridden that they had to be burned by the ton.

There seems to have been no distinction between the day couch and the night bed, though to us these offer different kinds of repose. There was usually a foot-panel to the bed, but no head-panel because there were no pillows as we know them. The parts of the bed were joined by lashings of linen cord or rawhide thongs, passing through slots in the legs, making a resilient joint that could stand the irregular strains imposed by the most plump and restless of occupants. In later work there are mortise-and-tenon joints. Angle-pieces were sometimes cut from natural L-shaped branches. The home-grown timber, being too fibrous, knotty and small for good surface work, was veneered with ebony or ivory, using casein glue made from milk.

2

Wooden furniture was often painted. The colour schemes were restricted, not unhappily, by the pigments to hand: the ochres offered a wide range of red, orange, yellow and brown, and there were plenty of blacks and whites; but greens and blues were limited. Royal beds might be sheathed in gold.

The supporting under-mattress was woven from cord and then lashed into place, or woven directly over the bed-frame, a method of about 5000 B.C. that is still in use in the Sudan. The 'pillows' were hard head-rests, usually of wood but sometimes of ivory or alabaster, richly decorated; they were high and curved, seemingly designed to protect an elaborate coiffure overnight. There was a folding head-rest made for travellers. Of the bedclothes, not a rag remains.

Queen Hetep-Heres of the Old Kingdom, about 2690 B.C., slept her last sleep among some fine bedroom furniture. Though the wooden core of her elegant bed has decayed, its gold plating has preserved the form, and the construction can be deduced. It has leonine legs, and a detachable footboard with an inlaid panel in a tenoned frame.

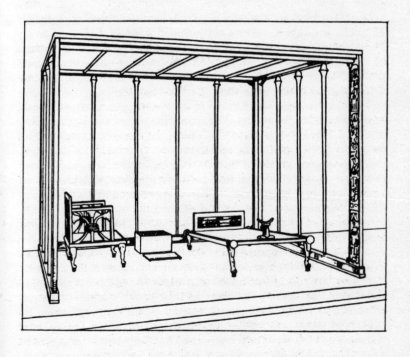

Bedchamber of Queen Hetep-Heres, c. 2690 B.C.

3

The tent-like portable canopy for hanging curtains over the bed-space could be dismantled for transport, and the various parts fitting into each other, like those of the bed, were copper-sheathed at the joints, and ingeniously stapled together by slotted bolts and wedges. The quick assembly of strong light-weight members is as well-contrived as in many a modern aircraft. The curtains were probably of mosquito netting. Herodotus tells us that even the common people used these:

... the contrivances which they use against gnats are the following. In the parts of Egypt above the marshes the inhabitants pass the night upon lofty towers, which are of great service, as the gnats are unable to fly to any height on account of the winds. In the marshy country, where there are no towers, each man possesses a net instead. By day it serves him to catch fish, while at night he spreads it over the bed in which he is to rest, and creeping in, goes to sleep underneath. The gnats, which, if he rolls himself up in his dress or in a piece of muslin, are sure to bite through the covering, do not so much as attempt to pass the net.

The furniture in the tomb of that over-publicised teenager Tutankhamen (about 1350 B.C.) included literally heaps of beds. These differ from earlier types in the use of curves, achieved perhaps by bending or cutting; more probably by using naturally shaped timbers. Their curves, together with the light construction and the use of animal forms, give them a lithe feline elegance. One ebony bed has not warped appreciably in thirty-three centuries. Its cross-members are deeply concave, to accept the sag of the woven string mattress. The legs are inlaid with ivory, and the gussets reinforcing the joints are of gold-sheathed hardwood. The panel at the foot, decorated with a group of household gods in triplicate, is of ivory, ebony and gold. (The god Bes, with his simian scowl, protruding tongue, and bow legs, looks rather a frightening overnight companion, but he was in fact the god of domestic fun, and is meant to be amusing—perhaps Walt Disney's lovable Goofy in a modern night-nursery would seem sinister to an ancient Egyptian.) From the same tomb comes another bed, of light wood painted white, made to fold up on bronze hinges, and easily carried by one man. There are three great gilt couches with their sides carved in the form of elongated animals—a lion, a cow, and one that may be either a hippopotamus or a crocodile. Each is made in four sections for carrying, joined by hooks and staples. There are head-rests of lapis lazuli faience, and of turquoise blue glass, and one made from only two large pieces of ivory. The skill of the ivory-carvers of Syria and Phoenicia is mentioned in the annals of the Egyptian kings, and in the Bible. The

4

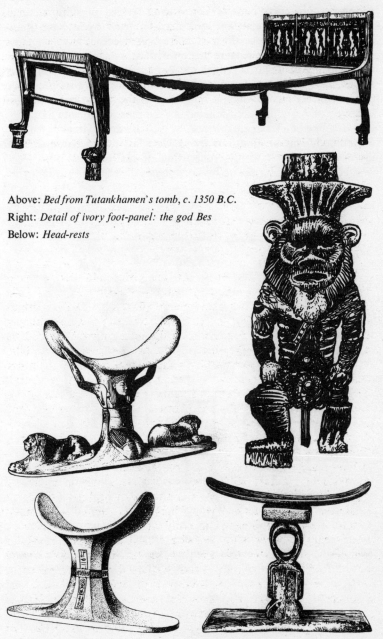

Above: *Bed from Tutankhamen's tomb, c. 1350 B.C.*
Right: *Detail of ivory foot-panel: the god Bes*
Below: *Head-rests*

prophet Amos uses 'beds of ivory' as a symbol of sinful luxury. Ivory panels of Phoenician workmanship from Syria have been identified as bed-panels. From their erotic subjects it has been supposed that some of these were made for ritual marriage-beds used in the worship of Astarte (Ishtar or Ashtaroth of the Bible), the Phoenician goddess of fertility. Phoenician work has also been detected in a bed upon which a sculptor has put Ashur-bani-pal, the last king of Assyria; as Sardanapalus, 'the most effeminate and corrupt of a line of effeminate princes', he went down in Greek legend as the embodiment of luxurious living. The last act of Sardanapalus involved the simultaneous combustion of no less than 150 beds, whereon he and his wife and his concubines died in his suicidal pyre.

King Ashur-bani-pal, alias Sardanapalus, dines alone in bed, according to custom, while his wife (not, as she might seem, a bearded lady), sits apart

6

2
Biblical Beds

THE Hebrews borrowed freely from the forms of their neighbour nations, and particularly from Egypt during their long sojourn there; Moses was 'learned in all the wisdom of the Egyptians'. A bed in the *Book of Proverbs* is decked 'with coverings of tapestry, with carved works, with fine linen of Egypt'. But when we have sorted out, from the many mentions of beds in the Old Testament, the few that are not merely incidental to its favourite themes of sloth, adultery, incest and murder, we are left with little information. In the story of Judith, who got Holofernes drunk—'he drank much more wine than he had drunk at any time in the day since he was born'—and cut off his head while he was in bed, and put it in her bag of meat, and then went to prayer, all 'for the exaltation of Jerusalem', we learn of the bed only that it was in a tent, and had a canopy and pillars. Solomon's bed was of cedar of Lebanon; the pillars were of silver, and the bottom—whatever that may mean—was of gold. Everyday bedroom furnishing, that might be of any century, is found in *Chronicles*: the wealthy Shunamite woman built for the prophet Elias 'a chamber on the wall, and set therein a bed, a table, a stool and a candlestick'. The 45th Psalm sings of ivory 'wardrobes', but we defer discussion of this word of many meanings. The *Book of Esther* mentions Persian beds of gold and silver. A unique bed of the Old Testament, in that it was of iron, was that of Og the King of Bashan. It measured 9 cubits by 4 cubits,

7

which if you read the ordinary cubit was 15 ft. by 6 ft. 8 in., and seems adequate, but if you read the 'royal cubit', was 16 ft. 10½ in. by 7 ft. 6 in. The bed was already a status symbol, for this one was carried off and preserved as a trophy of war, and we must hope that it was collapsible. There was an odd bedroom in the Tower of Babel; for this Herodotus is the authority:

. . . on the topmost tower there is a spacious temple, and inside that temple stands a couch of unusual size, richly adorned, with a golden table by its side. There is no statue of any kind set up in the place, nor is the chamber occupied at nights by any one but a single native woman, who, as the Chaldeans, the priests of this god, affirm, is chosen for himself by the deity out of all the women of the land. They also declare—but I for my part do not credit it—that the god comes down in person into this chamber, and sleeps upon the couch. This is like the story told by the Egyptians of what takes place in their city of Thebes, where a woman always passes the night in the temple of the Theban Jupiter.

Whether the chosen lady guest really enjoyed the embraces of the god, or dreamed that she did, or whether the priest put on the appropriate hat and ensured by proxy that faith endured, we do not know.

As for the New Testament: apart from the man who was commanded to take up his bed and walk (which was supposed by at least one schoolboy, familiar with only one kind of bed, to have been a spectacular climax to the miracle) we can but note the odd fact that the Saviour, though he is born in a manger and is once found asleep in a boat, is never mentioned as going to bed.

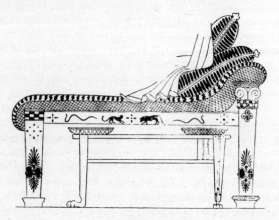

Greek couch and table

8

3

Homer Nods

HOMER tells us a lot about the beds and bedrooms of his
time, though we are vague as to when his time was—
somewhere between the sixth and ninth centuries B.C. The
society he describes is an aristocratic one, of wealthy land-
owners and shipowners. He gives us details of four houses which
no doubt have some foundation in reality: those of Priam in the
Iliad, and of Alcinous, Menelaus and Odysseus in the *Odyssey*. The
Greek house plan had evolved from the round nomadic hut with a
conical roof. From this it developed into a straight-sided plan with
the entrance at one end and a semi-circular apse at the other, partitioned off as a sleeping-chamber (*thalamos*). Next the apse was
squared, and the whole plan became rectangular, with a dominant
hall (*megaron*) and a low attached bedchamber. A great house would
be a complex of living-rooms, sleeping quarters, stables and store-
houses, arranged round courtyards. (In the palace of the prolific
Priam there were fifty rooms for his sons, and twelve for his married
daughters.) The *megaron* with its hearth was the heart of the dwelling. The bedroom of the master of the house was often in the women's
quarters.

Odysseus' home is not a palace, but more like a country manor.
A do-it-yourself man, he builds his own bed about the trunk of an
olive tree, shaping it to form the base. Next to his bedroom is a
bathroom, fitted with tubs. Penelope's bedroom, away from the
women's quarters where the concubines and servants live, is on a
terrace above the *megaron* and is reached by an outside stair. The
bedroom of Telemachus, the only son, is also upstairs, 'in the highest
part of the building'. There is a guest-bed in a 'coved entry', and the

housemaids range other beds under the 'sun-porch'. A bedroom, like most other rooms, was lit only through its large and lofty doorway, the double doors being usually left open, but guarded at night by servants watching or sleeping outside. When Nausicaa retired to bed, a fire was lighted in her room. Meanwhile the bondmen slept by the hearth in the hall, as they were to do for centuries throughout Europe.

The Greeks led an austere home life. The rich did not display their possessions, for the state enjoyed the right to own all property. In Athens *hoi polloi* had the upper hand, and understood 'the squeezing of the rich like sponges'; ours is not the first Age of the Common Man. Fine furniture was made chiefly for the temples and other public buildings. A bedroom would hold little more than the bed; perhaps a few coffers and light chairs. Following oriental forms, the bed (*kline*), like the Egyptian type, was a light couch with short legs, easily moved about. Odysseus' fixed 'treen' bed was exceptional, and by no means so rustic as it might sound, for it was encrusted with silver, gold and ivory. Homer gives us the name of the craftsman Icmalius who made Penelope's couch of like materials. He describes the bedclothes repeatedly, and almost with relish: the stuffed mattress, dyed purple; the linen sheet, as used by Odysseus even on shipboard; the 'choice fleeces' and 'lovely purple blankets covered smoothly with rugs, and thick woollen cloaks on top of all'. Nausicaa's laundry list includes a set of 'glossy bed-covers'. We are even told that Telemachus' bedroom door has a bolt, and that beside his 'fretted, inlaid bedstead' there is, rather oddly in Lawrence's translation, one 'clothes peg'. But Homer's luxuries are hardly typical. It was not until the decadent days that glossy bed-covers became common, and that the Sybarites slept on beds of roses and would have no cocks to crow within earshot.

The bedgoing of the Spartan soldier was subject to Spartan rules. When eligible at the age of 20, he joined a squad of fifteen men who shared one tent until the age of 30. If married, he could visit his wife briefly on a 'late pass' after supper, but he could not 'sleep out' until he was 30 and a full citizen.

In death, the Greek was exposed on a ceremonial bed—Hector, for nine days, and Achilles (who had however been roughly embalmed) for seventeen.

In Crete, among the splendid if somewhat over-restored remains of the great palace of King Minos at Knossos, the search for beds is disappointing. We know only that there were suites of bedrooms, lit by internal courts to avoid the fierce winter winds and blazing summer sun, with bathrooms and even water-closets adjoining, all magnificently frescoed; but the beds and bedclothes are dust.

10

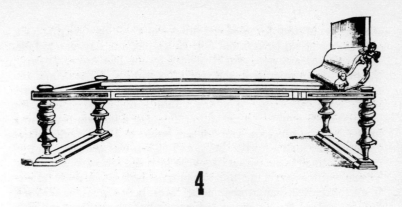

4

Roman Repose

THE Romans learned many of their ways from Greece, and for a long time they showed a Grecian simplicity in their home life. Only after they had conquered 'the world' did military habits and austere living give way to oriental luxury. Even then, the private houses (*domus*) in Rome were far fewer than the high blocks of poor apartment houses (*insulae*). The aristocratic mansions of Pompeii and Herculaneum are no guide to the general standard.

The private house followed a set plan dictated by custom. Two square courts surrounded by arcades were open to the air in the centre, but had awnings for summer and winter. The *atrium* was the main court, in which were the *penates* or household gods, the hearth which was the altar of family life, and opposite to the door the decorated *nuptiale* or marriage-bed. Should the householder die, he lay in state for seven days on the *lectus funebris*, clad in his best toga and surrounded by flowers and foliage, and on it was borne to his grave. The *atrium* was the general reception and living-room, rather like the Greek *megaron*, but it was not the dining-room. In the dining-room and the study were ornamented day-couches, for the Roman seems to have been able not only to read and write while reclining, but to eat elaborate meals without getting in a mess. In the dining-room there might be couches made for three or even for as many as six.

The bedrooms (*cubicula*) were small closets rather than rooms, closed by curtains or doors, disposed about the sides of the courts. Even in the best houses and in the best weather, the natural lighting must have been rather dim. The windows could be closed only by

11

shutters or curtains, for there was little or no sheet glass; so that heat, cold or rain could be kept out only by keeping out daylight and air. Larger apartments were usually divided by curtains into three parts: the first for an attendant, the second as a dressing-room, and the third for the bed (*cubile*) which was almost the only article of furniture there. Some people, like Pliny the Younger, might keep a chair for visitors; there might be a chest for valuables, a bedside mat, and a *lasanum* or chamber-pot. Only in one house, at Herculaneum, have rooms been found with two beds, and as this was probably an inn, there is nothing to show that they were intended for married couples. Roman writings never mention two or more beds in one room, except in the overcrowded apartment blocks. Most beds were single (*lectuli*), but as well as the ceremonial marriage-bed there were ordinary double beds (*lecti geniales*). Wooden beds were of oak, maple, cedar, terebinth or *arbor vitae*. Some, of inferior woods, had imitation graining, or fine figured veneers. Others were inlaid with tortoise-shell, silver or gold; some cast in bronze; Petronius describes the millionaire Trimalchio's bed as being of solid silver. Some had bronze feet and a wood frame; others ivory feet and a bronze frame. The under-mattress was still woven of webbing or cord. On this went a stuffed mattress (*torus*) and a bolster, both filled according to one's purse with straw, reeds, herbs, wool, feathers or swansdown. Between the next two coverings the sleeper lay, and finally there was a counterpane (*lodix*) or a gay damask quilt (*polymitum*). Silk had been rare in Greece, but it became common in Rome. Canopies, curtains and mosquito nets were sometimes fitted. Roman beds would not be wholly comfortable by modern standards, but they could look impressive. Martial tells of a gentleman who feigned illness and took to his bed so that his friends should see the marvellous bed-coverings he had received from Alexandria.

De Quincey says that the ancients 'went to bed like good boys, from seven to nine o'clock'. The habit in Rome was to rise at dawn, and even those who lay in late might start the day's work in bed by the light of a candle or *lucubrum*—whence the word 'lucubration'. Cicero, Horace, the Plinys, Marcus Aurelius and Vespasian are among the notable Romans who habitually lucubrated. The dark little *cubiculum* would not tempt the sluggard to breakfast in bed, and breakfast was seldom more than a glass of water. Getting up was a simple matter. The Roman did not strip at bedtime—nor does the oriental today. His various undergarments were worn day and night. He merely took off his toga, which he might put on the bed as an extra covering, and his sandals, under which he wore no socks, though he did sometimes wear a sort of puttees. 'They took good

12

care', says Carcopino, 'not to wear the toga when lying on their bed alive.' Putting on the toga properly would be the only troublesome task on rising. Modern actors and archaeologists alike have failed to find the secret: compare the elegant draping of Roman statues with the bundled figures of a modern play or pageant. If he cared to postpone this task, the rising Roman had merely to step into his sandals. He would not wash, knowing that he would go to the baths in the afternoon. In only one villa, that of Diomedes at Pompeii, has a wash-basin been found in a bedchamber. Even the emperor Vespasian could prepare himself unaided for his imperial duties within thirty seconds of rising. A lady's morning toilet took no longer. Like her husband, she slept in all her underwear: her panties (*strophium*), brassière (*mamillare*), corsets (*capitium*), and sundry tunics; sometimes to the final frustration of her husband she wore a mantle over all these on cold nights.

Even in these wealthier houses many elements of comfort as we know it were lacking, and life in the *insulae* was still less cosy. These high blocks often collapsed, or were torn down just in time to prevent it. Juvenal writes:

Who at cool Praeneste, or at Volsinii amid its leafy hills, was ever afraid of his house tumbling down? . . . But here we inhabit a city propped up for the most part by laths: for that is how the landlord patches up the crack in the old wall, bidding the inmates sleep at ease under the ruin that hangs above their heads.

In the better blocks, the ground floor might be let as a self-contained suite, and might have sub-floor heating, but the upper rooms were single 'bed-sitters', without heating, piped water or drainage. No person of mean degree would aspire to a proper bedstead, the privilege of the great. His bed might be no more than a masonry shelf along the wall, or a crude *grabatus* knocked together from a few timbers, covered with a pallet where bugs ran riot. Roman living is not necessarily synonymous with luxury.

13

Tenth-century bed as interpreted by Viollet-le-Duc

5

Byzantine Beds

FOR all those centuries between the breakdown or break-up of the ancient empires, and the reawakening of the Renaissance, household comfort hardly developed at all: the Ptolemies were as well bedded as the Plantagenets. The Merovingian kings of the sixth and seventh centuries did maintain some Roman ways, and rich furniture and precious stuffs are found in the Gallo-Roman period. Classical forms, with an Asiatic admixture, survived in Byzantine art. The Carolingians, from about A.D. 700 to 1000, imported furniture from the East, and their beds are much like couches of the old Roman kind. Such pictures of these beds as survive are mostly of religious subjects: some story from the Old Testament, a vision appearing to a saint in his sleep, or a Nativity in a nobly furnished stable. As evidence of contemporary design they must be taken with caution. So must another prolific source of information about early furniture, the drawings of Viollet-le-Duc, the nineteenth-century architect-antiquary. These are a shade too complete. He is never at a loss, however vague his sources, for the smallest detail of construction or decoration. There is a suspicious sameness about his supposedly factual records of the Gothic; he loves the grotesque, and can imbue even a bedstead with the kind of evil spirit that emanates from the famous gargoyle of Notre Dame.

14

With this reservation, we borrow his drawing of a tenth-century bed, based on a Bible illustration from the Imperial Library at Strasbourg. The metal bed, probably of bronze, is much higher at the head than at the foot, and the occupant sits rather than lies with a great pile of bolsters at his back. The mattress rests on a corded support of the ancient kind.

'Behold, it is the litter of Solomon; threescore mighty men are about it of the mighty men of Israel.'

In a twelfth-century picture of Solomon's bed, the mixed classical and oriental flavours are still evident. The perspective is odd, the lower half being drawn in side view, but the upper half as if looking downwards. As a result, it is not clear whether the framework seen behind Solomon's head represents a flat under-mattress of metal rods (consistent with the part seen at the other end) or a high bed-head (consistent with the propped-up attitude). It may be of course that the artist himself neither knew nor cared.

15

The death of Holofernes, as seen by the same artist, takes place under bed-curtains forming a sort of tent, hung from a central pole, with an opening for access at one side. This conforms with the Bible story in so far as Holofernes' bed was *in* a tent, but not necessarily with any twelfth-century practice.

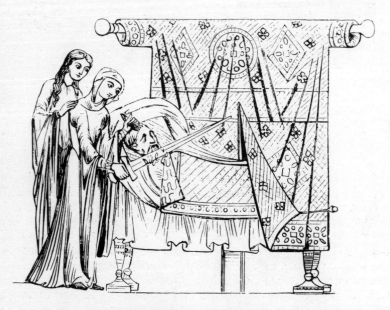

'*Then she came to the pillar of the bed, which was at Holofernes' head, and took down his fauchion from thence,*
'*And approached to his bed, and took hold of the hair of his head, and said, Strengthen me, O Lord God of Israel, this day.*
'*And she smote twice upon his neck with all her might, and she took away his head from him,*
'*And tumbled his body down from the bed, and pulled down the canopy from the pillars . . .*'
(Judith 13, 6–9)

Illustration opposite:
  '*Bedsteads*' *from an Anglo-Saxon MS. of the eleventh century*

16

6

Bench and Straw

WHEN the Saxons reached England, none of the old metal beds seem to have come with them; perhaps the last of them had been turned into weapons in some pre-invasion salvage drive. An echo of the Byzantine bed does occur in Anglo-Saxon pictures, but this need not mean that the artist ever saw such furniture; he would follow the accepted treatment for his traditional subject; that is to say, he would crib from an old picture. Among those who inherited the Roman ruins, the design of beds seems to have started afresh.

Pictures and descriptions of houses in Anglo-Saxon documents should not be taken too literally. The Saxons tend to boast, whether in their cups or not. They may well have depicted more ashlar walls and tiled roofs than they ever built. Even when they did use stone, their masons imitated structural forms proper only to wood, and this was their normal building material. Once the problem of roofing a fairly wide span with timber trusses had been solved, the same plan served for church, hall or barn: they made no distinction in architectural style whether they built for God, man or cow. Any ancient timber barn with side aisles gives a fair idea of the appearance of a Saxon 'hall'. The aisles could be divided into more or less separate bays, among which the cow-house and the hay-barn and the bed-chamber would be all much alike. The Saxons were farmers, and they lived in earthy intimacy with their retainers (significantly called 'hearth-men') all under one roof with their cattle and their produce. Long after this type of dwelling had disappeared from England,

17

farm workers still shared night quarters with the cattle: Elizabethan inventories record sheets, blankets and other bedding in the 'ox-houses'. Folk who spend the whole day labouring in the open, and are indoors only during the hours of darkness, do not ask high standards of comfort. Good furniture comes only with the habit of indoor life and sedentary occupations. Well into the Middle Ages, it was thought no hardship to squat or lie on the floor, or at best on a hard bench or bed put together with no more care for comfort than as if the underside of the human form, whether sitting or lying, were a flat surface. Nor was any distaste felt for sleeping in company closely huddled together. Warmth was valued above privacy. When the hearth was brought indoors and put in the middle of the floor, away from the combustible walls, with its smoke escaping as best it could through a hole in the roof, if offered heat and light as further inducements to sleeping in the hall. Moreover, in such lawless times there was safety in numbers. Beds of straw stuffed into sacks would be spread on the tables or the benches, or on chests in which the empty sacks could be kept. The lower orders, who did not merit such elevation above the draughts and damp and rats, would make their beds on the earth floor. Our expression 'making a bed' dates from the days when one was given a sack and some straw and did that very thing. One went to bed soon after supper, before the fire died or was covered. Not until later and merrier times would there be dancing and drinking and other fun between supper and bedtime.

To these one-roof houses, sundry external chambers were added from time to time, rather at random. Readers of Old English poetry will meet the phrase 'a bird in bure', that is, a lady in her bower or chamber. As 'bowers' these places sound more attractive than the crude lean-to sheds they probably were, built against the outside wall of the hall, or against the outermost fenced enclosure where they were even less likely to have any covered way to bed. Into them the lord and his ladies would retire, maybe scurrying through the rain, with or without a lantern. Even in the comparative comfort of the chamber, the bed was usually no more than the common sack of straw laid on a bench, for the words used to signify the bedstead and bedding are *baence* and *streow*: bench and straw. King Alfred's expression for 'make a bed' means literally 'prepare straw'. The bench was sometimes set in a recess, such as may still be seen in parts of Scotland and Northern Europe; the bed itself was called a *cota* (cot) or *cryb* (crib), and the bedchamber a *bed-clyfa* or bed-closet. The word 'bedstead' meant literally 'a place for a bed', and none but persons of rank would have what we now call a bedstead. The bedclothes, however, already conformed with modern ideas:

18

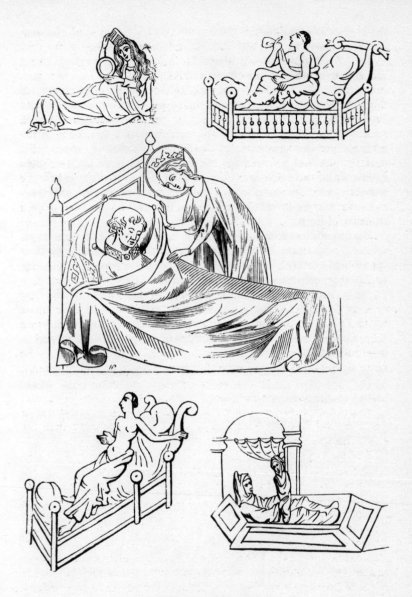

Anglo-Saxon Attitudes

19

the *bolstar* and *pyle* (pillow), the *scyte* (sheet), the *bed-felt* and *bed-reaf* (coverlets), and perhaps goatskins or bearskins over all.

The art of glass-making had been lost, and the windows could not give light without the chances of wind and rain. Defence, too, called for small windows. In the dark fireless chamber, the light-source might be no more than a mass of tallow plastered round a reed and stuck on a spike: the 'candle stick' or 'pricket' was then indeed a stick, and not a socket as now. Some had a *leoht-faet*, light-vat or lamp, probably a survival from the Roman occupation. We are told that King Alfred invented the candle-clock, an accurately weighed candle with twelve divisions marked upon it; but that it was because neither candle nor lamp would burn properly in his draughty bedchamber that he invented the lantern, that is, the *lant-horn* of thin translucent horn.

The Saxons had some rude washing, bathing and sanitary arrangements. Tacitus says of their ancestors on the Continent, with their 'fierce blue eyes, red hair and tall forms', that 'on waking from sleep, which they generally prolong into the day, they wash, usually in warm water, since winter bulks so large in their lives'. By the laws of King Edgar 'warm baths and soft beds' were banned as effeminate luxuries. As for sanitation: Roger of Wendover says that when King Offa's queen arranged the murder of her guest, King Ethelbert, in his chamber,

Near the king's bed she caused a seat to be prepared, magnificently, decked, and surrounded with curtains; and underneath it the wicked woman caused a deep pit to be dug.

The seat was so contrived that when the king availed himself of this treacherous convenience, he was tipped into the pit. But we must not assume that such installations were common, and when they were genuine, they cannot have improved the air of the bedchamber.

That 'most precious relic of Old English', the tedious Saxon romance of Beowulf, gives us some clues to the sleeping habits of a thousand years ago. When the hero Beowulf came with his men to the 'great mead-hall' of Hrothgar, king of the Danes, to deal with the nuisance Grendel, a monster who called at night to devour the sleepers, the visitors were lodged in the hall to await him:

Then he put off from him his iron byrnie, helmet from head; delivered to his esquire the richly decorated sword, choicest steel; and charged him with the care of his war-harness. Then did the valiant man Beowulf the Goth utter some vaunting words ere he mounted on the bed . . . Then the daring warrior laid him down; the pillow received the countenance of the lord, and round about him many a smart sea-warrior crouched to his hall-rest.

20

At dawn Hrothgar and his people, who had slept in the bowers, returned to find that Beowulf had dealt with Grendel by pulling an arm off him; Grendel had gone off to die. The day was devoted to a 'banquet of gladness', and on the second night

they cleared away the bench-boards; it was strewn throughout in beds and bolsters . . . At their heads they set the shields, the bright bucklers, there on the bench was over each etheling, plain to be seen, the towering war-helmet, the ringed mail-coat, the shaft of awful power.

But evidently the mead, too, was of awful power, for they slept so soundly that when Grendel's angry mother came in the dark, she was able to kill off one of Hrothgar's favourite nobles, retrieve the missing arm, and escape undetected. From this sorry affair we can deduce several facts germane to our subject: the chief guest sleeps on a raised bed, with a pillow, and there are benches and plenty of bolsters for the others. Nobody seems to undress for bed, except for taking off his ironwear. Even a favourite noble seems to have slept habitually in the common hall; he would not be there to help to deal with Grendel's mother, who was quite unexpected. The bowers must have been so remote from the hall that the rest of the household could sleep through the hullabaloo of the first night.

The conquering Normans thought these blond beasts a rude lot, and their ways uncouth. After the conquest the landowner's house or 'manor house' begins to show some care for everyday comfort. It develops in two forms: the Saxon 'end hall house' where the high ground-floor hall has a two-storey block of chambers attached at one end, and the less common 'upper hall house', of Norman origin, that has two storeys throughout. Whether upstairs or down, the hall is the focus of communal living. Although lords and ladies may retire to their chambers at night, all persons of lesser degree still lie in the hall, as even the nobles who wait on the queen will do as late as the reign of King John. Everybody turns in at about eight o'clock, according to the ancient custom of curfew, newly enforced by the Conqueror's law.

In the 'end hall house', one end of the hall gives access to the principal chamber, above which there is a more private one for the ladies or for important guests. In a royal establishment this may be solely an audience chamber, but in most houses it is a bed-sitting-room where visitors are received by day, regardless of the bed. In the manor house, even the field labourers report there cap-in-hand for their orders or their pay. It is known as the bower, chamber, parlour, solar or even cellar, all these variants variously spelt; and to confuse matters even further, 'solar' can be applied to any upper

21

room, loft or garret; originally it meant an open chamber in the roof which received plenty of sun. To simplify and to save ink we will call this multi-purpose room a 'chamber' until such time as it becomes simply and solely a bedroom. It is reached by a stair which at first is external, but later is built into the thickness of the wall; even if it extends into the hall, it is still an unpretentious private stair. When chimneys first appear in pictures, they are shown over the chamber, where the wall fire-place was first introduced. The chamber floor is strewn with straw or rushes. Being roofed at right angles to the hall, the chamber has free gables in which windows can be made. Norman windows are narrow, but being splayed inside they give more light than might be supposed, and with more settled times the chamber windows will be made as large as possible, and in as rich a style as the status of the house allows. The may overlook some 'pleasant pleying place', and the lattice may be entwined with vines, roses or honeysuckle; more like one's idea of a bower than those sheds of old.

Sir Launcelot at the queen's window
Children will be quicker than adults to understand this early fourteenth-century picture showing the relation of the hall (left), *chamber* (lower right), *and solar* (upper right). *Adults will be quicker to understand the story behind it, quoted in another context on page 37*

22

7

Painted Chambers

THE natural endurance of massive masonry tends to a belief that our forefathers liked internal walls to be of cold bare stone, a belief still firmly held in Hollywood. But these walls would at least be whitewashed, and by the twelfth century would normally be plastered and decorated with *red okyr*, *yelowe okyr*, and *rodel* or raddle such as still serves for marking sheep. The inmost layer of the plaster that was so recklessly hacked off by nineteenth-century 'restorers' was often original, and decorative painting was often destroyed with it. Neckam in the late twelfth century describes the chamber walls as covered with curtains, or with tapestry which was now being made in England. This would be hung on a fixed wooden rail like a picture-rail, so that it could be changed from time to time, or could go with its owner on his travels. Beside the bed, says Neckam, there should be a chair, and at the foot of the bed a bench. Near the bed was the 'hutch' or chest for valuables: in tales of pillage, the soldiery always rush first to the chambers,

23

whether the beds are occupied or not. On one side of the chamber the *perche*—a rod, pole or perch—was for hanging clothes, and there might be a similar one on the other side reserved for falcons, which if they are to be properly trained, have to live day and night with their master.

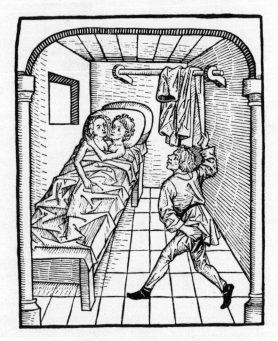

The Perche, fifteenth century

Beds still show the heavy hand of the carpenter, with his broad-bladed adze. The joiner, with his saw and his comparatively light framing and panelling, has yet to appear. The massive timbers are merely nailed together or iron-bound. Pictures of these beds are not easily interpreted, because the artist invariably runs into trouble with his perspective and tries to look from two directions at the same time. Usually he shows four square posts, 3 or 4 ft. high, with round knobs on top, and simple squared stretchers which presumably carry, hidden under the bedclothes, a boarded top or a corded mattress. Sometimes there are boarded sides below forming a chest. The bed may be high enough to call for a little stool by which to mount.

There may be a raised head-board, or a raised foot-board (not both), crudely ornamented by the carpenter.

We gain some intimate glimpses through the keyholes of royal bedchambers of the twelfth century from Lady Stenton's *English Society in the Early Middle Ages*. The first is from an account, written by one Walter Map, of court life as he had known it under Henry I with its mixture of pomp and homeliness:

'Who', says Walter Map, 'can conceal the little jests of so merry and gracious a man, not so much the emperor or king as the father of England?' The king's chamberlain, Pain fitz John, every night took a single measure of wine in case the king was thirsty during the night, and he never asked for it more than once or twice a year, so that Pain and the servants often safely drank it all early in the night. One night the king looked for the wine and it was not there. Pain got up and called the servants but found nothing. The king caught them hunting for the wine and not finding it. 'What's this,' said he to a trembling and fearful Pain, 'do you not always have wine ready?' Pain timidly replied: 'Yes, my lord, every night a single measure, but you are so rarely thirsty that we drink it either late at night or after we have slept awhile, and having told the truth we throw ourselves on your mercy.' Then the king said 'Do you get no more than one measure a night?' 'No,' said Pain. 'That', said the king, 'was very little for two of us; in future get two measures from the butlers every night, one for you and one for me.'

The royal household was organised in three main divisions: the chapel, the hall and the chamber. The first officer of the chamber was the Master Chamberlain, whose successor today is none less than the Lord Great Chamberlain himself; a great officer of state could still be a household servant in daily personal attendance on the king, though he would not for instance actually make the bed. That was one of the duties of the Usher of the Chamber, who had '4*d*. a day for the king's bed every day when the king went a journey'. Everyone, from king to serf, thought his bedroom the safest place for his valuables, and it is in the king's chamber that the Treasury too has its origins. That Edward the Confessor had kept his money by the bedside, we know from the story in Camden's *Remains*:

. . . one afternoon lying in his bed with the curtains drawn round about him, a poor pilfering courtier came into his chamber, where, finding the king's casket open . . . he took out so much money as he could well carry and went away, but an insatiable desire brought him again, and so the third time, when the King, who lay still all this while and would not seem to see, began to speak to him, and bade him speedily be packing . . . for if Hugoline [the chamberlain] came and took him there, he were not only like to lose all that he had gotten, but also stretch an halter.

25

The household accounts of Henry I show that one of the chamberlains, William Maudit, is paid 14 pence a day, and also

... continuously eats in the house and has one large candle, 13 pieces of candle, and 2 packhorses with their livery. The porter of the king's bed eats in the house and has 3 halfpence for his man and a packhorse with his livery ... The ewerer has double food and when the king goes a journey a penny for drying his clothes, and when the king has a bath 3 pence, except on the three great feasts of the year. Touching the laundress there is a doubt.

In King John's time the cost of the royal bath went up to 4*d.*, and then to 5½*d.*, but the doubt about the laundress must have been cleared up, for Florence the laundress regularly received '18 pence for shoes'. It is probable that gentlefolk undressed for the night, but there is no evidence about nightclothes. King John had a furred cloak for use when he got up at night, but the fact that this purpose was worth mention suggests that such a 'dressing-gown' was not usual. The word 'wardrobe' begins to appear in the chancery records of John, and at first seems to mean only the room where his valuables and clothes were kept, a sort of combined store-room, dressing-room and lavatory adjoining the chamber. By Henry III's reign (1216–72) it comes also to mean a whole administrative department staffed by the Clerks of the Wardrobe; but this king still uses the word in its old sense when he complains that the 'privy chamber' in his 'wardrobe at London' smells badly. The better-appointed wardrobe would contain a 'laver' or wash-basin, with 'running water' until its reservoir was empty, and a 'waste system' until its bucket below was full.

Throughout this reign buildings were going up apace. The new cathedrals of Salisbury and Wells exemplified the lighter and loftier Early English style superseding the massive Norman. Henry's copious household accounts show that in the eighteen establishments which he owns in various parts of the country, the chambers are becoming places of greater comfort, on which he spends a lot of money. New chambers are added, rather haphazardly if we judge by the many mentions of connecting alleys, passages, stairs and penthouses. Henry's most impressive bedroom, the 'Painted Chamber' at Westminster, lasted until a fire in 1834, and is well documented. This was the combined audience and bedchamber of his principal palace. Although dwarfed by the adjoining Great Hall, still there, it was no less than 80 ft. long, 26 ft. wide, and 31 ft. high. Its mural decorations are of special interest, and nineteenth-century copies exist of its many holy subjects: two pairs of Virtues and Vices, St.

Edward with the Pilgrim, the Coronation of the Confessor (over the bed), and Soldier Guardians (flanking the bed). These guardians are those of Solomon's bed, described in the *Song of Songs*:

Behold, it is the litter of Solomon; threescore mighty men are about it of the mighty men of Israel. They all handle the sword, and are expert in war: every man hath his sword upon his thigh, because of fear in the night.

It seems to be by something more than chance that the belief in their power of protecting a sleeper brings to mind the old nursery prayer:

Matthew, Mark, Luke and John,
Bless the bed that I lie on.
Four corners to my bed,
Four angels round my head;
One to watch, and one to pray,
And two to bear my soul away.

This invocation was known as 'The White Paternoster'; in 1656 it was quoted as a 'Popish charm'. There have been many versions, including one in German, and in most of them the saints or angels are set at the head, sides and foot of the bed, protecting in all directions. A derivation has been supposed, by way of half-magic and half-Christian charms, from ancient Jewish cabbalistic prayers against 'terrors that threaten by night', thus linking Solomon's fears with those of the modern nursery.

The 'little wardrobe' at Westminster is 'painted of a green colour to imitate a curtain', a scheme borrowed from the adjoining Painted Chamber. At Winchester the panelling of the king's chamber is painted green with gold stars, and there are roundels for picture-stories from the Bible, which were especially popular in days when few could read it; at his bedside is a 'tablet' where the Soldier Guardians again dispel 'fear in the night'. In 1238 Henry orders windows of white glass for the queen's wardrobe at Winchester, 'so that the chamber may not be so windy as it used to be'; this is one of the the first records of window glass in a secular building. The chimney-breast is to be painted,

. . . and on it to be pourtrayed a figure of Winter, which as well by its sad countenance as by other miserable distortions of the body may be deservedly likened to Winter itself . . .

not a very jolly subject, and hardly an appropriate one to depict just after having shut out the cold. In 1240 at the Tower of London he orders the queen's chamber to be panelled, whitewashed, and painted with roses. In 1245 the 'posts' in his chamber at Ludgershall are to be painted 'the colour of marble', and window glass is to be put in the queen's chamber at Guildford 'with panels which can be opened and closed'. Over the chamber fire-place at Clarendon are to be painted a Wheel of Fortune and a Tree of Jesse, and they are to

. . . paint that wainscot of a green colour, and to put a border to it, and to cause the heads of Kings and Queens to be painted on the borders and to paint the walls of the King's upper chamber the story of Saint Margaret Virgin and the four Evangelists, and to paint the wainscot of the same chamber with a green colour, spotted with gold, and to paint on it heads of men and women, and all these paintings are to be done with good and exquisite colours.

Next the History of Alexander is chosen to adorn the queen's chamber at Nottingham. His own is to be paved with 'plain tile', though a 'plastered' floor is good enough for the queen at Winchester. In 1251 at Guildford he is more ambitious:

. . . the whole roof ridge of our chamber to be remade 5 feet higher and the walls raised so that there can be made 3 glass windows similar to the new window lately made in the same bedroom. The passage between the hall and the said bedroom to be panelled and earthed over and better windows to be made in the passage, and the panelled bedrooms to be painted green. The downstairs wardrobe of the bedroom of Edward our son to be panelled and a stone vault to be made in it, in which our shrines and relics can be put . . . The wall outside our bedroom to be thrown down and moved 15 feet from the bedroom and rebuilt at its present height, and a herb garden made between our bedroom and the wall.

Green paint and gold stars recur at Geddington, and then in 1256:

. . . the King, in the presence of Master William the monk of Westminster, provided for the making, in the wardrobe where the King is wont to wash his head, at Westminster, of a picture of a king who was rescued by his dogs from the sedition plotted against him by his subjects . . . Philip Luvel, the Treasurer, and the said Edward are to pay Master William the cost of making this picture, at once.

The subject of this prepaid picture is indeed topical, for Henry's spending is making his overtaxed subjects restive. In the same year he gives orders

. . . to paint the queen's wardrobe with green paint and golden stars . . . to pave the chamber of Edward the king's son with flat tiles; to put forms round the king's chamber.

Green paint must be running short by this, but the favourite colour scheme does not pall after twenty-five years, for in 1262 it makes a last appearance in the royal chambers at Windsor.

The bedroom of Edward I conformed with custom in being open to much coming and going, for we know that he paid forfeits to such ladies of his court as could catch him in bed on Easter Monday morning. In 1287 the windows in his chamber in the Tower of London are being glazed, at a cost of 4*d.* a foot for white glass and 6*d.* for coloured. The small size of the pieces that can be made brings about the use of the leaded diamond lattice, a feature of 'Ye Olde' that will outlive its necessity by several centuries. At Nottingham in 1313 Edward goes in for thorough draught-proofing, with

... 3 great screens, one opposite the door of the King's wardrobe, another at the door of the chamber, and the third at the King's head ... [and] boards for a screen hanging over the fireplace between the hearth and the King's bed.

The head that wears a crown does not lie so uneasy, then, by the fourteenth century. We have progressed well beyond Beowulf's barbarous bedgoing when Chaucer writes:

> ... of downe of pure dovis white
> I wol yeve him a fethir bed,
> Rayid with gold, and right well cled
> In fine black sattin d'outremere,
> And many a pillow, and every bere
> Of cloth of Raines to sleepe on softe;
> Him thare [need] not to turnen ofte.

Chaucer may be taken as an expert witness, for at the age of 27 he had been 'Yeoman Valet to the King's Chamber', whose duties included bed-making.

As always, luxuries descended the social scale to become everyday necessities. They spread more quickly in the peaceful south of England, where soon the lord of the manor could retire, by day as well as by night, into his glass-windowed, fire-lit, decorated chamber, to enjoy its cosy privacy; severing the old intimate relations with his former 'hearth-men' that were implicit in the house plan.

29

Neolithic stone bed at Skara Brae, Orkney Islands

8

Sooty Bowers

RECORDS of royal chambers are plentiful, but those of the beds of 'pore menne' are sparse. The shakedown of the labourer, who did not enjoy even the communal straw of the hall, has remained primitive for so long, that the Irish peasant of yesterday, and the charcoal-burner and the bark-peeler of today, lie in hovels that stem from prehistory, and from prehistory their slight story can conveniently begin.

Put a wild animal into new surroundings, and it will seek shelter before it seeks anything else. So presumably with wild man, and such man-shelters as caves, roofed pits, screens of interlaced boughs, and huts of branch and leaf, doubtless contained rude beddings of fur—but anybody's guess is as good as that of the wisest prehistorian. It is too easy to weave jejune fancies about the habits of that rather phoney character Early Man. Perhaps because of a spate of anthropological finds being made about sixty years ago, he became a popular figure in the funny papers, and for at least a generation there was a sure laugh for drawings of a Stone Age in which fur-kilted Early

30

Men pedalled stone bicycles, or rode about in stone motor-cars wearing stone top-hats; inevitably they were depicted as sleeping in stone beds. Here at least the humorists stumbled on a truth, for when a Neolithic settlement was dug from beneath the drifted dunes of Skara Brae in the Orkneys, there indeed was a very stone bed, cosily adjacent to the stone hearth, not far from the stone sideboard. But here one must beware of what might be called the Survival Fallacy, for which even professional archaeologists have fallen. They have told us, for example, that Early Man invariably went into the gloomy depths of a remote cave to do his paintings; not being themselves artists, they do not see that no real painter confined to 'canvases' of rock could have resisted the temptation of the great pristine slabs available in the open, out in the sun, to be seen and admired by all. Naturally it is the protected works in the weather-proof cave—as likely to have been an art school as a hide-out of esoteric ritual—that have alone survived. So with the bedroom furniture; there may have been a thousand wooden beds for every stone one, and what Orcanian would elect to hammer out a stone bed, and lie hard, if his island had trees?

From the slight evidence found, it does seem that the earliest furniture was 'built-in'. (The prairie pioneer still prefers to build a bedstead of only three timbers against a corner of his log cabin, instead of a free-standing one needing at least eight.) A Neolithic house uncovered in Württemberg had two rooms, sharing a hearth formed in the partition, and in the bedroom were the remains of supports for a built-in wooden bed.

The circular hut, probably the first dwelling that deserves the name, formed of stakes thrust into the ground and forked or tied together at the top, is still built all over Europe by shepherds, or charcoal-burners, or bark-peelers as in the English Lake District, where men will live in such this very summer, with a hearth and two beds. This is the surviving prototype of the mediaeval 'booth'. As late as the year 1202 the permanent village dwelling—like these summer shelters—was so flimsy that an evildoer could be accused in court of having 'cut the posts of that house through the middle so that that house fell down', and Froissart says that when the Scots returned from a border foray to find that the English had meanwhile been razing the Scottish dwellings, they remarked philosophically that 'with six or eight stakes they would soon have new houses'. An English town house could be pulled down, in case of fire, by a mere hook and rope kept for such an emergency. The two-room dwelling was the normal standard; fire regulations of the year 1212 required 'that all chambers and hostelries be removed so that there may

31

remain only the house [that is, houseplace or hall] and bedroom'. Chaucer in *The Tale of the Nun's Priest* describes a widow's two-room house of this sort:

> Fful sooty was hir bour and eke hire halle

—sooty because there was no chimney. While the widow and her 'daughter two' slept in the bower, chanticleer and his seven wives shared the hall with the swine. In Scotland these two apartments would be the 'but and ben'. If the householder aspired to three rooms, the 'but' would be the kitchen, the 'ben' the parlour, and the 'farben' the bedroom; all on the ground floor. Not until the inverted 'V' house of inclined timbers (such as the surviving Teapot Hall, 'all roof and no wall') gave way to upright post construction with cross-beams, could the bedroom go upstairs.

Illustration opposite: *From* The Romance of the Holy Grail
Below: *Fourteenth-century bed with turned legs*

32

9

In Camisiam Jacere

ALL our pictures of European beds to date have one feature in common: the occupant is shown propped up so high, on a pile of bolsters or with his mattress curved up against the bed-head, as to be almost sitting, even when he is clearly asleep. He cannot lie flat and he never looks really comfortable. Many seem to accept that this semi-sitting bed-posture was customary; some even hold that it was adopted so that the sleeper might be quicker on the draw if attacked at night. More plausible explanations might be found. Any mediaeval artist who took as his model an actual sleeper, snuggled down with the covers up to his chin, would have little to depict but a face, and the result would lack the dignity proper to an important personage. The king portrayed in *The Romance of the Holy Grail* does lie rather lower than most, and so is on the verge of losing face in both senses; although the bedclothes are below his shoulders, it is partly his homely attitude that makes him so reminiscent of Soglow's 'little king' from *The New Yorker*.

Royal families of today are not photographed in bed alive, but if they were, they would assuredly sit up. These artists had something in common with the Chinese artist in Bramah's *Kai Lung*, who spent some years learning to draw a set of useful stock characters, but all facing the same way, wherefore he could illustrate processions but not conversations. The mediaeval formulae for faces were unlikely to include one for the difficult foreshortened features of a supine sleeper. Sometimes it would be easier, as it was when drawing the bed, to combine two viewpoints. In any case a human figure was thought incomplete without arms and feet, even if an inappropriate gesture had to be contrived for a sleeper's arms, and his feet had to peep out into the cold. Despite the pictorial evidence, our forefathers probably did stretch and relax quite normally in bed. Nor did kings and queens sleep wearing their crowns, which were added only to identify royalty.

It was the custom to sleep naked, except perhaps for a kerchief like a turban on the head, though from some pictures it seems that one wrapped the sheet around one closely before pulling the coverlet over. We see a thirteenth-century lady in bed wearing a head-dress with a bunch of flowers in it, but nothing else. Even the Virgin Mary wears no night-dress; nor any of the ladies throughout a fourteenth-century Bible, though Rachel does wear a veil over her head and shoulders. In 1279 a priest includes, in a list of the vows that a wife may not undertake without her husband's consent, '*in camisiam jacere*', to sleep in a chemise. An old French saying exemplifies

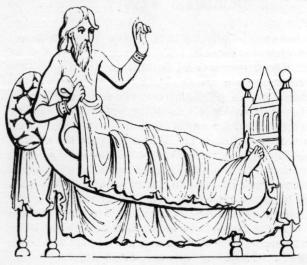

The 'Hutch' was a bedside chest for valuables

a promise hard to keep, by 'a wife intending to wear a chemise in bed'. In Chaucer's *Merchant's Tale* there is an exception, for a man is described as sitting up in bed in his shirt and night-cap. A man's inmost garment was his shirt, and a woman's her chemise, and these were the only night-wear available to the coy or the chilly. In the romance of *Launcelot du Lac* there is one who 'took not off his shirt nor his breeches' for bed, but it is implied that the omission is unusual. In the *Roman de la Violette* the lady Oriant is thought eccentric when she goes to bed in a chemise, until it is explained that she wishes to hide a blemish. In another tale an unusually pudent damsel, sleeping with her host's daughters and maidservants, amuses them by her reluctance to strip until the candle is out. The rules of one household require the servants 'to extinguish their candles, before they go into bed, with the mouth or with the hand, and not with their chemise', suggesting that the usual procedure was to take off one's chemise when in bed and shy it at the candle. The chamber being cosier than of old, and candles cheaper, reading in bed became more feasible. One ecclesiastic, who indulged in this habit, fixed his candle to the end of his bed, but fell asleep; the straw-filled bed caught fire, and set light to the 'wooden arches and planks' of his bedstead: an accident that has recurred regularly throughout bedroom history, and despite the obsolescence of the candle, continues in the age of the cigarette.

We do not find much information about bedding in early wills or inventories, for a curious reason: the bedding was normally a perquisite of the servants of the bedchamber, and being divided among them immediately after a death, it does not appear in the list. Mattresses have changed a lot, but the bedclothes have been much the same from the thirteenth century until today.

35

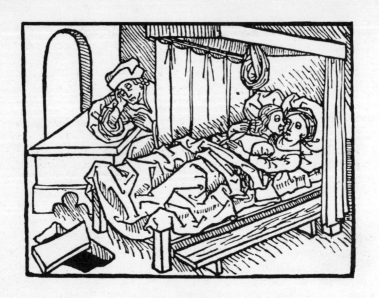

10

Virtuous Adultery

'COME up and see me sometime' is a very ancient invitation. In the Middle Ages a lady could quite properly entertain friends and lovers in her bedchamber. In the fabliau of *Guillaume au Faucon* a young 'damoisel'—that is, a noble youth—visits his lord's wife when the lord and the maids are away. He opens the door without knocking, and she is sitting on her bed; she greets him with a sweet smile and invites him to sit there too, and there 'he laughed, and talked, and played with her, and the lady did the same'. In the romance of *Ywayne and Gawaine*:

> In at the dore she him led
> And did him sit upon hir bed.
> A quylt ful nobil lay tharon,
> Richer saw he never none,
> She said if he wolde any thing
> He sold be served at his lyking.

Sir Gawaine's reply to this offer is a shade ungallant:

He said, that ete wolde he fain,
She wente, and come ful sone again.
A capon rosted broght she sone,
A cleane klath and brede tharon.
And a pot with rich wine,
And a pece to fil it yn.

A fixed table was rare in the bedchamber, but one could 'sett a borde' on 'trestes' for a meal, and put a bathtub before the fire for the visitor.

Even if we look into the bedchambers of the great days of chivalry in a spirit of pure research into matters of furnishing and upholstery, it is constantly forced on our notice that knightly morals do not shine with so white a light as they did in our school-books. Much depends on which text you are allowed to read. The bed is more prominent in the originals, and there is more popping in and out of bedchambers. Sir James Knowles says that his edition of *King Arthur and his Knights* of 1862 is 'little else than an abridgement of Sir Thomas Malory's version', but the two do not tally. According to Sir James, Launcelot du Lac 'had the greatest name of any knight in the world', and he would have us believe that Launcelot's love for Guinevere is platonic, spiritual and quite above-board, but Malory's words are:

Then Sir Launcelot took his sword in his hand, and privily went to a place where he had espied a ladder toforehand, and that he took under his arm, and bare it through the garden, and set it up to the window, and there anon the queen was ready to meet him. And then they made either to other their complaints of many diverse things, and then Sir Launcelot wished that he might have come in to her. Wit ye well, said the queen, I would as fain as ye, that ye might come in to me. Would ye, madam, said Sir Launcelot, with your heart that I were with you? Yea, truly, said the queen.

So Launcelot (as depicted on page 22) breaks the window bars, cutting the 'brawn' of his hand in the process, and leaps into the chamber.

So, to pass upon this tale, Sir Launcelot went to bed with the queen and he took no force of his hurt hand, but took his pleasaunce and his liking until it was in the dawning of the day; and wit ye well he slept not but watched, and when he saw his time that he might tarry no longer he took his leave and departed at the window, and put it together as well as he might again, and so departed,

leaving the blood from his cut hand to cause trouble later. As for Sir Tristram of Lyonesse, he is speared by the jealous King Mark while on his way to visit the wife of Sir Segwarides in her chamber, but he presses on regardless, and bleeds on the lady's sheets just as Launcelot did; Sir Segwarides finds this evidence, and makes so much fuss that the saintly Tristram has to kill him off. Next we find Tristram being 'taken naked abed with La Beale Isoud', the bride of King Mark who has been entrusted to his care. Even when Tristram does at last marry and settle down,

When they were abed both, Sir Tristram remembered him of his old lady La Beale Isoud. And then he took such a thought suddenly that he was all dismayed, and other cheer made he none but with clipping and kissing; as for other fleshly lusts Sir Tristram never thought nor had ado with her.

When Sir Pelleas trusts his friend Gawaine to intercede for him with the lady Ettard, wit ye well Gawaine goes to bed with her himself:

And therewith Sir Gawaine plight his troth unto Sir Pelleas to be true and faithful unto him; so each one plight their troth to other, and so they changed horses and harness, and Sir Gawaine departed, and came to the castle whereat stood the pavilions of this lady without the gate. And as soon as Ettard had espied Sir Gawaine she fled in toward the castle. Sir Gawaine spake on high, and bade her abide, for he was not Sir Pelleas; I am another knight that have slain Sir Pelleas. . . . And then he [Sir Pelleas] yede to the third pavilion and found Sir Gawaine lying in bed with his lady Ettard, and either clipping other in arms, and when he saw that his heart wellnigh brast for sorrow, and said: Alas! that ever a knight should be found so false; and then he took his horse and might not abide no longer for pure sorrow. And when he had ridden nigh half a mile he turned and thought to slay them both; and when he saw them both so lie sleeping fast, unnethe he might hold him on horseback for sorrow, and said thus to himself, Though this knight be never so false, I will never slay him sleeping, for I will never destroy the high order of knighthood; and therewith he departed again. And or he had ridden half a mile he returned again, and thought then to slay them both, making the greatest sorrow that ever man made. And when he came to the pavilions he tied his horse unto a tree, and pulled out his sword naked in his hand, and went to them theras they lay, and yet he thought it were shame to slay them sleeping, and laid the naked sword overthwart both their throats, and so took his horse and rode away.

After which show of indecision, one feels less sympathy for the ineffectual Pelleas.

Clearly more tolerance was practised in sex-life than was preached. Provided one observed the forms of polite society, adultery was an accepted upper-class diversion, almost a fine art. A doughty knight had to have a 'lady' to worship; preferably a married lady whose husband was of higher rank than himself, for a knight should keep

38

his mind on higher things. For her sake he would undertake the silliest exploits—one too many, in the case of Sir Moritz von Craun, who at last reached his lady's bed so worn out by his feats that he promptly fell asleep there, and the frustrated lady not unnaturally showed him the door. The cult of knightly love, sung in France by the *trouvères*, in Germany by the *minnesingers*, and in England by the troubadours, so sublimated and wrapped up all this real or would-be adultery that it seemed somehow quite pure. '*Honi soit qui mal y pense*', murmured the seeker of the Holy Grail as he sneaked through the bedroom window, having first invoked the aid of the Virgin Mary in the affair. The nineteenth-century historians tend to dodge the point, going no further than such cold comment as

. . . a tone of gallantry which could hardly produce a high degree of morality, but the details on this subject, though very abundant, are in great part of a description which cannot here be entered upon.

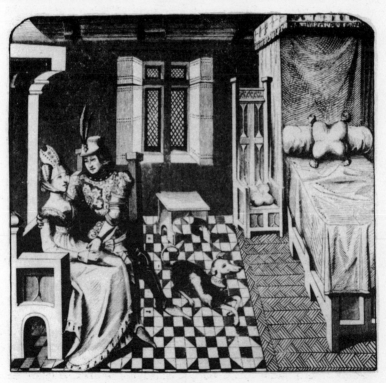

Knight and lady in bedchamber, fourteenth century

39

It is only fair to these chevaliers to mention that the ladies are often the suitors, and even less restrained than the gentlemen, their language and conduct being, in the words of the same historian as he again looks disapprovingly over his spectacles,

. . . loose beyond anything that those who have not read these interesting records of mediaeval life can easily conceive.

The heroine of *Blonde of Oxford* does not invite the gentlemen of that honourable seat of learning to visit her bedchamber. She throws a mantle over her shoulders and visits theirs. The Chevalier de la Tour-Landry tells a story to his daughters by way of moral instruction:

There was a young lady, the daughter of a very gentle knight, who quarrelled at the game of tables with a gentleman who had no better temper than herself, and who, provoked by the irritating language she used towards him, told her that she was known to be in the habit of going by night into the men's chambers, and kissing and embracing them in their beds without candle.

The chevalier's point, which is the point of the story here, is not that the young lady's conduct was abnormal, candle or no, but only that people who speak ill of others run the risk of having their own failings exposed.

The bed was a kind of seat-of-honour during the daytime. Christine de Pisan offered her book of poems to her patroness in her bedchamber, and Froissart there presented his *Book of Love* to Richard II. It would be troublesome to have to rearrange the bed every time a visitor called, and this led to the reintroduction of the classical day-bed or couch. The couch proper offers a brief comfort quite different from the deep recuperation of the bed; a *chaise longue* is essentially a long chair, not a narrow bed. Perhaps the earliest mention of an English 'couch' appears when Henry III in 1221 orders two silken ones, for his cousin Alienor and for Princess Isabella of Scotland; later, when he gives one to the King of Scotland, it is to be made by his tailor; tailoring included upholstery until the eighteenth century. In one of the 'chambers of pleasaunce' prepared for Lord Grautehuse, Ambassador from Charles of Burgundy to Edward IV, there was a 'rich couche with ffether beddis hanged with a tente knytt lyke a nette', but 'couch' and 'bed' are not always clearly distinguished apart, and the couch proper is rare until the sixteenth century, and seldom found outside a lady's chamber. Alienor de Poitiers says firmly that none but a royal dame should place her couch before the fire, and that some ladies of the Low Countries who violate this rule 'merit the ridicule of all'. But by the fourteenth century even a retail tradesman could lie in some luxury: a French cloth-merchant could boast a suite of three bedrooms, each with a richly curtained bed; the best was hung with tapestry, and the very carpets were worked with gold thread; the sheets were of Rheims linen, and his own pillow of crimson silk was embroidered—impressively if uncomfortably—with pearls.

The birth of a noble infant was the occasion for dressing up the bedchamber as a special showpiece. The state bed prepared for the expectant Philippa, the queen of Edward III, was of green velvet, embroidered with golden sea-sirens bearing shields wrought with the arms of England and Hainault. The bill, still to be seen among the Exchequer Rolls, was for £500. The sheets were of fine lawn, the blankets of Naples fustian, and the 'head-sheet' of the best 'cloth of Reynes' from Rennes in Brittany. The 'pane' of crimson velvet was 'wrought in Venice gold', bossed with pearls and furred with ermine. The twelve carpets on the floor cost £60. When the infant opened its eyes for the first time, it must have been much impressed. On the other side of the natal chamber, under an emblazoned 'sparver', was the *lit de misère* from which the mother would be hurried back into the state bed as soon as the midwife's offices allowed. Between the two beds stood a chair of state in crimson cloth-of-gold, with an ermine rug before it. A bench with a 'baudekyn' (a patterned silk from, or named from Baghdad) was provided for the gossips. On a canopied buffet were ewer and basin, wine, cups, spice-plate, and gold and silver *drageoirs* with comfits and sweet-meats for the visitors. Here my lady stayed and entertained for a full month, with the windows curtained day and night. Even the colours of the natal chamber had to conform with rules of rank. Philippa's crimson and green seem to have combined English and French codes: in France, *la chambre verde* was the privilege of queens and princesses, though white had been correct for them in earlier days. Thus, throughout the lying-in of Isabella of Bourbon, five large green beds remained empty, like state coaches waiting for passengers, until the christening ceremony began, when the guests climbed aboard. There is no record of anybody having felt silly on such occasions.

Durham Cathedral Priory (Benedictine): The dorter, now a library

11

The Dorter

ROYAL and noble bedchambers still take up an undue share of the records. We learned our domestic habits as much from the monastery as from the court, and much of our furniture found its form there. The very scantiness of mediaeval furnishing derives from the monastic idea.

The planning of buildings round a cloister was common to most of the orders. The focus of the plan, the church, was on the south side. In Benedictine and Cistercian plans the dorter, or dormitory, is normally on the east side. The Carthusian plan is very different, having no dorter, for Carthusian monks lived almost isolated, in self-contained little dwellings ranged round the cloister.

The dorter generally extended over the whole length of the eastern range, raised on a vaulted undercroft. For easy access to the church for night services, a 'night-stair' went down from a vestibule next to the dorter, into one of the transepts. Several dorters still have their roofs and are used now for other purposes: those at

Durham and Westminster are libraries, and one at Forde is part of a private house. They must have been fine great rooms: during a royal visit to York in 1327, the queen held court in the dorter and was able to seat sixty ladies at table. In early times the dorter was open from end to end, the beds ranged with their heads to the wall, leaving a gangway down the centre. The Cluniacs introduced partitions for privacy, and other orders followed suit, using curtains, wainscoting, or even stone. At Gloucester there were eighteen cubicles on each side, and the bases for the partitions still remain. At Durham there are stone-vaulted cubicles, two of which share each window. Attached to the dorter by a bridge was the 'reredorter' or sanitary wing, with seats in long rows, and a drain or a natural stream flowing beneath. There was no heating in the dorter, though there was a fire in the 'farmery', or sick-bay, where the aisles were divided into separate chambers, and sometimes 'private wards' were built on. An early ordinance that the abbot and prior should sleep in the dorter was soon abandoned, but a corridor to the dorter from the abbot's lodging allowed some 'snap checks' of behaviour at night, until the abbot took to a separate and sometimes palatial lodging of his own.

The life of a monk during the English winter is not to be envied. Every act of his day was strictly regulated, and the smallest breach of the endless rules might be reported and punished. For the novice's first year his master stayed with him day and night watching for error. The natural day, from sunrise to sunset, was divided into twelve 'canonical hours' varying in length according to the season. It began at midnight with Matins, the first and longest service. Just when sleep was sweetest, the monk was aroused by the sub-prior's bell, or more cruelly by a rattle, made in various cacophonous combinations of wood, nails and metal clappers. He put on his outer habit and his soft leather 'night-boots', said a prayer, and sat waiting on his bed until a bell tolled; then went down the night-stair to the icy church, where he was expected to sing and pray with fervour for an hour and a half. During the service the 'circator' came round with a lantern peering to see that he did not drowse. If he did, the circator put the lantern before him and shook him awake before going back to his own place. The sleepy one had then to take the lantern round until he in turn found a drowsy brother, when the cycle would be repeated. Returning at last to the dorter for his second sleep, he was roused again at daybreak, and was in trouble if he was not seated in the choir before the bell stopped, for more worship before the morning wash. Only the lay brothers, who did most of the hard labour, were allowed to sleep on until after this service. After Compline, the last office of the day, the brethren returned in procession to the dorter. Even there, rules governed every move. They must not leave the dorter until Matins. No brother might sing or read there, or even sit near a light, or have a candle of his own. He might go to the dorter by day to change his sheets, but he must not linger there, nor might a stranger enter. Feather-beds were of course proscribed. The rules about night-clothes varied; some orders banned these altogether; Bishop Hugo Gratianopolitanus forbade the monks to wear boots in bed, anticipating Elsa Lanchester's plaint:

> But he didn't oughter come to bed in boots, dear;
> It's the little things that fidgets me, you see.
> I never mind him sleeping in his suits, dear,
> But why can't he sleep in stockings, same as me?

Some slept in shirt, drawers and gaiters, taking off only the boots and outer habit. For those who undressed further there was a drill: the brother might not stand upright while doing this, but must sit on the bed, and then put his legs decently under the coverlet before taking off his clothes. When he was in bed, the lantern-beam dwelt upon him as the circator made a final tour, and then, with his senses numbed and his intelligence dulled by a routine from which death was the only escape, he could fall asleep—until Matins.

A well-behaved monk

44

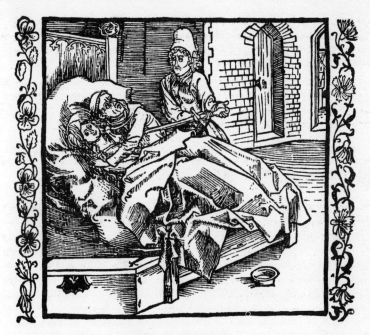

A less well-behaved monk

The dorter was under the care of the chamberlain. He was to provide fresh straw for the mattresses once a year. He was to find a laundress of good reputation and character to wash the sheets, once a fortnight in summer and once in three weeks in winter. The sub-chamberlain was to supply and tend lamps for the dorter. The division of duties was so exactly laid down, that the sacrist supplied the dorter bell, but its cord came from the chamberlain.

By the time of the Dissolution, life in the monasteries had grown easier, and the common dorter had gone out of use, but something very like it and its rules survived in large shops and business houses for apprentices, and survives in public schools today.

The monastery was the inn of the Middle Ages. In 1235 Abbot John at St. Albans built 'many bedchambers, very handsome, with their closets and fire-places, for lodging guests'. The hosteller looked after the guests; he was to provide

... mattresses and blankets, and sheets not merely clean but untorn, quilts of full width and length and pleasing to the eye; in winter, candles, and candlesticks, a fire that does not smoke; writing materials; the whole guest-house kept clear of spiders' webs and dirt, and strewn with rushes

45

underfoot . . . he should have a faithful servant, who is not to go to bed until the guests have retired. He should be up early when the guests leave, to see that they do not forget a sword or knife, and that the property of the convent is not accidentally taken away.

The guests seem to have been more liable to take away the property of the convent 'accidentally' than to forget their own, for at Dover the prior spoke with feeling of guests

who were such wasteful destroyers that it is impossible to keep things in order . . . they packed up the tablecloths, napkins, sheets and coverpanes and such things as they could lay hold of.

It was probably because the monasteries took the cream of the traffic that the secular inns, well established from the time of Edward I 'for the receipt, relief and lodging of wayfaring persons', were well below one-star rating. The guests slept in a common hall, but instead of sharing a common meal as they would have done at home or in the monastery guest-house, they did their own catering, unless their host perhaps offered a farthing bowl of soup. Candles likewise cost a farthing; beds cost a halfpenny; these were the prices paid in 1331 by a warden and two fellows of Merton College, Oxford. Not until the fourteenth century were English inns recognised and regulated, and this because the patrons were complaining about their bills. In 1349 a law required all 'hostlers and herbergers' to charge fairly, under the penalty of paying the swindled guest double his money—a law that has presumably been repealed.

Chaucer's *Tabard* inn is quite recognisable to the modern traveller, with its sign, its landlord ('right a mery man'), and its final reckoning; but the company of Canterbury pilgrims shared rooms there; moreover, on arrival at Canterbury they all shared one room, and one candle. A traveller had to holiday on the Continent to find

. . . all sorts of comforts; painted chambers, and soft beds, raised high with white straw, and made soft with feathers; here within is hostel for love-affairs, and when bed-time comes you will have pillows of violets to hold your head more softly; and, finally, you will have electuaries and rose-water, to wash your mouth and your face . . .

all of which sounds quite four-star.

Illustration opposite: *The birth of St. Edmund, according to an artist of about 1400, takes place in well-appointed surroundings*

46

12

Tarteryn and Baudekyn

URING the fourteenth century, according to the social historians, a new and prosperous middle class is emerging. The wide gap between lord and villein is being filled up. The substantial yeoman farmer and the merchant are a-building, and there are more and larger houses between the castle and cottage levels. Instead of a dominant all-purpose hall and only one or two chambers, we find whole suites of rooms; the hall survives, but it begins to lose its importance. The growing taste for privacy is reflected in the new house plan, formed round a more or less enclosed court. The chamber, though it still contains a bed, becomes more of a private parlour. There is more tapestry; the

47

principal chamber is sometimes called the *chambre encortinée*. More than one naughty tale depends upon the ease with which an illicit visitor can be hidden behind the 'arras', or tapestry from Arras. (There is a sorry reason for the destruction of much of this otherwise durable stuff: it often contained gold thread, and in lawless times it was burned to ashes merely to recover the few shillings'-worth of specie.) For the less wealthy there are the cheap hangings made in, and named after, the busy little village of Worsted. In the better houses the floor of the principal chamber may be matted, and even have little Spanish rugs at the bedside:

> Tapets of Spayne on flor by-side,
> That sprad shyn be for pompe and pryde.

The bed stands out squarely into the room, with the head to the wall. The bed-curtains of earlier times had been merely hung from the ceiling joists, or on cords stretched from the walls; now an important bed will have a 'tester', a square canopy hung on rods or chains, but not yet carried on posts. The 'full tester' covers the whole bed; the 'half-tester' only the head. The 'dorsar' is a rich hanging above the pillows; in armigerent families it will be crested. Curtains hang from the tester down to the floor, and are closed at night; perhaps pinned together if the chamber is draughty. 'Under the curtain' comes to mean 'in bed'. The full tester may be so large as to form almost a room within the room, enclosing a chair or even a second bed, and a lamp may be hung within.

The joiner, rediscovering an ancient principle, is now making furniture in which a comparatively light frame carries panels of tongued-and-grooved boards; but the bedstead, though its parts are properly dovetailed together, is still a solid and simple frame, hidden by 'costers' or valances. The *bed* still means the hangings and coverings, not the mere *bedstead*. In most inventories the bed, in this sense, is described in detail, and the bedstead is not mentioned at all. The bed is by far the most important of chattels: it may even deserve a distinguishing name of its own, as for example the Earl of Arundel's pet bed 'Clovis'. A lord will carry his bride over the threshold to a particularly splendid new one, and by an odd custom this will become next day a perquisite of the head of the bedchamber. When Princess Elizabeth, daughter of Edward I, married the Earl of Holland, Sir Peter de Champvent thus claimed the once-used bed, a huge affair that had needed two sumpter-horses to carry it to Ipswich, and as the newlyweds liked it and wanted to keep it, they had to pay for it again. When Philippa of Hainault married Edward III, Robert de

48

Vere the Earl of Oxford claimed not only the bed, but the laver in which she had washed on the auspicious night, and even her bedroom slippers; he was talked out of this, and took a hundred marks instead. When a noble was attainted and his household gear was confiscated, the bed was the great prize, and often went to the king. Thus Sir Simon Burley's was claimed by the Bishop of Salisbury, but the king insisted on having it; it was a fine thing of 'green tarteran, or Chinese cloth of Tars, embroidered with ships and birds', but the king paid the bishop only 20 marks in compensation. Such beds were made to last: the will of Ralph Lord Basset in 1389 bequeathed to 'that person, whosoever he should be, who first bore his surname and arms', the *use* of his great velvet bed *for life.* Henry V left to the Duke of Exeter a bed of arras, embroidered with scenes of hunting and hawking, but only on condition that there were funds to meet all his other bequests; which evidently there were not, for the duke had to pay for it. The first item of an inventory made at Dartington Hall in Devon in 1400 is a bed, and these recur throughout:

... there are on the day of the present Inquisition within the manor of Dertyngton divers goods and chattels which were of the same late Earl of Huntingdon ... namely one bed of silk embroidered with bulls and divers other arms with iii curtains of tarteryn [an unpatterned oriental silk, named after the Tartars] covered with gold foil with bulls ... also one bed of baudekyn embroidered with the arms of England and Hainault with iii curtains of red sendell [silk] ... Also one bed of red tarteryn embroidered with letters with a curtain of red tarteryn belonging to the same bed ... Also one bed of baudekyn with iii curtains of red tarteryn ... Also one bed of green baudekyn with a celer [canopy] and iii curtains of green tarteryn ... Also one old bed torn of baudekyn with iii curtains of blue tarteryn. Also one other old bed of Norfolk with iii curtains of card [probably coarse linen]. Also an old bed of red worsted embroidered with oak leaves ... Also one covering for a bed of silk pal of red and white ... Also ii mattresses and one canvas [slung to support the mattress].

Although this long document, of which only a fraction is quoted here, lists everything of value down to the frying-pans, there is no mention of bedsteads. When a great man travelled, his bed went with him, but his bedstead did not. There was a great deal of travelling to be done by the king, or by any landowner who was lord of several manors, and for the same reason. They depended on the revenues of their estates, most of which were paid in kind and would be bulky for transport. The easiest way to enjoy this produce was to move the whole household to each palace or manor in turn, staying there until its annual contribution had been consumed on the spot.

To have duplicated the furniture in every house, for the sake of a few weeks' use in the year, would have been expensive, and to have left it in vacant rooms would have been to invite the robber and the moth. Most household belongings were therefore designed to be portable: faldstools, or folding chairs, for example, were being made long before chairs of the modern kind, but they folded in order to save space on the road, not in the house. *Meuble* and *mobilier* (furniture) originally meant 'movables', as opposed to *immeubles*, or houses and buildings. *'Faire marcher les chambres'* was to travel about with one's furniture, complete even to the wall-hangings. A *chambre portative* was not a tent, but a set of bed-hangings and covers. Only the timbers of the bedstead would be left in place, hence their simple form and negligible value. In the will of an Earl of Arundel, a bed of red silk left to one of his daughters is distinguished as that 'usually' at his manor at Reigate, and another daughter gets a blue one 'usually' at his house in London. One looks in vain for evidence of some standardisation of these interchangeable beds and bedsteads, but something of the sort may well have been arranged. During a 'flitting', orders would be sent ahead to provide food and drink, and possibly clean linen, but everything else came by pack-horse or wagon in countless special trunks. The officers responsible for this 'running wardrobe' were the 'yeomen hangers' or 'yeomen bedgoers'. The household book of the Percys, who had about twenty residences, lays down the routine:

> Yt is Ordynyd at every Remevall that the Deyn Sub-dean Prestes Gentilmen and Children of my Lordes Chapell with the Yoman and Grome of the Vestrey shall have apontid theime ij cariadges at every Remevall: Viz. One for ther Beddes Viz. For vj Prests, iij Beddes after ij to a Bedde. For x Gentillmen of the Chapell, v Beddes ij to a Bedde. And for vj Children, ij Beddes after iij to a Bedde. And a Bedde for the Yoman and Grome o'th Vestry. In all xj Beddes for the furst Cariage.

Priests and gentlemen of the chapel two to a bed, and children three to a bed.

In France an oppressive privilege, the *droit de prisage*, allowed furniture to be commandeered without notice for the use of travelling royalty, and many subjects found themselves left to sleep on their floors. Philippe le Bel managed to entertain Edward III and his queen at Pontoise entirely with furniture so seized. A fire broke out in the night, and the beds were consumed, the royal guests escaping in their shifts; and the angry owners of the ashes, denied recompense, protested so loudly that the law was changed.

Richard III is the first monarch we know to have taken his bedstead with him as well as his bed when travelling. When he died on Bosworth Field in 1485 this bedstead (most unlikely to have been a four-poster, as it is often described), stripped of its rich hangings, was left at the *Boar's Head* at Leicester where he had slept his last night. About a century later the landlord of that inn became suddenly rich, for a gold coin had dropped out of the bedstead and led to the discovery that its double bottom had been Richard's travelling safe-deposit.

The usual place for valuables was still the chest in the chamber, where even a sleeper offered some guard for them. Most mediaeval pictures of beds show an iron-bound and padlocked wooden chest at the foot, used as a seat; occasionally at the side and used as a bed-step. It might also hold clothes (which at this date were seldom hung up) mingled with armour, saddlery, pots, pans and bottles; it was a sort of all-purpose container in days before the drawer was invented. A small inner box just under the lid was for herbs to sweeten the clothing. Among the *Paston Letters* is an account of the looting in London during Jack Cade's rebellion:

. . . the captain sent certain of his meny [retinue] to my chamber in your rents, and there broke up my chest, and took away one obligation of mine that was due unto me of 36L. by a priest of Paul's and one other obligation of one Knight of 10L., and my purse with 5 rings of gold, and 17s. 6d. of gold and silver; and one harness [suit of armour] complete of the touch of Milan; and one gown of fine perse blue, furred with martens; and 2 gowns, one furred with bogey [lambskin] and one lined with frieze.

This was indeed a roomy chest, as were those in which, according to naughty tales, lovers surprised in their mistresses' chambers were so often concealed; or that antique piece with a self-closing lock in the story of *The Mistletoe Bough* wherein the young lady lies during a game of hide-and-seek, to be found years later, a skeleton. Since the cash was kept there, the chamber could conveniently serve also as a counting-house: in 1459 Margaret Paston writes to Sir John to say that she has measured his chamber, and finds that if his 'cofers' and his 'cownterwery' are put between the bed and the door, he will not have room to sit beside them. God, as well as Mammon, could be served from the bedchamber; a private chapel was often attached to it for the owner 'to make his sacrifice when he arose and when he went to bed'.

13

Hanggyd Beddes

AN account of a pillage in 1306 mentions a mysterious summer snowstorm, which proved to be caused by the troops cutting open the pillows in search of loot; but feathers seem to have been scarce; servants were warned not to lose any when re-covering the bedding. Chaucer's 'fethir bed' was a luxury. Down was even rarer, although it was plucked repeatedly from the live birds; without unduly annoying them, if we believe in the willingness of the goose in the rhyme:

> Cackle, cackle, Mother Goose,
> Have you any feathers loose?
> Truly have I, pretty fellow,
> Half enough to fill a pillow.
> Here are quills, take one or two,
> And down to make a bed for you.

(Hence the later definition of 'government' as 'plucking geese without making them cackle'.) Payments for straw and 'litter' are frequent in the royal household books, and certain townships had to deliver regular fixed quantities to the crown. At Cardigan in 1428 we find '*4 slyddys de gorst ad implenda lecta*', that is, gorse for stuffing the beds; hardly a restful material, even though 9*d.* worth of 'litter' was added. Seaweed and peapods cannot have been much better. The hair-mattress had not yet come in, unless we swallow the splendid boast quoted in an anthology of *gasconnades*:

I would have you know that the mattresses on which I rest my limbs are stuffed with nothing but the moustaches of those my sword has vanquished!

An account of 1444 includes the cost of straw for the Duke of Orleans' bed, to be provided because somebody has stolen his '*pailles*'. The straw does not seem to have been neatly enclosed in fabric, but merely tied into a truss, until the *paillasse* (the 'pally-ass' of the modern army) appears in 1492:

> Gromes palets shall fyl and make liter,
> Six fote on length withouten diswer [disarray],
> One fote y wys it shall be brode,
> Well watered, and wrythen be craft ytrode.
> Wyspes drawen oute at fote and syde,
> Well wrethyn and agayne that tyde.

Straw formed the base even for a feather-bed. The household regulations of Henry VII detail the procedure for the whole solemn business of bed-making. The groom of the wardrobe brings in the loose straw and lays it reverently at the foot of the bed. The gentleman-usher draws back the curtains. Two squires stand by the bed-head, and two yeomen of the crown at the foot. One of these, with the help of the yeoman of the chamber, carefully forms the truss, and rolls up and down on it to make it smooth and to ensure that no daggers or such are hidden in it. (As this is done afresh every day, a king must use 365 times as much straw as a monk.) A canvas is laid over the straw, then the feather-bed, which is smoothed with a bed-staff. The yeomen next place and tuck in the various coverings: the 'fustians' or blankets, of which the best formerly came from Chalons in France, but are made in England by the 'chaloners'; Chaucer calls blankets 'chalons'; the sheets, maybe 'linen of Reynes'; the 'pillow-beres' of Naples fustian; all of these perfumed:

The gromes schell gadyr for the kinges gowns and shetes and othyr clothes the swete floures, herbis, rotes, and thynges to make them breathe more holesomely and delectable.

Over all goes a 'pane' of ermine, turned down to expose the embroidered head-sheet. The foot-sheet is a costly cover at the foot of the bed, on which the king sits for his bedtime toilet. Finally the usher opens the curtains again for a squire of the body to sprinkle holy water on the bed; the curtains fall, and the bed can be considered made.

In France the royal beds were by now so big, that the nightly routine required the *fourrier* to poke and thwack the bedding thoroughly with his bed-staff, not in order to smooth it, but to make sure that no intruder was hiding in it.

The English court followed royal example, and the merchant class in turn imitated the court; their bedchambers were by no means ill-appointed. A townsman of Bury in Suffolk in 1463 bequeathes to his niece:

... my grene hanggyd bedde steynd with my armys [painted with my arms] therin that hanggith in the chambyr ovir kechene, with the curtynez, the grene keveryng longgyng therto; another coverlyte, ij blanketts, ij peyre of good shetes, the trampsoun [pelmet], the costerys [valances], of that chambyr and of the drawgth [withdrawing?] chambyr next, tho that be of the same soort, a great pilve [pillow] and a small pilve; the fethirbeed is hire owne that hire maistresse gaf hire at London.
... And I geve hire the selour [bed canopy] and the steynyd clooth of the coronacion of Our Lady, with the clothes of myn that long to the bedde that she hath loyen in, and the beddyng in the draught chamber for hire servaunth to lyn in; and a banker [bench] of grene and red lying in hire chambyr with the long chayer [couch]; and a stondyng coffre and a long coffre in the drawth chambyr.

William Honyboorn, also of Bury, bequeathes to his wife in 1493:

... my best ffether bedde with the traunsome, a whyte selour with a testour thereon, with iij white curteyns therto, a coverlight white and blewe lyeng on the same bedde, with the blankettes ... [and to his daughter] a ffether bedde next the best, a materas lyeng under the same, iiij peyr shetys, iij pelowes, a peyr blankettes.

A bed 'next the best' need not be a mean affair, and when Shakespeare left his 'second best bed' to Anne Hathaway, the bequest was not necessarily meant unkindly. In other middle-class wills we find 'coveryng of arasse', 'a testour steynyd with fflowers', 'a coverlyght with fflowre de lyce, a selour and a testour steynyd with Seynt Kateryn at the hed and the crucifix on the selour'. These evidences of well-bedded households do not support the conclusions drawn by many writers from a much-quoted account by the Reverend William Harrison. This was written in 1577, but it refers back to the conditions of at least a generation earlier:

Our fathers yea and we ourselves have lien full oft upon straw pallets, covered only with a sheet, under coverlets made of dagswain or hop harlots (I use their own terms) and a good round log under their heads instead of a bolster. If it were so that our fathers or the good man of the house had a mattress or flockbed and thereto a sack of chaff to rest his head upon, he thought himself to be as well lodged as the lord of the town, that peradventure lay seldom in a bed of down or whole feathers. Pillows were thought meet only for women in childbed. As for servants, if they had any sheet above them, it was well, for seldom had they any under their bodies, to keep them from the pricking straws that ran oft through the canvas of the pallet and razed their hardened hides.

This passage has been taken to prove that middle-class comfort dates only from the middle Tudor period, but its value depends on what social class this country parson had in mind, and on what he meant by 'our fathers': he may have meant our remoter 'forefathers'. Even in 1500 it would hardly have been true of the average household. The growth of the wool trade was not only adding to the luxury of the manor house, and subsidising the building of some splendid churches; it was relieving poverty all round. During the fifteenth century, according to the social historians, a new and prosperous middle class was emerging.

55

Charles VI of France (1380–1422) gives audience, more or less in bed

14

Lit de Parade

THE household accounts, wills and inventories of the next
three centuries are full of colour, especially in France, where
the bed—always the most important item in the list—may
be of *serge violette, camelot jaune, cendal vermeil, tartaire
vert rayé d'or, velours bleu semé de fleurs de lis d'or, soie vermeille,*

56

satin vert brodé de cerfs-volants, cendal bleu clair enrichi de fleurs de lis de cendal jaune, satin blanc semé de roses, velours cramoisi orné de franges d'or, satin cramoisi et blanc frangé d'or avec damas broché d'or et semé de roses, velours figuré incarnadin garny de clinquant d'or et d'argent, toile damassée d'or, with *pommes dorées, trèfles d'argent* ... but those whose visual digestion is strong enough should consult the long and luscious descriptions in Havard's *Dictionnaire de l'Ameublement.* The queen of Philip V sleeps in a bed of red silk, embroidered with parrots bearing the arms of France, and butterflies bearing those of her native Burgundy, arrayed on a ground of silver shamrocks. Her husband favours pale blue silk with yellow *fleurs de lys* and heraldic embroidery. The *ciel de lit*, the underside of the canopy, over the bed of Charles V, is decorated with an orchestra of angels playing among red roses.

The bed becomes the symbol and setting of royalty, virtually a throne. The *lit de parade* or state bed develops from the *lit de justice* dating from the reign of St. Louis:

> *Seroit le lict a tousjours mis*
> *En tous lieux ou les roys seroyent*
> *Pour jugement, et que tiendroient*
> *De France la sainte couronne.*
> *... Et l'appel' on lict de justice,*
> *Qui est a ramembrer propice,*
> *Toutefois que roy proprement*
> *Doit venir en son parlement*
> *Ou qu'il sied pour justice alliours.*

('The bed would always be placed wheresoever the kings who held the holy crown of France might sit in judgement ... and it is called the bed of justice, to be propitiously erected whenever the king duly attends his parliament or else sits in judgement'.)

'The bed of justice,' remarked Fontenelle sourly, 'is the place where Justice sleeps.' Set up on a dais seven steps high, the king would more or less lie, while the princes sat, the higher officials stood, and the lesser ones knelt, thus clearly depicting the hierarchy in the eyes of all; everybody literally knew his place. On the bed the king displayed himself on all manner of court occasions; even after his death, when he would lie there fully robed, crowned, barbered, powdered and painted, for the public to queue and stare. This custom gave rise to a difficulty when a sick king neared his end: the state bed made an inconvenient sick-bed, but the king must die in it. Though he might be nursed in a simple little cot nearby, as soon as it was evident that he was entering his last agonies he would be unceremoniously whisked across into the state bed to expire in the

57

proper setting. The new king would start his coronation procession towards the cathedral by climbing out of a bed set up in the adjoining archbishop's palace. When a princeling was to be christened, a bed would be set up inside the royal chapel. The royal bed itself, even when unoccupied, became the object of a cult. Persons entering the bedchamber, even princesses of the blood, genuflected towards it as if it were an altar. Whether or not it had a protective balustrade round it, ordinary mortals would not approach. It had its own specially appointed guard. Dogs, who did not understand the rules, were a problem, and dog-stoppers of various kinds had sometimes to be laid over the bed or set around it like cages. At the *château d'Angers* in 1471 the dignity of the state bed must have been somewhat impaired by the '*grant treillis de bois*' erected for this purpose. But favoured dogs might share the royal couch, and puppies were sometimes trained as foot-warmers, rather as they are depicted in stone on knightly tombs. Hence perhaps the old saw, '*A coucher avec les chiens on attrape des puces.*'

By an extension of the idea of the divinity that hedges a king, the bed came to be thought a fit setting for a saintly image. Thus in a gatehouse at the Porte du Chatelet in Paris there was displayed a bed, richly decked up as for royalty, in which lay an effigy of St. Anne. The clergy were not content to crown the Virgin with gold and jewels: she surely deserved the honour of a bed, and when occasion offered she was given one, as in the Nativity painted at Rheims in 1548, in which the stable at Bethlehem houses a canopied bed in red and gold.

When royalty was abed, lords and ladies-in-waiting stayed in all-night attendance, but they slept on *paillasses* on the floor. Although a *chaalis* or bedstead was provided for one of those serving Charles VI, this was conceded only because the bedroom floor was unusually damp. In 1492 Anne of Brittany had six *paillasses* for her maids-of-honour. But a favourite lady-in-waiting might share a queen's bed in the king's absence. The dimensions of these beds allowed of such hospitality, and in all classes of society it was usual for members of a family not only to share a bed, but at need to make room for a guest. The idea that immorality requires bed-sharing, and *vice versa*, is a fairly modern one. Joinville tells of a queen who works herself up into such an anxiety state because her husband has gone crusading, that she begins to see Saracens in every corner of her bedchamber, and has to have a young chevalier to lie on her bed all night. Charles VIII, as a mark of reconciliation, invites the Duke of Orleans to share his bed. The chevalier Bayard (*sans peur*) shares his with his comrade Bellabre (*et sans reproche*); Francis I with Admiral Bonnivet.

Wax effigy of Henry IV on his lit de parade, *1610*

After the battle of Montcour the victorious Prince de Condé beds with his defeated but noble captive the Duc de Guise. Louis XIII seems to have been the first monarch known to have objected to bed-sharing.

A neat answer to the problem of the courtier or servant sleeping in attendance was provided by the 'truckle-bed', 'trundle-bed' or 'wheel-bed'; in France a *chariolle* or *sourlict* or *roulleret*—a little low bed with wheels at one end, occasionally at both, looking rather like a porter's truck, which could be pushed out of sight under the bigger bed, or under some other piece, or into another room, during the day. It was allotted to the squire when he accompanied his knight

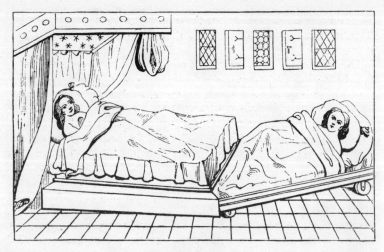

The Truckle-bed

on adventures. Falstaff has 'his standing bed and truckle-bed'. In a university the Master of Arts had his pupil in his room to sleep on a truckle-bed. In the illustration from the romance of *Le Comte d'Artois*, the count lies in the canopied bed while the truckle-bed is occupied by his valet (or so he thinks, though as it happens this is his wife in disguise). There is hardly headroom here for the occupant of the lower berth when it is pushed below the upper one, as the artist seems to suggest, but he is only trying to show how the device works. Sometimes the upper bed was in fact high enough to allow the valet to

> . . . lie upon the Truckle-bed
> Whiles his young maister lieth o'er his head.

In royal bedchambers the truckle-bed might be allotted to a person of some rank: in the queen's room, to the first maid-of-honour. Louise of Savoy, suspecting that the English Mary is an unfaithful wife to Louis XII, arranges for her stepdaughter Mme Claude to sleep in Mary's truckle-bed as a watch-dog.

A piece of bedroom furniture common from the fifteenth century is the 'aumbry', a little bedside cupboard for food and drink. In Thomas Tusser's *Five Hundred Points of Good Husbandry United to as Many of Good Huswiferie* we read how

> Some slovens from sleeping, no sooner be up,
> But hand is in aumbrie, and nose in the cup.

60

The aumbry was superseded by the 'livery cupboard', a larger affair. 'Liveries' were little stores of food and drink to prevent night-starvation.

There are many early references to *lits de camp* or 'trussing-beds', that is, folding 'camp-beds'; the first on record may be that used by Charles the Bold at the siege of Beauvais in 1472, but they were not necessarily for military occasions. Some were very elaborate, and many were made for ladies. Marguerite of Austria in 1523 had no less than one hundred on her inventory, including one of the earliest known four-posters. Louis XII gave one to the Cardinal d'Amboise that was *'faict à porsespiqz'*, not, that is, made of porcupines, but decorated with spiky knobs. Henry II of France, when he married Catherine de Medici, had one made of red velvet, embroidered with golden trees bearing fruit sewn with pearls. This cost 1300 *livres*; a rich affair, by whatever standard one might try to evaluate the *livre*; but two years earlier his father had given one to Henry VIII of England that had cost ten times as much. Such *lits de camp*, then, were not quite what we now call 'camp-beds'. Though made to fold in various ingenious ways, they had canopies and curtains and trappings much like the heavier fixed beds. As well as for journeying, they were used for prolonged camping, for which some elaborate tenting was made. In 1414 the Duke of Burgundy lived for more than a month in a forest camp with the Duchess, in tents complete with *salle, chapelle, chambres à parer et à couchier*. The 'Field of the Cloth of Gold' was a tented camp. Louis XV camped at Compiègne with 'tents' of wood, anticipating the modern army's prefabricated huts but doubtless better appointed and decorated: each had an audience chamber, a bedroom and a *cabinet de toilette*.

The introduction of the screw-cutting lathe had an indirect effect on the design and even the decoration of the bedstead. With metal screws instead of permanent tenon joints, the bedstead could now be dismantled at will and need not be left at home. This made it more worth while to decorate it, and the cabinet-maker began to divert some business from the upholsterer. It is significant that at the time of this change—about the mid-sixteenth century—the *châlit* is first called a *lit*, and the bedstead called a bed. With woodwork to be carried too, there is even more packing and carting and unpacking and assembling of beds in the accounts of royal journeys, and much bad temper when the beds travel more slowly than their weary owners. But Henry IV of France makes the best of this misfortune, when he goes to a first meeting at Lyons with his bride-to-be Marie de Medici. His bed fails to arrive, providing a neat excuse for anticipating the wedding night.

15

Elizabeth Slept Here

DURING the sixteenth century, according to the social historians, a new and prosperous middle class was emerging. After the Wars of the Roses, the English house plan could be adapted to still more tranquil times. Even a modest manor, though its moat might be dry, had till now made some slight gesture of defence with its walled courtyard and its gatehouse. Now, it could be built with big windows looking boldly outward over a peaceful countryside. Battlements and towers might persist, but they need not be taken seriously. Although architects in the modern sense had yet to emerge, builders were beginning to see that accurate 'draughts' or plans made beforehand, with plenty of right-angles, could save trouble later. The Gothic house seems to grow out of the ground almost naturally, like a rambling plant, but the Tudor house is an exercise in geometry. It is rectilinear and above all symmetrical, at some expense of indoor convenience. Contrary to modern tenets, outward show comes first, and the elevation dictates the plan. Typically this is an 'H' or more often an 'E', though this is not necessarily meant as a compliment to Queen Elizabeth. The short central arm of the E is the porch, and the side wings contain suites of chambers. The hall becomes a mere vestibule; its furniture is scanty and is often listed in the Tudor inventories as 'old'. Even the servants no longer eat or sleep in the hall: they have their own 'servants' hall' to live in. Many of them still sleep in the kitchen; as late as 1526 a King's Ordinance requires somebody to

... provide and sufficiently furnish the said kitchens of such scolyons as shall not go naked or in garments of such vileness as they now do, nor lie in the nights and days in the kitchen or round by the fireside.

Failing a shakedown among the pots and pans, the servants are relegated into long low attics where beds by the dozen may be ranged under the roof, an arrangement that survives in royal establishments until the last years of Queen Victoria.

Henry VIII denounced the disuse of the hall and the decay of communal living, but private apartments multiplied, and the old halls, as well as the abbey buildings taken over as dwellings, were being subdivided by the insertion of floors and partitions. There was not much new building work in Henry's time except that for himself and Wolsey, but soon after Elizabeth's accession, important new houses began to go up. She herself built little, but she made a 'progress' every summer, and her wealthier subjects vied to offer her fit hospitality. A great many 'lodgings' were needed in a house upon which the whole court might descend, a lodging being a suite of rooms in one of the side wings overlooking the courtyard. Some of these would-be hosts built and furnished so far beyond their means as to cripple their family fortunes for generations to come. If it is true that 400 six-horse vehicles were commandeered for one such progress—even if it is only one-tenth true—no mean house would have served. As well as historic families such as the Howards, the Nevilles and the Talbots, there were the new rich: the Cecils, the Cravens, the Spencers and the Verneys, newly equipped with coats of arms and pedigrees. Setting up as country gentlemen, these too could hope to entertain royalty. The unexpected truth about most of the houses where guides assert that 'Queen Elizabeth slept here', is that she did.

In the 'Great Chamber', the visiting queen would sleep and give audience. Dr. Andrew Boorde in 1542 advises that the Great Chamber, and as many other chambers as possible, should have windows looking into the chapel. It must have been highly convenient to be able to attend service and yet hardly have to get out of bed.

The upper floor, reached by a fine staircase, was now more important, and no longer all given over to bedchambers. A new and wholly English feature, the 'Long Gallery' upstairs, provided for

63

gentle exercise and games in wet weather, and served also as a picture gallery as the family portraits proliferated. The Long Gallery at Aston Hall measured 137 ft. by 16 ft. by 18 ft. high, and the existing one at Hatfield is even larger. There has been some argument as to the main purpose of such generous apartments. They were certainly used sometimes as dormitories, if only during a progress or other such influx of guests. There were two Long Galleries at Cowdray, one on each side of the court, and in the *Book of Household Rules* drawn up by Lord Montague in 1595 the 'Yeoman of the Wardroppe' is to

see the galleryes and all lodginges reserved for st[r]angers cleanly and sweetly kepte, with herbes, flowers and bowes in their seasons and the beddes of such as shall hither resorte att their firste cominge to be mayde and the better sortes of quiltes of beddes at any tyme to be used at nightes taken off, and Yrish Rugges layd in their places.

The 'withdrawinge chamber' must also have been used at times for sleeping, for 'Rule 20' instructs 'the Yeoman of my Chamber' that

everye morning they doe ryse att a convenient hower to remove the pallettes (if there be any) out of my said withdrawinge chamber.

Tradition says that some 200 persons slept in this house, and none of the large all-male staff was allowed to 'lodge abroad'. The Yeomen of the Chamber had to act as housemaids, and with the help of 'boyes of the kytchen' had to keep the chambers 'cleane and sweete'. Despite the use of living-rooms for sleeping, some great houses did still overflow. Wolsey, when first appointed King's Chaplain in his youth, had to share a bed with old Lord Darcy of Templehurst, and may have remembered this in his great days when he employed forty-six yeomen in his chamber at Hampton Court 'to attend upon his person', and eleven more in his 'wardrobe of beds'. At the royal manor of 'Okyng' Henry VIII had to order 'a grete long shed in the utter courte wyth viij new partycions in it for offycers to lye in'.

The walls of the chamber might be plastered, as at Little Saxham Hall whose owner paid in 1509 for

lathing and laying wt. here [with hair] and morter of iiij chambres, wt. pergettyng and white casting thereof.

'White casting' was moulded decorative plastering, a craft that was to develop into the repetitive elaboration of the late Tudor and Jacobean ceilings. The walls might be decorated in 'water-work'

Early Renaissance bed at the Chateau of Pau, belonging to Jeanne d'Albret, Queen of Navarre and mother of Henry IV. It is of oak, and bears the carved date 1562

(coloured distemper) direct on the plaster or on stretched canvas. An Elizabethan writer describes the chambers as

either hanged with tapestry, arras work or painted cloths, wherein either divers histories, or herbs, beasts, knots and such like are stained; or else they are ceiled with oak of our own or wainscot brought hither out of the east countries, whereby the rooms are not a little commended, made warm and much more close than otherwise they would be.

French bed, walnut and silk brocade, sixteenth century

Falstaff recommends to Mistress Quickly that

a pretty slight drollery, or the story of the Prodigal or the German hunting in water-work, is worth a thousand of these bedhangings and these fly-bitten tapestries.

The Tudors so loved painted decoration that in most years their Sergeant Painter was paid more than any other craftsman or contractor. Everything that a brush could reach was coloured: wooden ceilings; the plaster ceilings that we now see dead-white; even stonework. Wood was painted to look like marble or brick; brick to look like stone; stone to look like marble; plain wainscot, new or old, to look like marquetry. They seem to have had no love for the natural colours and textures of materials. One cannot merely say that Tudor rooms were gay—one might say that they were hilarious.

For a chamber window one might still use 'paper, or lyn clothe, straked a crosse with losynges' to make 'fenestrals in stede of glasen wyndowes'. Nor do floor-coverings seem to have improved. A ground-floor chamber might be paved with stone or tiles, but perhaps only with beaten earth. Elizabeth Cavendish instructs her servant Francys Wytfelde to 'cause the flore of my bedchamber to be made even either with plaster claye or lyme'. This would be matted, or strewn with rushes as of old. A much-quoted description by Erasmus of the dirty rush-strewn floors of an English house has led to a belief that the new rushes were merely spread on top of the old, but this can hardly have been so, for the occupants would soon have been wading knee-deep in a house such as Lord Willoughby's, where in 1561 up to 10s. a month was being spent on rushes. The 'herbes, flowers and bowes in their season' ordered at Cowdray were for the floors. Levinus Lemnius, a Dutch physician who visited England in 1560, contradicts Erasmus when he remarks how

their nosegayes finely entermingled wyth sundry sortes of fragraunte floures in their bedchambers and privy roomes, with comfortable smell cheered me up and entirelye delyghted all my sences.

A popular device in Elizabethan rooms was the 'posy', a pithy saying or rhyme inscribed decoratively over the fire-place or round the frieze. Thomas Tusser's suggestions for bedchamber posies include one that warns the guest so sternly how to behave, that it brings to mind the modern landlady's little notice about leaving the bathroom as one finds it:

With curtain some make scabbard clean, with coverlet their shoe:
All dirt and mire, some wallow bed, as spaniels use to do.
The sloven and the careless man, the roynish nothing nice,
To lodge in chamber comely decked are seldom suffered twice.

The ancillary furniture was still rather sparse in the state bed-chambers, and might still consist only of what a guest brought with him. When the Cardinal de Chatillon stayed at the royal palace of Sheen in 1568, Lord Buckhurst, who was in charge of the arrangements, had to lend his own bed, sheets, ewer, basin and candlesticks to the guest, who complained about this to the Privy Council. But most bedchambers would have at least a bed, meaning now a bedstead, for the cabinet-maker was ousting the upholsterer, and heavy wooden four-posters whose curtains were subsidiary were replacing the tester-beds, in which little woodwork had been visible. There might be several beds in one room; few of the principal chambers would have less than two. At Crook Hall in Durham in 1577 there were nine beds in three principal chambers, which had three, four and two beds respectively.

In the more modest household, with its bedrooms in constant use by the same occupants, furniture was more plentiful. In 1564 Margaret Cotton, of Gateshead, a widow of no very high social standing, had in her parlour

. . . one inner bed of wainscot, a stand, a bed, a presser of wainscot, 3 chests, a Dantzic coffer . . . a feather bed, a bolster, and a cod [pillow], 2 coverlets, 2 happgings [coarser coverlets], 3 blankets, 3 cods, with an old mattress . . .

The Rev. William Harrison says that even small farmers 'garnished their beds with tapestry and silk hangings'. But the labourer's 'silly cote' was as primitive as ever:

> At his bed's-feete feeden his stalled teme;
> His swine beneath, his pullen ore the beame . . .

New cottage building was discouraged, to deter the poor from pasturing on the common, and from perhaps burdening the local rates, and an act of Elizabeth 'against the creating and maintaining of cottages' was to stay on the statute book for some two centuries. The Tudor *cottage* was by no means the sort of thing that the term now suggests: our pretty country retreat of brick or half-timber, with its four or more rooms, if genuinely Tudor, was originally a 'yeoman house'. The miserable Tudor cottages have long since tumbled down.

68

The Great Bed of Ware (Victoria & Albert Museum) *measures 10 ft. 8½ in. wide and 11 ft. 1 in. deep—about the average size of the Tudor state beds of its time. It bears the carved date '1460' but was made more than a century later. It first became known at the* Crown Inn *at* Ware. *There, early in the eighteenth century, six citizens and their wives came from London and 'for a frolick' slept in it together. It is mentioned in* Twelfth Night, *in Ben Jonson's* The Silent Woman, *and in Farquhar's* The Recruiting Officer *thus:*

Serjeant Kite: *Oh! a mighty large bed! bigger by half than the great bed of Ware— ten thousand people may lie in it together, and never feel one another.*

Coster Pearmain: *My wife and I would do well to lie in't, for we don't care for feeling one another. But do folk sleep sound in this same bed of honour?*

S.K.: *Sound! ay, so sound that they never wake.*

C.P.: *Wauns! I wish again that my wife lay there.*

16

Ye Olde Four-Poster

THOSE who take special pride in the remote dates attached to their antique pieces should perhaps avoid lending or selling them to museums. When experts catalogue them, they tend sometimes to lose a century or two: the carved oak 'cradle of Henry V', for example, illustrated as such in several histories of furniture, and lent by the crown to the London Museum, is now dated 'late fifteenth century'; and the famous Great Bed of Ware, bearing the carved date '1460', is put by the experts of the Victoria and Albert Museum between 1575 and 1600. Not until the sixteenth century does the four-poster, so redolent of Ye Olde Englande, first lumber on to the English scene. It consists of a great shallow wooden box, raised above the floor, and carried on four tall posts, or sometimes on short independent legs within free-standing posts. The tops of the posts are connected by wooden rails or cornices. The 'sperver' or ceiling of the bed, and the vertical 'tester' behind the bed (which must not be confused with the older horizontal 'tester'), may be of wood or of fabric. Despite elaborate carving, all Tudor furniture is rather cumbersome, and the typical four-poster is especially so. Blackened by time, its oak looks even heavier today. Although it purports to follow classical forms, and may indeed look something like a Roman temple, beds are not buildings, and no Roman would think it anything but barbarous. The 'antique taste' has become adulterated on its way from Italy. Raw Dutch gin has got into the wine, and the final admixture of English beer does not improve the flavour. Although the first Renaissance work seen in England was by the hands of a few good Italian carvers working for Henry VII and for Wolsey, a very different kind of classicism came in with the Protestant refugee craftsmen from Flanders: vigorous perhaps, but clumsy; humorous, but without grace; its classical detail bungled by hands trained to a Gothic that had itself gone stale. A love of Ye Olde as such must be blind indeed if it can embrace these forms without a qualm: the posts with their illogical combination of the spindly and the bulbous in the same structural member; the coarse mouldings; the ill-digested ornament copied from the Dutch pattern-books, and unrelieved by any contrast of plain surface. God did not make good hard English oak for the purpose of finicky carving. A craftsman should respect his material; subdue it perhaps, but not torture it.

The bed was still far from being an efficient machine for sleeping in. All the necessary materials for making a comfortable spring mattress had been to hand for centuries, and there was no lack of craftsmanship: a swordsmith who could make a fine flexible rapier might surely have been able to turn out coiled springs; or at least an armourer who could tailor a comfortable chain-mail waistcoat might have made a chain-link mattress. But no thought seems to have been given to such possibilities. Beneath the splendour of carved wood and rich hangings, even royal backbones still lay on a base of straw, and a pile of 'brissel ticks' or feather mattresses—as warm in summer as in winter, and liable towards dawn to have formed a flat valley enclosed by two hillsides. At Bretton Park in Yorkshire, Sir Thomas Wentworth, Marshal of the Household of Henry VIII, kept the prodigious bulk of 'sixe stone' of feathers in stock. (Even prisoners in gaol were entitled to feather-beds if they could pay for their hire, as we learn from the record of a complaint lodged by the prisoners in Ludgate against their gaoler in 1533. He was denying them their right to have their own beds brought in, because he could then charge them 1d. a night for the use of a feather-bed, complete with blankets and covers; and furthermore he was making two or three share a bed, and charging them the full penny each.) Sheets were still something of a luxury, according to the inventory of a Cheshire house of 1605, which shows over twenty beds but only ten pairs of sheets.

71

The choice between night-wear and nudity still depended on climate, season and status. A woman of any social standing would wear a night-smock of cambric, with embroidery and openwork, perhaps heavily perfumed. Over this she might wear a 'night mantle', a thin sleeveless cape. In 1589 the 'Linnen List' of Winnifred Barrington includes '2 night quayfes' (coifs) and 'night cross-cloths' apparently worn across the brow. The 'night-gear' was kept by day in a 'cushion cloth' or night-dress case. The night-cap was *de rigueur*. Followers of Vaughan's *Treatise on the Preservation of Health* would wear one with a ventilating hole on top, and it was even held that a night-cap was highly necessary for the preservation of the teeth. A nobleman's might be rather splendid: the Duke of Rutland sported one that was 'wrought with gold' and cost 22*s*. John Corbett's 'beste velvet night cappe' was good enough to be worth mentioning in his will in 1577. The ordinary man would wear

> A knit nightcap made of coarsest twine
> With two long labels buttoned to the chin.

The 'night-gown', as is evident from the quantity and quality of its materials, was not for sleeping in; we would call it a dressing-gown. Anne Boleyn's night-gown is made of black satin—bound with black taffeta and edged with black velvet. Queen Elizabeth's 'winter night-gown' is also black, of velvet 'wrought with passanet lace of murry silk and gold, and lined with fur'. In 1568 she accepts the gift of a 'night-rail of cambric wrought all over with black silk'. It seems perhaps tactless in a virgin queen that when she is ordering 12 yards of purple velvet 'frized on the back syde with white and russet sylk' for another night-gown, she should include in the same order for 14 yards of murry damask 'for the making of a nyghtgowne for the Erle of Leycester'.

Bedroom manners still allowed a freedom that would lead to raised eyebrows today. Knights were still bold: Sir William Roper of Eltham called one day 'pretty early' on Sir Thomas More with a view to choosing one of his daughters for a wife; Sir Thomas took the visitor to his own bedchamber, where the two girls lay asleep in a truckle-bed, and whisked off the sheet to reveal them 'with their smocks up as high as their armpits'. Waking up, they both turned modestly over on to their faces, whereat Sir William remarked, 'I have seen both sides'; patted one on the bottom and announced 'Thou art mine'. 'Here', ends Aubrey, 'was all the trouble of the wooing.'

When Sir James Melvil, Gentleman of the Bedchamber to Mary Queen of Scots, came on a mission to Elizabeth's court, it was quite in order that the queen should take him to her bedchamber 'to show him some miniatures', and that he should find the Earl of Leicester and secretary Cecil there. When Elizabeth was being wooed by the eighteen-year-old Duke of Alençon, whom she called 'her frog', she took his soup to him in his bed, and let him keep her night-cap and her garter among his souvenirs; though she was very shocked when Mary Queen of Scots sat at the bedside of her lover Darnley when he had measles.

Elizabeth's 'Bodyguard of the Bed' comprised '5 beddes marshalls, 4 sewers, 2 surveiors, 2 yeomen, 2 groomes, 2 pages and 1 clark'— eighteen in all. In 1598 a tourist describes the beds of Henry VII, Henry VIII and Edward VI, all as being 11 ft. square, and Elizabeth's as not quite so large. (Sizeable beds these, but compare the marriage-bed of Phillipe le Bon and Isabella of Portugal, which was 18 ft. long and 12 ft. wide.) One of Elizabeth's beds deserves mention for its especial splendour. It was of 'walnut tree', carved, painted and gilt. The selour, tester and valance were of cloth-of-silver, figured with velvet, lined with taffeta that could be changed when its pattern palled, and deeply fringed with Venice gold, silver and silk. The tapestry curtains were 'curiously worked' with gold and silver lace, caught up with long loops and buttons of bullion. The head-piece was in crimson Bruges satin edged with a 'passemayne', surmounted by six

Dutch bedchamber, early sixteenth century

73

ample plumes containing seven dozen ostrich feathers of various colours. The counterpane was of orange satin, quilted with gold and silver cut-work. Finally, to relieve any drabness, the counterpane and even the ostrich feathers were garnished with gold and silver spangles. Had this very bed survived and been set up on the stage of the Royal Opera House for *Gloriana*, performed in the coronation year of Elizabeth II, John Piper might have been criticised for a scenic design of excessive fancy.

But as her end neared, Elizabeth was determined to avoid the risk that if she took to her bed, she might never rise from it again, and she passed the last four days and nights of her life lying on cushions on the floor, 'laid for her in the privy chamber hard by the closet door'.

Horace Walpole has described Mary Queen of Scots' state bedchamber at Hardwicke:

. . . the bed has been rich beyond description, and now hangs in costly golden tatters. The hangings, part of which they say her Majesty worked, are composed of figures as large as life sewed and embroidered on black velvet, white satin, etc., and represent the virtues that were necessary for her or that she was forced to have, as Patience and Temperance etc.

Another bed belonging to that tragic, black-gowned, black-bedded queen has been cited as evidence to blacken her name with complicity in murder. Her husband Darnley lay at the lonely house of Kirk o' Field in a new black bed, and alongside it was a bath. Just before going away for a night to attend a wedding, Mary had the bed taken away because, she said, the splashing of the bath might spoil it. An old purple couch was put in its place. That night, in her absence (unless we believe the story that she was there dressed as a man), Darnley was suffocated in his sleep, and the house was blown up with gunpowder. Mary's enemies have deduced that she knew of the intended murder, and was so cold-blooded as to want to save the bed.

Darnley's bedside bath cannot have been a very impressive affair —its cover was made from one of the house doors—but a few bathrooms adjoining bedchambers do appear in the records. Elizabeth had two, their walls and ceilings lined with mirror-glass. She even had a water-closet, the invention of her godson Sir John Harington, but his idea did not catch on. The 'house of office' or 'privy closet' adjoining the bedchamber was not water-flushed. The old 'garderobe' of the Middle Ages, a seat set over a shaft formed in the wall, was no longer being built. The substitute was a 'close-stool', an upholstered seat containing a pot, no more savoury than the old form of sanitation, but often kept at the bedside.

Late fourteenth-century Inn

17

Host and Hostess

THE Reverend William Harrison could speak highly of the Tudor inn:

> . . . Here in England everie man may use his inne as his owne house, and have for his monie how great or little varietie of victuals, and what other service himself shall thinke expedient to call for . . . Our innes are also verie well furnished with naperie, bedding, and tapisterie, especiallie with naperie, for beside the linnen used at the tables, which is commonlie washed daily, is such as belongeth to the estate and calling of the ghest . . . Each commer is sure to lie in cleane sheets, wherein no man hath been lodged since they came from the laundress. If the traveller have an horsse his bed dooth cost him nothing, but if he go on foot he is sure to paie a penie for the same. If his chamber be once appointed he may carie the kaie with him. If he loose ought whilest he abideth in the inne, the host is bound by a generall custome to restore the damage.

(No provision is made, we notice, for the 'ghest' who loses his 'kaie', but this is perhaps attached to a woundy great chain.) By the sixteenth century the distinction between the tavern and the inn—

still important today—is legalised. The tavern-keeper, whose proper business is victuals and drink, is forbidden to provide beds, but as is only fair, the innkeeper is forbidden to let his guests tipple. Old stories of old inns suggest that while the landlord often cheated the guest, the guest as often cheated him; the authors' sympathies seem to lie with the guest in either case. Tarlton, who was Court Jester to Queen Elizabeth, and 'could *undumpish* her at pleasure', makes advances to the hostess of the *Christopher* at Waltham:

. . . an exceeding merry honest woman, yet would take anything: which Tarlton hearing, as wise as he was, thinking her of his minde, he was deceived: yet he askt her if the biggest bed in her house were able to hold two of their bignesse; meaning himself and her. Yes, saies she, and tumble up and down at pleasure. Yes, one upon another, saies Tarlton. And under, to, saies she. Well, to have their custom she agreed to everything, like a subtill oastesse: and it fell so out that Tarlton, having her in a room at her house, askt her which of those two beds were big enough for them two. This, said she: therefore, goe to bed, sweetheart, Ile come to thee. Masse, saies Tarlton, were my boots off, I would, indeed. Ile help you, sir, saies she, if you please. Yes, thought Tarlton, is the wind in that doore? Come on, then. And she very diligently begins to pull, till one boot was half off. Now, saies she, this being hard to doe, let me try my cunning on the other, and so get off both. But, having both half off his legs, she left him alone in the shoemaker's stocks, and got her to London, where Tarlton was three houres, and had no help.

After which, Tarlton must have needed some undumpishing. But a score is made for the guests versus the hostesses by George Peele, whose *Merrie Conceited Jests* are related in 1600:

George lying at an old widow's house, and had gone so far on the score that his credit would stretch no further; for she had made a vow not to depart with drink or victuals without ready money. Which George, seeing the fury of his froward hostess, in grief kept his chamber; called to his hostess, and told her, 'She should understand that he was not without money, how poorly soever he appeared to her, and that my diet shall testify; in the meantime, good hostess,' quoth he, 'send for such a friend of mine.' She did: so his friend came; to whom George imparted his mind, the effect whereof was this, to pawn his cloak, hose, and doublet, unknown to his hostess: 'For,' quoth George, 'this seven nights do I intend to keep my bed.' Truly he spake, for his intent was, the bed should not keep him any longer. Away goes he to pawn his apparel; George bespeaks good cheer to supper, which was no shamble-butcher stuff . . . His friend brought the money, supped with him: his hostess he very liberally paid, but cavilled with her at her unkindness, vowing that, while he lay there, none should attend him but his friend. The hostess replied, a'God's name, she was well contented with it: so was George too; for none knew better than himself what he intended. But, in brief, thus he used his kind hostess. After his apparel and money was gone, he made bold with the feather-bed he lay on, which his friend slily conveyed away, having as villainous a wolf in his belly as George, though not altogether so wise, for that feather-bed they devoured in two days, feathers and all; which was no sooner digested, but away went the coverlets, sheets, and the blanket; and at the last dinner, when George's good friend perceiving nothing left but the bed-cords . . . he left George in a cold chamber, a thin shirt, a ravished bed, no comfort left him but the bare bones of deceased capons. In this distress George bethought him what he might do: nothing was left him; and as his eye wandered up and down the empty chamber, by chance he spied out an old armour, at which sight George was the joyfullest man in Christendom; for the armour of Achilles, that Ulysses and Ajax strove for, was not more precious to them, than this to him; for he presently claps it upon his back, the halbert in his hand, the morion on his head; and so gets out the back way, marches from Shoreditch to Clerkenwell, to the no small wonder of those spectators that beheld him.

Being arrived to the wished haven he would be, an old acquaintance of his furnished him with an old suit and an old cloak for his old armour. How the hostess looked when she saw the metamorphosis in her chamber, judge those bomborts that live by tapping, between the age of fifty and three-score.

An even worse-behaved guest was that quarrelsome traveller Benvenuto Cellini, who took umbrage at an inn between Chioggia and

Fifteenth-century Inn

77

Ferrara when the host insisted on being paid in advance, even before Benvenuto went to bed:

We had, I must admit, the most capital beds, new in every particular, and as clean as could be. Nevertheless I did not get one wink of sleep, because I kept on thinking how I could revenge myself. At one time it came into my head to set fire to his house; at another to cut the throats of four fine horses which he had in the stable . . .

but finally, going back to the inn on a pretext, when the baggage is safely away,

I went upstairs, took out a little knife as sharp as a razor, and cut the four beds that I found there into ribbons. I had the satisfaction of knowing I had done a damage of more than 50 crowns.

Let us remember, in fairness, that for every innkeeper who may be heard to complain of the behaviour of a guest, there are hundreds of guests who may complain of him.

A manual of foreign conversation in seven languages, published in 1589, was so popular that it ran into seven editions. It gives a rather strange dialogue to help travellers to deal with chambermaids:

My shee frinde, is my bed made? is it good?
—*Yea, Sir, it is a good feder bed, the scheetes be very cleane.*
—I shake as a leafe upon the tree. Warme my kerchif and bynde my head well. Soft, you bynde it to harde, bryng my pillow and cover me well: pull off my hosen and warme my bed: drawe the curtines and pinthen with a pin. Where is the camber pot? Where is the privie?
—*Follow mee, and I will shew you the way: go up streight, you shall finde them at the right hand. If you see them not you shall smell them well enough. Sir, doth it please you to have no other thing? Are you wel?*
—Yea, my shee frinde, put out the candell, and come nearer to mee.
—*I wil put it out when I am out of the chamber. What is your pleasure, are you not wel enough yet?*
—My head lyeth to lowe. My shee friende, kisse me once, and I shall sleape the better.
—*Sleape, sleape, you are not sicke, seeing that you speak of kissyng. I had rather die than to kisse a man in his bed, or in any other place. Take your rest in God's name, God geeve you good night and goode rest.*
—I thank you, fayre mayden.

In the morning, under the heading 'Communication at the oprysing', the traveller calls to the boy, 'Drie my shirt, that I may rise', and has forgiven the unwilling chambermaid, for he departs with 'Where is ye maiden? hold my shee freend, ther is for your paines.'

78

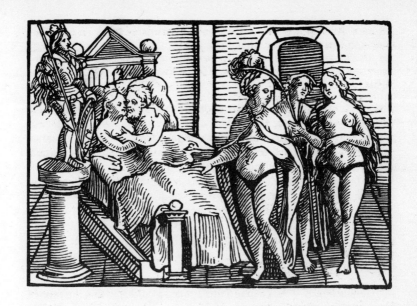

18

Stuart Frolics

IN seventeenth-century England, according to the social historians, a new and prosperous middle class was emerging. New houses were going up apace. Timber was getting scarce, and except in a few southern counties, the art of building had passed out of the hands of the carpenter into those of the mason and bricklayer. The so-called 'Jacobean' style was only a continued development of the 'Elizabethan'. The house plan was still based on external drama—symmetrical massing and striking silhouette—'uniform without,' says Francis Bacon, 'though severally partitioned within'. Architects were still reluctant to give space to circulation, and thus provide privacy. Their unpractical planning was frowned upon by Sir Henry Wotton in his *Elements of Architecture* of 1624:

. . . they do so cast their *partitions* as when all *Doors* are open a man may see through the whole *House*, which doth necessariely put an intollerable servitude upon all the *Chambers* save the Inmost, where none can arrive, but through the rest; or else the Walles must be extreame thicke for secret passages. And yet this also will not serve the turne, without at least *Three* doores to every Roome: a thing most insufferable . . . I cannot commend the direct opposition of such *Overtures*, being indeede merely grounded upon the fond ambition of displaying to a *Stranger* all our *Furniture* at one Sight.

The relations between the householder, the family and the servants were still so intimate, that much coming and going through bed-rooms that would today be intolerable intrusion, was then a matter of course. There is a foretaste of better domestic planning to come, in the house at Coleshill built in 1662 by Sir Roger Pratt, a friend of Inigo Jones. It is much in advance of its time, with circulation on modern lines. Absolute symmetry does not deny internal convenience. The two bedrooms on the ground floor, and the four above, all have separate access from a corridor, with dressing-rooms, fire-places, and good light. Except for the housekeeper's room, no servant's room is in the basement; they are in the roof, which has generous dormers. Celia Fiennes describes this house:

. . . the fine house of Sir George Pratt's called Coalsell . . . on the tope of the stairs you enter in ye midde into a dineing roome, within that a Chamber on each side with two closets to each bigg Enough for a little bed, with chimney's convenient for a servant and for dressing roomes, one of which has a doore also out into that passage and soe to the back staire . . . They are all well and Genteel'ly furnisht, damaskes Chamlet and wrought beds ffashionable made up. Over this runs a Gallery all through the house, and on each sid severall garret roomes for servants ffurnished very neate and Genteele . . .

The taste for tall houses, for the sake of external effect, can be instanced in Chastleton and in Fountains Hall, both with five floors. This arrangement incidentally improved the access, the lighting and the height of the bedrooms. Inigo Jones had shown how to handle classical forms with scholarly elegance, and the English interior now looked more like the work of a gentleman. Counterfeit materials were more rare. The naïve fancies of the 'Sergeant Painter' were discouraged; decoration and colour were sobered. Bedrooms were now panelled against cold and damp. There was still a strong Flemish influence in furniture, and little classic grace in it as yet, but the English craftsman had begun to drop the bad habit of making furniture as if it were architecture. Under the Commonwealth, the simplification of living and of design insisted upon by the Puritans was in some ways salutary. By the time of the Restoration, furniture had become austerely comfortable, almost functional. When Charles II and his fellow-exiles returned from the Continent with gay ideas, the revival of rich furnishing was restrained by some moderation learned during the Puritan years. In the bedroom, the heavy four-poster was dismantled, and the upholsterer, with his fine Genoa velvets, won back his former supremacy over the cabinet-maker. The canopy of the bed, with a lighter moulded cornice, was raised almost to the ceiling, and as the rooms were high, the curtained bed assumed an elegant proportion quite unlike the squat Tudor structure. Celia Fiennes, writing in about 1698, thinks it a fault when a bed does not reach the ceiling, for she notes at Newby Hall

... 6 or 7 Chambers off a good size and lofty, so that most of the beds were two foote too low which was pitty they being good beds, one was crimson figured velvet, a damaske bed, the rest moehaire and camlet.

At Burghley House, the home of the Duke of 'Excetter', then recently altered and refurnished, she describes in breathless prose into which some punctuation has been inserted by her editor:

... parlours dineing rooms drawing roomes and bed-chambers, one leading out of another at least 20 that were very large and lofty and most delicately painted on the top, each roome differing, very fine Carving in the mantle-pieces and very fine paint in pictures, but they were all without Garments or very little, that was the only fault, the immodesty of the Pictures especi-ally in my Lords appartment; his bed chamber was furnish'd very rich the tapistry was all blew Silke and rich gold thread, so that the gold appeared for the light part of all the worke; there was a blew velvet bed with gold fringe and very richly embroidered all the inside with ovals on the head piece and tester where the figures are so finely wrought in satten stitch it looks like painting; there is also my Ladys appartment; severall roomes very richly furnish'd and very fine tapistry with silver and gold in most, there was at least 4 velvet beds 2 plaine and 2 figured crimson green severall coullours together in one, severall damaske beds and some tissue beds all finly embroydered . . . there is a Chamber my Lady used to lye in in the Winter a green velvet bed and the hangings all Embroydery of her Mother's work, very fine, the silk looks very fresh and figures look naturall.

(This was not the only occasion when immodest pictures upset Celia: at 'Lord Sandwitch's' house she saw 'a fine picture of Venus were it not too much unclothed'.)

Once again, royal mistresses set the pace and the people followed. Charles Cotton, the burlesque writer, comments on the trend:

> Anthony feigns him Sick of late,
> Only to shew how he at home,
> Lies in a Princely Bed of State,
> And in a nobly furnish'd Room

Adorned with pictures of Vandike's,
A pair of Chrystal Candlesticks,
Rich Carpets, Quilts, the Devil, and all:
Then you, his careful Friends, if ever
You wish to cure him of his Fever,
Go lodge him in the Hospital.

State beds still featured in court ceremonies. A spectator describes
the scene at the marriage of the 14-year-old Prince of Orange to
the 10-year-old Princess Mary Stuart, solemnised in Her Highness'
bedchamber:

The Princess was disrobed in the Queen's chamber, and placed in the
state bed of blue velvet, called the bed of parade, which was richly framed
with gold and silver, with buttons and embroidery of gold and silver,
surmounted with four grand white plumes . . . The King himself [Charles I]
introduced the Prince, who was in his *robe de nuit* and *pantoufles*. His
Majesty had some difficulty in conducting him through the crowd to the
side of the bed where the Princess was lying in state. The Prince kissed his
two brothers-in-law, the Prince of Wales and the Duke of York, and bade
them both good-night before he entered the bed, which he did very gently.
He then kissed the Princess three times, and lay beside her about three-
quarters of an hour, in presence of all the great lords and ladies of England,
the four Ambassadors of the United States [of Holland], and the distinguished personages who attended him in London.
When the King intimated it was time for him to retire to another
chamber which had been prepared for his use, the Prince bade adieu to his
little bride, kissing her thrice. But on leaving the bed one of his *pantoufles*
was missing, which after a search was found near the Princess.
As soon as he had recovered his *pantoufle*, he knelt to the King and
asked his blessing, and that of the Queen, and having received the bene-
diction of both, he was conducted by His Majesty to the chamber where he
slept.

This formal 'bedding' was part of the marriage contract, however
young the pair; they must appear in the same bed before the whole
court. Saint-Simon takes charge of the ceremony for the dauphin
and the Spanish infanta. The king undresses the prince, and the
queen the princess. All have to witness the closing of the bed-curtains,
but Saint-Simon takes the precaution of having the Duc de Popoli and
the Duchesse de Montellano slip inside unseen to keep an eye on
the newlyweds, who, they report, lie there quite happily eating sweets.
As soon as the witnesses have gone, they are let out. (The marriage,
however, was not a success.) The ceremony might even be carried
out by proxy in the absence of the bridegroom, as with the Emperor
Maximilian's bride:

82

She was publickly contracted, stated as a bride, and solemnly bedded; and, after she was laid, Maximilian's ambassador put his leg, stript naked to the knee, between the espousal sheets.

The gathering of the wedding-guests within the nuptial chamber to see the bride and groom into bed was not confined to royal occasions or the marriage of minors. It was a normal part of the fun at weddings at every social level until the nineteenth century. Evelyn, as a guest at a Jewish wedding in the ghetto at Venice, in 1644, was 'brought into the bride-chamber, where the bed was dressed up with flowers, and the counterpane strewed with works'. The custom survived into living memory in English villages, where it involved much bucolic horse-play, and it survives still in many lands. The bride having promised, at the church door, to be 'buxom in bed and at board', was escorted by the 'bridegroom men', while the 'bridemaids' escorted the groom. When the hour came for retiring, the bride was undressed by her maids and put to bed, while the men undressed the groom, and led him in. There was singing and dancing in the bedchamber, and 'flinging the stocking', a rite by which the guests might divine which of them would be next to wed. They would not withdraw until the bed, and the pair in it, had been blessed by the priest. It is said that some priests asked an extra fee if they performed this office

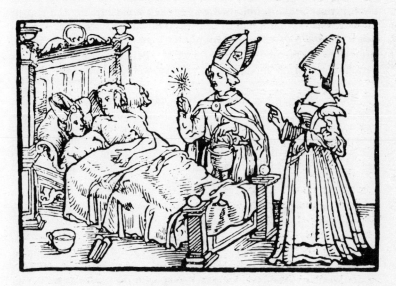

The Bishop blesses the Marriage Bed

83

before midnight; a tax on the impatient, who otherwise risked excommunication. Even then they were not left in peace, for

... though the yonge parsones, beynge weery of the bablyng noyse and inconuenience, comes ones towarde theyer rest, yet can they haue no quietnesse. For a man shall fynd unmanerly and restlesse people, that will first go to theyr chambre dore, and there syng vycious and naughtie balates that the deuell may haue his triumphe now to the uttermost.

Such bawdy customs long persisted. When Shelley eloped with Harriet Westbrook, and took a lodging in Edinburgh, the landlord allowed them credit and advanced funds for the wedding, on condition that Shelley would treat him and his friends to supper on the wedding night. The supper over, no sooner were the pair alone than the landlord tapped at their door, announcing 'It is customary here at weddings for the guests to come, in the middle of the night, and wash the bride in whisky.' 'I immediately', said Shelley, 'caught up my brace of pistols, and pointing them both at him, said to him, "I have had enough of your impertinence; if you give me any more of it I will blow your brains out"; on which he ran or rather tumbled down stairs, and I bolted the door.'

At Gilbert White's village of Selborne they recall the accident on the wedding night of one of the older inhabitants, still flourishing there, whose brass double bed was broken amidships by the weight of the guests, so that it had to be carried down the street to the blacksmith, welded together, and brought back amid cheers in time for the climax of the ceremony. The point of Mr. Pepys' account of such an occasion is that its 'modesty and gravity' were exceptional:

... and so, after prayers, soberly to bed; only I got into the bridegroom's chamber while he undressed himself, and there was very merry, till he was called to the bride's chamber, and into bed they went. I kissed the bride in bed, and so the curtains drawn with the greatest gravity that could be, and so good-night. But the modesty and gravity of this business was so decent, that it was to me indeed ten times more delightful than if it had been twenty times more merry and jovial.

But among Mr. Pepys' more fashionable friends there is less 'modesty and gravity', and many bedroom romps:

... and going to my Lady Batten's, there found a great many women with her in her chamber, merry—my Lady Pen and her daughter, among others, where my Lady Pen flung me down upon the bed, and herself and others, one after another, upon me, and very merry we were.

Italian Beds: c. 1600, from the Davanzati collection, Florence

c. 1650, from the Salvadori collection, Venice

85

. . . my Lady Castlemaine, a few days since, had Mrs. Stuart to an entertainment, and at night began a frolic that they two must be married—and married they were, with ring and all other ceremonies of church service, and ribbons and a sack posset in bed, and flinging the stocking; but, in the close, it is said that my Lady Castlemaine, who was the bridegroom, rose, and the King came and took her place. This is said to be very true.

Which recalls the remark of the Victorian lady who went to see *Antony and Cleopatra*: 'how unlike the home life of our own dear Queen!'

Nell Gwynn's bedroom at No. 79 Pall Mall was lined with mirrors from floor to ceiling. The bedstead was of solid silver, made by John Coques the silversmith whose shop was near by. At 2*s*. 11*d*. an ounce, it cost over £900. Its ornamentation included the king's head, some slaves and cupids, eagles and crowns, and—of all things—a figure representing the popular rope dancer Jacob Hall. Many have puzzled over this odd choice, but a solution may be offered. Mr. Pepys passes on to us a bit of gossip from his actress friend Mrs. Knipp, who appeared in the same theatre as Hall: my Lady Castlemaine, the king's official mistress, was 'mightily in love' with Hall. The figure of Hall, on the bed which the king doubtless shared, may well have been there to remind him, to the ease of his conscience and to Nell's advantage, that my Lady Castlemaine was as unfaithful to him as he to her. In any case, Hall is the last link in a vicious circle: Nell lies with the king, the king with Lady Castlemaine, Lady Castlemaine with Hall, and Hall (if only in effigy) shares Nell's bed; *la ronde* is complete.

To Evelyn it is quite an everyday matter that he should visit the king, the queen, Princess Henrietta, the Lord Chancellor, and the Duchess of Newcastle in their respective bedchambers, but he is a more sober character than Pepys, and even less approving of the court frolics:

Following his Majesty this morning through the gallery, I went with the few who attended him, into the Duchess of Portsmouth's *dressing-room* within her bedchamber, where she was in her morning loose garment, her maids combing her, newly out of her bed, his Majesty and the gallants standing about her; but that which engaged my curiosity was the rich and splendid furniture of this woman's apartment, now twice or thrice pulled down and rebuilt to satisfy her prodigal and expensive pleasures, whilst her Majesty's does not exceed some gentlemen's ladies in furniture and accommodation.

. . . Surfeiting of this, I . . . went contented home to my poor, but quiet villa. What contentment can there be in the riches and splendour of this world, purchased with vice and dishonour?

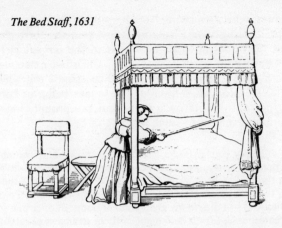

The Bed Staff, 1631

19

And so to Bed

THROUGHOUT the nine years of Mr. Pepys' diary (1660–9) the bedroom recurs as a background for his joys, woes and fears. His bed is a place for music, for reading, for the instruction of his wife and servants, for quarrels and reconciliations. In the bedroom, 'a little troubled and melancholy', he plucks his lute, or plays his pipe out of the window, or with his wife sings to the flageolet until they fall asleep. Mr. Greatorex the stationer shows him 'the manner of the lamp glasses, which carry the light a great way', and he decides to buy one for his lucubrations. He makes the boy Will construe at the bedside Latin verses from the Bible, and by night he teaches his wife 'things in astronomy'. He shares a bed with Mr. Hill, and they lie 'talking till midnight about Berkenshaw's music rules, and so to sleep'. He is mightily troubled with his snoring, and knows not how to cure it. On St. Valentine's Day there is some charming informality:

This morning comes betimes Dick Pen, to be my wife's Valentine, and came to our bedside. By the same token, I had him brought to my side, thinking to have him kiss me; but he perceived me, and would not; so went to his Valentine: a notable, stout, witty boy.

As he prospers, he often improves and refurnishes his house, and there is much changing around of bedrooms and beds; fitting new blue hangings in his own room, 'very handsome'; putting the old red ones in the dressing-room; hanging tapestry in the 'best chamber' in place of the 'sad stuff' that now goes to the servant girl in the 'long chamber'. Poor Mrs. Pepys (whose Christian name we never learn) 'works like a horse' at all this, then spends the whole day 'making herself clean, after four or five weeks being in continued dirt', and they not only throw a party, but can proudly lodge their guests overnight, subject to some juggling of beds:

... I did lodge my cousin Pepys and his wife in our blue chamber. My cousin Turner, her sister, and The. in our best chamber; and myself and my wife in the maid's bed, which is very good. Our maids in the coachman's bed, the coachman with the boy in his settle-bed, and Tom where he uses to lie. And so I did, to my great content, lodge at once in my house, with the greatest ease, fifteen, and eight of them strangers of quality.

He completes his bedroom appointments by putting up a 'spitting sheet' which he finds 'very convenient'. (This we must suppose to have been hung on the wall by the bedside as a target that would call for less accuracy than the spittoon. Expectoration in England has never approached American standards of marksmanship. At least it was preferable to the habit noted by Molière in one of his *Caractères*—drawn from life—who, because there are guests in the bedroom, *crache dans ses draps*.)

Next we see Mr. Pepys bringing home a perquisite of his job at the Admiralty:

Home with my wife, and saw her day's work in ripping the silk standard which we brought home last night, and it will serve to line a bed, or for twenty uses, to our great content ...

a perquisite probably no more authorised than the parachute silk that so often ended as nightwear during World War II.

The duties of the servants, one of whom usually sleeps in the Pepys' bedroom, include helping to dress and undress their master, reading to him, dancing, singing, playing sundry instruments, cutting his hair, and combing his head—a very necessary process of disinfestation, until soon after this time it became fashionable to have one's hair cut off and replaced by a periwig. Men at home and at their ease would replace the wig with a soft silk or velvet night-cap, even by day, and wear what Pepys calls a 'nightgown', but still what we would call a dressing-gown. The night-shirt had become as elaborate as the day-shirt, with lace at the neck and down the sleeves, and

88

ruffles at the wrist. The wig was dressed with powder, hence the 'powder-closet' where this dusty job could be done behind a closed door. The powder-closet would often conceal a 'close-stool', bringing to mind the modern euphemism 'powder-room'; but Mr. Pepys seems to have found a chamber-pot adequate in the bedroom, for his 'very fine close-stool' was kept in the drawing-room.

To bed, and this night began to lie in the little green chamber where the maids lie; but we could not a great while get Nell to lie there, because I lie there and my wife. But at last, when she saw she must lie there or sit up, she, with much ado, came to bed.

Nell seems to have been the only maid who took a twentieth-century view of this sleeping arrangement, but perhaps she had divined her master's way with wenches.

Abroad to buy a bell to hang by our chamber door to call the maids . . . [and then, two days later:] My wife waked to ring the bell to call up our maids to the washing about four o'clock, and I was, and she, angry that our bell did not wake them sooner; but I will get a bigger bell.

About the middle of the night I was very ill—I think with eating and drinking too much—and so I was forced to call the maid, who pleased my wife and I in running up and down so innocently in her smock.

He is a constant victim to wakeful fears, most of them quite imaginary, and his courage seldom rises above the point of sending a servant to seek out the thief or ghost while he awaits the outcome in safety:

To bed, a little troubled that I fear my boy Will is a thief and has stole some money of mine . . . [and the next night:] after we were all abed the wench (which lies in our chamber) caused us to listen of a sudden, which put my wife into such a fright that she shook every joint of her, and a long time that I could not get her out of it. The noise was the boy, and we did believe, got in a desperate mood out of his bed to do himself or William some mischief. But the wench went down and got a candle lighted, and finding the boy in bed, and locking the doors fast, with a candle burning all night, we slept well but with a great deal of fear.

About eleven o'clock, knowing what money I have in the house, and hearing a noise, I begun to sweat worse and worse, till I melted almost to water. I rung, and could not in half an hour make either of the wenches hear me; and this made me fear the more, lest they might be gagged . . . At last Jane rose, and then I understand it was only the dog wants a lodging, and so made a noise.

The truth is, my house is mighty dangerous, having so many ways to be come to; and at my windows, over the stairs, to see who goes up and down; but, if I escape tonight, I will remedy it. God preserve us this night safe! So, at almost two o'clock, I home to my house, and, in great fear, to bed, thinking every running of a mouse really a thief; and so to sleep, very brokenly, all night long, and found all safe in the morning.

. . . . an accident last night, that our young gib-cat did leap down our stairs from top to bottom, at two leaps, and frightened us, that we could not tell well whether it was the cat or a spirit, and do sometimes think this morning that the house might be haunted.

Over the years, domestic trouble mounts to a head in the Pepys' bedroom; nothing very serious at first; he goes to bed 'in a discontent' or 'in a pet', and when his wife buys 'a laced handkercher and pinner' without his leave, they 'do not sleep friends'. After an argument 'about the dog's being put down into the cellar, which I had a mind to have done because of his fouling the house', they 'lie all night in a quarrel'. Then the real trouble starts:

. . . after supper to have my head combed by Deb., which occasioned the greatest sorrow to me that ever I knew in this world; for my wife, coming up suddenly, did find me embracing the girl. I was at a wonderful loss upon it, and I endeavoured to put it off; but my wife was struck mute and grew angry, and, as her reason came to her, grew quite out of order: and I to say little, but to bed, and my wife said little also, but could not sleep all night, but about two in the morning waked me . . . But after her much crying and reproaching me with inconstancy, I did give her no provocation, but did promise all fair usage to her, and love, till at last she seemed to be at ease, and so toward morning a little sleep.

Deb keeps her job for a while, but Mrs. Pepys takes over Deb's duty of helping Mr. Pepys to dress and undress; good resolutions are made, but are broken even after Deb has been dismissed; soon Mrs. Pepys is

. . . upon her bed in a horrible rage afresh, calling me all the bitter names: and, rising, did fall to revile me in the bitterest manner in the world, and could not refrain to strike me and pull my hair, which I resolved to bear with, and had good reason to bear it . . . by and by into a raging fit she fell again, worse than before, that she would slit the girl's nose: at last W. Hewer came in and came up, who did allay her fury, I flinging myself in a sad, desperate condition upon the bed in the blue room. . . .

I to bed, not thinking but she would come after me . . . and I now and then praying her to come to bed, she fell out into a fury, that I was a rogue and false to her. I did, as I might truly, deny it, and was mightily troubled, but

90

A Lady of Quality, 1686

all would not serve. At last, about one o'clock, she came to my side of the bed and drew the curtain open, and with the tongs red hot at the end made as if she did design to pinch me with them; at which, in dismay, I rose up, and with a few words she laid them down, and did by little and little, very sillily, let all the discourse fall; and about two, but with much seeming difficulty, came to bed. . . .

My wife mighty peevish in the morning about my lying unquietly a'nights, and she will have it that it is a late practice from my evil thoughts in my dreams . . . she did believe me false to her with Jane, and did rip up three or four silly circumstances of her not rising till I come out of my chamber, and her letting me thereby see her dressing herself, and that I must needs go into her chamber; which was so silly, and so far from truth, that I could not be troubled at it, though I could not wonder at her being troubled, if she had these thoughts.

Not that he was incapable of watching a wench dressing, for when he visited Mrs. Turner, she was dressing herself by the fire in her chamber, and

. . . there took occasion to show me her leg, which indeed, is the finest I ever saw, and she not a little proud of it. . . .

and when Lady Peterborough sends for him to talk business, he notes how 'she loves to be taken dressing herself, as I always find her'. When he visited Mrs. Penington at Greenwich,

. . . at last, late, I did pray her to undress herself into her night-gown that I might see how to have her picture drawn carelessly (for she is mighty proud of that conceit), and I would walk without in the street till she had done. So I did walk forth, and whether I made too many turns or no in the dark, cold, frosty night between the two walls up to the Park gate I know not, but she was gone to bed when I came again to the house upon pretence of having some papers there, which I did on purpose by her consent.

Nor was he quite free of the 'evil thoughts in his dreams' that Mrs. Pepys suspected, though the only such dream recorded in the diary features neither Deb nor Jane:

. . . something put my last night's dream of Lady Castlemaine into my head, which I think is the best dream that ever was dreamt. And I dreamed that this could not be awake, but that it was only a dream, and that I took so much real pleasure in it, what a happy thing it would be if when we are in our graves (as Shakespeare resembles it) we could dream, and dream but such dreams as this, that we should not need to be so fearful of death as we are at this plague-time.

20

Births, Marriages and Deaths

THE curtains of the state bed still rose on such performances as lyings-in, births, christenings, marriages and deaths. Thus in 1612:

about this day sevenight, the Countess of Salisbury was brought a bed of a daughter, and lyes in very richly, for the hangings of her chamber being white satin embroidered with silver and pearl, is valued at fourteen thousand pounds.

The cost of the bed was more important than the weight of the baby, an item inescapable today but never mentioned then. The staging of the Salisbury accouchement would not have been judged particularly impressive in France, where expectant mothers of quite modest social standing would be abed in ample time to receive their friends beforehand, and would resume the party as soon as the baby was presentable. In higher circles, the proper period for such entertaining became so extended, that twenty balls could be held in the Duchess of Burgundy's bedchamber between her bedgoing and the delivery. A birth might be made the occasion for the painting of a family group centred on the natal bed. A bride was expected, on the day after her wedding, to take to her bed again to receive visitors of either sex. According to La Bruyère, who disapproved of the whole thing, it was open to anybody, acquainted or not, to come in and see the show. The Marquise of Rambouillet suffered so from rheumatism, that she had to wear a sort of bag round her legs at all times, and the doctors would not let her discard it even for this ceremonial occasion; but a lady of her rank need not have worried, for though the bag drew much attention, her visitors hastened to follow suit, and leg-bags immediately became fashionable, regardless of medical need. Saint-Simon mentions, as if it were the most ordinary of matters, that his wife the duchess, the day after their wedding, received *'toute la France'* on her bed. When a princess married, the king would join the court in visiting both newlyweds, fully dressed but in bed. Even crazier routines developed. We find the mother and even the sister of the bride taking to their beds for the nuptial occasion. Mme de Montespan receives congratulations from her bed, the day after the marriage of her niece. Mme de Maintenon goes one better when she and her newlywed niece go to bed simultaneously. Soon, any sort of happy or unhappy event justifies getting into bed, as when Mlle de Fontanges has been made a duchess and granted a pension—nobody present, remarks Havard, would have dreamed of drawing the obvious parallel between the attitude in which the duchess received her congratulations, and that in which she had earned her rewards. The finest shades of respect due to rank could be nicely observed in the bedroom setting. When the Doge of Genoa visited Versailles, the de Guise family received him standing, the dauphin and dauphine seated, the duchess in bed but dressed, the Princesse de Conti and Mlle de Bourbon in bed and in *deshabillé*. When Cardinal Richelieu was about to arrange with English ambassadors for the match between Charles I and Henrietta of France, negotiations almost broke down over a matter of two or three paces to be taken over the floor—protocol required that the distances walked should be apportioned, according to rank, between those meeting—but the cardinal neatly avoided the issue by taking to his bed, and opened the talks from there under indisputable rules. Voltaire found this sort of thing rather tedious—he thought that 'if anyone had suggested to Scipio that he should get between two sheets, to receive a visit from Hannibal, he would have found the ceremony very funny'. The sixth Duke of Somerset, as first peer of the realm, used to insist on his two youngest daughters standing in turn by his bedside throughout his afternoon nap, and when he awoke one day to see that Lady Charlotte, being tired, had sat down, this breach of decorum cost her £20,000 which he deducted from her legacy. The *bourgeoisie* joined in the game, and close friends and relations might be brought to the bedside at any hour of the day. Men imitated the ladies, despite some mockery, and not all of them were obviously queer characters like the Duc de Roquelaure, who amused himself on the day after his wedding by dressing up as a lady, and accepting in a dimly lit bed the congratulations intended for his bride; or that odd ecclesiastic the Abbé d'Entragues, who used a fan, lipstick, mascara, and hair-ribbons, and received in bed while working at his embroidery. A judge might execute his magisterial functions from the pillow. Rousseau tells a painful tale of M. Simon, the *Juge-Mage*, a man of brilliant intellect but weird physique:

His height was certainly not three feet. His legs, straight, thin, and tolerably long would have made him look taller, if they had been vertical; but they formed an obtuse angle like those of a wide-opened pair of compasses. His body was not only short, but thin, and in every way indescribably small. When naked, he must have looked like a grasshopper. His head, of ordinary size, with a well-formed face, noble features, and nice eyes, looked like a false head set upon a stump. He might have spared himself much expense in the matter of clothing, for his large wig alone covered him completely from head to foot.

He had two entirely different voices . . . one was grave and sonorous; if I may say so it was the voice of his head. The other—clear, sharp, and piercing—was the voice of his body.

. . . As he desired to make the most of his advantages, he liked to give audience in bed; for no one, who saw a fine head on the pillow, was likely to imagine that that was all. This sometimes caused scenes, which I am sure all Annecy still remembers.

One morning, when he was waiting for some litigants in, or rather upon, this bed, in a beautiful fine white nightcap, ornamented with two large knots of rose-coloured ribbon, a countryman arrived and knocked at the door. The maidservant had gone out. 'Come in', . . . came out of his mouth with his shrill utterance. The man entered, looked to see where the woman's voice came from, and, seeing in the bed a woman's mobcap and top-knot, was going to retire with profound apologies. M. Simon became angry, and cried out in a still shriller voice. The countryman, confirmed in his idea and considering himself insulted, overwhelmed him with abuse, told him that he was apparently nothing but a prostitute, and that the Juge-Mage set anything but a good example in his house. M. Simon, full of fury, and having no other weapon but his chamberpot, was going to throw it at the poor man's head, when his housekeeper came in.

Condolences would be offered at the bedsides of the bereaved, and grief was displayed in bed for periods graded to suit one's rank: up to six weeks between the sheets for a widowed queen of France, and so down in a diminishing scale. 'Blacke clothe hangings 3 yardes deepe and foure and a halfe yardes longe', together with a black bed, were kept in store at Claydon by the Verneys for the use of any member of the family who might suffer bereavement. Gentlefolk in mourning wore black night-clothes; the *Verney Memoirs* of 1651 mention '2 black taffety nightclothes with black night capps'. A young Verney widow has to be excused to her visiting relatives for having a white counterpane.

One French princess was exhibited abed in the period between her death and the autopsy, and it was obligatory on the ladies of her bedchamber to attend both ceremonies. Even an ignominious death did not disqualify a sufficiently noble corpse for public bedding-out. Important persons who were to be executed, and could pay in advance for the service, could have their heads 'sewed on againe' before burial, and so could lie in state in one piece, with the help of a disguising scarf. A royal mistress was entitled to symbolise her occupation by lying on the royal bed after her death: Marion Delorme, mistress of Richelieu and of at least seven other notables, was exposed wearing a *couronne de pucelle*, until the priest who had heard her last confession reconsidered her right to a virgin's crown, and put a sudden end to what he belatedly decided was a bad show. A macabre scene occurred while one defunct princess of the blood was on public view by the flickering light of funeral candles. A curious visitor in the queue, one M. Donnesan, could not believe his eyes when the deceased, propped on her pillows, seemed momentarily to raise a hand to her face. Watching more carefully, he clearly saw the hand holding a handkerchief, take another hasty dab at the royal nose. Others had seen this too, and there was something of a panic. When it happened a third time, the crowd began to fight their way out. The Chevalier de Castellux kept his head, and having some acquaintance with the chief chambermaid, who admitted him to the alcove behind the bed, he solved the mystery. The princess had been suffering from an affliction that still made it necessary, every now and then, for a maid hidden behind the bed to insert an arm through the curtains and tidy up the exhibit.

By extension of the idea that it was in order to sit on one's host's bed, it was still so when one attended his obsequies. When Henry IV lay dead on his bed at the Louvre, several courtiers sat on the queen's bed as they tried to console her, but the Councillor of State sat alongside the corpse. Not until the mid-seventeenth century does it become bad form to sit on another's bed: when the Prince de Conti sits on the Pompadour's bed, it is calculated to annoy. When the Czar of Russia visits St. Cyr he is judged uncouth, not because he enters Mme de Maintenon's bedroom without knocking, but because he opens the bed-curtains before opening the conversation.

Chambre de Parade *by Daniel Marot, seventeenth century*

The great personage would not normally sleep on the *lit de parade*, but on a rather more practical bed in an adjoining chamber. The *petit lever* was a less formal getting-up ceremony, held in the inner bedchamber for more intimate guests, than the *grand lever* in the *chambre de parement*. All this involved a good deal of climbing in and out.

At Versailles a valet sat on guard all day inside the enclosure round the state bed, even if the king was away. One quite practical object of this was the prevention of sorcery: an ill-wisher could have sprinkled the bed with some spell-bearing mixture, and the king would have languished. One cannot mock at this belief after learning that Nicole Mignon was burned alive in 1600 for having tried that very thing. At night the guard still slept on the floor on *paillasses*, so that there was plenty of straw about; the infant Louis XIII could thus play a rather charming game in which stooks representing enemy soldiers were set up on the nursery floor, with a powder-train laid between them and ignited to make a pretty climax to the battle. There were 298 such *paillasses* on the Versailles inventory until the night in August 1682 when Mme la Dauphine gave birth to a son, whereat a royal bed-guard, awakened by the hubbub within and excited by the news, rushed into the courtyard and there set light to his *paillasse* with joyful cries, showing more loyalty than discipline.

Bed by Daniel Marot

On seeing this blaze, the happy courtiers began setting fire to every inflammable object in sight, including the royal furniture. One of the servants—to be precise, the servant of the valet to the principal *valet-de-chambre*—even tore off his clothes and added them to the bonfire. The happy father, advised of these unrehearsed celebrations, had no comment but *'pourvu qu'ils ne nous brûlent pas!'* and next day gave to the servant of the valet of the principal *valet-de-chambre* a new outfit and 50 louis in cash. Things seem often to have got out of hand in such ways on these natal occasions. At the accouchement of the Duchess of Burgundy in 1704, the *accoucheur* was heard by a valet to exclaim *'Je le tiens!'*, and assuming the birth of a prince, which was what was wanted, triggered off the lighting of bonfires and the galloping of couriers in all directions. Unfortunately, the doctor had merely been asking for the cradle to be put ready, and made the remark on seeing it already there. The couriers could not be recalled, but the story ended happily with the birth of a boy anyway. It was not sufficient for two or three reliable witnesses to be present at the royal delivery. Princes and princesses of the blood, secretaries of state, dukes and duchesses, marshals and ministers had to check the obstetric details to guarantee against fraud. Before the midwife had finished her services to Marie de Médicis, there were more than 200 persons in the room, and to the midwife's protests the king—who had himself been nearly bowled over by the crowd—replied

Tais-toy, tais-toy, sage-femme, ne te fasche point. Cet enfant est à tout le monde; il faut que chacun s'en réjouisse.

Favoured bed-guards, who might be persons of some rank, had little *lits-de-veille* or watch-beds. Mme de Montespan was such a nervous sleeper that her maids were expected, not only to keep watch all night with dozens of candles burning, but to be found merrily chatting, eating, or playing games, at any hour when she might happen to awake.

Serving so many purposes, the bedchamber had to be arranged and furnished accordingly. The space between the bedside and the wall had long been specially designated the *ruelle*, that is, a *petite rue* or alleyway, for which there is no elegant equivalent in English. Perhaps the first mention of this feature is in an account of the assassination at Rouen, in 1415, of one Pinel by one Jehan. Pinel, it seems, had found Jehan in a lady's bedroom, in this convenient hiding-place. For centuries the *ruelle* was associated with such goings-on, especially when the bed-curtains came to be extended to screen it off. Any notorious gallant was liable to be execrated, or

99

admired, as a *'coureur de ruelles'*. Mme Olonne had a cupboard in her *ruelle* containing a trap-door, giving quick access to a corresponding cupboard in the room below, and as an added precaution the trap-door was covered by a rug and a chair. The furnishings of some *ruelles* indicate their size: one of them has four armchairs, four stools and eight other chairs. When Marguerite of Valois receives a parliamentary deputation in her bedchamber, there are choirboys in the *ruelle* singing to the lute. Mazarin goes there to confide in *La Grande Mademoiselle*. Mme de Maintenon sups there with a guest. Poets read their verses there to their patrons. When Marie Leczinska, wife of Louis XV, tires of her husband's infidelities and has her bed at Fontainebleau moved to the wall, eliminating the *ruelle* on the side at which a gentleman would enter the bed, this important gesture is regarded as a *divorce d'ostentation*. But it was not entirely without cause that Louis became an inconstant bedfellow. Marie was very susceptible to cold, and insisted on such a deep feather bed and so many eiderdowns and quilts, that Louis suffered many *'nuits sudorifiques médiocrement agréables'*. The Duc de Luynes relates that on more than one occasion poor Louis, suffocated into a state of nightmare, flung himself out of bed and awoke bruised on the floor. He could have entered a counter-plea of incompatibility of temperature.

Falling out of bed seems to have been an occupational hazard of royalty, to which the Bourbons were particularly prone. In 1685 the dauphin, who walked in his sleep, tripped over the steps of the dauphine's bed, was badly bruised, and indeed nearly fell down the adjoining staircase. In 1717 another dauphin, who had already dived from his cot on to his head in infancy, became old enough for the ceremonial *'coucher'*. When the spectators departed, he relieved his boredom by an attempted somersault across the bed, but being short-sighted, he misjudged the distance, and was saved only by the alertness of a valet who interposed himself between the royal head and the nursery floor. (Those confused by the long series of dauphins appearing in Louis XIV's reign should recall that he was Louis XV's *great-grandfather*.) When Louis XV's daughter Louise-Elizabeth, future infanta of Spain, inherited the habit and likewise dived from her cot, she began an endless argument of future years, as to whether this was the cause of her head being too big, and her intelligence too great, for a Bourbon.

Illustration opposite: *'Winter Bed' of Marie Antoinette at Fontainebleau*

21

Riches Litz

WELL may an inventory of the beds belonging to Gabrielle d'Estrées, mistress of Henry IV of France, be headed '*Riches Litz*', for there are twelve beds of every colour, combined with silver and gold, one of them embroidered with birds, beasts, flowers and sundry grotesques in coloured silks, its coverlets sown with pearls; and these are only her 'winter beds'; there is a separate list of the summer ones. With so many changes to be rung, there would be never a dull moment with Gabrielle. The next monarch, Louis XIII, does not seem to have encouraged luxury in the bedroom. His own tastes were simple, considering his background. He managed at most times with only two beds: the black and silver, or the purple and gold. He was content for most of his lifetime with a wooden bath-tub, and only when too old to argue did he agree that marble was more fit. The trouble about Louis, from the upholsterer's point of view, was that there were not enough women about the place. But the mistresses of his successors soon revived business. The domination of a court by *'belles et séduisantes impures'* has always led to some elaboration in furniture design; not because these ladies have interesting ideas when out of bed, or are persons of taste, but because, if they read even a little of the history of royal love, they have the sense to collect all the perquisites they can while the going is good. The bedroom furnishings are personal belongings, and the more valuable they are, the safer are the declining years of the uncrowned ex-queens. Furthermore, the existing royal apartments offered a draughty and comfortless luxury. 'If I have to stay any longer in the king's chamber', writes Mme de Maintenon, 'I shall end up paralysed. None of the doors or windows closes. You are buffeted by wind like an American hurricane'. Hence her new bedchamber at Versailles. Should the king be in a mood for work there, his chair and table were supplemented by two bureaux, a writing-table, a seat for his secretary, and a place for his briefcase. Should she share this mood, she had a chair and a table in a near-by recess. The walls were hung with alternate bands of red, green and gold damask. The great bed was 9 ft. high, with columns topped by plumes, its hangings green and gold outside, red inside. Alongside it was a small *lit de repos* to match. A third bed was in a little wooden enclosure, less than 6 ft. by 2 ft. 10 in. by 8 ft. 6 in. high, crowned by four vases of flowers carved in wood, gilt and painted, upholstered with the same bands of red, green and gold, closed by curtains. In this tiny retreat, perhaps glad to escape even further from grand spacious draughty living awhile, the lady spent whole days on end. To complete the room there were three armchairs, twelve folding chairs, four upholstered seats, two mirrors, and in a shady corner a *chaise d'affaires* or close-stool which, according to Saint-Simon, the king sometimes 'honoured by his contact'. Mme de Maintenon was known to be so fond of this room, that when the Duc d'Antin wooed her, and invited her to stay with him at Petit-Bourg, he provided there an exact replica of it. He had bribed her valets to allow a quick but accurate survey of the original, down to the last details—even the books in their order, and one or two slight irregularities in the furniture. She stayed one night, and it is to be hoped that he found it all worth while.

The *lit de repos* or day-bed was especially popular in these days of gallantry, and it plays a big part in naughty literature. Until the seventeenth century, any casual siesta would usually be taken on an ordinary bed. The earliest existing example of a day-bed in England

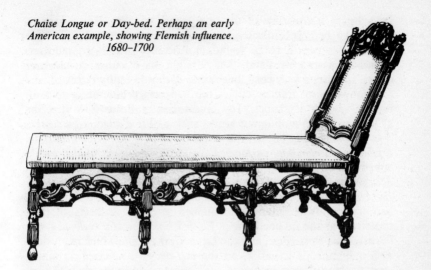

Chaise Longue or Day-bed. Perhaps an early American example, showing Flemish influence. 1680-1700

is in the Tudor gallery at Hardwick Hall. It is of oak, with panelled ends raking outwards, painted chocolate-red, with floral arabesques and the arms of Talbot and Cavendish. It is 7 ft. 3 in. long, and has a long loose mattress of red damask embroidered in coloured silks and gold. There is a similar one at Knole. In 1650 when the Prince de Conti was put under arrest, he was found on his day-bed, and as he would not deign to rise or speak, he was carried away on it to gaol, still silent and dignified. In 1673, for some unaccountable reason, Molière owned 100 day-beds; none of his plays has such a large cast that they might have been explained by rehearsals at his home prolonged into the night. Mme de St. Hérem, who was terrified of lightning, used to lie under hers during a thunderstorm, and as an extra protection she required all her maids to pile in together above. The wounded hero the Maréchal de Villars, installed at Versailles on his day-bed, had another one set alongside it for the use of the monarch when he deigned to call; the royal day-bed was of course made a few inches higher. Richelieu had done the same for Louis XIII. A Versailles inventory lists forty-eight day-beds of Louis XIV, some over 7 ft. long and up to 3 ft. wide. Gradually they are replaced by *chaises longues, duchesses,* ottomans, and all manner of variations on the sofa, one of which usually stands against the foot of any important bed.

Bancs-lits or *banlits* were what we now call 'box-divans', and appeared in the south of France in about 1600. During the day these looked like ordinary seats, and perhaps contained the bedclothes.

103

In ordinary households of the seventeenth century, many ways of hiding the bed were devised. Some were made in cupboards, the *lit clos* that is still to be found in Brittany, the Low Countries, Scandinavia and Scotland. These might have either curtains or doors, offering a very cosy, but rather dark and stuffy retreat.

Meanwhile in grander circles the bed was proliferating into an infinite variety of shapes. The inventories of Louis XIV describe at least twenty-five different kinds, such as *lits d'ange, à baldaquin, à la dauphine, à la duchesse, à hauts piliers, en housse, à impériale, à pente, à la romaine, en tombeau, à la turque*; many of the names ephemeral ones that cannot now be identified. The Siamese ambassador, taken on a tour of the royal bed-store, was shown sixty of the more impressive specimens, and there were 353 more to have seen had time allowed. Many were named after the subjects of their tapestries, as the *Lit des Satyres, Lit de l'Enlèvement d'Hélène, Lit de l'Histoire de Proserpine*, and the *Lit du Cerf Fragile* which is presumably a humorous variation on the *cerf-agile*, the heraldic running stag. Mme de Guise increased the collection by one, when she bequeathed to the king a bed embroidered with pearls, on which she had worked for ten years. As for *Le Triomphe de Vénus*, this bed to end all beds occupied the skill of Simon Delobel the *tapissier* for twelve years. It is still to be seen, but Venus has given place, on the underside of the canopy, to *The Sacrifice of Abraham*, for Mme de Maintenon thought that for pictorial illustration this legend of death was more suitable than the facts of life. Louis XIV was in the habit of giving beds as birthday or wedding presents to his various more or less illegitimate offspring; he even gave one to his doctor Félix. The quality of the bed-trappings is evidenced by the fact, related in *Curiosités de Paris*, that in the church of St. Nicholas-des-Champs the splendid altar-cloths reserved for Corpus Christi were presented by a merchant who had originally made them for a royal bed; they were good enough for the service of God but not, it seems, for that of the Sun God. The famous *tapissiers* Messrs. Bon were kept so busy that normal delivery time was twelve months. Gilding in particular became so elaborate that Louis, resentful that ordinary mortals should sleep in glory, forbade 'Registrars, Notaries, Attorneys, Commissaries, Ushers, merchants and artisans, and their wives', to own beds or other furniture embodying gold or silver, under pain of fine and confiscation, and with penalties for the makers too. Nobody seems to have observed this rule for very long.

Molière mocks the worldly follies of others, but sees no absurdity in himself sleeping in a bed with eagles' feet in bronze; a head-piece carved, painted and gilt; a dome of azure blue, with four eagles,

Lit à impériale

Lit à la turque

Lit à la romaine

Lit à la dauphine

Lit d'ange

Lit à la duchesse

Lit à quenouilles

Lit clos

Lit en tombeau

State Bedchamber of Louis XIV (1643–1715) at Versailles

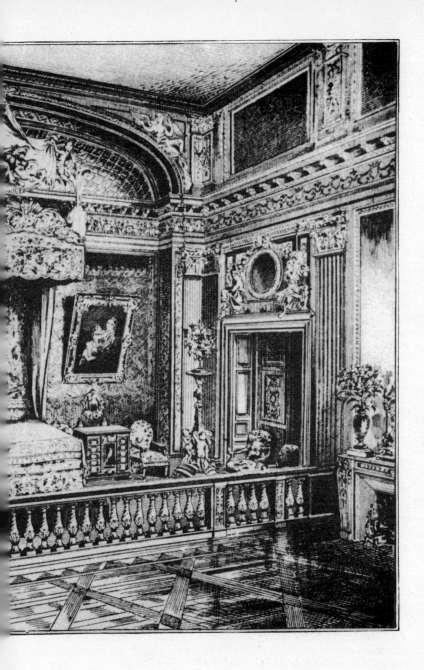

four pineapple finials; pink and green taffeta pelmets and valances with fringes; an inner dome carved and gilt; flowered brocade curtains . . . and the rest. An inventory made at his death shows that he left eighteen *chemises-de-nuit*, thus outdoing his father, who had left only four.

The young Louis XV lived comparatively simply, making do with one bed. The ceremonial of the bedchamber became less formal; almost homely, according to Horace Walpole's account of his presentation at court in 1765:

> You are let into the King's bedchamber just as he has put on his shirt; he dresses and talks good-humouredly to a few, glares at strangers, goes to mass, to dinner, and a-hunting. The good old Queen, who is like Lady Primrose in the face, and Queen Caroline in the immensity of her cap, is at her dressing-table, attended by two or three old ladies, who are languishing to be in Abraham's bosom, as the only man's bosom to whom they can hope for admittance. Thence you go to the Dauphin, for all is done in an hour. He scarce stays a minute; indeed, poor creature, he is a ghost, and cannot possibly last three months. The Dauphiness is in her bed-chamber, but dressed and standing; looks cross, is not civil, and has the true Westphalian grace and accents. The four Mesdames, who are clumsy plump old wenches, with a bad likeness to their father, stand in a bedchamber in a row, with black cloaks and knotting-bags, looking good-humoured, not knowing what to say, and wriggling as if they wanted to make water. This ceremony too is very short; then you are carried to the Dauphin's three boys, who you may be sure only bow and stare . . . The whole concludes with seeing the Dauphin's little girl dine, who is as round and as fat as a pudding.

The alcove was a new feature of the bedchamber, replacing the *ruelle*, so that the *coureurs de ruelles* became *alcôvistes*. The Marquise de Rambouillet is supposed to have introduced the alcove into France, probably from Spain; the word comes through the Spanish *alcoba* from the Arabic *al Koba*, the tent or pavilion in which the Arab sleeps. The idea was imitated by the fashionable, especially by the *précieuses* for whose literary parties the alcove made a perfect setting. It was part of the bedchamber, but separated by an opening, often with columns, sometimes with a balustrade, sometimes up a step or two; a room within the room. It contained seats as well as the bed, looking rather like a high-class Punch and Judy show. Architects like Marot and Lepautre have left designs for alcoves of monumental proportions. The distinction between those who may, and those who may not approach the bed, is even more clearly marked.

In the eighteenth century the alcove, like the bedchamber itself, becomes smaller and cosier. It is no longer a place for receptions; it becomes secluded and discreet:

Alcove at the Palais-Royal, by Roubo fils

> *Dans une alcôve parfumée,*
> *Impénétrable au dieu du jour,*
> *La Pudeur, sans être alarmée,*
> *Dort sur les genoux de l'Amour.*

> (In an alcove's perfumed shade,
> Hidden from the god of day,
> Modesty is unafraid;
> On Cupid's lap she sleeps away.)

So sang the Abbé de Bernis, future cardinal and ambassador, thanks largely to his services to the god in whose lap he, too, is said to have slept. Voltaire puts Agnès Sorel

> *Dans le réduit obscur d'une alcôve enfoncée,*
> *Point trop obscure et point trop eclairée.*

> (In a safe shady alcove, away from the light,
> That should not be too dark, but by no means too bright.)

An erotic gadget first devised for Louis XIV enjoyed a brief revival, when the naughty pictures painted on the undersides of bed-canopies '*pour encourager les plus refroidis*' were replaced by mirrors. Apart from the objections raised by moralists to the '*miroir indiscret*', it literally fell out of favour when the well-known *voyeur* M. de Calonne narrowly escaped vivisection as his mirror, too rudely shaken, dropped and shattered on the bed. After this accident, notes Havard, such mirrors are found only in certain '*alcôves impures*'.

Leading ladies now took their settings with them when they transferred their allegiance to new management—not only their beds, but even their alcoves. This scene-shifting must have left their former protectors with some large bills for 'making good'. But by the time of the Revolution, which in the light of the foregoing chapter one might have expected to occur sooner, the alcove had shrunk to a modest recess, with room for nothing but a couch.

The Revolution broke the continuity of fashion in the decorative arts, which in any case might well have run into a stale dead-end. Under the Empire, when the means and the taste for fine things returned, two new influences were at work: the recent discoveries at Pompeii, and the archaeology sponsored by Napoleon during his campaign in Egypt. The republican and imperial associations of

Bedchamber in the Pompeiian manner by Percier and Fontaine

110

Alcove of the Restoration period

Rome were politically appropriate, and aesthetically they offered a new flavour. Scholarship was not so widespread that a whiff of Egyptian amid the Pompeiian would offend. Hence the 'Empire style', the backdrop for the Napoleonic tragedy. No other exponents need be quoted than Napoleon's architects Percier and Fontaine. It is significant that their *Receuil des Décorations Intérieures* is so titled. The 'interior decorator' has come in to oust the architect and the cabinet-maker, to both of whom decoration had been only a carefully controlled adjunct to structural form. Percier at first makes the bedroom a fairly architectural *atrium* on whose walls every decorative motive to be found in the latest measured drawings from Pompeii is accurately reproduced. If this chilly cubage is heated, no means is visible save a pair—inevitably a pair, in balance—of braziers. Soon the hangings, valances, pelmets and curtains escape from their architectural frame, and spread over the walls; the very doors and windows are upholstered. This makes for some splendid bedrooms, given that all the world's a stage, but Napoleon himself complains that one of these striped tent-like rooms is like a cage for wild beasts. The bed becomes a classical day-couch, but outsize; with symmetrical patterned covers, looking as formal and about as flexible as a carpet, that no sleeper surely would dare to crumple. The pillows are pure

111

cylinders which none would even be able to dent. It is as if the architect's working drawings had included the bed-clothes. Percier and Fontaine think nothing of hanging the bed-curtains from great pointed spears and arrows, piling helmets and swords and shields around like Christmas presents, or enthroning a god on the top of a wardrobe. It is all glorious fun while it lasts. It does not last long. Percier and Fontaine's partnership dates from 1794 to the significant date 1814. Most of their projects are unexecuted; the business ends with Waterloo—won in the dormitories of Eton.

At this notable milestone, it will be convenient for a while to abandon historical sequence. We find ourselves accumulating some side-issues better treated by subject than by period. The histories of such things as the school dormitory, the railway sleeping-coach and the alarm clock, have not been fragmented for piecemeal insertion according to dates; each will have its self-contained chapter.

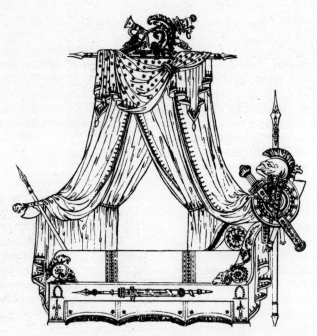

'O, who would not sleep with the brave?'

112

*Napoleon's state bed at Fontaine-
bleau, and one of his iron camp-beds*

22

Murdered in our Beds

INNKEEPERS do not go out of their way to tell customers that
their bedrooms are haunted, but some doubtless are, for horrid
events have occurred overnight in many of them. In 1613 the
widow of that landlord of the *Blue Boar* at Leicester who, as
already related, had found Richard Crookback's gold in his bedstead, was murdered there for the sake of what coin remained. The
guilty maidservant had no less than seven male accomplices, making
a fine hanging. In April 1654, a Mr. Kidderminster vanished while
travelling in Essex, carrying the sum of £600, and it took his widow
nine years to find out what had become of him. He had put up at the
White Horse at Chelmsford, where some queer things had happened
that night. Mary Kendall, the chambermaid, had found herself
unaccountably locked into her bedroom until morning. She had
then noticed that the *King's Bedroom* was closed for the next eight
weeks. When it was reopened, she was sent there to fetch something,
and found Mr. Kidderminster's sword, hat and boots. She kept
silence for nine years, when the finding of 'the bones of an unknown
person' in a Chelmsford back-yard, and then her own evidence, led
to a murder charge against the landlord, his wife, and Moses Drayne
the ostler (for whom no crime writer could have invented a better
name). Sewell, the landlord, died mysteriously before the assizes,
and it was believed that his wife had poisoned him to prevent his

confession. Moses Drayne was hanged, but Mrs. Sewell, though implicated in one murder and strongly suspected of a second, seems to have got off.

A 'whodunit' with a nice twist at the end was staged at Jonathan Bradford's inn at Oxford, to which came a Mr. Hayes and his servant, making the same mistake of carrying a large sum of money. Two other guests, hearing frightful groans in the night, found landlord Jonathan, with lantern and knife in hand, stooping over the bloody bed in which Mr. Hayes was expiring. Nobody could have been blamed for suspecting Jonathan, nor indeed for hanging him despite his protests of innocence. But years later, Mr. Hayes' servant made a death-bed confession: he himself had done the deed, and the landlord had arrived on the scene, with the same intention, a minute too late. In the circumstances, we may call Jonathan 'a vera clever chiel, but nane the waur o' a hanging'.

The classic masterpiece of all inn crimes, for scale, for method and for the one fatal slip-up, is the series of murders at Colebrook related by Thomas Deloney. The genial Jarmans, host and hostess of the *Crane*, had been so long in the habit of doing away with wealthy guests, that they would agree the deed by a set formula:

. . . this was alwaies their terme, the man to his wife, and the woman to her husband: wife, there is now a fat pig to be had, if you want one. Whereupon she would answer thus, I pray you put him in the hogstie till to-morrow.

The wealthy Thomas Cole of Reading, coming there one night on his way home with 'a great store of money', found himself unaccountably melancholy, even after taking a quart of burnt sack. He asked for pen, ink and paper, meaning to write a letter.

Ha, how say you hoast (quoth he) is no this well? I pray you read it. His hoast looking thereon, said, why Master *Cole*, what have you written here? you said you would write a letter, but me thinks you have made a Will, what neede have you to doe thus? thanks be to God, you may live many faire yeares. Tis true (quoth Cole) if it please God, and I trust this writing cannot shorten my daies, but let me see, have I made a Will? Now, I promise you, I did verily purpose to write a letter: not withstanding, I have written that that God put into my mind . . .
. . . With that scritch owle cried piteously, and anone after the night raven sate croking hard by his window.
Jesu have mercy upon me (quoth hee), what an ill favoured cry doe yonder carrion birds make, and therewithall he laid him downe in his bed, from whence he never rose againe.

115

The guest's bedroom was above the kitchen, and Jarman, who had been a carpenter, had fitted up some sinister devices:

... the best bedstead therein, though it were little and low, yet was it most cunningly carved, and faire, to the eye, the feet whereof were fast naild to the chamber floore, in such sort, that it could not in any wise fall, the bed that lay therein was fast sowed to the sides of the bedstead: Moreover that part of the chamber whereupon this bed and bedstead stood, was made in such sort, that by the pulling out of two yron pinnes below in the kitchin, it was to be let downe and taken up by a drawbridge, or in manner of a trap doore; moreover in the kitchin, directly under the place where this should fall, was a mighty great caldron, wherein they used to seethe their liquor when they went to brewing. Now, the men appointed for the slaughter, were laid into this bed, and in the dead time of the night, when they were sound a sleepe, by plucking out the forsaid yron pinnes, downe would the man fall out of his bed into the boyling caldron, and all the cloaths that were upon him: where being suddenly scalded and drowned, he was never able to cry or speake one word.

Then they had a little ladder ever standing ready in the kitchin, by which they presently mounted into the said chamber, and there closely take away the mans apparell, as also his money, in his male or capcase: and then lifting up the said falling floore which hung by hinges, they made it fast as before.

The dead body would they take presently out of the caldron and throw it downe the river, which ran neere unto their house, whereby they escaped all danger.

The murder went off nicely, but then one little thing went wrong: Cole's hired horse escaped before Jarman could secure and disguise it, and was found and returned to its owner. Jarman as usual told all enquirers, including a messenger from Cole's wife, that his guest had ridden homeward before day; now suspicion was mounting, and Jarman lost his nerve and fled. His wife confessed; he was caught; both were hanged, after confessing that they had murdered by that means 'LX persons'. Whatever the proportion of truth in the tale, nervous visitors to Colebrook need not fear that they may sleep unknowingly in this dreadful bedroom, for

When the King heard of this murder, he was for the space of vii daies so sorrowfull and heavie, as he would not heare any sute, giving also commandement, that the house should quite be consumed with fire, wherein *Cole* was murdered, and that no man should ever build upon that cursed ground.

The bedroom is indeed splendidly adapted for murder. If we could tabulate all the kills made in all the other rooms—the impromptu

116

shootings in the living-room, the poisonings at the dinner-table, the knifings in the kitchen, the kings speared in the privy-closet, the brides in the bath—all these would not add up to a tithe of the horrid harvest of the bedroom; and its very advantages make the *known* total there a much smaller fraction of the whole. It might have been designed specifically for doing the occupant to death undetected. We know he will be there at the chosen hour, unconscious or sleepily off-guard; that shadows offer us a lurking-place; that no witness is likely to intrude, or to see us come and go. Pillows and bedding are at hand to stifle our victim's cries, or to soak up the blood, or to wipe our hands clean afterwards. Even let the wretch wail like a cat, or screech like an owl, no rescuer will stir. Husband, wife or lover (who between them form such a high proportion of murderers) can approach without causing alarm; thus Isabella, the Duchess of Bracciano, gladly let her Paolo embrace her as he leaned over her pillow, that night in 1577, while his henchmen from the room above lowered a noosed cord through a little hole in the ceiling, just above her head. The deed done, the cord was silently withdrawn; the little hole may still be seen today.

We learn an even more safe and subtle method from Thomas Hardy, who may have been recalling an old wives' tale with some

One would not readily guess, either from the style of the bedroom furnishings, or from the nonchalant bearing of the company, that this illustration from an early French manuscript translation of Josephus, *represents the death of Nero*

117

truth in it, when in *Her Second Husband Hears Her Story* he told of the perfect bed-murder—or was it only manslaughter? A widow marries again, and on the wedding night she tells her new husband, with dreadful casualness, how she killed her first. While he was in a drunken sleep, she took needle and thread, and patiently stitched him up into his bed-clothes, so tightly that by morning he was dead. Before anyone came she had taken all the stitches out, and 'thus 'twas shown to be a stroke'.

> 'And this same bed?'—'Yes, here it came about.'
> 'Well, it sounds strange—told here and now to me.
> 'Did you intend his death by your tight lacing?'
> 'O, that I cannot own.
> I could not think of else that would avail
> When he should wake up, and attempt embracing.'
> 'Well, it's a cool queer tale!'

One would not use the word 'corny' of a great poet, but one might say that Hardy was not always at the top of his literary form.

As with murder, so with self-murder: despite all the shootings in the gun-room, the Roman deaths in the bathroom, the hangings in the woodshed, the squalid gassings in the back kitchen, the bedroom has always been favoured by suicides, from Evelyn's diary entry of 1647:

Lord Clifford, late Lord Treasurer . . . wrung me by the hand, and, looking earnestly on me, bid me God-b'yc, adding, 'Mr. Evelyn, I shall never see thee more' . . . I have heard from some who I believe knew, he made himself away, after an extraordinary melancholy . . . locking himself in, he strangled himself with his cravat upon the bed-tester; his servant, not liking the manner of dismissing him, and looking through the key-hole (as I remember), and seeing his master hanging, brake in before he was quite dead, and taking him down, vomiting a great deal of blood, he was heard to utter these words, 'Well; let men say what they will, there is a God, a just God above'; after which he spake no more. This, if true, is dismal . . .

to Orwell's tale of the bed cell in the casual ward at Cromley:

A tramp had managed to smuggle a razor into his cell and there cut his throat. In the morning, when the Tramp Major came round, the body was jammed against the door, and to open it they had to break the dead man's arm. In revenge for this, the dead man haunted his cell, and anyone who slept there was certain to die within the year; there were copious instances, of course. If a cell door stuck when you tried to open it, you should avoid that cell like the plague, for it was the haunted one.

This also, if true, is dismal.

23

Afrayd of Sprights

THE murder-room, the suicide-room; certainly the ghost-room too. Who ever met a proper ghost in the larder or the bathroom? In the cellar or the attic perhaps; the dining-room just possibly; but it is nearly always in the bedroom that the chill falls on the air, and something is about.

> Must we to bed indeed? Well then,
> Let us arise and go like men,
> And face with an undaunted tread
> The long black passage up to bed.

Thus Stevenson, on a fear that Walter de la Mare also has understood:

The daylight ebbs away, the blinds descend, the curtains are drawn, the clock strikes: it is bed time; and Childe Roland pale, hollow-eyed, speechless, sets off to keep his nightly tryst in the Dark Tower.

119

By day, it is but a few seconds' run from the top floor to safety and companionship downstairs, but at night the faint sounds of music and laughter below are hopelessly remote. There seem to be more closed doors, more flights of grey stairs, in between. Charles Lamb, haunted for years by a Bible picture of the Witch raising up Samuel ('O that old man covered with a mantle!') did not dare even in daytime to enter his room without keeping his face turned to the window, away from the bed where his 'witch-ridden pillow' was. It is all, we know, imaginary; we have to learn, like Forrest Reid,

... to conquer this senseless, superstitious cowardice. And an easy way to conquer it was to remember God was with me in the dark. He wasn't; he never had been—unless he was a tall smiling figure with long, pointed yellow teeth, that I saw one night standing at the foot of my bed.

Walter de la Mare has listed some of the Things that can lurk in the night nursery: the Spoorn, the Puckle, Clap-cans, Church-grim, Jack-in-Irons, Old Bendy, the Shriker, Gally-trot, the Phooka, the Neugle, the Gabble Raches. What use, he asks, for parents to explain that the departed beast cannot possibly have been a *real* bear? For how can bolts and bars or the most loving of parents keep out a bear that isn't real? Not, he adds, that fear of the supernatural is confined to children:

We fear what we cannot explain, and what we cannot explain is less any particular phenomenon than its influence upon us. To a child a hanging dress in a dark closet, a door ajar into the vacancy of a lightless house, a vagrant moth, a wailing as of the wind, the shriek of a night-bird, is a decoy, a spell, an invocation; and it is what is invoked that troubles his entrails and chills his blood. The adult has whittled down the invocations: but *if* there is no wind to account for the sigh in the dark, or only the faint *whirr* and tapping *as of* a moth, if the pendent dress stir, swell, remove itself from the hook and come forward, what kind of hero is he then?

Most level-headed adults, no doubt, claim to take these Things as philosophically as Hobbes, whose

... work was attended with Envy, which threw severall aspersions and false reports on him. For instance, one (common) was that he was afrayd to lye alone at night in his Chamber; I have often heard him say that he was not afrayd of *Sprights*, but afrayd of being knockt on the head for five or ten pounds, which rogues might think he had in his chamber.

Some would reject even such authenticated accounts as that

120

True and most dreadful discourse of a woman possessed with the devil; who in the likeness of a headless bear fetched her out of her bed and in the presence of seven persons most strangely rolled her through three chambers and down a high pair of stairs on the 4 and 20 of May last 1584 at Ditchet in Somersetshire.

But would they have remained sceptical in the bedroom of Caisho Burroughs, in Stuart times, whose betrayed lover committed suicide?

At the same moment she expired, she did appear to Caisho at his Lodgings in London. Colonel Remes was then in Bed with him, who saw her as well as he; giving him an account of her Resentments of his Ingratitude to her, in leaving her so suddenly, and exposing her to the Fury of the Duke, not omitting her own Tragical EXIT, adding withall, that he should be slain in a Duell, which accordingly happened; and thus she appeared to him frequently, even when his younger Brother (who afterwards was Sir John) was a Bed with him. As often as she did appear, he would cry out with great shrieking, and trembling of his Body, as anguish of Mind, saying, O God! here she comes, she comes, and at this rate she appeared 'till he was killed; she appeared to him the morning before he was killed.

Mr. Pepys, no kind of a hero, thought ghosts an ill subject for joking:

. . . late to bed; Sir William telling me that old Edgeborrow, his predecessor, did die and walk in my chamber, did make me somewhat afeard, but not so much as, for mirth sake, I did seem. So to bed in the Treasurer's chamber . . . Lay and slept well till three in the morning, and then waking, and by the light of the moon I saw my pillow (which overnight I flung from me) stand upright, but, not bethinking myself what it might be, I was a little afeard, but sleep overcame all, and so lay till nigh morning, at which time I had a candle brought me, and a good fire made.

Boswell's terrors were so powerful that he could never sleep alone until he was 18, and throughout his life, had anything creepy been said towards bedtime, he had to share his bed with a friend. When he toured Italy with Lord Mountstuart they were always in the same room.

[We] talked about superstitions. I was afraid that ghosts might be able to return to earth, and for a time wished to get into bed with my Lord. But I lay quiet.

Nobody who had truly known what these night-fears mean, would ever resort to spooky practical jokes, like that played on Mr. Fiddis, a minister, and told by Abraham de la Pryne:

. . . some had out of roguery fixed a long band to the bedclose where he lay. After half a houer after he was got to bed they began to pull, which, drawing the bedclose off by degrees put him into a suddain fright, and looking up, he did really think and believe that he saw two or three spirits stirring and moveing about the bed . . .

or that more brutal jest by Casanova, who tugged at a sleeper's sheets until he awoke; not taken in, the laughing victim grabbed in the dark and caught a hand—the hand of a corpse, brought by Casanova—and became 'stupid and spasmodic' for the rest of his life.

It is often remarked that the anticipated ghost never materialises. But that is not necessary: the fear of fear is enough, and *is* real, as Poe well knew:

Sleep came not near my couch—while the hours waned and waned away. I struggled to reason off the nervousness which had dominion over me. I endeavoured to believe that much, if not all of what I felt, was due to the bewildering influence of the gloomy furniture of the room—of the dark and tattered draperies, which, tortured into motion by the breath of a rising tempest, swayed fitfully to and fro upon the walls, and rustled uneasily about the decorations of the bed. But my efforts were fruitless. An irrepressible tremor gradually pervaded my frame; and, at length, there sat upon my heart an incubus of utterly causeless alarm.

These moving draperies are peculiarly dreadful; it is a theme that keeps recurring among the horrors of the bedroom: the long grey

The bedroom in Chelsea where Turner died in December, 1851

122

garment hanging on the door; the eiderdown on the other, empty bed, slithering to the ground; the crumpled linen in M. R. James' little masterpiece *Whistle and I'll Come to You*:

... the reader will hardly, perhaps, imagine how dreadful it was to him to see a figure suddenly sit up in what he had known was an empty bed. He was out of his own bed in one bound, and made a dash towards the window ... This was, as it turned out, the worst thing he could have done, because the personage in the empty bed, with a sudden smooth motion, slipped from the bed and took up a position, with outspread arms, between the two beds, and in front of the door. Parkins watched it in a horrid perplexity. Somehow, the idea of getting past it and escaping through the door was intolerable to him; he could not have borne—he didn't know why—to touch it; and as for its touching him, he would sooner dash himself through the window than have that happen. It stood for the moment in a band of dark shadow, and he had not seen what its face was like. Now it began to move, in a stooping posture, and all at once the spectator realised, with some horror and some relief, that it must be blind, for it seemed to feel about it with its muffled arms in a groping and random fashion. Turning half away from him, it became suddenly conscious of the bed he had just left, and darted towards it, and bent and felt over the pillows in a way which made Parkins shudder as he had never in his life thought it possible. In a very few moments it seemed to know that the bed was empty, and then, moving forward into the area of light and facing the window, it showed for the first time what manner of thing it was.

Parkins, who very much dislikes being questioned about it, did once describe something of it in my hearing, and I gathered that what he chiefly remembers about it is a horrible, an intensely horrible, face *of crumpled linen*. What expression he read upon it he could not or would not tell, but that the fear of it went nigh to maddening him is certain.

In the end it was agreed—if that is any comfort to the nervous reader—that

... There seemed to be absolutely nothing material about it save the bed-clothes of which it had made itself a body. The Colonel, who remembered a not very dissimilar occurrence in India, was of opinion that if Parkins had closed with it it could really have done very little, and that its one power was that of frightening.

But are *you*, reader, nervous? Perhaps at this very moment finishing this chapter, alone and a shade uneasy, in some not quite friendly bedroom? What comfort can be offered to you about ghosts? Well may your heart miss a beat—might it not be best to drop this book and *get out*? For what use will comfort be to YOU in a few moments' time, when you realise that THERE IS SOMETHING IN THE ROOM WITH YOU NOW?

'King Charles' Bedroom' at the Saracen's Head, *Southwell*

24

Cold Harbours

THE troubled travels of the Stuarts have added much to the tales of old inn bedrooms. Charles I slept at the *White Hart Royal* at Moreton-in-the-Marsh in 1644, on his way to Evesham. In his room, in the oldest wing of the house, some landlord long ago has put up the inscription:

> When friends were few and dangers near
> King Charles found rest and safety here.

There is another *King Charles' Bedroom* at the *King's Head* at Monmouth, though this inn is too old to have taken its name from a Stuart; Henry V, who was born in Monmouth Castle, is the more likely. In 1646, when Charles met the Scottish Commissioners at Southwell, he stayed at the *Saracen's Head*, and invited them to dine there; having enjoyed his hospitality, they took him prisoner, and sold him to the Roundheads for £400,000. His room and his four-poster are still to be seen. A bishop of New Zealand, who lay awake in this historic bed one night in 1858, was so affected by its associations that he arose in the night and wrote a poem on the subject, too long and not quite bad enough to be funny.

One September evening in 1651 a party of three persons arrived at the modest *Sun* inn at Cirencester: a Mr. Lassels, his kinswoman Mrs. Jane Lane, and a roughly dressed young man Will Jackson, a farmer's son. Will Jackson was given a truckle-bed in Mr. Lassels' chamber. But it was Mr. Lassels who slept in the truckle-bed, for Will Jackson was Charles Stuart, already Charles II, in flight from the battle of Worcester with a price on his head.

Less happy, though uncertain associations hang about the *King's Head* at Kirbymoorside in Yorkshire. Although some historians hold that the 'witty and sparkling debauchée' George Villiers, second Duke of Buckingham, died 'between two common girls' in the house of one of his tenants there, Pope in his *Moral Essays* has him die

> In the worst inn's worst room, with mat half hung,
> The floors of plaster and the walls of dung,
> On once a flock-bed, but repaired with straw,
> With tape-tied curtains, never meant to draw,
> The George and Garter dangling from that bed
> Where tawdry yellow strove with dirty red,
> Great Villiers lies—alas! how changed from him,
> That life of pleasure, and that soul of whim.

The Kirbymoorsiders insist that it was the *King's Head*—its walls no longer of dung—that was so honoured. Connoisseurs of squalor may take their choice.

In travellers' tales of inns and lodgings we find rooms and even beds being shared, and sometimes shared with strangers, often without comment. A companion might be introduced after one was asleep, and if he were the more important, one might be turned out to make room for him. There is not much more care for privacy, nor coyness about bedgoing in company, in the seventeenth century, than in the Middle Ages. A Polish officer in Sweden notes how the ladies there undress completely for bed in the presence of the foreign troops billeted on them, and a French general in Baden is distracted by the presence of two girls of about 19 naked in the next bed. One Lieutenant Hammond, travelling to Canterbury in about 1650, meets a 'light and sprightly Mademoiselle', and at the inn there

... this pretty she-rider at that time held it no nicety, nor point of incivility, to disrobe and bed her little, tender, weary'd corps in our presence, which I

125

understood afterwards is common and familiar amongst them of that nation.

Mr. Pepys passes many nights at inns, and nearly all of them comfortless, but for some reason hardships seem to amuse him mightily, and the worse the lodging, the greater the mirth. At Dartford:

... we returned to our inn and to bed, the page and I in one bed, and the two captains in another, all in one chamber, where we had very good mirth with our most abominable lodging.

At Ashtead:

... we got a lodging in a little hole we could not stand upright in ... to bed, where with much ado yet good sport, we made shift to lie, but with little ease, and a little spaniel by us, which has followed us all the way, a pretty dog.

At Boremans:

... Pierce and I to bed together, and he and I very merry to find how little and thin clothes they give us to cover us, so that we were fain to lie in our stockings and drawers, and lay all our coats and clothes upon the bed.

At Rochester (where he goes to see Lord Brouncker in his bedchamber and is startled to find a watchman with a halbert on guard at the bedroom door) he stays at the *White Hart*, and has a bed 'corded' for himself and Mr. Creed; that is, a cord mattress stretched taut by means of a 'bed-twitch', a regular task that needed the efforts of a strong man. (A bed-twitch is to be seen at York Castle Museum.) But there are no sheets to be had, only 'linen to our mouths', meaning presumably pillow-slips. When Mr. Pepys travels with his wife and Deb Willet their maid, the three always share one room, and they ring all the changes, except the forbidden one that is constantly in his mind. Thus at the *Reindeer* at Bishop's Stortford:

... and so to bed, my wife and I in one bed, and the girl in another, in the same room, and lay very well ...

but at the *Rose* at Cambridge:

... after supper to cards and then to bed, lying, I in one bed, and my wife and girl in another, in the same room, and very merry talking together, and mightily pleased both of us with the girl ...

126

and then at Brampton:

. . . my wife and I in the high bed in our chamber, and Willett in the trundle bed, which she desired to lie in, by us . . .

but the next night, in the same house:

. . . I lay in the trundle bed, the girl being gone to bed to my wife, and there lay in some disquiet all night, telling of the clock till it was daylight.

With his wife and two maids riding pillion, he goes to see the great ramparts of Old Sarum, 'prodigious, so as to fright me', and losing the way they come late at night to a little inn, where his sense of humour stands a sterner test:

. . . we were fain to go into a room where a pedlar was in bed, and made him rise; and there wife and I lay, and in a truckle-bed Betty Turner and Willett . . . Up, finding our beds good but lousy, which made us merry.

At Welling, he and Mrs. Pepys not only sup well, but enjoy a splendid sleep, splendidly described:

. . . had two beds in the room, and so lay single, and still remember it that of all the nights that I ever slept in my life I never did pass a night with more epicurism of sleep; there being now and then a noise of people stirring that waked me, and then I was a little weary, that what between waking and then sleeping again, one after another, I never had so much content in all my life, and so my wife says it was with her.

But at Parson's Grove, 'a heathen place', he finds a 'miserable inn' where

. . . about twelve o'clock or more, to bed, in a sad, cold chamber, only the maid was indifferent handsome, and so I had a kiss or two of her . . . and so to sleep, but was bit cruelly, and nobody else of our company, which I wonder at, by the gnats.

We may suppose that apprentice fisher-boys of those days slept in their masters' boats, rather as apprentice shop-boys slept under the counter, for Mr. Pepys tells us that at the *Crown* at Rochester

. . . [we] made ourselves merry with the poor fisher-boy, who told us he had not been in bed the whole seven years since he came to 'prentice, and hath two or three more years to serve.

127

Finally, back to London for a night out:

. . . Creed and I, it being about twelve o'clock and past: and to several houses [inns], but could get no lodging, all being in bed. At last we found some people drinking and roaring; and, after drinking, got an ill bed. I lay in my drawers and stockings and waistcoat till five of the clock, and so up; and, being well pleased with our frolic, walked to Knightsbridge.

A generation later, Celia Fiennes, travelling about Britain on horseback, is seldom luckier than Mr. Pepys in her choice of lodgings. At Buxton Hall, which belongs to the Duke of Devonshire but is run as an inn,

. . . its the largest house in the place tho' not very good, they are all Entertaining houses and its by way of an Ordinary, so much a piece for your dinners and suppers and so much for our Servants besides; all your ale and wine is to be paid besides, the beer they allow at the meales is so bad that very little can be dranke, you pay not for your bed room and truely the other is so unreasonable a price and the Lodgings so bad, 2 beds in a room some 3 beds and some 4 in one roome, so that if you have not Company enough of your own to fill a room they will be ready to put others into the same chamber, and sometymes they are so crowded that three must lye in a bed; few people stay above two or three nights its so inconvenient: we staid two nights by reason one of our Company was ill but it was sore against our wills . . .

A brilliant idea this, to raise the other charges and offer the beds free, for what guest could reasonably complain of overcrowding in a bed for which he had not paid?

'At Haltwhistle (so named long before the railways) in Northumberland, Celia is refused hay at the one inn, and when she buys it elsewhere,

they were angry and would not entertaine me, so I was forced to take up in a poor cottage which was open to the thatch and no partitions but hurdles plaister'd; indeed the loft as they called it which was over the other roome was shelter'd but with a hurdle; here I was forced to take up my abode and the Landlady brought me out her best sheetes which serv'd to secure my own sheetes from her dirty blanckets, and indeed I had her fine sheete with hook seams to spead over the top of the clothes, but noe sleep could I get.

In Scotland she observes not only that their miles are long, but that few towns except 'Edenburough Abberdeen and Kerk' can offer a bed fit to lie in, and that most travellers therefore go from one

128

nobleman's house to another. At a little market town just within the Scottish border, she compares the houses unfavourably with booths at a fair:

... there is no roome in their houses but it is up to the thatch and in which are 2 or 3 beds even to their parlours and buttery; and notwithstanding the cleaning of their parlour for me I was not able to beare the roome; the smell of the hay was a perfume and what I rather chose to stay and see my horses eate their provender in the stable then to stand in that roome, for I could not bring my self to sit down.

Boswell and Johnson find a variety of beds on their tour of the Highlands and the Hebrides. At an inn at Aberdeen, there is a 'little press bed' for Boswell in the Doctor's room, but the disciple thinks this intrusive, and has it wheeled into the dining-room. When they penetrate to wilder parts, we find them lying, with a third companion, in a row on the hay in an outhouse. At Flora Macdonald's house in Skye, the Doctor sleeps in the very bed in which Bonnie Prince Charlie lately lay during his flight from Culloden—though not in the sacred sheets, kept ever unwashed, to be used one day as old Mrs. Macdonald's winding-sheets. Johnson is less susceptible than Boswell to the associations of this bed—'I have had no ambitious thoughts in it.' At Corriatchin, where they are held up for some days by bad weather,

... the good people had no notion that a man could have any occasion but for a mere sleeping-place; so, during the day, the bed-rooms were common to all the house. Servants eat in Dr. Johnson's; and mine was a kind of general rendezvous of all under the roof, children and dogs not excepted.

Thomas Campbell the poet, at an old Scots inn where the Moffat carriers slept, had got snug into bed after his tumbler of toddy, when there was a knock at the door, and in came the pretty maiden who had given him supper, in her 'short-gown' and petticoat. 'Please, sir, could ye tak' a neebor into yer bed?' 'With all my heart,' said the delighted poet, starting up. 'Thank ye, sir, for the Moffat carrier's just come in a' wat, and there's no a single ither place.' And in came the 'huge and reeking' man.

The inns of Scotland had an ill name for centuries, even from Burns and Walter Scott, and Dickens was to describe one in the Highlands as 'a mere knot of little outhouses'.

Few travellers seem to have lain much easier on the Continent. Evelyn, doing the Grand Tour, finds some sorry inns. At a village in the Italian alps his bed is stuffed with leaves, which so crackle and prick that he cannot sleep. At a 'cold harbour' in Switzerland

. . . we went to bed in cupboards so high from the floor, that we climbed them by a ladder; we were covered with feathers, that is, we lay between two ticks stuffed with them, and all little enough to keep one warm.

Worse still, at St. Maurice, the inn being full, he has one of the hostess' daughters turned out of her bed, moves into it while it is still warm, and soon afterwards goes down with smallpox, which he attributes to this obliging girl. Boswell writes from France:

I came at night to a tolerable inn. I sat up too late writing, and I suppose astonished the people of the house, who are used to see their guests tumble into bed immediately after supper. By the by, the French soft feather beds are destroying me by relaxing my nerves. The inns of this light-headed nation are very seldom good, for the rooms are cold and comfortless and dirty, the sheets damp, and snuffers difficult to be found. Old England live for ever, for thy inns are more excellent than are palaces anywhere else!

Horace Walpole says that in an Italian inn he had to heap *saddles and portmanteaus* on the bed to keep off the cold. When Casanova engages a troupe of actors and has to lodge them, they tell him, 'Sir, we are twenty, and shall require six rooms with ten beds.' On another occasion he himself offers no objection to sharing a bed with the cook—although a male cook—but finds that his trunk has to be put under the bed, for the very good reason that the bed completely fills the room. Rousseau, at Turin, pays one *sou* a night for a bed in a room shared with his landlady, five or six children, and such other lodgers as may come and go—'she was a good woman, who swore like a carter, whose breast was always exposed and her hair untidy, but kind-hearted and obliging'. In the Balkans one still does not rent a room at an inn; one rents so many beds. Not until Sterne's *Sentimental Journey* of 1786 does it become rather naughty to share a room with an unknown lady, and not until Mr. Pickwick's adventure at the *White Horse* at Ipswich does it become unthinkable—to an Englishman, that is; for many Europeans still think otherwise; we learn from Lord Alexander that when he visited the Russian Marshal Tolbukhin's headquarters in Hungary in 1945, a 'female valet' was expected to sleep on a settee in his room. So un-English a practice had to be rejected: 'I didn't think that was quite the thing, and she spent the night outside the door'.

130

25

Sleep's Foes

THROUGHOUT history, man has shared his beds with one or more of that tormenting trio, the louse, the bug and 'sleep's foe, the Flea, that proud insulting Elfe'. As an ancient writer puts it,

You must own that for the quelling of human pride and to pull down the high conceits of mortal man, this most loathsome of all maladies [*pediculosis*, or lousiness], has been the inheritance of the rich, the wise, the noble and the mighty—poets, philosophers, prelates, princes, Kings and Emperors.

The Reverend Doctor Kirby, the 'Father of English Entomology', refused to believe 'that man in his pristine state of glory and beauty and dignity could be the receptacle of prey so loathsome as these unclean disgusting creatures'. To resolve this dilemma, he had to date the creation of the louse *after* the Fall of Adam. The Carthusians claimed to be free from lice for the unexpected reason that they— the monks, and so perhaps the monastery lice—were vegetarians. Some devout persons would deliberately introduce fleas into their own beds—if they were lacking—so that they should be awakened to devote part of the night to prayer, contemplation, and the examination of conscience. The mediaeval housewife seems to have been engaged in a constant warfare against the triple alliance. The

131

'*Ménagier de Paris*', in his instructions to young wives, written in 1392, gives six recipes for combating the flea:

In summer take heed that there be no fleas in your chamber nor your bed, which you may do in six ways, as I have heard tell. For I have heard from several persons that if the room be scattered with alder leaves the fleas will get caught therein. Item, I have heard tell that if you have at night one or two trenchers of bread covered with birdlime or turpentine and put about the room with a lighted candle set in the midst of each trencher, they will come and get stuck thereto. Another way which I have found and which is true: take a rough cloth and spread it about your room and over your bed and all the fleas who may hop onto it will be caught, so that you can carry them out with the cloth wheresoever you will. Item, I have seen blankets placed on the straw and on the bed and when the black fleas jumped upon them they were the sooner found and killed upon the white. But the best way is to guard oneself against those which are within the coverlets and furs and the stuff of dresses wherewith one is covered. For know that I have tried this, and when the coverlets, furs or dresses in which there be fleas are folded and shut tightly up, in a chest straitly bound with

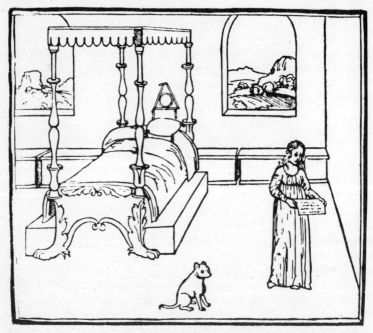

From Francesco Colonna's Hypteromachia, *published in Venice in 1499. Note the monastic austerity of mediaeval furnishing, confined here to a bed and a row of chests serving as benches*

132

straps or in a bag well tied up and pressed, or otherwise compressed so that the said fleas are without light and air and kept imprisoned, then they will perish and die at once.

From which unconvincing suggestions, the *ménagier* goes on to deal with flies and mosquitoes:

> I have sometimes seen in several chambers that when one has gone to bed in them, they were full of mosquitoes, which at the smoke of the breath came to sit on the faces of those who slept and sting them so that they were fain to get up and light a fire of hay to smoke them off.

Again he offers six infallible recipes: a mosquito net; sprigs of fern hung up; a bowl filled with a lethal mixture of milk and hare's gall, or with the juice of raw onions; a bottle containing a rag dipped in honey, or a string dipped in honey and hung up; fly-whisks to drive them away; closing up the windows with oiled cloth or parchment; all rather like the current Civil Defence precautions against the atomic bomb. Had the *ménagier* relied less on hearsay, and carried out a properly controlled experiment, using all twelve methods at once, he might have learned which of them, if any, were effective— though his bedroom would have looked strange. The subject has been thought worthy of poetic treatment:

> *Toute la nature sommeille:*
> *Mais non, j'ai tort; je m'aperçoi*
> *Que dans ce beau lit où je veille,*
> *Les puces veillent avec moi.*
> *Le bois de cet auguste lit*
> *Est de vieille menuiserie,*
> *Et tout son chevet s'embellit*
> *Des placards d'une confrérie.*

> (All nature's children are at rest:
> But no, I notice my mistake;
> For with me in my sleepless nest
> My flea companions watch and wake.
> The timbers of this august bed
> Are so antique in all regards
> That, dotted round its curtained head,
> Bug-visitors have left their cards.)

A manual for hunters dated 1585 recommends the wearing overnight of a wolf-skin cloak, which repels fleas, lice and bugs 'like fire'. Yet another antipuce is offered by the Elizabethan versifier Thomas Tusser:

133

While wormwood hath seed, get a bundle or twain,
To save against March, to make flea to refrain.
Where chamber is swept and that wormwood is strown,
No flea for his life dare abide to be known.

Fleas prefer blue blood, according to an old belief recalled by Mr.
Pepys:

> The Doctor and I lay together at Wiard's, the surgeon's, in Portsmouth:
> his wife a very pretty woman. We lay very well and merrily; in the morning,
> concluding him to be of the eldest blood and house of the Clerkes, because
> that all the fleas came to him, and not to me.

But on one occasion he maligns the fleas—and his maids—without
cause:

> I have had a bad night's rest tonight, not sleeping well, as my wife
> observed; and I thought myself to be mightily bit with fleas, and in the
> morning she chid her maids for not looking the fleas a'days. But when I
> rose I found that it is only the change of the weather from hot to cold . . .

Evelyn notes that most of the bedsteads in Italy are of 'forged iron
gilded, since it is impossible to keep the wooden ones from the
cimices'. At Ely (where an earlier traveller noted the 'turfy sent and
fenny posture' of the inhabitants) Celia Fiennes finds her inn bedroom free from all the usual parasites, but some unusual creatures
in their place:

> . . . the dirtyest place I ever saw, not a bitt of pitching in the streetes so its a
> perfect quagmire the whole Citty . . . it seems only a harbour to breed and
> nest vermin in, of which there is plenty enough, so that tho' my chamber
> was near 20 stepps up I had froggs and slow-worms and snailes in my
> roome—but suppose it was brought up with the faggotts.

Cimex lectularius is a resistant enemy—he can live for twelve months
between meals, and is willing to travel right across the bedroom from
his hide, to obtain them. The average life of *Pulex irritans* is only a
few weeks, 'but he lives merrily if not long'. A 6-ft. man who could
proportionately match his high jump could achieve about 350 ft., and
in the long jump event, about 1200 ft. With *anopheles*, in some
countries better-named *zanzara*, it is the female that makes most of
the noise, and does most of the biting. *Pulex* and *anopheles* in alliance
can pose a frightful dilemma—whether to be cold and mosquito-
bitten, or warm and flea-bitten—probably ending with both.

134

26

Requisate Foolerys

B Y the end of the seventeenth century, bedchambers were less draughty, and all-round protection for the bed no longer essential, so that the old 'half tester' came back into fashion; Celia Fiennes described it as 'the new mode' when at Windsor Castle she saw

... two bed-chambers, one with a half bedstead as the new mode, dimity with fine shades of worstead works well made up, there are good Pictures; the next roome has such a bed but that is fine Indian quilting and embroidery of silk ...

The low balustrade isolating the holy-of-holies was still in use at Hampton Court, and at Windsor it had been heightened to enclose the state beds in almost a cage:

... next is the Queenes Chamber of State all Indian Embroidery on white sattin being presented to her by the [East India] Company on it is great plumes of white feathers; there is very good tapistry hangings full of gold and silver but they are large old figures; here's a silver table and stands and glass frame; there was a raile set across at the beds feete which reach each side of the roome made of sweate wood frames and open wires in the middle, and was to be doubled together in leaves as a screen, this was

135

instead of the raile use to be quite round the king and queens beds to keep off companyes coming near them . . .

The austerity that is said to have ruled at the court of William III is not in evidence in these Windsor bedchambers. One might have expected that when not displayed in the gilded cage, he would have slept content in some modest cot, but even his 'constant bed chamber' is far from austere:

. . . thence into the Kings constant bed chamber being one of the halfe bedsteads of crimson and green damaske inside and outside the same hangings, and chaires and window curtaines the same; it was lofty and full, with good fringe and there was such another screen or raile at the feete of the bed that tooke the length of the roome [and] looked very glorious and was newly made to give audience to the French Embassadour to shew the grandeur and magnificence of the British Monarch—some of these foolerys are requisate sometymes to create admiration and regard to keep up the state of a kingdom and nation.

A little later, Defoe sees there a 'Chints Bed . . . the Chints being of *Masslapatam*, on the Coast of *Coromandel*', and at Hampton Court the late queen's little bathroom, 'made very fine, suited either to hot or cold Bathing, as the Season should invite'; but such minor comforts were set in surroundings little cosier than Versailles. A tour through the royal suites, now open to the public, followed by a check of Wren's plan, shows that the king, going to bed and starting from the head of the 'King's Great Staircase', had to traverse the Guard Chamber, the First Presence Chamber, the Second Presence Chamber, and the Cartoon Gallery *or* the Audience Chamber and the Drawing Room, before reaching his bedroom. The Queen, starting from the 'Queen's Staircase', had to traverse seven apartments, her bedroom being 220 ft. from the head of the stair. By all means let an ordinary mortal have to pace this out, to earn the honour of seeing royalty abed, but not a sleepy queen. Royal living is royal living, and one must not confuse Hampton Court with Kosy Kot, but could not Wren have planned some quick private access for off-duty days?

For the funeral pomps of the palaces, the corpse was now, rather illogically, coffined on its bed. Inigo Jones had devised the bed of state for the funeral of King James I, showing the skill and something of the economy of an experienced stage designer:

. . . he made 4 heads of the Cariatides (which bore up the canopie) of playster of Paris, and made the drapery of them of white callico, which was very handsome and very cheap.

136

The death of Charles I was hardly an occasion for such show; still less that of Cromwell; but after Charles II had been 'surprised in his bed-chamber with an apoplectic fit', the new king James II received homage and condolence there:

> There came over divers envoys and great persons to condole the death of the late King, who were received by the Queen-Dowager on a bed of mourning, the whole chamber, ceiling and floor, hung with black, and tapers were lighted, so as nothing could be more lugubrious and solemn.

William's queen Mary died in December 1694, but she did not lie in state until February 1695, and she was not buried until twelve days later, when William

> . . . omitted noe ceremony of respect to her memory and remains, which lay in State in Whitehall in a bed of purple velvet all open.
> . . . a halfe pace [a dais] railed as the manner of the princes beds are; this in a roome hung with purple velvet, full of large wax tapers, and at the 4 corners of the bed stood 4 of the Ladyes of the Bed Chamber—Countesses —with vailes; these were at severall tymes relieved by others of the same.

After which ceremony at Whitehall,

> . . . to Westminster Abby where was a sermon, in which tyme the body of the Queen was reposed in a masulium in form of a bed with black velvet and silver fringe round, and hanging in arches, and at the four corners was tapers and in the middle a bason supported by cupids or cherubims shoulders, in which was one entire great lamp burning the whole tyme.

As the Georges died—not always to the unmingled sorrow of their subjects—the setting for the coffin became a simpler catafalque, without the bed-like hangings; at lyings-in-state in Westminster Hall nowadays, the association with the bed is forgotten.

It became the fashion, when a wife died, to commission a painting of the family, grouped around the death-bed—a race between composition and decomposition. The eighteenth-century doctor Van Buchell went one better than this. Losing his first wife, he had her embalmed by Dr. Hunter, who injected the blood-vessels with carmine and inserted glass eyes. Decked with silk and lace, she was put to bed in the sitting-room, and for years she was introduced to every visitor, until for some reason the second wife objected.

State bedroom by Sir James Thornhill, c. 1720

27

Hail, Glorious Structure!

WITH the eighteenth century came a changed relationship between the English architect and his patron, who was no longer content to trust an expert and foot the bill. He would now hire a dog and bark himself. He considered himself well up in the arts, if he had done the Grand Tour and had perhaps collected a few antiques. He had ideas he thought his own, and the wise architect would defer to them, and forego any credit for the result. Because these ideas came from books rather than from real training and experience, the outcome might be a somewhat arid intellectual exercise rather than a work of high imagination. Moreover, Vitruvius and Palladio had known nothing of the English climate or the English way of life, and the noble *dilettanti* who bowed to their rules would make no concession to practical domestic needs. A house in the Grand Manner is the very opposite of 'a machine for living in'.

138

'Thanks, sir,' cried I, "'tis very fine,
But where d'ye sleep, or where d'ye dine?'

says Pope, and mocks the 'imitating fools' who

. . . call the winds thro' long arcades to roar,
Proud to catch cold at a Venetian door;
Conscious they act a true Palladian part,
And if they starve, they starve by rules of art.

Lord Hervey describes the new Burlington House as

Possessed of one great hall of state
Without a room to sleep or eat

and when General Wade complains of the inconveniences of his new
town residence, Lord Chesterfield can only advise him to take a
house on the opposite side of the street, from which he may enjoy
the prospect of its magnificence in comfort. Not that comfortless
splendour was a Palladian innovation—Wren had already shown
what monumental inconveniences could be inflicted on royalty, and
Vanbrugh's Blenheim of 1705 was practically uninhabitable. It has
four major bedroom suites on the ground floor, all the rooms connected through each other, but few connected independently to any
main circulation: the apartments *are* the circulation. As for the lesser
rooms, it is a common drawback of monumental planning, that these
must make do with the odd spaces left over, after the 'great shapes'
have been assembled. The Palladian mansion always has one or two
suites of fine state bedrooms and dressing-rooms, but the others are
fitted into residual spaces, with only such lighting and access as can
be contrived. Nobody will sleep comfortably, the important persons
because their bedrooms are too large, the rest because they are too
small, ill-shaped, airless, dark. Only in the smaller houses, where the
country builders kept up the Wren tradition, but on a modest scale
and with an eye to the facts of everyday living, did comfort survive.
Of Mereworth Castle in Kent, a copy of Palladio's *Villa Almerico*
at Vicenza, the architect Colen Campbell says, 'I shall not pretend
to say that I have made any improvements in this plan from Palladio';
nor has he. All is sacrificed to symmetry, and the bedgoing guest
climbs a dark narrow spiral staircase of about 50 steps, arriving on
an open gallery, around which guests in search of their rooms, and
servants carrying chamber-pots, must circulate in full view of the
great hall below. Each of the four portico pediments contains a vast

139

bedroom about 40 ft. long, lit only by a single bullseye window about 4 ft. in diameter. Unless partitioned, it is a mere barrack-room; if partitioned, no room save one has air or light. The entrance front is flanked by two distant buildings, one devoted to stabling, the other to additional bedrooms that cannot have been popular with guests on a wet winter night. At Holkham, the demands of the grand plan likewise lead to most of the guests being expelled into a virtually separate building. An invitation to stay does not yet mean that one is socially so acceptable as to live as one's host lives. Doctor Johnson, after a comfortless night at Kedleston, reports it

... very costly but ill-contrived ... the grandeur is all below. The bed-chambers are small, low, dark and fitter for a prison than a house of splendour. The kitchen has an opening into the gallery by which its heat and fumes are dispersed all over the house.

He might have added, had he known, that there were three servants' bedrooms opening directly off the kitchen.

In town houses, with their deep narrow sites and blind party-walls, the lighting and access to all but the best front bedrooms were seldom satisfactory. Plans from the drawing-boards of Isaac Ware and John Wood show dark, ill-ventilated bedrooms accessible only through one another, and dressing-rooms reached only by crossing the common stair-landing. Again, the servants came off worst. Ware recommends for 'an ordinary town house', that as well as lodging servants in the garrets, beds should be 'contrived to let down into the kitchen', which is in the basement, though he does considerably add that 'the necessary care for these people's health' requires that the kitchen walls shall be boarded. In a country-house, he says, servants of the meaner kind may be lodged over the hen-houses, 'that the common thieving of hen-roost robbing will be avoided'. The window-tax, instituted in 1696, continued through the eighteenth century, and many windows were bricked up to reduce the imposition. 'It is a dreadful thing to pay as we do,' says a landlady in *Tom Jones*; 'Why now there is about forty shillings for Window lights, and yet we have stopped up all we could: we have almost blinded the house, I am sure.' We may safely assume that the servants' windows were among the first to be blinded. Sir William Chambers recommends that over the smaller main apartments, where even with a coved ceiling the proportion will not be tolerable, mezzanines should be contrived for 'servants' lodging rooms, baths, powdering rooms, wardrobes and the like'.

Below these rambling warrens, the monumental principal bedroom suites were still used for the reception of visitors, but the dressing-room was taking over the functions of the former parlour-bed-chamber:

> . . . a dressing-room in the house of a person of fashion is a room of consequence . . . The morning is a time many chuse for dispatching business; and as persons of this rank are not to be supposed to wait for people of that kind, they naturally give them orders to come about a certain hour, and admit them while they are dressing. This use of the dressing-room shows also the necessity of a waiting-room.

Though it was not too difficult, given a good 'crib' and a drawing-board, to produce a Palladian house or even a Vitruvian bedchamber, neither Palladio nor Vitruvius had left any models for the furniture, and this had to be invented. Architects seldom stay long enough in the workshop to understand furniture design, and once again, beds looked like scaled-down temples; more elegant than the Elizabethan four-posters, but 'no more like Greek or Roman furniture than Pope is like Homer'. About 1720, Sir James Thornhill was designing state beds on strictly architectural principles, but the flowing draperies of a bed are not easily confined within the frame of a classical order, even if it leans to the baroque. The upholsterer, for the sake of harmony, must make some concessions to the cabinet-maker, and treat his fabrics more rigidly than is natural to them; the cabinet-maker too must meet half-way by softening his lines, if the bed is to be a coherent unit. A particular weakness observable in most of the architectural four-posters of the period, is that the strong structural lines of the column, its important junction with the entablature, and the capital implied by its ornate base, are masked by the fabric pelmet. Too often the canopy and the bed are of equal size and importance, so that neither dominates.

The more inventive cabinet-makers now began to run wild among Chinese, Gothic and naturalistic sources of inspiration, and even mixed these ingredients. In 1742 Batty Langley was recommending what he called 'the Saxon style', its supreme outcome being Horace Walpole's house at Strawberry Hill, the forerunner of the Gothic Revival. ('Lord God! Jesus! What a house!' said old Lady Townshend.) By 1760 the 'Chippendale style', a blend of rococo, pidgin-Chinese, and pseudo-Gothic, was well established. Chippendale's *Gentleman and Cabinet Maker's Directory* appeared in 1754. He has been credited with vast quantities of furniture not made by him, nor in his time; often not resembling his work. It has been doubted whether he himself drew many of the designs in his book, though he did sign them all. Mr. R. W. Symonds doubts whether in the eighteenth century Chippendale was considered anything more than a successful

Lacquered and gilt bed from Badminton, probably by Chippendale, c. 1760. (Victoria
& Albert Museum)

tradesman, and one specially noteworthy for making furniture of very good quality. Though fanciful, and 'ephemeral as the best confectionery', Chippendale furniture is usually comfortable, and beautifully made. The beds with which he is known to have been associated include one made for the Earl of Pembroke at Wilton, and another made for Sir Edward Knatchbull at Merstham Hatch in Kent, that was sent from London by sea. A painted wooden bedstead from Garrick's villa at Hampton is now in the *Victoria and Albert Museum*. Garrick's total furniture bill was for nearly £1,000 —Chippendale had to sue him for two-thirds of it. Fanny Burney describes another bed at Hampton, a 'Press Bedstead' which was an inlaid cabinet of rosewood and fustic (a tropical American or West Indian wood) concealing a folding bed. Other 'probable Chippendales' are a bed in the Blue Bedroom at Dumfries House, Ayrshire, and the famous Chinese Bedroom at Badminton. This room was hung with imported Chinese wallpaper: paper had hitherto been thought of as a mere substitute for better materials, but it was now more fashionable than panelling. The bed, in black japan with gilt details, but without its hangings, is now in the '*V. & A.*' together with some of the furniture. Chippendale was also concerned, with the architects John Carr and Robert Adam, in the state beds and other furniture for Harewood House, in 1770. Chippendale's bill totalled £6,326: no mean amount at then values. An anonymous poet, seeing the results, exclaims

> Hail, glorious structure! noblest of our isle,
> Finished by artists bred on every soil,
> What gold can finish or what taste can show
> Beyond conception strike the astonish'd view
> Such costly furniture, such beds of state!

Other so-called 'Chinese Chippendale' jobs include a Chinese bedroom at Eastbury, in the attic storey, 'excessively droll and pretty, furnish'd exactly as in China, the bed of an uncommon size 7 ft. wide by 6 ft. long.'

Hepplewhite seems to have done better when executing the designs of the brothers Adam than when working on his own. Little is known of him beyond his pattern-book *The Cabinet Maker's and Upholsterer's Guide* of 1787, and not one piece of furniture can confidently be attributed to him. 'Chippendale', 'Hepplewhite' and 'Sheraton' are convenient labels, like 'Spanish Sauternes'. Fashion was so ephemeral that Sheraton could write of Hepplewhite's book, when it was sixteen years old, that 'this work has already caught the decline, and perhaps in a little time will die in the disorder'. Sheraton was addicted to complicated draperies, and like Chippendale he was sometimes tempted to be silly. There were countless other cabinet-makers; the *trade* subscribers to these two books numbered over 800. Their status had improved—*The London Tradesman* could already say in 1747 that the 'upholder'

. . . was originally a species of Taylor, but by degrees has crept over his Head, and set up as a connoisseur in every article that belongs to a house. He employs journeymen in his own proper calling, cabinet-makers, glass grinders, looking-glass framers, carvers for chairs, Testers and Posts for Beds, the Woollen Draper, the mercer, the Linen Draper and several species of smiths and a vast army of tradesmen of the other mechanic branches.

Such firms undertook, like the 'universal providers' of today, the whole job of decorating, equipping and furnishing the house, even to organising funerals. They had impressive showrooms, ran 'mail-order' business, and sent their goods all over the country: the state bed for Erthig House in Denbighshire (which is still there), made by Mr. Hunt 'at ye Looking Glas & Cabenet at East end of St. Paul's Church Yard', travelled over 200 miles by wagon, together with such fragile items as gilded mirrors up to 10 ft. high, over some of the worst roads in the country.

In 1759 Samuel Norman, of the 'Royal Tapestry Manufactury, Soho Square', provides among other things a 'Grand State Bed' for Woburn; his prices are high, and his bill is for £378, but the Duke of Bedford makes him knock £20 off. At Lancaster, Mr. Gillow's 'ware rooms' are said in 1772 to be the best stocked outside the metropolis. The English makers are not so well known as the French, who were highly organised, and had their names registered. Each *maître* would stamp his own mark on every piece, except those made for the crown.

Oak, more fit for stout structure than for slender whimsy, was long since out of favour, and there was little English walnut after about 1725. Most beds were now of mahogany, which gives such freedom to the designer that it can be used almost like a synthetic material. In this lies the danger, of excess of detail masking the construction. Some of the forms are refined to the verge of flimsiness. Pine-wood overlaid with gesso and gilding was used for some of the fruitier of the baroque beds, a technique borrowed from Italy.

Although native designers flourished, the 'French taste' persisted. The versatile French-trained Daniel Marot had worked for William and Mary, styling himself on his drawings '*Architecte de sa Majesté*

Design for a State Bed by Chippendale, 1761, which he 'submits to the Judicious and the Candid, for their approbation. There are found Magnificence, Proportion and Harmony. If the Pedestals of the Bedstead, the Pillars, Cornice, and Top of the Dome, are gilt with burnished Gold, and the Furniture is suitable, the whole will look extremely grand, and be fit for the most stately Apartment. The ingenious Artist may also, in the Execution, give full scope to his Capacity. The Bedstead should be 6 or 7 feet broad, 7 or 8 feet long, and the whole height 14 or 15 feet. A Workman of Genius will easily comprehend the Design. But I would advise him, in order to prevent mistakes, to make first a Model of the same at large; which will save both Time and Expense'

English State Bed by Sheraton, 1803
'The cornice, pillars, etc., are adorned with various symbolical figures expressive of the different branches of the British Government. There are various figures supposed to represent, or be symbolical of Democracy, Aristocracy, and Monarchy; the crown is supported by Justice, Clemency and Liberty; and other figures are Law, Obedience, Authority, Counsel, etc. etc.'

146

Britanicque', and his influence was strong among the English 'upholders'. Fine French furniture was still imported by great men like the fourth Duke of Bedford, who had been Ambassador in Paris, and had furnished the Embassy there in such splendour that even the footmen and housemaids had *lits à baldaquin*. He brought back some important pieces to Bedford House, and to Woburn where the *French Bedchamber* and the *Printed Cotton Bedchamber* of his time may still be seen. The Duchess' bed in Paris was '*à la turque*', that is, with padded 'boards' not only at the ends but along the wall, the whole surrounded by a light and elegant tester from which curtains fell from head to foot; this may well be the same bed as the 'double-headed Couch bed . . . with a Doom canopy and a Gotheroon cornice' in a Woburn inventory. ('Doom' for 'dome' incidentally gives a sound eighteenth-century precedent for the pronunciation of James Thurber's coloured cook, who when the hot-water tank went wrong, unnerved him by speaking of 'the doom-shaped thing in the kitchen'.)

In England the custom of receiving visitors in bed was going out of fashion. Thus *The Spectator*:

I could heartily wish that there was an act of parliament for prohibiting the importation of French fopperies.

The female inhabitants of our island have already received very strong impressions from this ludicrous nation . . . I remember a time when some of our well-bred country-women kept their *valet de chambre*, because forsooth, a man was much more handy about them than one of their own sex . . . About the time that several of our sex were taken into this kind of service, the ladies likewise brought up a fashion of receiving visits in their beds. It was then looked upon as a piece of ill-breeding for a woman to refuse to see a man because she was not stirring; and a porter would have been thought unfit for his place, that could have made so awkward an excuse. As I love to see everything that is new, I once prevailed upon my friend Will. Honeycomb to carry me along with him to one of these travelled ladies, desiring him, at the same time, to present me as a foreigner who could not speak English, that so I might not be obliged to bear a part in the discourse. The lady, though willing to appear undrest, had put on her best looks, and painted herself for our reception. Her hair appeared in a very nice disorder, as the night-gown which was thrown upon her shoulders was ruffled with great care. For my part, I am so shocked with everything which looks immodest in the fair sex, that I could not forbear taking off my eye from her when she moved in her bed, and was in the greatest confusion imaginable every time she stirred a leg or an arm. As the coquets, who introduced this custom, grew old, they left it off by degrees; well knowing that a woman of threescore may kick and tumble her heart out, without making any impressions.

147

28

The Celestial Bed

IN 1778, with the laudable object of

> . . . the propagation of Beings, rational and far stronger and more
> beautiful in mental as well as in bodily Endowments, than the present
> puny, feeble and nonsensical race of Christians . . .

Doctor Graham introduced the nobility, gentry, and persons of
learning and taste to his Celestial Beds. He had already been

demonstrating, at his Temple of Health in the Adelphi, such wonders as

the celestial Brilliancy of the Medico-Electrical Apparatus . . . the Effects of Electricity, Air, Music and Magnetism when applied to the Human Body . . . the display of the Celestial Meteors . . . the Electrical Fire. (*Note*: *Ladies and Gentlemen Electrified*.)

The demonstrations and lectures were presided over by 'Vestina, the Rosy Goddess of Health', who in private life was Emma Lyon, a blacksmith's daughter, later to become Lady Hamilton, and successive mistress to a queue of gentlemen culminating in Lord Nelson. Vestina, then, was an authority on beds. These first Celestial Beds were merely the Magneto-Electric type, sundry ills being curable by lying on them at a fee of £50 a night. But the real show-piece, in the later Temple of Hymen in Pall Mall, was *The* Celestial Bed.

It is placed on the second floor, in a large and elegant hall, on the right hand of my orchestra, and immediately before my charming hermitage. In a neighbouring closet is placed a cylinder by which I communicate the celestial fire to the bed-chamber, that fluid which animates and vivifies all, and those cherishing vapours and Oriental perfumes, which I convey thither by means of tubes of glass. The celestial bed rests on six massy and transparent columns; coverings of purple, and curtains of celestial blue surround it, and the bed-clothes are perfumed with the most costly essences of Arabia: it is exactly similar to those that adorn the palaces in Persia, and to that of the favourite sultana in the seraglio of the Grand Turk . . . I have omitted none of the precautions which decency and delicacy have a right to exact. Neither I, nor any of my people, are entitled to ask who are the persons that rest in this chamber, which I have denominated the Holy of Holies. This bed is never shown to those who come only to view the accessory parts. This precaution is as proper as it is delicate; for is there a being frigid enough to resist the influence of that pleasure, of those transports which this enchanting place inspires? It furnishes the grossest imagination with the means of refining its enjoyments, of multiplying its pleasures, and of carrying them to their highest degree. But the consequences are cruel; such dangerous refinements on the pleasures of the senses abridge the period of life, and relax the springs of body and mind.
. . . The chief elastic principle of my celestial bed, is produced by artificial lodestones. About 1500 pounds weight of artificial and compound magnets, are so disposed and arranged, as to be continually pouring forth in an ever-flowing circle, inconceivable and irresistibly powerful tides of the magnetic effluvium, which every philosophical gentleman knows, has a very strong affinity with the electrical fire. These magnets too, being pressed, give that charming springyness—that sweet undulating, tittulating, vibratory, soul-dissolving, marrow-melting motion; which on certain critical and important occasions, is at once so necessary and so pleasing.

The fee for one night's use (the customer providing his own companion) was at first £100, but as the supply of wealthy impotents ran out, it fell to £25 and even less. Finally, after about five years, the Temple closed its doors, and the paraphernalia came under the auctioneer's hammer; Dr. Graham died in poverty. The various offices of the Temples of Health and Hymen survive today only in the separate ministrations of the psychiatrist's couch, the electrotherapeutic clinic, and the strip-tease club.

Drawing by Robert Adam: A Bed for Osterley Park, 1775

29

Adam to Pugin

THE architect dominated the cabinet-maker and all the other craftsmen, in the person of Robert Adam. The whole house, complete with its decoration and furniture, would be designed in detail on his drawing-board. The result, if somewhat severe, was always a unified whole. His first known authentic furniture designs are those he made for the 'Queen's House', now part of Buckingham Palace, in 1761. His state bed for Queen Charlotte Sophia of Mecklenburg-Strelitz, the consort of George III and the grandmother of Queen Victoria, is now at Hampton Court, though not in its proper setting. It has a Greek flavour, with its anthemion acroteria crowning the slender posts; it is draped in beautifully embroidered lilac satin. Adam did not eschew all fantasy, for at Kedleston, despite the severely classical setting, he put in the state bedroom the Palmtree Bed, whose four posts are palm trunks, rising from gnarled roots to a luxuriant cresting of palm-fronds. Perhaps his masterpiece among beds is at Osterley, an Elizabethan mansion which he remodelled for Robert Child the banker. The modestly proportioned state bedroom is dominated by this vast domed bed, which exactly follows in every detail his surviving drawings dated 1775–6, as also does the carpet, which is so much part of the room that four circular spots in its pattern mark the precise positions for the four double-columned bed-posts. Horace Walpole thought this bed

. . . too theatric, and too like a modern head-dress, for round the outside of the dome are festoons of artificial flowers. What would Vitruvius think of a dome decorated by a milliner?

But had Adam seen Walpole's *Great North Bedchamber* at Strawberry Hill, he in turn might fairly have asked what the Gothic masters would have thought of a bed of Aubusson tapestry, with festoons of flowers on a white ground, lined with crimson silk, and topped with ostrich plumes, in a Gothic setting. Walpole's own comment on seeing this completed for him was that it 'would become Cleopatra on the Cydnus, or Venus if she was not past Cupid-bearing'. Strawberry Hill is in fact Gothic only in detail; its bones are classical and its spirit in some ways akin to Adam's.

At William Beckford's fantastic Gothic 'Abbey' at Fonthill, built from 1796, on such a scale that it offered an uninterrupted internal vista of 307 feet, Beckford's own bedroom was little more than an unheated monastic cell, with one small window, on the second floor of a tower. But in the *Lancaster State Bedchamber* the honoured guest slept in a massy ebony bed with crimson damask hangings, under Henry VII's purple silk quilt.

Ackermann's *Repository of Arts* for 1813 sets out to 'display the decorations of some of the principal apartments of a mansion in the Gothic style'. The bedroom is illustrated by a gloomy plate, thus captioned:

The walls are divided into compartments of mullions and tracery. The hangings are of blue silk; and the ornaments, velvet, of a darker colour. The bed is formed on the principle of the Gothic crosses of Queen Eleanor, and of wood corresponding with the yellow or orange wood of the mullions: portions of this are gilded. From the pinnacles rise groined arches, to support a Gothic canopy, from which are suspended the hangings of the bed, of a tent-like character. The base of the bedstead extends on each side, where steps are made to rise, as the steps to a throne. The hangings are of orange silk lined with blue and with blue ropes and tassels.

We are not told how many minutes the chambermaid was allotted for the dusting.

A Gothic Bed: from Pugin's Gothic Furniture, *1835*

Augustus Welby Pugin was a better Gothic scholar than any of these; he was responsible for the fine Gothic detail of the Houses of Parliament. His name falls into this period only because of his early death, in 1852, at the age of 40. *Pugin's Gothic Furniture* of 1835 shows some extremely Gothic beds. He seems to have enjoyed a sense of humour, for it is not one of his critics, but Pugin himself, who remarks that

a man who remains for any length of time in a modern Gothic room, and escapes without being wounded by some of its minutiae, may consider himself extremely fortunate.

Very few such rooms were in fact built, and few restless sleepers were stabbed by crockets or finials. The full horrors of the Gothic Revival were yet to come; its high priest Ruskin was not born until 1819. The classical tradition died slowly, if it can be said to have died at all.

30

Pioneers! O Pioneers!

THE little ship, of a mere 180 tons burden, that dropped anchor at Plymouth, Massachusetts, on December 11, 1620, must have presented a strange sight, with her deck cargo piled half-way up the mast—for how else would she carry the quantity of furniture guaranteed to have been imported in the *Mayflower*? Although indeed English and Dutch furniture did come over in the seventeenth century, it was not long before good cabinet-makers and joiners were plying their trade in New England and New Amsterdam, and fashion was only a few months behind that of Europe. Mr. Wallace Nutting has been able to illustrate nearly 5,000 native examples dating up to the early nineteenth century.

The pioneer has no time for frills, and his bedstead might be much like the 'jack bed' still used by the hill-billies of the southern Appalachian highlands. A single post is set about 6 ft. from one wall and about 4 ft. from another. From it, bearers extend to the walls, carrying slats of springy poles on which lies the sack filled with straw, corn-husks, reeds or rags. Panels may be added below to form a cupboard for extra bedding. In the Dutch colony, the *betste* was a 'press-bed' set in a recess, much like a cupboard, with doors closed during the day. This was so much a built-in affair that it might

154

appear in the contract for the house, as in that for the ferry-master at Brooklyn in 1665:

... to wainscot the east side the whole length of the house, and in the recess two bedsteads [*betste*] one in the front room and one in the inside room, with a pantry at the end of the bedstead.

Adam Roelandsen, the first New York schoolmaster, and Jan Peeck, the founder of Peekskill, both had *betstes*. The *sloep-banck* or *slaw-bunk* was a folding bed, hinged about 2 ft. from the head, and with two hinged legs, made to disappear behind curtains hung from a tester; sometimes behind cupboard doors. Parson Chandler as late as 1755 said that the beds in Albany were simply wooden boxes, each with a feather-bed, under-sheet and blanket. The *sloep-banck ap rollen* or *trecke-bedde* was a truckle-bed. The settle-bed, another space-saver, perhaps an idea of Irish origin, was a long box-seat with a high back and arms; the seat could be drawn forward with its front panels resting on the floor, to form the bed. The 'sleigh-bed' was made to fit along the wall, so that its decoration if any was confined to one side. The 'under-eaves bed' was a low bed made to fit under a sloping ceiling, often with elaborately but clumsily turned foot-posts, but no head-posts.

Bed foundations took several forms. For a low bed, straw mattresses might be put on the floor itself. Some beds had solid boarding. Most of them were corded, and better ones had sail-cloth, which could be fixed at one end to a roller and tightened up, being held taut by a ratchet. Above this went one or more straw mattresses; then, in better homes, a deep goose-feather bed. The blankets were thick homespun. An ample linen-store was a matter of pride: Francis Rombout, mayor of New York, died in 1690 leaving linen valued at $500, including no less than fifty-one plain and ten checked 'pillow-bears'. Two years later Captain Kidd of New York set up house with four beds, of which three had 'suits' of curtains and valances. His bedroom equipment also included:

4 feather beds, bolsters and pillows
10 blankets
2 dressing-boxes [perhaps combined dressing-table and chest-of-drawers, like a sea-chest]
1 close stool
1 warming-pan
2 bed-pans [warming-pans were called 'bed-pans' in England; the distinction is not clear; these can hardly have been what the modern hospital calls a 'bed-pan']
3 quilts
1 parcel of linen sheets.

155

The better-off had four-poster beds from early days, and Captain Kidd's may have been such, but until about 1750 the 'bedstead', as in earlier times in England, would be valued at only a few shillings in an inventory; the 'bed'—that is, the hangings and bedding—was the important item. Only the head of the household was likely to have a four-poster. Its canopy top was originally of solid wood panels, but cloth soon replaced these, and with the eighteenth century came some graceful and charming 'field-' or 'tent-beds'. These may have derived from the canvas tent-beds used by officers in the field during the Revolution; they were known, but uncommon, in England. They have delicate spindly posts and light lacy hangings, almost transparent. The ogee arch top was especially popular in America. Its dome-like form needs a fairly lofty room, and does not consort happily with a low ceiling; nor does it look right when hung, as it sometimes was, from a ring above—a dome should be supported from below, not dangled like a dish-cover.

American beds made under Chippendale influence are markedly simpler than other contemporary furniture. Well into the nineteenth century there is a tradition of Puritan austerity. The Dutch influence for some reason survived mainly in day-beds, with their ball-and-claw feet and elaborate carving. From about 1830 the four-poster gave way to the fashionable low 'French' bedstead. The American craftsman made rather heavy weather of the Empire style, in which, if the job would not run to real mahogany, he often used a rather fierce red paint. The massive Empire sleigh-bed, especially popular in the South, is too reminiscent of Napoleon's red porphyry tomb in the *Invalides*. By the mid-century, as in England, the machine was ousting the craftsman; a notable symptom is the 'spool-bed' with a profusion of turned knobs, like an abacus, on every member. The ways divided towards antique-collecting for some, period reproduction for others.

The American inn does not seem to have bedded its guests very comfortably in the early days, except in Boston and in the South. It was not called an inn, but an 'ordinary', until late in the seventeenth century when it became a 'tavern', which to the English traveller would now suggest a mere pot-house. In the eyes of the law, even the most sumptuous of American inns are still taverns.

Rooms and beds were often shared with strangers, though wagon teamsters, a tough lot and not encouraged to mix, might have a special stair; at the *Pease Tavern* at Shrewsbury, Massachusetts, they had to reach their beds on the top floor by climbing up toe- and hand-holes cut in the outside weatherboarding.

The first inn mentioned in New York was *Kriger's Tavern* in 1642.

In 1651 *The King's Arms* in Boston had thirteen beds; its rooms were named, in the English manner, as *The Exchange, London, The Starr Chamber, The Court Chamber*. So were those at the Boston inns *The Blue Anchor, The Rose & Sun, The Cross Keys*, and *The Anchor & Castle*.

In 1704 Mrs. Sarah Knights, a Boston widow, went 'by post'—that is, on horseback in company with the postman—from Boston to New York, and kept a journal of the trip. At an 'ordinary' at Rye, New York,

... being very hungry I desired a Fricassee which the landlord undertaking managed so contrary to my notion of Cookery that I hastened to Bed supperless. Being shew'd the way up a pair of Stairs which had such a narrow passage that I had almost stopt by the Bulk of my Body; but arriving at my Apartment found it to be a little Lento [lean-to] Chamber furnisht among other Rubbish with a High Bedd and a Low one, a Long Table, a Bench and a Bottomless Chair. Little Miss went to scratch up my Kennell whch Russelled as if shee'd bin in the Barn among the Husks and supose such was the contents of the Tickin—nevertheless being exceedingly weary down I laid my poor Carkes never more tired and found my Covering as scanty as my bed was hard. Anon I heard another Russelling noise in the room—called to know the matter—Little Miss said she was making a bed for the men; who when they were in Bed complain'd their Leggs lay out of it by reason of its shortness—my poor bones complained bitterly not being used to such Lodgings, and so did the man who was with us; and poor I made but one Grone which was from the time I went to bed to the time I riss which was about three in the morning Setting up by the fire till light.

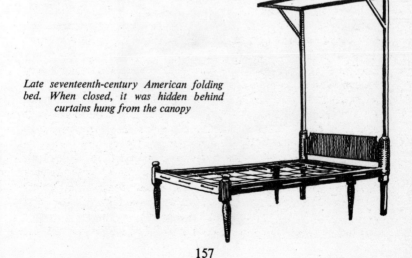

Late seventeenth-century American folding bed. When closed, it was hidden behind curtains hung from the canopy

A Mr. Twining has recorded that after he was asleep the landlord came, candle in hand, and escorted a stranger into his bed; and a Mr. Thurlow Weed, that anyone who objected to this sort of thing was regarded as unreasonably fastidious. A Mr. Wansey noted that in a Boston lodging-house in 1794 the beds were 'generally two in a room, and not very cleanly, for we were much pestered with bugs', and he met *Cimex lectularius* again in the best tavern in Philadelphia. In the same year an unusual view was expressed by an Indian warrior staying in New York, who remarked on the want of judgement among the palefaces, in having their bedrooms upstairs:

Walking upwards is so unnatural, especially when there was so much room on the ground; besides, you were in that situation so easily surprised by the enemy, who could put a fire under you, and burn you, while you were asleep.

American 'Sheraton' bed with ogee canopy frame, by Israel Sack, 1790–1800

At an 'ordinary' in Virginia in 1799, the English actor John Bernard found

. . . a bed stuffed with shavings, on a frame that rocked like a cradle, and in a room so well ventilated that a traveller had some difficulty in keeping his umbrella erect, if endeavouring, under this convenience, to find shelter from the rain while in bed.

By 1818 the *Exchange Coffee House* in Boston, rebuilt after a fire, had over 200 bedrooms, and by 1827 one Boston hotel had water-closets and bathrooms, though in the basement. Charles Dickens, travelling in America in 1840, found much to criticise in the hotels —but Dickens had little good to say for any American, after he found that they were pirating his books. He says that however comfortable the hotels may be in other respects, the bedrooms are always 'very conducive to early rising'. They are very barely furnished. Only in one does he find enough water to wash, and curtains to his bed—though he admits that he never uses these at home. In another, his wardrobe is 'an unusual luxury', but its dimensions 'may be estimated from the fact of my having lived for fourteen days and nights in the firm belief that it was a shower-bath'. Yet by 1853 the *Mount Vernon Hotel* at Cape May, New Jersey, was far ahead of Europe, offering a bath with hot and cold running water to every bedroom.

31

Pickwick slept Here

THE first of the two great periods of prosperity for the English
inn was the coaching era. This was brief; it lasted only from
the making of good fast turnpike roads in the last years of
the eighteenth century, until the spread of the railways a
generation later. (The second such period was to come with the motor-
car.) The 'post inn', where the public coach changed horses, was the
equivalent of the railway station, but there was little night travel.
Those who have driven along English lanes in the 'blackout' years
of the war, with no headlights, dimmed sidelights, and no 'cat's-eyes'
on the road, will understand why. This meant an enormous demand
for bedrooms, and many inns were enlarged at this period—happily,
one when architecture was of fine quality. These additions often
included a new feature, the 'Long Room', usually on the upper floor,
for big functions, dinners and dances. It seldom survives, but an
exploration of the bedrooms may reveal an alteration that explains
their incomplete ceiling mouldings, and the presence of fire-places
far too grand for such small chambers: the old Long Room has
been subdivided. As it usually had a fire-place at each end, its former
length can be deduced from these. Some unexpectedly fine bedrooms
prove to have been formerly ante-rooms to the Long Room. In
1802 De Quincey, aged 17, arrived at the *Lion* at Shrewsbury to find
that such bedrooms as were not being redecorated were full, and he
was accommodated in the Long Room:

. . . I was received with special courtesy, and, so it happened, with something even like pomp. Four wax-lights carried before me by obedient mutes, these were but ordinary honours, meant (as old experience had instructed me) for the first engineering step towards effecting a lodgement upon the stranger's purse. . . . I have always looked upon this fine of 5s. or 7s. (for wax that you do not absolutely need) as a sort of inaugural *honorarium* . . . I stepped into the sumptuous room allotted to me. It was a ball-room of noble proportions—lighted, if I chose to issue orders, by three gorgeous chandeliers, not basely wrapped up in paper, but sparkling through all their thickets of crystal branches, and flashing back the soft rays of my tall waxen lights. There were, moreover, two orchestras, which money would have filled within thirty minutes. And, upon the whole, one thing only was wanting—viz., a throne, for the completion of my apotheosis.

But this was no place for a man of De Quincey's cast of mind to relax in. To an ordinary guest it would have been a windy night; to him,

. . . the whole atmosphere had by this time become one vast laboratory of hostile movements in all directions. Such a chaos, such a distracting wilderness of dim sights, and of those awful 'sounds that live in darkness' . . . and the local circumstances around me deepened and intensified these reflections, impressed upon them solemnity and terror, sometimes even horror . . . The unusual dimensions of the rooms, especially their towering height, brought up continually and obstinately, through natural links of associated feelings or images, the mighty vision of London awaiting me, afar off . . . their unusual altitude, and the echoing hollowness which had become the exponent of that altitude—this one terrific feature (for terrific it was in its effect), together with the crowding and evanescent images of the flying feet that so often had spread gladness through these halls, on the wings of youth and hope, at seasons when every room rang with music— all this, rising in a tumultuous vision, whilst the dead hours of the night were stealing along, all around me—household and town—sleeping, and whilst against the windows more and more the storm was raving, and to all appearance endlessly growing, threw me into the deadliest condition of nervous emotion under contradictory forces, high over which predominated horror recoiling from that unfathomed abyss in London into which I was now so wilfully precipitating myself.

Not, in fact, a very good night's rest.

The general layout of the typical English inn has shown little change. It is planned—if the word can be used for such picturesque haphazard—round a long stable-yard, with the upper floor carried across the gated entrance. An outside staircase from the yard leads to one or two tiers of open balustraded galleries above. These galleries run round two, three or very occasionally four sides, and offer the

161

only access to the bedrooms. Any bedroom window that does not open on the gallery is probably a later addition. A row of numbered bells on the yard wall will summon the chambermaid; a bell will wag long enough, on its coil spring, for the needy guest to be identified. The galleries are then enclosed to form corridors, and where no other windows can be contrived, the bedrooms must take what light and air they can across the corridor. The outside stair may also be enclosed, incidentally making it less easy to walk out with one's baggage and ignore the bill. The *George* at Southwark is the best-known surviving example of an inn with open galleries, and there are countless closed galleries still in use.

Baron Pückler-Muskau, touring England in the heyday of the coaching era, had nothing but praise for the inns, perhaps because

The White Hart Inn, Southwark, in 1827. The only access to the bedrooms is from the open galleries

162

he does not seem to have considered expense, for on at least two occasions he absent-mindedly left purses of gold behind him.

In the inns every thing is far better and more abundant than on the Continent. The bed, for instance, which consists of several mattresses laid one upon another, is large enough to contain two or three persons; and when the curtains which hang from the square tester supported on substantial mahogany columns, are drawn around you, you find yourself as it were in a little cabinet,—a room, which would be a very comfortable dwelling for a Frenchman. On your washing-table you find—not one miserable water-bottle, with a single earthen or silver jug and basin, and a long strip of a towel, such as are given you in all hotels and many private houses in France and Germany; but positive tubs of handsome porcelain, in which you may plunge half your body; cocks which instantly supply you with streams of water at pleasure; half a dozen wide towels; a multitude of fine glass bottles and glasses, great and small; a large standing looking-glass, foot-baths, &c., not to mention other anonymous conveniences of the toilet, all of equal elegance.
. . . Good carpets cover the floors of all the chambers; and in the brightly polished steel grate burns a cheerful fire, instead of the dirty logs, or the smoky and ill-smelling stoves to be found in so many of our inns . . . a stranger is never invited to eat, sit and sleep in the same room, as in the German inns, in which there are generally only ball-rooms and bed-chambers.

Such service was to become rare in the railway days, then imminent, though it is there anew for those who, like the Baron, drive up with an impressive vehicle and spend accordingly. A traveller of modest means would be less well received, and might be wise to carry his own bed-linen with him. The German Pastor Moritz, who toured England in 1782, made the mistake of going on foot, and was 'treated like a beggar but suffered to pay like a gentleman'. At Windsor, he was shown to a bedroom resembling 'a prison for malefactors', and when he asked for a better one, was advised to walk back to Slough. He took the room, which he had to share with a drunk who came to bed in his boots. The bill, including for a supper of an old, tough fowl, was 9s. Had he gone to a 'hedge-inn' he might have fared as well for 9d. Jonathan Swift, on his way from Moor Park to Leicester, had paid 6d. for a clean bed at a hedge-inn. Town lodgings were variable. Swift paid 8s. a week for a bedroom and sitting-room in London, which he thought 'plaguey dear', and moved to Chelsea where he paid 6s. for 'one silly room with confounded coarse sheets'. Benjamin Franklin's furnished room in Smithfield cost him 3s. 6d. a week until, when he talked of leaving, his landlady made an abatement of 2s., so that for the rest of his stay in London

163

he paid 1*s*. 6*d*. a week. Compare the French Ambassador who, arriving through Dover in 1762 with a suite of twelve persons, spent his first night at the *Red Lion* at Canterbury, and was charged the fantastic sum of £44 10*s*. 8*d*. for lodging with a light supper. It is good to hear that when this imposition became known, the *Red Lion* was blacklisted by so many travellers that the landlord had to put up his shutters.

Travellers of today who seek overnight associations in their inn bedrooms have a wide choice. At the *White Swan* at Stratford-on-Avon you may sleep in a room, with a curious little Gothic window looking down the road into the town, that was probably the 'solar' of the original house of about 1450. At the *Ancient Gate House* at Wells, you may have a Tudor four-poster in the room over the archway that leads to the cathedral precincts; at the *Speech House Hotel* in the heart of the Forest of Dean, a choice of three four-posters, two of them measuring 7 ft. by 6 ft. At the *Royal Castle* at Dartmouth, you may have a bed slept in by Sir Francis Drake; at the *Bull* at Gerrards Cross, one slept in by the highwayman Jack Shrimpton, who found this a convenient centre from which to waylay the London-to-Oxford coaches, until he was hanged in 1713. At the *White Horse* at Romsey you may enjoy a fragment of mediaeval wall-painting beside your bed. At the *Bell* at Thetford, which was standing when Columbus sailed for America, you may warm your pyjamas at a Tudor fire-place, though you probably have to put a coin in a meter first. At the *George* at Portsmouth, you may get the room where Nelson slept his last night in England before boarding the *Victory* for Trafalgar. At the *Hope Anchor* at Rye, an old smugglers' inn, you may choose your bedroom according to the view from its window, as expressed by its name, '*Trader's End*' or '*Starland*' or '*Western Watch*'. At the *Royal Fountain* at Sheerness, likewise dating from the days before rooms were numbered, three of them still bear their old name-plates in heraldic style, the '*Sun*', the '*Rose*' and the '*Star*'; a fourth, the '*Crown*', was lately stolen by a lover of past things. At the *Shakespeare* at Stratford-on-Avon you may choose '*Merrie Wives*' or '*Midsummer Night's Dream*' according to your mood. If you have visited the 'Old Curiosity Shop' in London with some belief that it has or ever had any connection with Dickens, you will no doubt sympathise with a former landlord of the *White Horse* at Ipswich: 'So this is where Mr. Pickwick is supposed to have slept?' said a visitor viewing the sacred bedroom. '*Supposed* to have slept?' said the ruffled landlord, 'He *did* sleep here, sir!'

164

After Rowlandson

32

Pestered with Buggs

HOUSING and hygiene had been improving during the eighteenth century, more than is generally supposed, but bugs were still a problem. About 1770, William Cauty advertised from 'King's Street, the corner of Bury-Street St. James's, London' (the simple idea of numbering houses not having yet struck mankind),

. . . bedsteads of every kind, sofas and chairs, finished so as no Vermin of any Denomination can ever possibly exist in either (Warranted Gratis) by a new and infallible method, never before found out, and done no where else but at the above shop . . .

The infallible method seems to have been lost, and Cauty does not seem to have prospered by it, for the Westminster City Rate Book a few years later records that he has not paid his rates, with a kindly marginal note, 'Poor, give him time.' In 1775 Andrew Cooke of Holborn Hill, 'Bug-Destroyer to His Majesty', was claiming to have 'cured 16,000 beds with great applause'. In 1786 Parson Woodforde stayed at the *Bell Savage* in London and

... was bit so terribly with Buggs again this Night that I got up at 4 o'clock and took a long Walk by myself about the City till breakfast time.

Nevertheless he patiently stayed on there, and the next night:

I did not pull of my Cloaths last Night but sat up in a great Chair all night with my Feet on the bed and slept very well considering and not pestered with buggs.

The Young Woman's Guide to Virtue, Economy and Happiness, which is undated, but is quoted here from a copy bearing a bookplate of 1819, adds to our list of infallible remedies: a strong solution of vitriol is to be rubbed into all the joints and crevices of the bed with a painter's brush. This corrosive 'should also be applied to the walls of the room to ensure success; and if mixed with a little lime, will give it a lively yellow'. After which dangerous if decorative procedure, the author goes on to picture a domestic scene at which the imagination boggles:

The boiling of any kind of wood work or new furniture in an iron cauldron, with a solution of vitriol, will prevent the breeding of bugs, and preserve it from rottenness and decay.

There might still be no peace for the occupant of the vitriolic bed, for if bugs still persisted, he must apply more vitriol to 'the lacings of the bed, the foldings of the curtains near the rings, and other parts where it is at all likely the bugs may nestle and breed'. As for mere fleas,

... the best remedy to expel them from the bed-clothes is a bag filled with dry moss, the odour of which is to them highly offensive. Fumigation with brimstone, or the fresh leaves of a penny-royal sewed in a bag, and laid in the bed, will also have the desired effect.

Two innovations did deter the bug: the introduction in the mideighteenth century of cheap cotton bed-clothing, in which the bug could be boiled to death without spoiling the fabric; and of the cheap metal bedstead in which no bug could 'nestle and breed'. In 1824 the Grand City State Bed in the Mansion House, measuring 9 ft. by

6 ft. 8 in., with damask satin curtains embroidered with gold, proved untenable by guests because of 'all sorts of vermin', and had to be burned. In Queen Victoria's reign a firm was still advertising as 'Bug-Destroyers to Her Majesty', and Mayhew gives an account of a bug-hunt in the Princess Royal's bedroom. As late as 1896, in the London Union of Journeymen Basket Makers' list of sizes and prices of work for the London district we find under 'Furniture Work':

Bug Traps (Slight Randed). To be made 11 inches wide, with six sticks. To be paid for at the rate of 3d. per foot.

The curious will find one of these wickerwork lobster-pots in the University Museum of Archaeology and Ethnology at Cambridge, and another in the London Museum of Pestology. Both were made by Mr. Thomas Okey, a basketmaker, who has described their use:

The trap was placed behind the bolster and between it and the head of the bed . . . the little anthropophagi after their nightly meal would retire to digest between the interstices of the wicker trap. The housemaid in the morning would take the trap into the yard or garden and shake out the victims, who would meet a violent death under her feet.

Toilet or Dressing Table for a Lady, by Chippendale, 1762.
'The glass, made to come forward with folding hinges, is in a carved frame, and stands in a compartment that rests upon a plinth, between which are small drawers. The drapery is supported by cupids, and the petticoat goes behind the feet of the table, which looks better. The ornamental part may be in burnished gold or japanned. The drapery may be silk damask, with gold fringes and tassels'

167

33

Nouryces use Lullynges

THE rocking of the cradle, like the beat of the dance, is one of the oldest sources of rhythmic song.

Nouryces use lullynges and other cradyl songes to pleyse the wyttes of the chylde

wrote John de Trevisa in 1398; and when an Anglo-Irish friar in the time of Edward II set down his lullaby

> Lollai, lollai, litil child,
> Why wepistou so sore?

he may have had in mind the ancient Roman nurse's

> *Lalla, lalla, lalla, aut dormi, aut lacte.*

As for

> Hush-a-bye baby, on the tree top;
> When the wind blows, the cradle will rock . . .

although this cannot be traced further back than the sixteenth century, it refers to an older practice of putting the cradle in the branches,

168

out of harm's way, to be rocked by wind-power. Tacitus says that the ancient Britons wove cradles in the tree-tops for both children and old men. Trees in the Indian reservations of North America are still festooned with papooses in their vertical birch-bark cradles, only the heads and shoulders visible; Chinese babies have rather similar affairs, of wicker, shaped like churns; the luxury model has a little charcoal heater below the baby's toes.

The traditional wood for a cradle is birch, the tree of inception, which drives away evil spirits. A child in an elderwood cradle will pine away, or at least be pinched black and blue by the fairies.

The ancient Greek child was laid in a cradle shaped like a winnowing-basket, symbolising newly harvested grain. A curved shield offered a ready-made and rockable cradle; it was upon a shield that the first Prince of Wales was introduced to his subjects. Manuscripts of the ninth and tenth centuries show cradles hollowed out from halved tree-trunks, with holes along the edges for straps or cords to keep the baby from falling out. Greek peasants were still using this type late in the nineteenth century. The 'Moses basket' (*moïse*), very like that in which babies are nowadays left to suffocate in closed motor-cars, is very old, though there is no record that it was so called before about 1800. Some mediaeval cradles were made like miniatures of an adult's bed, but on two curved rockers. A noble infant in *The Process of the Seven Sages* had three nurses, who

> . . . Wente out of the hall,
> And set the cradil under the wall.
> One gaf it souke als it would serve,
> Ye toder wasshes it and bathes,
> Makes the bed and dons the clothes.
> Ye third wasshes ye shetes oft,
> And rokkes it on slepe soft.

This subdivision of labour in the nursery was to be carried even further; here the nurse who washes the sheets also rocks the cradle, but later, a noble baby would have at least one full-time 'rocker'. It might have a costly cradle; when the men of Ghent despoiled the house of the Earl of Flanders in the fourteenth century, they destroyed all his furniture except the cradle—not out of consideration for the baby, but because the cradle was of solid silver.

The cradle that swung from two fixed supports—a different principle from the rocker, the pivot being above the centre of gravity instead of below—dates from the fifteenth century. It goes on rocking for some time with only an occasional push, and it would seem to offer a more gentle ride, with less tendency to eject the child; but

169

this we shall never know for sure, for no child small enough for a test would be articulate enough to report its conclusions. In French inventories the *berseil* (cradle) and the *bersouère* (stand) are listed as two distinct items. Until the sixteenth century the cradle was not curtained, because its place was under the parents' or nurse's bed-curtains, or in the *ruelle*.

In most early pictures the child is shown 'swaddled' like a chrysalis in its 'swaddling bands'. This practice was general until the eighteenth century, and still survives in remote corners of Europe and in the East. Dr. Mauriceau, a French obstetrician, said that it ensured *'l'attitude droite'*, producing an upright man, against the natural tendency to crawl like an animal on all fours. Children seem to have survived it without crippling or deformity.

Wallace Nutting has told (or killed) some stories of *Mayflower* cradles supposedly brought to America by the Pilgrim Fathers. In the Pilgrim Hall at Plymouth hangs a great painting of the lading of the *Mayflower*, in which a sailor is seen lugging an oak cradle aboard. The artist painted this from an actual cradle said to have been brought over by one Samuel Fuller. But Fuller, though a Pilgrim, was not a father—not even married—at this time, and as Mr. Nutting remarks, 'he would have shown great faith, even for a Pilgrim, to bring this cradle under the circumstances'. The story is further spoiled by the fact that this cradle is made mainly of good American white oak. Another '*Mayflower*' cradle in the Pilgrim Hall proves to be made of pine—'If the English before 1620 were making pine cradles,' says Mr. Nutting, 'it is interesting to know it.' Not that these are not both fine pieces of early American craftsmanship: the Samuel Fuller cradle has changed hands at prices rising from $250 to $2,500.

Some rocker cradles have the posts at the head lengthened and turned to form handles for rocking them, but no good housewife or nurse would have used such means; she would rest a toe on the tip of

170

the rocker, and thus leave both hands free to sew or spin. The cradle tends to decline with the rise of the rocking-chair; a settee combined with a cradle was invented, on which mother and child could rock together, one at each end.

In the royal nurseries of France, the rules to safeguard the precious heir, and the staff appointed to observe them, were both so numerous that more than one child was killed by kindness. The Duc de Beaumont was entrusted to a nurse with such a fear of cold—*'il vaut mieux suer que trembler'*—that after two months in an overheated nursery, being moved into a normal atmosphere, he died immediately.

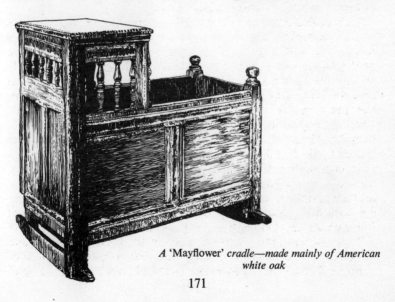

A 'Mayflower' cradle—made mainly of American white oak

171

Fourteenth century

Fifteenth century

*Seventeenth century,
beaten copper*

*Venetian, c. 1750,
painted wood*

Elizabeth I

Henry IV of France, born 1589   *King of Rome, son of Napoleon I*

Fifteenth century, painted wood

Sixteenth century

Berceaunette, 1878

Seventeenth century

'Victoria Regia Cradle', 1851

Iron cradle, 1890

173

The princess born to the Duchesse de Berry was laid in a cradle in an adjoining room, lit by blazing cressets and heated by a great fire, on a warm October day; there were five or six guest-beds almost filling the room, and a horrid smell was traced to the worm-infested mattresses lately unearthed from the *garde-meuble*; the child died with all the symptoms of asphyxia. To ensure watchfulness, the *femmes-de-chambre* were not allowed mattresses until the child was three months old, and even then, were expected to sleep one at a time and fully dressed, until it was three years old. In 1736 there were fourteen such women on call. Their respective duties were so exactly defined, that if a dauphin or dauphine anticipated its sanitary time-table and howled in discomfort, none dared lift and service it until the appointed moment and the appointed nurse duly arrived. Even English princelings required the attendance of governess, under-governess, wet-nurse, dry-nurse, rockers and maids—Charles II had eight of each—as well as laundress, sempstress, page and 'necessary woman'; the last-named, presumably, confined to the duties associated with the 'necessary house'. In the same way as the royal adult corpse would lie in state on a bed, the royal infant corpse might lie and even be buried in its cradle. Sophia, the two-day-old daughter of James I, having been embalmed, 'cered' by the wax-chandler, and laid in lead by the plumber, was entombed in a cradle monument, 'in which her *Effigies* lieth, done to the life'. Again like the adult, who had two beds, one for show and one for sleep, many noble infants had two cradles. The *berceau de parade* of the infant Henry IV of France so bristled with martial emblems, as to suggest that he was called up for his national service from birth; so with George III, who wore full military dress for a parade on his first birthday. His children, in their turn, had 'split-wicker' cradles, probably their second-best, but still no common objects, for a surviving bill from Catherine Naish 'the joiner' charges for them 'as usual' at £13 2s. each. As for the cradle ordered by Napoleon for his son the King of Rome, it was designed by Prudhon, occupied a skilled craftsman for six months, and cost a subsequent collector over £5,000. When this long-wanted heir was born, poor Napoleon paced the floor as anxiously as any commoner, and spared no safeguards: the Empress even wore a *chemise de Notre-Dame*, reviving a custom that dated back for centuries. It seems that the very *chemise* worn by Our Lady throughout her pregnancy was in the possession of the cathedral chapter of Chartres. Kings and queens of France, seeking holy aid in conception and in childbirth, would go afoot on pilgrimage to borrow this precious relic, together with an exact replica. The king wore the replica until conception was assured, and the queen the original until

174

A cradle made for Queen Victoria in 1850—by no means the first, for her seventh child was due, ten years after the marriage—was enthroned at the Great Exhibition. It was carved by the labours of Mr. Rogers in that rather intractable material turkey boxwood, which allows of all too much fine detail and is usually worked by the square inch. Mr. Rogers explained his intention

. . . that the entire object should symbolise the union of the Royal Houses of England with that of Saxe-Coburg and Gotha, and, with this in view, I arranged, that one end should exhibit the Arms and national motto of England, and the other those of H.R.H. Prince Albert. The inscription, 'Anno 1850', was placed between the dolphins by her Majesty's special command.

A connoisseur of the day described it as 'a fine piece of work which would not have disgraced the latter period of the Renaissance', and the Art Journal *believed it to be 'one of the most important examples of the art of wood carving ever executed in this country'*

the delivery. In 1582, when the royal pair returned to Paris complaining of sore feet (the double journey being nearly a hundred miles) the chapter simplified the procedure, and thereafter, when pregnancy was notified, they sent the replica only, which seems to have been equally effective.

Napoleon had his influence in the English nursery, where the lullaby in his time took a topical note:

> Baby, baby, naughty baby,
> Hush, you squalling thing, I say!
> Peace this moment, peace, or maybe
> Bonaparte will pass this way!

175

Walter de la Mare has recalled that 'Old Boney' was still a stock nursery menace in the 'eighties.

The future George IV first received company when twelve days old, in a golden cradle surmounted with a golden coronet; coronets were woven into his bibs and aprons. He lay under a canopy of state, enveloped in crimson velvet and gold lace, in a nest of white satin. On either side stood 'a fair mute, employed as occasion required, to rock the infant to sleep'. The public were admitted in batches of forty. The daily bill for cake was £40, and for wine, 'more than could have been conceived'.

The chore of rocking the cradle was now being avoided by the use of stupefying drugs, sold under such innocuous names as 'Dalby's Carminative' and 'Godfrey's Cordial'—a mixture of treacle, laudanum and brandy. Doubtless there was factual basis for an incident in a story by Charlotte Yonge, where a child dies from an overdose. Such things are now under better control—the drowsy syrup that renders you unconscious of your cough is at least labelled as unsuitable for young children. Not only opium for infants, but rocking too, is out of fashion; the cradle has given way to the cot, and has not survived into days when it would certainly have been rocked by an electric motor. It has been held that rocking, by inducing artificial anaemia, damages the brain. Today's unrocked and undoped babies seem somehow able to sleep; perhaps they are exhausted by the wear and tear of traffic and television. But meanwhile, more of them are killed by accidents than by all the infectious diseases put together, and most of the accidents occur in the home; high in the list of causes are strangulation by badly spaced cot-bars (there is a British Standard for these), guillotining by cot-sides that drop at the wrong moment, suffocation by soft pillows or by 'overlaying', burning in inflammable 'nighties'. Though we no longer dope them to death or rock them into imbecility, there are dangers still in the nursery.

34

Odd Jobs in Bed

THE bed has been the scene of many activities other than
sleep, love, birth or death; they range from mere authorship
to such oddities as making bread or milking cows. Authors
who have written in bed include Cicero, Horace, the Plinys,
Milton (it is largely in bed that 'the old blind schoolmaster hath
written a marvellous tale, all about Adam and Eve and the Garden
of Eden', and there 'at what hour soever, he rung for his daughter
to secure what came'), Swift (with a bedside fire), Rousseau, Voltaire
(of whom a striking portrait shows him still dictating while dressing),
Gray, Pope, Trollope, Mark Twain, Stevenson, Proust, Winston
Churchill, and Edith Sitwell ('but that,' says the housekeeper who
gives the fact to the press, 'is supposed to be a secret'). Hogg, in his
Life of Shelley, records that 'a fussy, foolish little fellow, a banker in
a country town' told him that much of Wordsworth's poetry was
written in total darkness, in bed. 'Any man who can write verses
in the dark must be a real genuine poet,' added the banker. Shelley
heard of this feat, and tried it, but he usually lost his pencil, or his
paper, or both, and the results were illegible. (It can, in fact be done,
if the lines are widely spaced; it can be recommended to followers of
Dunne's *Experiment in Time* who want to record their dreams
promptly and without fully rousing.) A blind Australian journalist,
broadcasting from London, has mentioned among the advantages of
his handicap, that of being able to snuggle down under the bed-
clothes in winter and read Braille in comfort.

Elinor Glyn, urgently needing £1,000 to meet a rash I.O.U. given by her husband, contracted to write a 90,000-word novel in three weeks—not the novel of that name—and took to bed. Fortified with coffee and brandy, she wrote all day and most of the night, with the haunting I.O.U. lying on her bed-table. She finished the job in eighteen days, and lay back exhausted. Da Vinci (strange bedfellows, these) liked to recapitulate his daytime studies in bed. Hobbes, the philosopher, would draw geometrical problems on his thighs or on his sheets. Sir John Suckling practised card-playing. Pepys cunningly planned to make the bed serve his purpose of talking business, safe from interruption, with the Deputy-Treasurer of the Fleet:

. . . and after a game or two at shuffle-board, home, and Creed lay with me; but, being sleepy, he had no mind to talk business, which indeed I intended by inviting him to lie with me . . .

Casanova was neither the first nor the last debtor to make his bed a refuge from creditors. Joseph Joubert, moralist and disciple of Diderot, liked to lie in bed for days on end in a pink dressing-gown, trying to think of absolutely nothing and to feel no emotion whatever; if he succeeded, it must have been hard to know whether he had stayed awake. D'Annunzio, having long deferred the urgent task of composing an inscription for a monument to Wagner, found that his staff had left sheets of paper, blank but for the heading 'Epigraph on Wagner', pinned not only to the bed, but to the Maestro's very pyjamas. Max Beerbohm no doubt wrote in bed, for did he not say that his ideal of happiness was a four-poster in a field of poppies? Salvador Dali, in a self-portrait, entered under the heading 'Proudest Symbol': 'The sign on my sleeping chamber, "POET WORKING".'

As for the artists: Fantin-Latour would draw in bed, wearing his overcoat and scarf and top hat, as we know because Whistler has so depicted him. G. K. Chesterton, himself no mean draughtsman, has said that lying in bed would be an altogether perfect and supreme experience if only one had a coloured pencil long enough to draw on the ceiling. Matisse, bedridden in his old age, achieved this joy, drawing on the wall from his bed with the aid of a long stick to which his charcoal was tied. William Morris set up a loom in his bedroom.

Moscheles in 1814 brought his piano arrangement of *Fidelio* to Beethoven, who was still in bed, but

. . . jumped immediately, and placed himself, just as he was, at the window looking out on the Schottenhastei . . . Naturally, a crowd of street boys collected under the window, when he roared out 'Now what do these confounded boys want?' I laughed, and pointed to his own figure. 'Yes, yes, you are quite right,' he said, and hastily put on a dressing-gown.

178

Glinka composed in bed; likewise Rossini, who was indeed a bed-lover; he had just completed the soprano. part of a duet, to be embodied in an opera due for first performance on that very night, when the manuscript sheet dropped off the bed and out of reach. Unable to face the misery of getting out of bed to seek it, he took the easier course, and having forgotten how it went, wrote an entirely new duet.

Homelier tasks have been done in bed: thus Negley Farson travelling in Roumania:

When we went to bed one old man and his wife went to the far end of the room and climbed on to the stove. Kostia and his wife lay down at this end—their child between them—then Feodor, stripped to his undies, lay down beside them, and I brought up the flank. The others lay in lines on the floor . . . About three I awoke, saw Kostia's wife, with the lamp lighted, bowing toward their ikon. Then she climbed back on the bed and began to knead some bread which was on the raised part of the stove.

Nearer home, and not long since, the Hon. Blanche T., at the age of about 70, took to her bed with a severe nose-bleed. When the doctor came this had ceased, but she now complained of a pain in her spine. On examination, he unearthed the cause, a huge rusty iron key which she had bid the coachman bring from the stables and drop down her back to cure the nose-bleed. In the process, his fingers were bitten by one of the four spaniels hidden under the bed-clothes. His next visit was even more memorable. He found the stairs covered with planks, and at his patient's bedside a cow and a pail; her prize Jersey was temperamental, and would let nobody else milk it. (Compare the converse arrangements made by Mme de Mezeray, who, falling into a consumption, adopted the bucolic practice of moving her bed into the cowhouse for several months; the cleaning of the floor was delayed to ensure a strong curative atmosphere.)

Animals a-plenty abound in bedroom history. Dogs predominate. Louis XI, confined to bed and debarred from hunting, had rats and mice coursed round his apartments. Cromwell's dog seems to have shared with him the room at Hampton Court that had belonged to Charles I, according to a long-accepted story: Charles, at the window of this room, had refused silver to a gipsy below, who had thereupon prophesied that his crown would fall, but that the death of a dog in that very room would herald its restoration. Cromwell, they say, knew of this prophecy, yet let his dog sleep there—need one add that he awoke one morning to find that the dog was dead? Evelyn noted that Charles II delighted to have his spaniels in the bedchamber, and the bitches pup and suckle there, 'which rendered it very offensive, and indeed made the whole court nasty and stinking'—from which comment we may judge that it was without permission that a cat kittened on Evelyn's own bed, incidentally leaving there one kitten having six ears, eight legs, two bodies from the middle downwards, and two tails. The Pompadour's bedroom had a special little alcove built for beds for her two dogs. Visitors to Voltaire at Ferney might be startled by his ape Luc peering through the bed-curtains. Boswell tells us that Lord Gardenstone, Judge in the Court of Session, carried his fondness for pigs to the point of letting one share his bedroom. Mrs. Celestina Collins, an 'Ornamental Hermit' of the eighteenth century, shared her bed with thirty fowls, a cock and a rat; until one day the rat attacked the cock, and Mrs. Collins, joining in, struck the rat a fatal blow for which she never forgave herself. 'As if this were not ample company,' adds Edith Sitwell, 'a nest of mice too was found in her bed.' Parson Woodforde had dog trouble in the bedroom:

Very much disturbed in the night by our dog which was kept within doors tonight, was obliged to get out of bed naked twice or thrice to make him quiet, had him into my room, and there he emptied himself all over the room.

After the battle of Waterloo, the inelegant Blücher quartered himself and his dog in the imperial suite at St. Cloud, and encouraged it to befoul Napoleon's magnificent couch.

Emily Brontë's savage tawny bulldog 'Keeper', who figures in Charlotte's novel *Shirley* under the name of 'Tartar', had the bad habit of stealing up the stairs at Haworth parsonage and sleeping on the delicate white counterpane of the best bed. Though he was also in the habit of flying at the throat of anyone, friend or foe, who struck him, Emily vowed punishment if he trespassed on the bed again. He did, and she dragged him downstairs growling while the others watched in frightened silence; there was no time to fetch a stick, 'for fear of the strangling clutch at her throat'—she beat him with her fists till his eyes were swelled up; but he forgave her, and walked first among the mourners at her funeral. 'Let us somehow hope,' says Mrs. Gaskell, 'in half Red Indian creed, that he follows Emily now; and when he rests, sleeps on some white bed of dreams, unpunished when he awakens to the life of the land of shadows.'

The Carlyles, living in Cheyne Row, Chelsea, in 1850, accepted the kennel-bedroom. When Jane was away from home, she wrote to their mongrel Nero:

. . . My dear good little dog! How are you? How do they use you? Above all, where do you sleep? Did they put you to bed by yourself in my empty

180

room or did you 'cuddle in' with your surviving parent? Strange that amidst all my anxieties about you it should never have struck me with whom you were to sleep; never once, until I was retiring to bed without you trotting at my heels. . . .

(Surely words like *surviving* and *anxieties* are rather long and difficult ones to include in a letter to a dog?)

Queen Victoria, when Albert's greyhound bitch had grown over-fat, gave orders that 'she must be well starved, poor thing, and not allowed to sleep in beds, as she generally does'. D'Annunzio favoured the same breed, and like Charles II, liked to watch the pups feed on his bed. These relationships, ranging from the pathetic to the emetic, bring to mind W. C. Fields' remark that no man can be wholly bad who dislikes babies and doggies.

The Hygienic Dog Bed
('sizes to suit all dogs'), 1938

Tastes have become more varied, and today's formula for a best-seller seems to be to lie down with the lioness, or smuggle owls into the dormitory at Eton, or share a bed with an otter.

Some of the more fantastic minor scenes of history and biography have been set in the bedroom. Thackeray records one at Richmond Lodge on June 14th, 1727, where a little man lies asleep—'he always slept after his dinner, and woe be to the person who interrupted him!' But an urgent visitor in jackboots demands admittance. The awakened sleeper, with many oaths and a strong German accent, asks who dares to disturb him. 'I am Sir Robert Walpole,' says the kneeling messenger, 'I have the honour to announce to your Majesty that your Royal father, King George I, died at Osnaburg on Saturday.' At which His Sacred Majesty King George II roars back, 'Dat is one big lie!'

Edith Sitwell paints two fine bedroom scenes of the eighteenth

181

century; the first features the famous sportsman Squire Mytton; thus his biographer 'Nimrod':

You have read that somebody set fire to Troy, Alexander to Persepolis, Nero to Rome, a baker to London, a rascally caliph to the treasures of Alexandria, and the brave Mucius Scaevok to his own hand and arm to frighten the proud Lars Porsena into a peace; but did you ever hear of a man setting fire to his own nightshirt to frighten away the hiccup? Such, however, is the climax I have alluded to, and this was the manner in which it was performed. 'Damn this hiccup,' said Mytton, as he stood undressed on the floor, apparently in the act of getting into his bed; 'but I'll frighten it away'; so, seizing a lighted candle he applied it to the tab of his shirt and, it being a cotton one, he was instantly enveloped in flames.

Edith Sitwell continues:

In the subsequent mêlée, during which two intrepid gentlemen knocked down and rolled upon the Squire in their attempt to put out the flames, and the flames did their worst against both nightshirt and hiccup, the two gentlemen won, for they tore his shirt from his body piecemeal. As for the hiccup, it was frightened away. 'The hiccup is gone, by G——,' said the Squire, as, appallingly burnt, he reeled into bed.

Secondly, Colonel Thornton of Thornville Royal, who tells his own story:

Arrested? Why, I have been arrested oftener than anyone in England, once, under the most atrocious circumstances. You must know I was lodging at Stevens', my wife was with me. One morning between 7 and 8 o'clock while we were in bed, a bailiff came into the room. 'I understand your business, my good fellow', said I. 'Wait below, I'll get up and dress, and accompany you to my solicitor, who'll do the needful.' He swore I should get up and go with him as I was. 'What, in my nightshirt?' said I. He insisted, I resisted, when the scoundrel went to the fireplace, drew out the poker which had been left in the fire all night, and thrust it, red as it was, in the bed between my wife and me. She, womanlike, as all women would do, jumped out of bed; not so your humble servant. There I lay, and there stood the scoundrel poking at me; and there, Sir, I would have remained had not the bedclothes taken fire. Now did I not choose to be burnt in bed, nor would I endanger the safety of the house, in which there happened to be many lodgers at the time, so up I got and dressed myself. I resolved to carry *that* point, and I did. Now I put it to you, as men, as *gentlemen*. Did I compromise my honour by giving in at last? But observe, gentlemen, 'twas as I told you, not until the bed took fire.

Yet another bedroom conflagration—limited, but embarrassing— broke out upon Baron Pückler-Muskau on Christmas night in 1828:

182

The bad habit of reading in bed occasioned me a laughable misfortune last night. My hair caught fire, and I was forced to bury my head in the bedclothes to extinguish it. The injury is horrible;—one entire half of my hair was destroyed, so that I have been obliged to have it cut almost close to my head all over. Happily my strength does not reside in my hair.

According to a story that cannot be authenticated here beyond saying that it is quoted by Daniel George, a certain baronet in Hampshire was nearly driven to distraction by the fact that, every night, he went to bed in a shirt, and every morning awoke naked, without a trace of the missing garment being found. The servants believed him mad; he began to fancy himself bewitched. Taking (rather late, for we are told that hundreds of shirts had disappeared) the obvious course of having a friend to watch in his room, he fell asleep, and as the clock struck one, rose, took a candle, walked the long route to the stable-yard, there took a pitchfork, and buried his shirt in the dung-heap before returning, still fast asleep, to bed. ·
Augustus Hare tells another tale of somnambulism:

A lady was awoke in the night with the disagreeable sense of not being alone in the room, and soon felt a thud upon her bed. There was no doubt that someone was moving to and fro in the room, and that hands were constantly moving over her bed. She was so dreadfully frightened, that at last she fainted. When she came to herself, it was broad daylight, and she found that the butler had walked in his sleep and had laid the table for fourteen upon her bed.

'The burglar under the bed' has nearly always been imaginary, for what burglar, however anxious to hide, would risk having to lie doggo for hours, and creep out an inch at a time at dawn? But he proved almost real one night in 1850, when the famous 'Boy Jones' was found under a bed in the royal nursery in Buckingham Palace. Not that he had burglarious intent; he had only a mania for harmless palace-breaking. He had made three such intrusions, managing to spend days there unseen, studying palace life, eating in the empty kitchen at night, until—treated with remarkable mildness, and unable to reap the journalistic rewards that would offer today—he was packed off to sea. This recalls a story told—though with some disbelief—by Charles Lamb:

In one of the state beds at Arundel Castle, a few years since—under a ducal canopy—(that seat of the Howards is an object of curiosity to visitors, chiefly for its beds, in which the late duke was especially a connoisseur) —encircled with curtains of delicatest crimson, with starry coronets interwoven—folded between a pair of sheets whiter and softer than the lap where Venus lulled Ascanius—was discovered by chance, after all methods of search had failed, at noon-day, fast asleep, a lost chimney-sweeper. The little creature, having somehow confounded his passage among the intricacies of those lordly chimneys, by some unknown aperture had alighted upon this magnificent chamber; and, tired with his tedious explorations, was unable to resist the delicious invitement to repose, which he there saw exhibited; so, creeping between the sheets very quietly, laid his black head upon the pillow, and slept like a young Howard.

Vehicles more unusual than the truckle-bed or the occasional pram have found their way into bedrooms. A gallant R.A.F. pilot was in the habit of staying in the mess bar at night until it closed, while his lovely foreign wife languished alone in a nearby guest-house, among a group of all-too-visibly devoted younger couples, to whom at last she cried:

You tink my hosband neglect me, but he don't! I tell you what he do a few days ago. He love me, all right. I am in bed. He come upstairs. What you think he do?

Nobody dared to guess. The answer was unexpected:

He bring my bicycle up to the bedroom, and before he go to bed, he take it to pieces, every little bit, and he clean it and oil it, every little bit, in the bedroom, and he put it all together again, like new!

Motor cycles, and 500 c.c. at that, have been raced between rows of beds in army huts, a sport more amusing to those who made it the climax to a party, than to the deafened sleepers. Even ruder the awakening of two inhabitants of Royton, in Lancashire, who recently found themselves, still in bed, on the roof of a runaway diesel train that had demolished their house. The bed itself becomes the vehicle, where the new sport of Bed Pushing is in vogue. Students of Dalhousie University in Nova Scotia set the bed rolling with a 350-mile marathon. The Ontario police having ordered a Queen's University team off the main streets of Kingston, they managed 1,000 miles in a week on back-street routes. The speed record has been claimed at 8·4 m.p.h., but this involved the doubtful practice of replacing the castors by cycle wheels, frowned on by all true Bed Pushers. Still less acceptable to the purists is motorisation. A bedstead fitted with a 197 c.c. engine, driven through Farnborough, led to fifty-two summonses against thirteen students of the Royal Aircraft Establishment, and the driver was fined a total of £13 and disqualified for one month, for being uninsured, not having 'L' plates fitted on the bedstead, having no excise licence, and not having an efficient braking system. Costlier engineering seems to have gone into Howard Hughes' self-propelled bed: when immobilised after an aircraft crash, this millionaire film-producer designed a hospital-bed, operated by thirty electric motors from an elaborate 'cockpit', in which he could tour the wards, move himself into any position, and by pressing buttons provide such luxuries as music and hot or cold water.

Aircraft sometimes intrude into bedrooms, and some even come into existence there, for glider pilots, faced with the problem of building wings of 25-ft. span without a workshop, have more than once filled bedrooms with shavings and dope-fumes. The tip of the wing, it should be explained, projects through the window. Brads in the bed-clothes are said to be the chief discomfort.

A last peculiar activity in connection with beds (both 'common' and 'garden'): an article in *The Observer* recommends the rhubarb-grower to get a second-hand wool flock mattress, and *dig it in*, at the rate of about a barrow-load to 4 square yards.

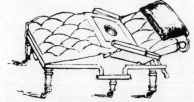

A Perfect Invalid's Adjustable Couch.

35

To Bedward Be You Merry

PHYSICIANS and philosophers have advised at length on the related problems of how to go to bed, how to get to sleep, how long to sleep, whether to sleep alone, how to wake, and when and how to rise. It may be instructive to compare their views on these points.

Edward IV lays down rules for his eldest son, requiring him

... to be in his chamber, and for all night livery to be set, the travers drawn anon upon eight of the clock, and all persons from thence to be avoided [sent out] except such as shall be deputed and appointed to give their attendance upon him all night, and that they enforce themselves to make him merry and joyous towards his bed.

Dr. Andrew Boorde in his *Compendyous Regyment, or a Dietary of Helth* of 1542, gives full directions for bedgoing:

Whole men of what age or complexion soever they be of, should take their natural rest and sleep in the night: and to eschew meridial sleep.

186

But if need should compel a man to sleep after his meat: let him make a pause, and then let him stand and lean and sleep against a cupboard, or else let him sit upright in a chair and sleep. To bedward be you merry or have merry company about you, so that to bedward no anger nor heaviness, sorrow nor pensivefulness, do trouble or disquiet you. To bedward and also in the morning, use to have a fire in your chamber, to waste and consume the evil vapours . . . In the night let the windows of your house, specially of your chamber, be closed. When you be in your bed, lie a little while on your left side, and sleep on your right side . . . Let your nightcap be of scarlet, and this, I do advertise you, to cause to be made a good thick quilt of cotton, or else of pure flocks or of clean wool, and let the covering of it be of white fustian, and lay it on the featherbed that you do lie on; and in your bed lie not too hot nor too cold, but in a temperance.

Robert Burton in *The Anatomy of Melancholy* of 1621 advises that

Many cannot sleep for witches and fascinations, which are too familiar in some places. But the ordinary causes are heat and dryness, which must first be removed: a hot and dry brain never sleeps well: grief, fears, cares, expectations, anxieties, great business and all violent perturbations of the mind, must in some sort be qualified, before we can hope for any good repose.

He thinks it good at bedtime to hear sweet music, or read some pleasant author, or to lie

. . . near some floodgates, arches, falls of water, like London Bridge, or some continuate noise which may benumb the senses . . . Piso commends frications, Andrew Boorde a good draught of strong drink before one goes to bed; I say, a nutmeg and ale, or a good draught of muscadine, with a toast and nutmeg, or a posset of the same, which many use in a morning, but methinks, for such as have dry brains, are much more proper at night; some prescribe a sup of vinegar as they go to bed, a spoonful . . .

Francis Bacon, too, liked a good draught of strong beer at bedtime, 'to lay his working fancy asleep', and William Harvey, the 'Doctor of Physique and Chirurgery' (says Aubrey)

. . . was hott-headed, and his thoughts working would many times keepe him from sleepinge; he told me that then his way was to rise out of his Bed and walke about his Chamber in his Shirt till he was pretty coole, i.e. till he began to have a horror, and then returne to bed, and sleepe very comfortably.

Harvey's 'horror', it should be explained, was only what we would call shivering.

Aubrey also tells of a lady who was whistled to sleep, though on one night this music had the wrong effect:

Sir William Petty had a boy that whistled incomparably well. He after wayted on a Lady, a widowe, of good fortune. Every night this boy was to whistle his Lady asleepe. At last shee could hold out no longer, but bids her chamber-mayd withdrawe: bids him come to bed, setts him to worke, and marries him the next day. This is certeyn true.

Thomas Hobbes the philosopher, at the age of 75, would play tennis just before going to bed, where he was 'well rubbed'; he too liked bedtime music:

He had alwayes bookes of prick-song lyeing on his table: which at night, when he was abed, and the dores made fast, and was sure nobody heard him, he sang aloud (not that he had a very good voice) but for his health's sake.

An Elizabethan herbal recommends 'A Bag to smell unto for melancholy or to cause one to sleep':

Take drie rose leaves, keep them close in a glass which will keep them sweet, then take powder of mints, powder of cloves in a gross powder, and put the same to the rose leaves, and put all these together in a bag, and take that to bed with you, and it will cause you to sleep, and it is good to smell unto at other times.

Some devotees of ancient lore have preferred to anoint the soles of their feet with the fat of a dormouse, which has obvious associations with sleep; others, to brush their teeth at bedtime with the ear-wax of a dog, for reasons less obvious. According to an unconfirmed American journalist, the Victorian philosopher Herbert Spencer travelled with a pillow stuffed with hops. Spencer's biographers, attentive to such details, do not mention this. The apparent association with the soporific beer is misleading, the main contribution of hops to beer being a matter of flavour. But the hop-stuffed pillow is still advertised today (12s. 6d. single; 20s. double).

Spencer could be difficult to please:

Mrs. G. . . . told us when once in his middle age she had visited him he was unwell and suffering very much from insomnia. He was in bed and not equal to talking himself, and yet wanted company with intermittent conversation. She was, therefore, bidden to his room, and was met with the remark—

188

'There may be just one question asked and one response given.'

With this permission she made a remark and duly received a reply.

Waiting what she considered the necessary interval, she then ventured upon a second observation. To her great discomfiture, a drowsy voice from the bed responded—

'I had just dropped off to sleep, and you wakened me,' which effectually crushed her for the time being.

Sir Thomas Browne thought it happy to go to bed 'with grand music, like Pythagoras' (as all too many still do, especially on hot summer nights when windows are wide open). Plato was reading in bed—a play of Aristophanes—on the night he died, aged 81. Burton liked to read, or be read to, until he fell asleep. Sir Henry Lee, says Aubrey, 'was never married, but kept women to reade to him when he was abed'. We find Mr. Pepys reading himself asleep while 'the wench' sits mending his breeches by the bedside, and Boswell writes:

I felt myself dreary at night, and made my barber try to read me asleep with Hume's *History*, of which he made very sad work.

Doctor Cheyne, in his *Essay of Health and Long Life* in 1724, puts the whole matter of winning sleep on a sound medical basis:

If anyone not suffering under any disease, is disturbed in his Sleep, 'tis certain his Stomach is filled with *Food*, or *Crudities*; or his *Guts* filled with *Wind*, *Choler*, or *Superfluous Chyle* . . . The sharp and crude Humours, *twitching* and *twinging* the *nervous Fibres*, and Coats of the *Bowels*, become like so many *Needles* and *Pins*, constantly running through them . . . The *unconcocted* Chyle stopping or circulating *slowly*, first in the Bowels, then in the smallest *Vessels*, begets these *Convulsions*, *Flatus*, *Night-Mares*, and *Oppressions* of *Spirits*.

Lying long abed, he adds,

. . . necessarily *thickens* the Juices, *enervates* the Solids, and *weakens* the Constitution.

He warns us of pernicious Easterly, and especially the North-Easterly winds, which in Winter

. . . bring along with them, all the *Nitre* of the *Northern* and *Scythian* Snows, *Mountains of Ice*, and *frozen Seas* thro' which they come . . .

189

and advises that one who has been subjected to such winds should take at bedtime

> ... a large Draught of warm Water-gruel, or of warm small *Mountain-wine* Whey, as an *Antidote* against the *nitrous Effluvia*, suck'd into the Body.

We recall Burton's taste for the 'continuate noise' of water when we learn from Boswell that the laird of Dunvegan chose his bed-chamber because there was behind it 'a considerable cascade, the sound of which disposed him to sleep', and again when Arthur Stanley in *The Bedside Book* says that he sleeps most happily on a rainy night, thanks to a spout from the roof close to his bedroom window, 'down which the rain slips very pleasantly, making a soothing sound like *googly-goo*'.

A leisurely clock is said to induce sleep because its beat is slower than that of the human heart; a fast-ticking watch has the opposite effect. A dog is said to sleep better near a clock because 'he thinks it is his mothers' heart'.

Brushing the hair has been recommended as a soporific. Dr. Macnish—who incidentally warns against sleeping in stockings—advises repeating some well-known rhyme until the monotony produces the desired unconsciousness; one of those recipes that would make for disharmony in a shared bedroom. Dr. Elliotson records the case of a lady who was sent to sleep by her husband rubbing the soles of her feet; John Philips the poet enjoyed the same treatment by an equally obliging mate; Anne, the Empress of All the Russias, preferred her feet tickled. Spanish mothers send their infants to sleep by rubbing the spine, Korean mothers by gently scraping the abdomen. The self-styled 'Professor Wells, Phrenologist', writing and publishing from Observatory Villas, Scarborough, in 1888, notes that 'thousands of brain-workers die for want of sleep', and gives precise directions for attaining it:

> Place the body in a straight position in bed, so as to avoid curvature of the spine, as seen in cut, Fig. 2; and, unless you want to poison your blood, do not put your head under the blankets . . . The bed must be clean and moderately springy, the room well aired, but not too warm; and there should of course be a mind at ease and a clear conscience. The wet compress around the body has a soothing effect, and a hot and cold foot-bath before retiring conduces to an equable circulation . . . One of the commonest causes of sleeplessness is cold feet. On retiring to bed put on a pair of cotton socks wrung out of cold or tepid water and draw over them a pair of dry thick lambswool stockings, and even a second dry pair may be donned if one is not sufficient, and keep them on all night . . . If the hands are also cold, or the skin very dry and inelastic, a pair of cotton gloves

may be drawn and kept on all night . . . Some people produce sleep by closing their lips when they lie down and by drawing the breath hard enough through the nostrils to produce an audible sound, and by listening to this sound the mind is withdrawn from distracting thoughts and refreshing sleep is produced.

One suspects that a pupil of Professor Wells would be an unwelcome bedfellow.

The head of the bed should of course point to the North. Many travellers—Charles Dickens among them—used to carry pocket compasses to ensure accurate orientation. They must have suffered when on shipboard, in immovable bunks, unless they could bribe the captain to steam at night according to the lie of the bunk, and make good his track by day. It seems a little inconsistent that they who were also particular on the railway to sit with their backs to the engine, should have chosen, when travelling round the earth's axis at speeds up to 29,000 miles a day or about 1,200 miles an hour, to go sideways. The Chinese poet Po Chu-I did indeed sleep with his face to the South, though we do not know whether he took the diurnal rotation head- or feet-first; and Mr. Hay Japp in 1880, supported by Mrs. Gladstone in 1884, advised that the body should lie in line of the earth's motion. But all others who think it matters at all are for the North-pointing bed, and no better answer can be found, to those who doubt, than that given by Elinor Glyn. When her belief was questioned, she retorted that it was 'pure common-sense'.

To Doctor Marie Stopes, who wrote (in 1956) that the head of the bed should be to the North *or* to the South, it was not a question of rotation but of magnetism. She held that for some people like herself 'a sense of the North . . . is just as clear and definite a sense as any other . . . one *magnetates* the North'. She always moved her bed if it was wrongly set; or, if it was too heavy to move, she lay diagonally or crosswise as required. It was in her spine, between her shoulder-blades and hips, that she magnetated; she did not need a compass. In the course of a rather odd conversation with a coastguard, who happened to pass her garden as she lay there on her camp-bed, she mentioned that this particular bed was not quite rightly set, being 4 degrees East of true North. Disbelieving to the point of laughter, he brought his compass, checked the bed, and found it indeed exactly 4 degrees E. of N. Well, Marie Stopes was a Doctor of Science, and one should not merely laugh like a coastguard, and dismiss her as the Elinor Glyn of medicine. But there is a snag. Unfortunately there are three different Norths. The North Geographic Pole or *True North* to which she refers does not coincide by a long way with the

North Magnetic Pole or *Magnetic North*, which when she camped in the garden was wandering somewhere about N.E. Canada. The difference, or 'variation' to navigators, was then about 8 degrees West in Dr. Stopes' garden. So the bed, if it was exactly 4 degrees East of *True North* as measured by a skilled coastguard, was in fact about 12 degrees East of the *Magnetic North* sensed by the Doctor. Readers to whom this is not crystal-clear should skip the whole paragraph, for there is more to come. No compass being perfectly accurate, we have a third North, *Compass North*, to which a particular compass points. The difference between *Compass North* and *Magnetic North*, called 'deviation', can be allowed for, or largely corrected by 'swinging' the compass. That coastguard would have allowed for it. It follows, then, that the Doctor, if otherwise right, must have been suffering from deviation to the extent of 12 degrees East. Reluctantly, but to avoid correspondence from navigators who might think the point had been overlooked, one has to add a note on *Magnetic Dip*. Lines of magnetic force are vertical at the Magnetic Pole and horizontal only at the Equator, so that a free compass needle in Doctor Stopes' garden in the 1950's would have pointed downwards between 60 and 70 degrees. Would she not have slept even better if tilted accordingly? Should not her followers carry—even if they need no compass—an Isoclinal Chart for dip, as well as an Isogonal Chart for variation; and watch their tendency to deviation, and if necessary be swung?

For insomnia, sheep-counting is so old a recipe, that counted millions, flocks to cover the earth, must have jumped the gates of imagination by the time that Dylan Thomas wrote of Salt Lake Farm where

. . . Mr. Utah Watkins counts, all night, the wife-faced sheep as they leap the fences on the hill, smiling and knitting and bleating just like Mrs. Utah Watkins.

But conversely, a Spanish proverb advises those who would *keep awake*, to 'borrow the pillow of a debtor'; while Groucho Marx recommends them to subtract sheep. (We may ignore as fictional the story of the sleepless boxer who tried counting sheep, but had to desist, because every time he got to nine, force of habit made him get up.) A respected but wakeful railway engineer living in South Kensington prefers ton-miles to sheep: 247 tons go 113 miles; how many ton-miles? On especially bad nights he may split his goods trains at junctions, so that 132 of the 247 tons go only 91 miles, and the rest all the way; how many ton-miles now? Others list alphabetically: Arnold, Browning, Chaucer; or Alvis, Bentley, Citröen; hoping to doze before 'X'. Some strain open eyes upward into the darkenss, as if trying to see their own eyebrows, and claim that they sleep from the instant when the eye-muscles are allowed to relax and the tired eyelids close. But the most sensible insomniacs accept the fact that they are awake in a spirit of 'so what?', and not caring whether they sleep or not, soon do so. How fortunate that Scottish ploughboy who complained that he never enjoyed a night's rest, because as soon as he put his head on the pillow it was time to get up again.

As for sleeping drugs, the ideal one produces a reliable hypnotic effect, does not cause a preliminary stage of excitement, does not upset the stomach, has no dangerous side-actions, does not produce tolerance or drug-addiction, and does not exist.

A Belgian invention to ensure fresh air for the sleeper who prefers his window shut

Van Gogh's bedroom in Arles

36

This Delicate Ambrosia

OPINIONS as varied have been offered as to how long to
sleep, and at what time to rise—not quite the same thing.

> Six for a man,
> Seven for a woman,
> Eight for a fool.

> Nature requires five,
> Custom takes seven,
> Laziness nine,
> And wickedness eleven.

Old ancient doctors of physic saith eight hours of sleep in summer and
nine in winter is sufficient for any man; but I do think the sleep ought to be
taken as the complexion of man is. *(Andrew Boorde)*

I have heretofore imputed the cause of agues or maladies, whereinto I
have falne, to the lumpish heavinesse or drowzy dullnesse which my long
sleeping had caused me, and ever repented mee to fall asleepe againe in the
morning. Plato condemnes more the excesse of sleeping than the surfet of
drinking. *(Michel de Montaigne)*

Seven or eight hours is a competent time for a melancholy man to rest, as Crato thinks; but as some do, to lie in bed and not sleep, a day, or half a day together, to give assent to pleasing conceits and vain imaginations, is many ways pernicious. *(Robert Burton)*

Who complains of want, of wounds, of cares, of great men's oppressions, of captivity, whilst he sleepeth? Beggars in their beds take as much pleasure as kings. Can we therefore surfeit on this delicate ambrosia? . . . Sleep till your belly grumble. *(Thomas Dekker)*

Jeremy Taylor lowers the average opinion considerably when he judges three hours sleep enough. When Dr. Johnson held that a sufficient quantity of sleep was between 7 and 9 hours, Boswell quoted Dr. Cullen's rule, that 'a man should not take more sleep than he can take at once', which brought the retort that if every man whose sleep was broken, must then get up, 'such a regimen would soon end in a long sleep'. Despite the Doctor's stated 9-hour limit, Boswell often found him still abed at noon, and he admitted that he often stayed there until 2 in the afternoon. 'The happiest part of a man's life,' he said, 'is what he passes lying awake in the morning.' But it is only fair to add that he held any man who went to bed before midnight to be a scoundrel. Boswell quoted Lord Monboddo, who

. . . awaked every morning at four, and then for his health got up and walked in his room naked, with the window open, which he called taking an air bath; after which he went to bed again, and slept two hours more. Johnson, who was always ready to beat down anything that seemed to be exhibited with disproportionate importance, thus observed: 'I suppose, Sir, there is no more in it than this, he wakes at four, and cannot sleep till he chills himself, and makes the warmth of the bed a grateful sensation.'

John Wesley allowed 6 hours; Gladstone only 4, but he took short naps during the day. William Pitt, exhausted by a series of political crises, once slept 16 hours and then had to be shaken to rouse him. Lord Brougham, after his defence in the trial of Queen Caroline, gave orders not to disturb him however long he might sleep, and to the astonishment—almost terror—of the servants, slept nearly 48 hours.

Russian peasants do *not* sleep continuously for months on end in winter; no peoples hibernate completely, but in parts where food runs short in winter, some practice quasi-hibernation; when the first snows fall, families shut themselves up in their huts, huddle round the stove and lapse into slumber, each member taking his turn to stoke the fire. Once a day, all bestir themselves enough to eat a little dry bread.

Dr. Kleitman, experimenting in the power of the will to resist sleep, managed to keep awake for just under five days. Boerhaave, after severe overwork, was without sleep for six weeks. There are several authenticated cases of persons who for years on end, though they have lain and rested, have never in the strict sense slept at all.

The time of rising was naturally earlier in the days when rush-lights, tallow candles or crude oil-lamps gave such a wretched light—'darkness visible'—that there was little incentive to sitting up late, and the labourer went to bed and rose by the sun. Andrew Boorde advises:

When you do rise in the morning, rise with mirth and remember God. Let your hosen be brushed within and without, and flavour the inside of them against the fire; use linen socks, and linen hosen next your legs: when you be out of your bed, stretch forth your arms and your body, cough and spit . . . After you have evacuated your body and trussed your points [that is, tied up the laces by which your long hose are attached to your doublet], comb your head oft, and so do divers times in the day. And wash your hands and wrists, your face and eyes and your teeth, with cold water; and after that you be apparelled, walk in your garden or park, a thousand pace or two . . .

from which it may be noted that a gentleman of such substance as to own a park, and to have a fire in his bedroom, has still to be advised by the doctor to wash on rising. It is not quite clear whether he wears his socks and hosen in bed. Sir John Harington's rules for his servants in 1592 require them to be up by 6 in summer, 7 in winter. Montaigne, though, says 'seaven of the clocke in the morning is to me an early houre'. Nicholas Breton in his *Fantastickes* of 1626 will have the thrifty husbandman 'rouse towards his rising' at 2 a.m.; the cock calls the servants at 3; and 'fie sluggards' at 5, at which hour there is at least the incentive to rising, that 'the alehouse door is unlocked for good fellows'. But even at 6 'the sun at every window calls sleepers from their beds', and not until 8 are 'good stomachs ready for their breakfast'. Lastly, at 9, 'the amorous courtier is almost ready to go out of his chamber'. Not long before, Stubbes in his *Anatomie of Abuses* had complained of the ladies that

Some of them lye in bed till nine or tenne of the clocke every mornyng; then, beyng rouzed forthe of their dennes, they are two or three howers in puttyng on their robes.

Clearly the time of rising was staggered according to social standing, as it still is today (when the pink *Financial Times* does not bud in the

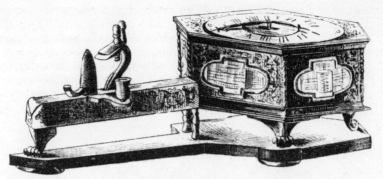

A candle-lighting alarm-clock (see page 208)

morning trains until an hour or two after the *Daily Mirror* is in full blossom).

'Waking that hurts, by all means must be avoided,' said Robert Burton in *The Anatomy of Melancholy*. Dean Swift achieved this by having a fire lit in his bedroom at 7 o'clock, and staying in bed until 11 'thinking of wit for the day'. Addison observed the widest seasonal variation known, for he rose between 2 and 3 on summer mornings, but not until 11 or noon in winter. Boswell spoke for millions of fellow-sufferers when he discussed with Dr. Johnson the pains of getting up,

... and wished there could be some medicine invented which would make one rise without pain, which I never did, unless after lying in bed a very long time. Perhaps there may be something in the stores of nature which could do this. I have thought of a pulley to raise me gradually; but that would give me pain, as it would counteract my internal inclination ... and as I have experienced a state in which rising from bed was not disagreeable, but easy, nay, sometimes agreeable; I suppose that this state may be produced, if we knew by what. We can heat the body, we can cool it; we can give it tension or relaxation; and surely it is possible to bring it into a state in which rising from bed will not be a pain.

'Bozzy' usually awoke 'heavy, confused and splenetic', or even 'dreary as a dromedary', but once up, he found that to 'cut two or three brisk capers round the room' was 'attended with most agreeable effects'. Wellington slept hard—even in his great house Stratfield Saye he used his camp-bed—and took so little pleasure in lying in late, that a hostess who had him called at 7 learned that he was

197

already fully dressed and packing his kit. Charles Lamb would neither lie down with his woolly namesake, nor rise with the lark:

At what precise minute that little airy musician doffs his night gear, and prepares to tune up his unseasonable matins, we are not naturalists enough to determine. But for a mere human gentleman—that has no orchestra business to call him from his warm bed to such preposterous exercises—we take ten, or half after ten (eleven, of course, during this Christmas solstice), to be the very earliest hour, at which he can begin to think of abandoning his pillow.

He imagined a splendid revenge for

... the detestable rap of an old hag of a domestic, who seemed to take a diabolical pleasure in her announcement that it was 'time to rise'; and whose chappy knuckles we have often yearned to amputate, and string them up at our chamber door, to be a terror to all such unseasonable rest-breakers in future.

A friend asked Oscar Wilde to call on him at 9 o'clock the next morning. 'You are a remarkable man!' drawled Oscar. 'I could never stay awake as long as that. I am always in bed by 5 o'clock.' George Moore, when he was an art student and life-class started at 7, wrote of 'glancing in terror down the dim and grey perspective of early risings' that awaited him; his valet had not only to remove the bed-clothes, but to lock them up in another room. G. K. Chesterton saw no virtue in early rising; he pointed out that misers get up early and burglars the night before.

Those of us who retire early, or rise late, or both, in the hope of keeping young and beautiful, are wasting our time, according to Dr. Firmin Nash. He has lately tested the effect of sleep on the ageing process. 188 men and 71 women confessed their ages, and the hours they slept. Other observers *guessed* their ages by appearance. The findings were:

Short-sleepers looked no older than their years, and 'lie-abeds' no younger. Some women who spent only six hours in bed appeared two or three years younger than they really were. Other women who spent nine hours between the sheets looked two or three years older.

So, beauty sleep is a myth.

37

Double or Twin?

THE issue is clearer-cut, and opinion hotter, when we turn to the long-fought battle between the two schools that Groucho Marx calls *monobedders* and *polybedders*. There are really three choices: the double bed, twin beds, or separate rooms. In ancient Rome twin beds were unheard of, and it was either the *lectus genialis* or two rooms for the married pair; among the aristocracy, who enjoyed much independence in the home, it was usually the latter. Humble folk with no room to spare never expected anything but a shared bed. Martial in one of his epigrams agrees to marry a rich old woman on the condition '*communis tecum nec mihi lectus erit*': that they need never sleep together; but he is not a confirmed *monobedder*, for he dwells all too fully on the joys that were witnessed by the nuptial bed of Calenus and Sulpicia. Montaigne is a *monobedder*:

I love to lie hard and alone, yea and without a woman by me, after the kingly manner; somewhat well and warme covered. I never had my bed warmed, but since I came to be an old man, if need require, I have clothes given me to warme my feete and my stomacke . . .

The refrain of an old French song is '*Plus aisé couche un seul que deux*', though most beds were then so roomy that few of the objections to doubling can have applied:

> . . . *Car deux ensemble la nuitie*
> *Est soufrir froidure et dangier:*
> *L'un sue, l'autre tosse ou crie;*
> *L'un veult dormir, l'autre veiller* . . .
> *Plus aisé couche un seul que deux.*

199

(One sleeps better than two;
For two together all night
Means suffering freezing and fright;
One coughs, one talks; one's cold, one's hot;
One wanting to sleep and the other one not—
Oh, one sleeps better than two!)

Even connubial beds have held three without friction. Laurence Sterne tells a story of the thirteenth century in which one Count Gleichen, taken prisoner on a Crusade, marries a Sultan's daughter. Though he already has a wife at home, polygamy is here permitted, and moreover when he takes his second bride home to Venice, the Pope grants him a dispensation to keep both. Sterne says that at Gleichen they still showed the bed in which all three slept peaceably together. Beaumont and Fletcher shared, not only the writing of their fifty-two plays, but the same clothes, the same bed and the same wench. Havard, although elsewhere he records the use of twin beds by Charles the Bold of Burgundy and his second wife Isabella in the fifteenth century, dates the first known example of twin beds at 1743. Dr. Graham of Celestial Bed fame, in 1783, holds that there is not

. . . anything in nature which is more immediately calculated totally to subvert health, strength, love, esteem, and indeed everything that is desirable in the married state, than that odious, most indelicate, and most hurtful custom of man and wife continually *pigging* together, in one and the same bed . . . to sleep, and snore, and steam, and do everything else that's indelicate together, three hundred and sixty-five times—every year.

Balzac in his *Physiologie du Mariage* tolerates double beds, prefers two rooms, and absolutely condemns twin beds ('*pernicieuse*' is his adjective) until after twenty years of marriage. Esme Wingfield-Stratford in *The Victorian Tragedy* writes:

Though it would have been violating a taboo to have said so, there was probably not a parent in the country who would not, in his or her heart of hearts, have approved Mr. Shaw's description of marriage, as combining the maximum of temptation with the maximum of opportunity. The double bed, otherwise so obviously inconvenient, is a silent witness to its truth. By the strange inversion of propriety that reigned behind closed doors, any suggestion of substituting two beds for one would have been regarded as not very nice. There are old-fashioned people, even today, who have not wholly cast off this prejudice.

Dr. Richardson in the Victorian magazine *Good Words* nevertheless comes out strongly as a *monobedder*, on the grounds that no two

Sheraton provides single beds but sociability in his 'Summer Bed in Two Compartiments', which is 'intended for a nobleman or gentleman and his lady, to sleep separately in hot weather'. There is a passage between the beds, but they share a curtained canopy. In a note that is not entirely clear, he seems to suggest a cross between the double and single beds:

'Some beds for this purpose have been made entirely in one, except the bed clothing being confined to two drawers running on rollers, capable of being drawn out on each side by servants in order to make them.'

persons require the same kind of bedding, and that they must disturb one another. He is supported by Mr. Hay Japp in 1880, who holds that

... such a thing even as a double Bed, should not exist, not to speak of the habit of several persons sleeping in one large Bed—the box-bed of the Scotch being simply intolerable.

He quotes in favour of the single bed the long-accepted idea that young persons are in some way robbed of vitality, and enfeebled, by sleeping with the aged. This is believed also by Professor Wells, who barely manages to approve bed-sharing even by married couples:

Two healthy persons may sleep together without injury when they are of nearly equal age, but it is not well for young and old to sleep together. Married couples, between whom there is a natural affinity, and when one sex is of a positive and the other of a negative nature, will be benefited by the magnetism reciprocally imparted; but, unhappily, such cases of connubial compatibility are not common.

Yet these views were being expounded at a time when the double bed was so much the throne and symbol of fruitful domestic felicity, that its brasswork shone with something of the sacred aura of the Roman *lectus genialis*.

What can the *monobedders* have thought about 'bundling'? This curious custom, by which courting couples were permitted to share a bed, though with certain precautions, was once widespread in the north of England, in Wales and in Scotland, and was exported to New England. There is an obvious reason for its final survival in the Hebrides, for it is an outcome of a cold climate, a bleak landscape, long winter nights, and cottage life. Winter is the time for courting, when the young men are idle at home, but the open air is uninviting, and the girl's parents occupy the living-room. She therefore goes to bed, but with her legs wedged into an outsize stocking or bag which her mother ties securely. There the young man may lie beside and woo her, experiencing—as Shaw might have said—the maximum of temptation with the minimum of opportunity. (Mayhew observes that female crime is prevalent in various counties, in 1850, in proportion to the prevalence of bundling.)

As for the Abyssinians, husband and wife share not only the same bed, but the same night-shirt, each being entitled to one sleeve.

38

Rise and Shine

WE still await Boswell's wonder-drug for painless rising, but meanwhile men have devised countless means of murdering sleep, most of them cruel, though a few do show some attempt to coax gently. Apart from natural alarm-clocks such as the rising sun or the crowing cock, the earliest artificial alarm-clock was a development of the oldest form of time-piece that could have been used in the bedroom: the *clepsydra* or water-clock, in which the water level of a graduated vessel with a slow leak showed the hour with a fair degree of accuracy. A second vessel set over the sleeper's face received the drops from the first, and would overflow at the chosen moment. Such an alarm had the advantage that it treated the prompt riser kindly, and built up a progressive discomfort for the sluggard until it made the bed untenable.

In the monasteries, to keep the sexton alert through the night watches, ready to ring the chapel bell at the proper times, an hourly warning was needed. Before mechanical clocks, this was achieved by an ingenious development of King Alfred's graduated candle: a set of tiny bells was embedded in the candle, so that at every hour one of these fell with a 'ping' into a metal dish. A similar and very old device was known as 'the weaver's alarm', because these operatives 'got weaving' so early. A weight was hung on a piece of packthread passed through the candle, which burned down until it broke the thread, to produce a rousing crash. Dr. Johnson seems to have thought this a new idea when he told Boswell

. . . that the learned Mrs. Carter, at that period when she was eager in study, did not awake as early as she wished, and she therefore had a contrivance, that, at a certain hour, her chamberlight should burn a string to which a heavy weight was suspended, which then fell with a strong sudden noise.

For centuries the night watchman patrolled the streets calling out the hour, giving a current weather report, and assuring his hearers that all was well (we find no record of what he said if all was *not* well) but the sleeping citizens must surely have become so inured to his cry, that they can hardly have relied on it to awaken them at their chosen hours. In the industrial towns of the North of England, the 'knocker-up' could be engaged to hammer on the street door in the morning. If late-lying neighbours objected to this, a length of thread (in which a fairly low breaking-strain was advisable) could be tied to the sleeper's toe and hung down from the window. The services of the knocker-up cost only a halfpenny a week, so that even the advent of the 5s. alarm-clock, representing more than two years' fees, did no great harm to the profession.

The date of the first pendulum clock, driven by a weight, is unknown, but probably lies in the thirteenth century. Not being portable, it was seldom used in the bedchamber. In the *Romance of Sir Degrevaunt* there is an 'orrlege' that rings the hours in the bedchamber of Myldore the Bright, and another such is mentioned in the *Romaunt de la Rose* of 1305. These weight-driven clocks could be used as alarms: an adjustable stop was fitted to the chain on which the weight descended, and this triggered off the striking mechanism. But few clocks of any sort were to be found in English homes until the fifteenth century, and evidently a watch was still a rarity in the lifetime of Thomas Allen the mathematician, born in 1542, who

. . . happened to leave his Watch in the Chamber windowe. The maydes came in to make the Bed, and hearing a thing in a case cry *Tick, Tick, Tick*, presently concluded that that was his Devill, and tooke it by the String with the tongues, and threw it out of the windowe into the Mote (to drowne the Devill). It so happened that the string hung on a sprig of an elder that grew out of the Mote, and this confirmed them that 'twas the Devill. So the good old Gentleman gott his Watch again.

Watch-stands in many forms were made for bedside use, but with a curtained bed the watch was handier—and its tick muffled—when

kept in a watch-pocket (*cartel de chevet*), pinned or hooked to the
inside of the curtains; a device that survived to be used by Mr.
Pickwick. In 1676 came the 'repeater' clock or watch that chimed
the nearest hour when interrogated by pressing a pin. There were
soon quarter-hour and even minute repeaters. Mr. Pepys borrowed
a 'larum watch' from his watchmaker while his own watch was being
mended. He thought an illuminated bedside clock worthy of note:

To White Hall; and Mr. Pierce showed me the Queen's bed-chamber,
and her closet, where she had nothing but some pretty pious pictures, and
books of devotion; and her holy water at her head as she sleeps, with a
clock by her bed-side, wherein a lamp burns that tells her the time of the
night at any time.

Before the days of matches, the getting of a light in the dark with
flint, steel and tinder was a fumbling business for a sleepy riser.
About the year 1500, one Carovagius is said to have invented a
device to solve this problem: an alarm-clock that lit a candle. This
was to be reinvented many times thereafter.

205

By the early fifteenth century the spring drive was replacing the weight, and greatly simplified the making of portable alarm-clocks. A monastic alarm-clock of about 1400 in the Germanisches Museum at Nuremberg has a 16-hour revolution—the 'Nuremberg hours'— and was intended solely for use at night. There are 16 'touch-pins' projecting from the hour-circle, by which to 'feel the time' in the dark. The alarm rings every hour by the half-revolution of a toothed wheel, briefly but 'enough to waken the dead'. Another in the same collection has a 24-hour dial, the daylight hours being on a white face, and the night on black. An early form of 'daylight saving' was in force in all the monasteries, and the proportion of day to night hours was changed according to the time of the year, thus:

8 day and 16 night on November 23
16 day and 8 night on May 25

varying intermediately.

Other early monastic alarm-clocks were made to strike the 'canonical hours', namely:

Prime	3
Tertia	2
Sexta	1
Nona	2
Vespers	3
Compline	4

A portrait in the Antwerp Fine Arts Museum shows an unknown man of the Burgundian court of 1440–50. In the background is a spring-driven clock which seems to have an alarm escapement. At the top of the picture are two quotations from the Bible: '*Hora est jam de sompio surgere*' ('Now it is time to wake up from sleep') and '*Quia novissima hora est*' ('It is as late as can be') and these seem to show that a clock could be taken into the bedroom to wake one up, and back to the living-room to warn when bedtime had come. In 1511 Dürer shows a bedroom clock supplemented by an hour-glass below it, though this need not imply mistrust of the newer device; we do not scrap our beloved grandfather clock because we have radio time-signals. Some of Henry VIII's clocks had 'larums' of some kind and were probably spring-driven. A German alarm-clock of about 1600 in the London Science Museum, its movement almost wholly of iron, has a 24-hour dial, and the alarm is set by rotating a similar inner dial. A 'drum calendar timepiece' in the same museum has a separate detachable alarm mechanism clipped to the top of the clock, and

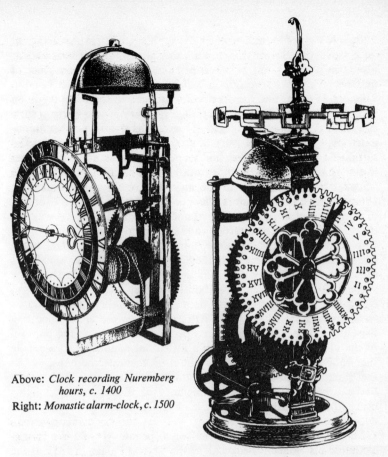

Above: *Clock recording Nuremberg
hours, c. 1400*
Right: *Monastic alarm-clock, c. 1500*

touch-pins on the hour-circle. Louis XIII had something of a passion
for alarm-clocks. He carried several with him when he travelled, and
had them put at his bedside so that he could set and regulate them
all nightly. The only thing that made him angrier than an inaccurate
clock was that anybody else should interfere with them. Louis XIV
too, despite the vast bedchamber retinue available to rouse him, had
his bedside alarm-clock, a rather mundane note amid such magnificence. The 'Friesland clock', a wall-clock in an ornate wooden case
with coloured carving in the rather bucolic manner of the Swiss
cuckoo-clock, very popular in early days in America, had a small
brass dial on the face that could be set for an alarm. Casanova often
mentions setting his 'alarum' at bedtime, especially when sharing a
bed in a tricky situation involving a returning husband; not a very
glamorous preliminary.

Joseph Tich of Vienna, in the eighteenth century, invents a variant on Carovagius' device that could work all too well if overloaded: his alarm sets off a charge of gunpowder, and this ignites a piece of tinder which then springs up into view. This clock is in the London Science Museum, but visitors are not allowed to load and try it. In 1762 M. Musy of Paris produces his '*veilleuse*' which burns a little candle. It gives a subdued light all night, tells the time on an illuminated dial, sounds a bell every hour if required to remind an invalid to take his medicine, offers hot soup at any time, and—if the user is not so exhausted by its ministrations as to sleep through anything —wakes him with a bell in the morning. An improved model of 1768, thanks to a spirit lamp, offers hotter soup. In 1781 M. Morgues of Marseilles produces a clock that not only lights a candle at waking-time, but draws the bed-curtains and opens the window. Most of the many candle-lighting alarms used a powder-pan, flint and steel, much like a pistol. An example from the School of Horology at Anet holds the candle horizontally until it is lit, when it springs smartly to the vertical. Robert Houdin's, of about 1819, has a candle with a head like a match, that strikes itself as it rises. In Gabry de Liancourt's '*veilleuse-pendule*' of the same date, instead of the clock operating the light-source, the light-source operates the clock: as the oil level of the night-light falls, it lowers a little float connected to a needle that shows the time on a dial—about as accurate, perhaps, as the fuel gauge on a modern car (whose owner, incidentally, if he happens to be French, perpetuates the memory of these dim watch-lights every time he speaks of dipping his headlamps as '*mettre les phares en veilleuse*').

For those whose slumber was sound-proof, Mr. R. W. Savage exhibited his 'Alarum Bedstead' at the Crystal Palace in 1851. If the bell was ignored, the bed-clothes were automatically removed. If the sluggard still snored, the mattress slowly tilted up sideways to 45 degrees, leaving him to end his sleep, if he could, on the floor. A variant shown at the Leipzig Fair a few years later was as thorough in its efforts, but coaxed more kindly. Only if a gentle alarm-bell failed did it resort to a loud one. If this too failed, the sleeper's night-cap was pulled off, and a notice 'Time To Get Up!' was thrust under his nose. Although he was finally tilted out of bed, the assault was followed by the apologetic offer of a cup of hot coffee.

In *Daily Wants* of 1858 we read of a 'new and economical alarum' of American invention and manufacture, which seems to have involved some unnecessary mental arithmetic:

The figures upon the face represent the number of hours required to elapse before the alarum shall be allowed to go off. Thus, if a person wished

to sleep five hours, he would calculate that number of hours from the time of his going to bed, which, if he retired at eleven at night, would extend to four o'clock in the morning. He would, therefore, set the hands of the alarum at the figure seven, and at the last moment of the fifth hour, which would be four o'clock, the alarum would go off with a loud ringing.

One's grasp of these instructions, if any, is further clouded by a suspicion that when the writer says seven he means five, or else that he set his alarm two hours before bedtime and forgot to say so. But another article in *Daily Wants* warns us that

. . . to arouse a person abruptly out of sleep by sudden violence or noisy exclamation, is a cause of serious injury to the brain and nervous system . . . and dangerous, if not fatal effects, have resulted from the mental terror evoked by a sudden and undefined noise startling the nerves before the judgement has had time to analyse the nature of its alarm.

It goes on to advise the application of burnt feathers or hartshorn to the nostrils; and that shouting in the ear should never be resorted to except in cases of coma or apoplexy.

In 1893 the 'Night Light Watch Holder' was advertised, complete with a box of lights, for 3*s*. 4*d*., but for those who were willing to spend from 27*s*. 6*d*. to 63*s*. to attain the same result in an impressively original way, the 'Electric Ceiling Clock' was offered in 1911. When a button was pressed, an image of the clock face was projected on the ceiling—not too ornate a ceiling, one hopes:

CLARKE'S "PYRAMID" NURSERY LAMP FOOD WARMER.

2s. 6d., 3s. 6d., 5s., and 6s. each.

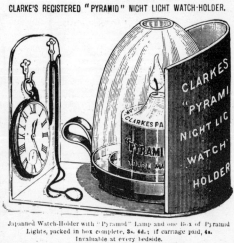

CLARKE'S REGISTERED "PYRAMID" NIGHT LIGHT WATCH-HOLDER.

Japanned Watch-Holder with "Pyramid" Lamp and one Box of Pyramid Lights, packed in box complete, 3s. 4d.; if carriage paid, 4s. Invaluable at every bedside.

New Pattern Electric Night Clock.

In Polished Oak, with 8-Day Movement.

Fitted with an intermittent Battery, which illuminates the Dial when the Button is pressed. The Battery is formed of the New Dry Cells, so that there is no liquid which can be upset when travelling. The Dry Cells last a year, and can be renewed at a trifling cost.

Size 7in. by 6¼in. by 3¼in. .... Price 90s.

From advertisements of 1896

210

. . . such a huge and plain reflection of face and hands, that anyone—even with the weakest eyesight—can see the time during the night. Artistic—well-made—of British manufacture.

Is it from fact, or from fiction, that one recalls that most unnerving of all alarm-clocks, which forced the sleeper not merely to rise, but to leap across the room, or to pay as a penalty the cost of a new clock? It stood on wheels, and as the bell rang, travelled slowly but inexorably along the mantelpiece. If the hypnotised owner delayed a second too long in saving it, it dived to the floor and shattered.

Then there is the most silent of all sounds that can ever have awakened man—that of the regular morning signal-gun to which the off-duty sailor became so inured, that he slept undisturbed by it until the day when he awoke with a violent start at the exact moment when, for once, it failed to go off.

Today we can be awakened, subject to arrangement, by our bedside telephone, or by radio automatically switched on. The tea-making alarm has reappeared from the past. Hundreds in camp, barracks, airfield or ship can be roused simultaneously, thanks to the public address system, by the honeyed but over-amplified voice of one Waac, Waaf or Wren, and kept 'rising and shining' by a blaring military march. One wartime officer in the R.A.F., driven desperate by this daily siren voice coming an hour or two after his night duty ended, cut the wiring to the speaker outside his door. Unfortunately he did not appreciate the difference between 'series' and 'series-parallel' wiring, and half the airfield was silenced, the other half deafened. Furtively, he repaired the break, whereat sound was restored to all, but in a stuttering whisper. Search parties traced the fault to his door, and suspicion fell upon a frivolous but innocent Group Captain sleeping opposite. Honour required that the culprit, feeling rather like Harry Wharton going to the Headmaster's study, should confess to the Station Commander. The present Commandant of London Airport may recall presenting an electrician's bill, together with some harsh words, to the present writer.

Let Dr. Marie Stopes be given the last word on the subject. Anyone who needs an alarm-clock, she says, should realise that this is a sign that more sleep is needed—and go to bed earlier.

211

Dormitory at Westminster, c. 1816

39

The Dorm

THE history of the school dormitory shows no steady heart-warming improvement in conditions for the little victims, either along the scale of time, or up the scale of fees and caste. We find mediaeval orderliness and Victorian barbarism. It is still axiomatic that he who has survived unbroken the rigours of a good public school is a man proof against all hardship. Hardship indeed seems to have been an intentional ingredient of student life in most ages. When newly founded, the schools and universities looked for the dedicated scholar, not the illiterate oarsman or the titled loafer. Living standards were those of the monastery, of which many a school formed a part. The fourteenth-century student rose at 5, and had attended a service in chapel before the first lecture at 6. St. Richard of Chichester and two fellow-students shared one room, one small bed, one gown, and one suit of clothes; while the first went out to lectures in the gown, the second wore the suit, and the third slept. The fifteenth-century statutes of the choir schools at Wells provide for packing two small boys with their pillow at the head of the bed, and the feet of an older one between. A story-teller of that time begins, as if it were an everyday matter,

When I was a youth, and lay in a square chamber, which had only a single door well shut from within, together with three more companions in the same bed . . .

At the Abbey of Bec, the schoolboy monks-to-be are roused before the brethren:

. . . the Master of the Boys should rise very softly and just touch each of the children gently with a rod, that he may awake from sleep; then let them rise as quickly as possible, and, leaving the dormitory, wash and comb and say their prayers . . . Let the masters sleep between every two boys in the dormitory, and sit between every two at other times, and if it be night, let all the candles be fixed without on the spikes which crown the lanterns, that they may be plainly seen in all that they do. When they lie down in bed, let a master always be among them with his rod and (if it be night) with a candle, holding the rod in one hand and the light in the other.

(The final detail suggests that some master may have put himself off his stroke, and produced a welcome blackout, by trying to wield the rod with the hand that held the candle.)

When Henry VI founded Eton College in 1442, he laid down standards for the scholars' sleeping quarters that were to be sadly ignored in centuries to come. The seventy boys were to be lodged in a series of small dormitories round a large quadrangle—but these were never built. At least three seniors were to keep order in each dormi-tory, and only boys under 14 were to sleep two to a bed. In 1560 the rule was to rise at 5, chant prayers while dressing, make the beds and sweep under them, and then go down to wash at 'the children's pump'; to bed at 8, chanting more prayers while undressing. At Christmas and Easter eves, they went to bed an hour earlier because of the coming midnight service, a custom that continued long after the service had been abandoned. There was no regular system of 'houses', but the Provost and the Fellows might let lodgings to the fee-paying 'Oppidans'. The 'Collegers', who were admitted free, lived in the notorious Long Chamber, among 'dirt, discomfort, rats and riots', where they were locked in without supervision from 8 p.m. until morning. Not until 1716, when their numbers were reduced from about seventy to fifty-two, did each have a separate bed. In 1818 the windows still had no glass, and a boy might awake in winter to find his bed covered with snow drifting in through the shutters. Each boy was issued with a tallow-dip, but no candlestick; he would contrive one by bending a book, punching a hole in it, and tying the candle with string. Only the seniors had wash-basins. If a boy had a chamber-pot, he had brought it from home. In 1838 a deputation petitioned for water to be laid on, but was told 'You will be wanting gas and turkey carpets next!' Below the Long Chamber was the Lower Chamber, which Coleridge described as 'the nethermost hell':

> Ye chambers three, ye foul abodes
> Which filth and bedsteads line,
> Where every instant adds fresh loads
> To Cloacina's shrine.

Bedtime sports included tossing new boys up to the roof in blankets —in 1832 one of these was 'completely scalped as with a tomahawk' in the process, but we are assured that 'beyond having the scalp sewn on again, and the natural irritation of the wound, he did not suffer either at the time or afterwards'. Another jolly game was to wait until a new boy was asleep, pull his bed out, and turn it up on end, head undermost. If granted the courtesy of a warning, he could get his head under the pillow and avoid the major injuries. Less effort was required, and a good effect produced, by setting the tassel of his night-cap on fire. More useful was the sport of 'rug-riding', rugs being taken from the small boys' beds and made into sledges on which they had to pull the upper boys around, thus polishing the floor. To complete the pandemonium, the pets kept in the Long Chamber included dogs, ducks, a pig (mentioned by Tennyson), and at least once, a stolen donkey. Rats were already available; the drill was to catch one in a stocking and then bang it to death against the bed-post. Edward Thring, a Headmaster of Uppingham, has summed it up:

Rough and ready was the life they led. Cruel at times the suffering and wrong; wild the profligacy. For after 8 o'clock no prying eye came near till the following morning; no one lived in the same building; cries of joy or pain were equally unheard; and excepting a code of laws of their own there was no help or redress for anyone.

Indeed, hardly the set-up that Henry IV had envisaged; but in 1846 the 'New Buildings' provided bed-sitting-rooms for fifty-five Collegers, and the Long Chamber became a dormitory for only fifteen, each with his own cubicle. Etonians are incurably conservative, and many

214

have professed regret for the passing of the dear old Long Chamber. Today every boy, except those fifteen who seem to survive, has a bed-sitter; in fact, if we are to believe a photograph in Christopher Hollis' book *Eton*, from which most of this material has been taken, life there is so respectable that they work the lathes in the school workshop wearing tail coats.

About the mid-eighteenth century, Eton and Westminster were in the lead, with Winchester fallen from first to third. Westminster has a dormitory rare in two ways: as a building for sleeping which has an independent elevational expression, and as an instance of Sir Christopher Wren losing an architectural competition—to Lord Burlington (and Wren an old boy!). In this draughty high-windowed hall, some shelter was provided, at the expense of supervision, by bed-curtains, which look rather the worse for wear in Pugin's etching. Taine, writing in about 1868, reports that at Westminster College [*sic*] two of the youngest boys get up at 3.30 a.m. to light the fire, heat water, and call the older boys at 4; he adds that as the older boys do not have to rise until 7.30, the small boys have to warn them of the time every half-hour. We must believe either that the seniors were willing to be roused eight times each morning, or that some Westminster fag pulled the inquisitive Frenchman's leg. (Taine is not always a quite reliable observer: he records that he watched a cricket match at Kew in which 'seven or eight youthful Englishmen' were 'throwing the balls to each other' in complete silence for an hour and a half.)

Tom Brown's Schooldays, nominally fiction but clearly autobiography, shows Rugby far more civilised than Eton in the days of William IV. There are twelve in the dormitory where Tom has 'a clean little white bed'. The sixth-form boy in charge has a bigger one, with white curtains, in a corner by the fire-place. Every boy has his own wash-stand, and his shoes are cleaned for him. Lights are put out by the verger at 10.15, but not when boys want to sit up to read. True, Tom is tossed in a blanket, but there is none of the lowering of fags out of the window at night, to go to the pub for gin, that we read of in *Eric, or Little by Little*. The moral tone is on the up-grade; especially after the night when little Arthur, a new boy, kneels by his bed to pray. Two or three cads sneer, and a 'big, brutal fellow' shies a slipper at the 'snivelling young shaver', but our hero Tom takes little Arthur's part (rather indelicately), throwing a boot at the bully's head.

It was no light act of courage in those days, my dear boys, for a little fellow to say his prayers, even at Rugby.

De Quincey, at Manchester Grammar School, fared even better, with a bedroom to himself, a piano for his sole use, and an occasional bottle of brandy.

In 1884 when the law demanded a minimum of 700 cu. ft. of air per head in workhouses, and 900 cu. ft. had long been recommended for prisons, many school dormitories still offered as little as 300 cu. ft. In some the only means of heating was to light the naked fish-tail gas-burners for an hour or two before bedtime, though Dr. Dukes thought *any* warmth an unnecessary luxury: 'It is better not to sleep too warm, for sanitary as well as moral reasons.' Dr. Dukes says that he does not propose to discuss the question of dormitory morality in its entirety, but his 'few essential remarks' on this occupy nine pages of *Health at School*. He objects to separate cubicles as being dark, airless, prison-like, and 'with every facility for secret vice'. Since then, boarding-school planners have vacillated between the open dormitory, screened but paired beds, single screened beds, and private rooms; the worried housemaster has not come out firmly for either multiple promiscuity or secret vice; apart from the headmaster's question of *quis custodiet ipsos custodes*? Happy that headmaster, quoted by Quentin Crewe, who could say that 'Eating in bed is the most disgusting thing a boy can do!'

40

He Gat No Heat

COLD beds have been a problem from the days of King David to those of the electric blanket. The oldest means of heating minor and hearthless rooms such as bedchambers was the brazier. Although by the fourteenth century the bedroom fire-place was quite a normal provision, the large hearth and chimney needed for a wood fire drew enormous quantities of cold air into the room through the ill-fitting doors and shutters. When St. Bernard retired sick to his cell, he could not be persuaded to indulge in the luxury of a fire, but his brethren, anxious for his life, are said to have practised a pious fraud upon him, and heated his cell without his knowledge by introducing hot air through the stone floor under his bed. But this is a rare, if not unique survival of the old Roman method of central heating. Charles the Bad of Navarre in his old age had his bed warmed with 'heated air', but this seems to have been by some more direct and dangerous method, for the bed caught fire, so that he died. It is clearly easier and quicker to heat the bed than the whole room; better a warm bed in a cold room, than a cold bed some way from the fire. Intermediately comes the method still used in the bitter winters of Northern Europe, where the family bed—to which guests too may be invited—has its communal cosiness enhanced by being made on the flat top of the stone-built or tiled stove.

One very effective bed-warmer, equivalent to an electric heater of about 100 watts, has been produced in enormous quantities, though it is not always obtainable: a human companion.

Now King David was old and stricken in years; and they covered him with clothes, but he gat no heat. Wherefore his servants said unto him, Let there be sought for my lord the king a young virgin: and let her stand before the king, and let her cherish him, and let her lie in thy bosom, that my lord the king may get heat. So they sought for a fair damsel throughout all the coasts of Israel, and found Abishag a Shunammite, and brought her to the king. And the damsel was very fair, and cherished the king, and ministered to him: but the king knew her not.

In the words of John Cotgrave:

> Make me thy maiden chamber-man,
> Or let me be thy warming-pan.

Dramatic results were obtained from the human warming-pan when Sir William Petty, the seventeenth-century surgeon, about to dissect the corpse of a poor wench lately hanged for felony, changed his mind, and

. . . put her to bed to a warm woman, and, with spirits and other means, restored her to life. The young scholars joined and made a little portion, and married her to a man who had several children by her.

Reginald Reynolds quotes a recent traveller in Newfoundland whose bed was warmed by putting a baby in it awhile first. Most vivid of all, the words of Dylan Thomas, whose Mr. Edwards, 'the draper mad with love', cries

Throw away your little bedsocks and your Welsh wool knitted jacket, I will warm the sheets like an electric toaster, I will lie by your side like the Sunday roast.

A hot stone from the fire, wrapped in a cloth, was probably the first artificial bed-heater. The warming-pan, of copper or silver, for hot coals, was common by the fifteenth century. Louis XI had one, a 'bassinoelle pour bassiner le lit', bought from Loys Boutard the poeslier for 30 sols in 1481. Henry VIII's was of copper-gilt. Queen

218

Elizabeth's was fine enough to appear in an inventory of her jewels and plate; Horace Walpole observes: 'one bed-pan, having the Queen's arms enamelled at the end. Here was luxury, magnificence and taste!' In the sixteenth century the warming-pan inspires the Muses— Pierre Delarivey devotes a sonnet to it. Francis Bacon, chilled by a snowstorm,

. . . went to the Earle of Arundel's house at High-gate, where they putt him into a good bed warmed with a Panne, but it was a damp bed that had not been layn-in in about a yeare before, which gave him such a colde that in 2 or 3 dayes as I remember Mr. Hobbes told me, he dyed of Suffocation.

The pan, rightly used, is still the best of all bed-warmers, but it was hardly fair to expect one to dry out a bed that had not been used for a year.

Sir Hugh Platt in his *Jewel House of Art and Nature* (1594) says that it was from a 'conceipted chaffing dish to keepe a dish of meate long hote' that there sprung the invention of 'froes, or pans, to heat beds with, and cast one into a kindly sweat'. A ship's captain presents Mr. Pepys, whose job is at the Admiralty, with 'a noble silver warming-pan', which we suspect is a bribe when Mr. Pepys is 'doubtful whether to take it or no'. A cool and empty one was an excellent vehicle in which to smuggle a new-born baby into a natal chamber, when a badly needed royal or noble infant was stillborn —or had never existed. James II is among the husbands said to have been thus deceived. So popular was this trick, that elaborate procedures were worked out to defeat it; after which it was certain at least who the mother was. Louis XIV had ten silver warming-pans; Molière only two, copper ones. In the comfort-loving seventeenth century they became almost as numerous as in the antique-loving twentieth. In a genuine and used antique brass pan, the metal will have scaled through repeated heating; the brass of modern copies is of better quality and does not scale. There should properly be an inner ember-pan to subdue and prolong the heat; this is omitted from most fakes; without it, it is easy by over-loading or inattention to scorch the sheets, if not to set the bed on fire. The earliest brass pans used in England were imported from Holland; home-made brass pans date from about 1585. The older handles are of metal, not of wood. From about 1730, simpler and much lighter pans of rosy-hued copper replaced brass. From about 1770, they were being drop-stamped, being therefore shallower than the hand-beaten kind. Antique or fake, it is a pity not to take ye olde warming-pan from the wall in frosty times and use it. In skilled hands, its temperature

Bed-wagon or moine, *eighteenth century*

will have fallen, by the time of getting into bed, to a point where the
pan can even be left in to toast the feet; for this, the short-handled
type is best.

The 'bed-wagon' was a light wooden framework in various forms,
containing a hanging pan of hot charcoal. In France this was known
as a '*moine*', doubtless by way of some bawdy jest about a monk in
the bed. It should of course be removed before getting in. Saint-
Simon tells how the Princesse de Furstemberg was found in bed
complaining that she was dying of some sudden fever; her symptoms
included a fast pulse, a splitting headache and a profuse sweat; it
was found that the *moine*, still glowing, had been left in the bed.
(The home handyman can make a serviceable modern version by
enclosing a 100-watt lamp in a cylindrical cage of laths.)

Rather like a *moine*, but for a different purpose, was the device
used by an inventive gentleman of Melton in Suffolk, not long since.
He used to insist on a wickerwork linen-basket being put temporarily
between the sheets while the bed was made, because he hated having
to squeeze into a bed too tightly tucked in. Another peculiar bed-
making arrangement was that devised by Herbert Spencer, and
described by his housekeeper:

. . . he retired the first evening after his arrival at an earlier hour than was
his custom subsequently in order to see that the bed had been prepared
for him after the approved plan.

This was as follows. A hard bolster was placed under the mattress,
raising thereby a hump on which the small of his back rested. The clothes
had a pleat in them right down the centre, so that they were never strained,
but fell in loose folds on either side of him, an arrangement which, though
we were assured it was most comfortable and restful, certainly looked
peculiarly untidy.

Our earliest reference to the hot-water bottle comes from France.
The Bishop of Avranches, who had suffered from cold feet since

infancy, was using a tin bottle in 1681, and has mentioned that these were then commonly sold for the purpose. Despite this, the French in 1770 were importing them as the new '*bassinoires anglaises*', justly advertised as incapable of singeing the sheets. There was also the stoneware 'belly-warmer', a large round affair with one side made concave so that it fitted the person snugly; we are not told whether customers were measured. The standard form of stoneware bottle, well into the present century, when rubber superseded it, had a flat base and an arched top. The stoneware screw-threads of the neck and stopper were none too accurate, and it was wise to keep them uppermost. Perhaps the least forgivable thing that we know of Mr. Gladstone is, that it was his habit to take one of these to bed, filled

Belly-warmer, eighteenth century

221

with hot tea, which he drank from it when he woke. In full households, short of hot-water bottles, a beer flagon wrapped in a sock has been found a serviceable if inelegant substitute; but any used bottle brought downstairs should be carefully segregated. This has caused trouble in one family: a relation who was none too abstemious opened the flagon standing before him at dinner, and poured out— an ugly shock—a glass of water. Such was his hurt rage at the seemingly calculated hint, that none has ever dared to explain.

A London stores catalogue of 1929 still offers a vast choice in the hot-water bottle field. The shapes include cylinders plain or fluted, arch-tops, ovals, and a flat round thing looking like a land-mine. Covers for these are available in lambswool, plush or velour. There is a copper bed-warmer shaped like the old warming-pan, but for hot water. The 'belly-warmer' is still offered, but it is now of metal, and has become a genteel 'stomach-warmer'. There are hot-water beds, like air mattresses, and hot-water pillows, both being sold, rather oddly, by weight, at 7s. 6d. a pound. (The only choice at the same store in 1880 had been between the warming-pan and the stoneware bottle.) But despite this variety in 1929, there is no mention of the rubber hot-water bottle, available in some stores, but still slightly suspect.

The rubber hot-water bottle, though not mass-produced until our time, is a far older idea according to Fournier, the historian of inventions; he says that the Indians of the Amazon had it in the sixteenth century. It has found a place in literature, for Wodehouse has woven a tale around the devilish practice of surreptitiously puncturing a hated rival's bottle while he sleeps. Dr. Stopes rejected it as late as 1956, for she held that the cramp in the legs that she suffered on winter nights was due, not to the cold, but to the 'stink' given off by the hot rubber. The newspaper obituary of a gentleman dying in 1960 allows him the sole claim to fame, that he invented the *seamless* rubber bottle. In many households it is now to be found bearing the words, in indelible relief,

THIS HOT WATER BOTTLE IS THE PROPERTY OF A DIRECT MEMBER OF THE BRITISH HOTELS AND RESTAURANTS ASSOCIATION, AND IS PROVIDED FOR THE COMFORT OF GUESTS WHILST HERE

—the last two being the operative words. The current cosy companion is to be had moulded into rather repellent cuddly animal forms for kiddies' cots; while for adult males, the best-selling hot-water bottle of 1960 literally took the form of a bikini-clad bathing beauty. One wonders what the Indians of the Amazon would have said of that.

The electric blanket got off to a bad start, because too many were marketed without safety devices—before the designers had, as they say, 'ironed out the bugs'. Many were far from fool-proof in 1956, in the light of some disconcerting facts then published. According to a survey by the Fire Protection Association, these and other bed-warmers caused over 2,600 of the fires reported to British insurance companies. In three years, electric blankets had caused twenty deaths. From over 200 models, the Consumers' Association tested thirteen. For safety and reliability, only seven of these were up to the minimum required by the British Standard, and none would pass the more stringent tests of the U.S. Underwriters' Laboratories. There are three types on the market: the *mains voltage*, *low wattage* type gives a gentle heat; the *mains voltage*, *high wattage* type warms up more quickly but is controlled by a thermostat; the *low voltage*, *low wattage* type, operated through a transformer, is as warm as the others, but with little risk of a shock if anything goes wrong. Any blanket up to the British Standard is safe, provided a few simple rules are observed: do not fold or crease it, or pile clothes on it, when switched on; do not put pins in it; and unless it is of the low voltage type, do not use it if it is wet or worn, and switch it off before getting into bed. All reputable makes are now quite safe, and some certainly efficient, if we are to accept the photograph in *Life* showing a smiling blonde resting, with the electric aid, under the *peine forte et dure* of a load of ice-blocks. They are coming within the means of all, according to a report from the U.S.A., where an inexplicable consumption of electricity in unoccupied houses has been traced to the one-night visits of tramps who carry their electric blankets with them.

Another recent invention is the mattress inflated with, and slowly exuding, air pre-conditioned for winter or summer, enabling those who feel uneasy in hot weather under a mere sheet to keep cool under normal bed-clothes. This converse problem of keeping cool in bed has been considered in the past. The 'Dutch Wife', a large bolster loosely filled with feathers and laid parallel to the sleeper, which sometimes puzzles the Englishman abroad, makes a cool bedfellow on a summer night. Disraeli liked to have two beds in hot weather, transferring himself from time to time into the cooler one. Benjamin Franklin had long since done the same, but he found that he needed four.

41

Terribly Strange Beds

EMBARKING on an eerie search through

> . . . many an old decaying room
> Hung with the ragged arras of the past,

we find—to borrow Wilkie Collins' title—some terribly strange beds.
His story of the great four-poster, whose canopy descends slowly and
silently to suffocate its victim, is pure fiction, but we need not go to
fiction to find beds fantastic, beds funny-queer, beds funny-ha-ha,
beds macabre. First among them (for who will prove it fictional?)
must come the Bed of Procrustes, whose name means 'the stretcher'.
A robber, dwelling near Eleusis of the Mysteries, he boasted that his
bed exactly fitted every guest, the long and the short and the tall.
The short were stretched on the rack, and the long chopped down,
to fit; presumably some lucky customers came the right size. Next—
centuries before Salvador Dali—come those surrealist Egyptian beds
of the eighteenth dynasty, whereon the god Osiris was depicted in
shapes filled with seed which, duly watered, grew to form a horrid
tapestry of living vegetation. Julius Caesar had a normal Roman bed
as far as we know; but a most strange bedroom, if we are to believe
John de Fordun's *Schotichronicon* of the fourteenth century. There
used to stand, near Falkirk in Scotland, a circular domed building
of stone known as 'Arthur's O'on' or 'King Arthur's Oven'. De
Fordun suggests that it was a portable sleeping-chamber used by

Caesar on his travels, 'with each stone separate, and built up again from day to day wherever they halted, that he might rest therein more safely than in a tent'. This structure, which certainly existed and has been measured and drawn, was some 20 ft. in diameter, and its masonry up to 4 ft. thick, so it is to be hoped that Caesar did not go to bed too early, nor sleep too long, when making a 'one-night stand'.

'St. Kevin's Bed' at Glendalough in Ireland is a recess in a cave cut in a rock cliff some 30 ft. above a lake. Some archaeologists will have it to be a tomb, but according to tradition it was used as a sleeping-place by the sixth-century St. Kevin, as well as by the later and celebrated St. Lawrence O'Toole. In the unlikely event of either saint wanting a morning plunge, he would have had only to jump from the doorway. It was here that St. Kevin sought refuge from the amorous attentions of the King's daughter:

> 'Here at least,' he calmly said,
> 'Woman ne'er shall find my bed.'
> Ah! The good Saint little knew
> What that wily sex can do . . .

Awakened one night on his mossy couch by the sudden onslaught of her kisses, the saint took quick advantage of the local topography:

> Sternly from his bed he starts,
> And with rude, repulsive shock,
> Hurls her from the beetling rock.

The very opposite of a crazy bed is 'St. Hilary's Bed' in a church at Poitiers, which restores the sanity of such demented characters as can be induced to sleep in it.

The physician Charles de l'Orme, who is said to have had 'useful ideas on every subject relating to beds', slept in one built of bricks, complete with a built-in stool-pot, and recommended the idea to all. Several incurious writers have been content to repeat this unsatisfying story, and leave it at that, as if a brick bed needed no explanation. It has proved worth while to explore the matter further. De l'Orme, we find, had a terror of dying from cold. He would pray to St. Lawrence (of gridiron fame, and thus an expert) to intercede for a constant supply of '*la principe de la vie*', the warmth necessary for life. His 'brick bed' was not so much a bed, as an oven to enclose one. It was 3 ft. wide, 5 ft. high, with a brick arch roof, and a wooden bedstead (with stool-pot) was built in by the bricklayer. As it was only 5 ft. long, the head of the bed must have been outside. The end opening, 2 ft. wide, was curtained, the floor inside matted, and the

225

brickwork insulated by layers of fur. At bedtime, hot bricks wrapped in linen were laid along the sides and at the foot of the bed. It seems unlikely that this bed was either draughty or cold, but as a final precaution, de l'Orme's night-wear included six pairs of stockings and a pair of leather ankle-boots lined with cotton wool.

Brick beds are found in China, built across the backs of the rooms, touching three walls and occupying up to three fourths of the floor space. Some of these have built-in heating: 'When the tail of the Great Bear was directly to the north,' writes Nora Waln, 'windows were sealed and fires lit in the beds.' In northern China, Persia, Korea and Japan, a charcoal fire is sunk in the middle of the floor and covered first with a lid, then with a great bedspread under which a whole family may sleep, radiating like troops in a bell-tent, feet to the fire. 'Headache', we are told, 'is *always* produced', and sleepers are often found suffocated. Some Chinese avoid this risk by slinging hammocks above the brick bed, or by piping the heat into the bed from another room. A traveller in Poland has noted, in a cottage, a square structure of branches entwined with twigs and daubed with mud, which 'serves for kitchen, chimney, stove and bed'. On top and at the sides, 'both sexes of all ages sleep together like pigs, on straw or furs, without undressing themselves'. Similar

Scandinavian bed
226

arrangements have been reported from Archangel, Moscow, Nanking and Cairo.

Ludwig II of Bavaria had a bed shaped like a Gothic cathedral. Thomas Bushell, of Cromwell's time, was an earlier lover of the Gothic; in his 'howse in Lambeth marsh':

. . . In the garret there is a long Gallery, which he hung all with black, and had some death's heads and bones painted. At the end where his couch was, was in an old Gothique Nich (like an old Monument) painted a Skeleton recumbent on a Matt. At the other end, where was his pallet-bed, was an emaciated dead man stretched out. Here he had severall mortyfying and devine Motto's . . . In the time of the Civill Warres his Hermitage over the rocks at Enston were hung with black-bayes; his bed had black Curtaines, etc., but it had no bed-posts but hung by 4 Cordes covered with black-bayes instead of bed-posts. When the Queen-mother came to Oxen to the King, she either brought (as I thinke) or somebody gave her, an entire Mummie from Egypt, a great raritie, which her Majestie gave to Mr. Bushell, but I beleeve long ere this time the dampnesse of the place has spoyled it with mouldinesse.

Peter I of Russia contrived an equally macabre bedroom ornament for his wanton wife Catherine. When she betrayed him with one William Mons, Peter had her lover beheaded in her presence. She seemed quite unaffected, and refused to admit the sin; so Peter had the head pickled and set at her bedside. Still denying that Mons interested her, she lived with it so unmoved, that Peter gave up and restored her to favour. (At least the head was real, and to that extent less dreadful than the inverted and tattooed head on the bedroom mantelpiece in H. G. Wells' *Pollock and the Porroh Man.*) A colder case of Russian cruelty is told of the Empress Anne. A noble dotard at her court had sunk to the status of a court jester and a butt for royal humour. He was, by her order, married with all ceremony to an equally ancient crone who served her bedchamber. Meanwhile, on the frozen river Neva, a house had been built and furnished entirely with ice, and to this the newlyweds were carried on the back of an elephant, to be installed together in a bed of ice, and shut in with an ice door. They just survived the night.

The bedroom of the Comte d'Artois, in the time of Louis XV, rates as a strange one, for so martial were his tastes, that not only was the bed bristling with weapons and topped by helmets; the pilasters of the chimney-piece were in the form of cannons, and the very fire-irons were decorated with bullets, bombs and grenades. Compare the milder tastes of Sir Richard Owen, who at his country seat had his bed hung just below the ceiling, so that he might watch the deer in his park. (This recalls Marco Polo's story of the light canework beds in which the nobles of southern India were hauled up to the ceiling by cords, and thus defeated all nocturnal pests from fleas to tarantulas.) As for Squire Waterton at Walton Hall, he never slept in a bed, but on the floor, wrapped in his cloak and with a block of wood for a pillow. Prince Metternich at the Palace of Furstemberg in 1820 chose to decorate his *rocaille* twin beds with lizards, toads and bats, in *bois-doré*, and set them in an alcove lit by a hanging lamp in the form of an owl carrying a globe; when the globe was extinguished the owl's eyes still shone and stared all through the night.

Jacob von Falke, in *Art in the House*, describes a bedroom of strange charm, as an example of 'Art outdone by Nature':

I once saw a chamber in a little inn on the south coast of England, through the window of which an immense ivy-branch had grown, covering the walls and ceiling with a dense curtain of shining dark green foliage, and entirely surrounding the fire-place, in which the fire burned brightly. The little room, with its luxuriant verdure illuminated by the ruddy light of the flame, was infinitely lovely; but if any one should attempt to decorate a room similarly by painting, the absence of charm and poverty of effect would at once convince us of our mistake.

There is something faintly reminiscent of the pickled head of William Mons in the bedroom arrangements made for Queen Victoria after Prince Albert's death: every bed in which she slept had to be double, and above 'his' empty pillow had to be hung a framed photograph of his corpse, surrounded by immortelles. Year after year, his night-clothes were neatly laid out at the bedside, and the wash-basin had water ready for his ghostly hands. (Compare Marilyn Monroe, over whose bed hung a portrait of—guess whom? Abraham Lincoln.)

D'Annunzio evolved a queer bedroom, not wholly by design, when living with a keen ornithologist. The only room available for the poet was full of glass cases of stuffed birds, which he hated, and to hide them he bought eighteen high screens. The final result was disconcerting in a different way, for the bed could be reached only by way of a maze, and to miss the way by night was to be faced by some dreadful bird. The bed, incidentally, was covered with forty red damask cushions (his motto was *Non per dormire*), and these came into Austrian hands, or rather under Austrian rumps, in the retreat from Caporetto. Surrealism recurs in d'Annunzio's bedroom at the *Vittoriale*, its only ornament being a Greek statue, a female nude, standing over his bed. Awakened one night by an earthquake, the terrified poet saw the lady toppling upon him, leaped out just in time, and thereafter lived without her.

The canopy of this Russian bed is not, as it might seem, intended to descend and crush the occupant; the design is based on pure aesthetics

Salvador Dali's own real-life bedroom is disappointing: he does not curl up into his usual foetal sleeping-position in a four-poster built of crutches; no camembert bedspreads or putrescent pillows; only Edwardian twin beds of curly brass, and a wall-draping topped by a Napoleonic eagle, that might be from any mews-flat bedroom pictured in *Vogue*. Even when we are shown him sleeping in the sea— pillowed in sand in a few inches of water—we doubt whether the cameraman did in fact creep up unseen, or that the pose was held after the click. Dali, who feels that he is a reincarnation of Da Vinci, has invented 'sleep-masks which stimulate technicolor dreams', but gives us to understand that these are not yet perfected. He has lectured on 'The Surrealist and Phenomenal Mystery of the Bedside Table', and as a further contribution to our subject, elects to record that he wet his bed until he was eight years old 'for the sheer fun of it'.

A strange bed used to be seen at fun-fairs: hung behind a protective net, it held a more or less glamorous lady wearing a night-dress that betrayed the presence of warmer garb beneath. When a target was hit by a wooden ball (at 7 for 6*d*.) the bed tilted on hinges and dropped her into a canvas pool below. Sir Leslie Joseph, the fun-fair tycoon, has lately explained why 'Tip the Lady Out of Bed' has lapsed: 'We ran clear out of ladies.'

There is a famous training stable at Newmarket where the horse-boxes are so splendidly appointed as to have drawn pilgrims from all parts of the horsy world—so well appointed, indeed, that when a box is vacant and the weather fair, the servants, who are by no means ill-housed, compete for the luxury of sleeping in it. Privacy is worth some sacrifice. It would be tactless to name the English

229

Bedstead in carved ebony, 'Renaissance style', shown by M. Roulé of Antwerp at the Great Exhibition, 1851

village where a picturesque local Diogenes, whose ammunition boots and overcoat and sombrero are all oversize, not caring to share the family roof with a somewhat unsympathetic sister, is to be seen once a week bearing home the armful of straw on which he sleeps untroubled in the dog-kennel. Meanwhile, almost within sight of his little door, there is a hollow on the hillside under the roots of a great old tree, showing clear evidence that it is rightly called 'the tramps' nest'. Only one man, at any one time, can be the worst lodged in the world.

How uncomfortable can a bed be? As the story of the princess and the pea illustrates, comfort is relative. The party of supermen who lately climbed the North face of the Eiger in winter spent four nights on its ice cliffs, and slept standing on ledges, roped to *pitons*, but such an arrangement hardly rates as a bed. (We pause to note that when they descended to a hotel and were offered beds and pyjamas, only one of the party proved ever to have seen such a garment before.) Galton writes of a hardy Cameronian who, when bivouacking with his son in the snow, noticed that the boy had rolled a snowball to make himself a pillow, and kicked it away, with the stern rebuke of 'No effeminacy, boy!' The fakir on his bed of nails might seem to be in the running for the worst bedded man in the world, but he may not fully deserve his reputation for hardihood. It does not always occur to the wondering observer that the *more* nails there are, the

230

less the risk of pain. Laying aside our pen to make a simple experiment with a letter-scale and a reasonably sharp new nail, we determine what load on its point can be tolerated by the epidermis. Using for convenience the rather sensitive palm of the hand, we find that ¼ lb. is hardly felt; ½ lb. is on the threshold of pain but quite tolerable; 1 lb. is mildly painful, and briefly marks but does not pierce the skin. At about 1½ lb. one has not yet drawn blood, but loses enthusiasm for the experiment. Hence, even if a hardened fakir's back were as tender as a writer's palm, and the nails as sharp as new, a 6-stone man (and fakirs, who 'can live for a week on the skin of a dirty onion', average less) should lie easy on a bed twenty nails long by ten nails wide.

The actor Peter O'Toole has told how he and a companion, hiking from Stratford to London, wormed their way after dark deep into a haystack, becoming only gradually aware, towards dawn, that it was in fact a manure-heap. For combined physical amd moral discomfort, that is noteworthy, but for purely moral discomfort, consider the ordeal of a certain Fellow of the Society of Antiquaries and his wife, likewise hiking, and in search of a secluded dell in which to lay their sleeping-bags. Rejecting one spot after another, they grew weary, and in intense darkness they settled for a grassy couch under a spreading tree. They awoke in sunlight to find themselves on a small green triangle in a busy suburb, already objects of interest to the schoolgoers, and faced with the choice of rising and dressing in public, or cowering in their bags, deaf to all enquiry, until night should fall again.

War has shown that to an exhausted man, who will sleep on the march until the road bends and he goes straight on into the ditch, sleep is bliss whatever the bed. The sleeping-bags used on the winter

Most Japanese have always slept on mats on the floor, but their royal family used this bed

231

journey in the Antarctic made by the 'Cape Crozier Party' of Scott's last expedition, described in *The Worst Journey in the World*, may well rate as the worst beds in the world. Complete darkness, day and night, combined with temperatures down to 107 degrees of frost. At bed-time, a man might take an hour to get out of his armour of clothing and fight his way into a frozen bag, taking so much ice in with him, that he might not become warm enough to thaw it out.

It was far too cold to keep a hole open through which to breathe. So all night long our breath froze into the skins, and our respiration became quicker and quicker as the air in our bags got fouler and fouler; it was never possible to make a match strike or burn inside our bags! . . . For me it was a very bad night; a succession of shivering fits which I was quite unable to stop, and which took possession of my body for many minutes at a time until I thought my back would break, such was the strain placed upon it. They talk of chattering teeth; but when your body chatters you may call yourself cold.

On emerging, they would quickly stuff their gear into the mouth of the bag before it could freeze; this made a removable plug and offered a frozen hole for entry. When the temperature rose to only —27° F they enjoyed the comparative comfort of 'a pleasant wet kind of snipe-marsh' inside the bags. Towards the end they were getting frost-bitten even in bed, and in the morning, never rolled the bags up, but opened the mouths wide before they froze, and carried them flat and stiff on the sledge. Yet of such beds Cherry-Garrard could say:

. . . the more horrible the conditions in which we sleep, the more soothing and wonderful are the dreams which visit us . . . We slept not only soundly the greater part of these days and nights, but with a certain numbed pleasure.

Prisoners of war, already lying hard, have willingly surrendered their bed-boards for use as tunnel-linings, some replacing them by mattresses woven of string saved from Red Cross parcels. Prisoners in Japanese hands have been more than content with beds of coral (not unlike broken glass) or with the gap between two coconut logs laid together, or a 9-inch channel-iron along the side of an over-crowded ship's hold. Back home after release, many of them have found normal beds untenable, and for weeks have been able to sleep only on the floor. It was no unusual thing, around 1940, to step from a London Underground train across the sleeping-bag of some placid grandmother who would have been exasperated in 1939 by a dripping tap near her bedroom.

42

Charms and Omens

MEDICINE and magic have never lived wholly apart, and they certainly mingle among the charms, omens and superstitions associated with the bedroom. 'Go to bed with the skin of a mole round your left thigh'—magic, or medicine? Parson Woodforde cured his nightly cramp by taking a piece of brimstone to bed with him, and holding it near the affected parts, with immediate results—superstition, or faith-healing, or electro-therapy? A roast mouse, as a remedy for bed-wetting, was mocked at recently in print, whereat a mother wrote to endorse its efficacy; she serves her children only with clean well-bred white mice from Harrod's. Rheumatism—some say, cramp—can be cured by putting a cork—some say, a whole bag of corks—between the sheets—some say, under the mattress. It is possible that a Royal Warrant is given to this idea: the evidence lies in a peculiar feature of a photograph of King Edward VII lying on his death-bed. Hung casually round the bed-post near his head is a sort of necklace, made of string and about twenty of what are almost certainly ordinary bottle-corks. This was not the later lying-in-state in Westminster

Hall, so it is not a matter of surrounding the deceased monarch, like a Pharaoh in his tomb, with household objects appropriate to his life in the other world. The point deserves research.

To prevent bed-sores, put two buckets of fresh spring water under the bed every day—but never use cold *boiled* water, which angers the Devil and brings bad luck. This has been explained on the grounds that water once boiled will not freeze, and the Devil may want it to do so; unfortunately (for motorists in particular) boiled water in fact freezes at the normal rate. Speaking of the Devil: look under the bed before retiring, to ward him off (not in any hope of seeing him), and note that no good hand at cards ever has the four of clubs in it, this being a picture of the Devil's four-poster bed.

Best known of the occult dangers of the bed is that of getting out on the wrong side, though which is the wrong side has never been clearly agreed. Some say it is the opposite side to the one at which we get in; others, that it is the left, or *sinister* side.

It is unlucky to sweep out a guest's bedroom until he has been gone for an hour. A cynical explanation might be offered for this: if he has dropped any valuables there, it is better not to find them until he is well beyond recall.

The lunatic influence of moonlight on the bed is known the world over; it not only turns men mad, it turns black men white. When the new moon is first seen (not of course through glass), the usual drill is to turn one's money over, but some say that the housewife should quickly turn a bed.

Sir James Frazer records two forms of homeopathic magic concerned with the bed. Among the Galelareese, when a young man goes wooing at night, he sprinkles a little earth from a grave on the roof just above the spot where the girl's parents lie, and they then sleep like the dead. The aboriginals of South-east Australia, like the ancient Greeks, believe that a man may be injured by sticking sharp objects into the mark left by his sleeping body, causing the acute pains which the ignorant European puts down to rheumatism. That is why it is important on rising to smooth the hollow in the bed-clothes.

There are several causes of nightmare, such as sleeping on a feather bed which has been turned on a Sunday; but several cures, such as hanging your stockings crosswise at the foot of the bed with a pin stuck in them, or putting your shoes under the bed with the toes pointing outwards, or laying an iron or steel object such as a knife under the foot of the bed, or hanging up a stone with a natural hole in it. If your cattle have nightmares (and you somehow know about this), this last is said to be equally effective in the cowhouse.

234

At All Hallow's Eve—the eve of the Celtic new year—a girl may conjure up the ghost of her husband-to-be. The procedure varies: if she eats an apple in front of her mirror at bedtime, combing her hair the while, he may appear dimly reflected behind her. He may come in a dream, especially if a slice of bride-cake or an onion (not both, one hopes) is put under the pillow. It will help if the slice of cake is first drawn three times through the wedding-ring. The Scottish procedure is more elaborate: the maiden must stand three pails of water in her bedroom, pin three leaves of green holly to her night-dress, and go to sleep. She will duly be aroused by yells and laughter, followed by the appearance of her future husband; if he loves her, he will move the pails. Aubrey has it differently:

To know whom one shall marry. You must lie in another county, and knit the left garter about the right legged stocking (let the other garter and stocking alone) and as you rehearse these following verses, at every comma, knit a knot.

> This knot I knit,
> To know the thing, I know not yet,
> That I may see,
> The man that shall my husband be,
> How he goes, and what he wears,
> And what he does, all days, and years.

Accordingly in your dream you will see him: if a musician, with a lute or other instrument; if a scholar, with a book or papers.

Child-bed precautions include nails in front of the bed to ward off elves; the bed must not be turned until the child is a month old.

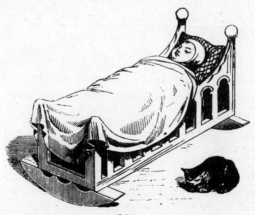

235

Lacking a baby-sitter,

> Let the superstitious wife
> Near the child's heart lay a knife;
> Point be up and haft be down;
> While she gossips in the town
> This 'mongst other mystic charms
> Keeps the sleeping child from harms

In China, a knife under the bed likewise protects a child's entry into the world; it may be supplemented by a dummy sword fashioned of 'cash' strung together, scissors cut from red paper and pinned to the bed-curtains, a tiger-skin inside the mattress, and pictures of fierce wild animals pasted on the walls, doors and windows.

> Teach me to live that I may dread
> The grave as little as my bed

says the hymn, to the puzzlement of at least one child who, having heard but not read it, assumed a comma after 'grave', and the last words to be descriptive of the grave's dimensions. There have always been cross-associations between grave and bed. In Welsh, *bedd* means either. There is a form of wooden grave-board not only resembling, but known as a 'bed-head', though most of these have by now ended in the church heating chamber. 'If I could please myself,' wrote Barbellion, 'I should have my coffin made and kept under my bed. Then if I should die they could just pull the old box out and put me in it'—and many have so pleased themselves.

The death-bed is especially haunted by portents and dangers. Omens of death include triple knocks at the bed's head; a white bird fluttering around it; even the squeak of a mouse behind it. If three persons take part in making a bed, there will be a death in the house that year. A little dust from the church floor, sprinkled on a death-bed, eases the pains. No one can die comfortably under a cross-beam, nor in a bed set crossways to the floor-boards, nor on a mattress of pigeon's feathers, from which the dying person should be lifted in his sheet and laid on the floor—but, given a mattress of game-feathers (no contradiction here, for pigeons do not rate as game but as vermin) it is *impossible* to die.

236

43

Springs and Stuffings

I T was its easy folding and portability, rather than cheapness or a wish to discourage bugs, that first led to the revival of the metal bedstead, out of use since the last days of the Roman Empire; it came back as a 'camp-bed' for travellers. Iron beds were used in Sicily from the late sixteenth century, but generally they were thought fit only for hospitals or prisons. A document of 1569 records a bed of iron and copper, with brass posts, and four brass satyrs in lieu of guardian angels, but this is a rarity. In 1623 a bene-factor leaves a fund to the *Hôtel-Dieu* hospital in Paris, to provide iron beds, but not until late in the eighteenth century are they made commercially in any numbers. In the infant Louis XVII's nursery the governess, the nurse, the numerous women, and the royal babe itself, all sleep on metal beds. A French advertisement of 1772 offers them as '*non sujets aux punaises*'—bug-proof. There are several early nineteenth-century patents: Wingfield's for 'Tubes or Rods for Furniture' in 1827, 'Bedsteads from Hollow Tubes' in 1831, and 'Metallic Bedsteads' in 1841. These last were full- or half-testers. But iron and brass did not come into their own until the Great Exhibition, where some glorious examples were on show. Havard, as late as 1890, notes that in France metal beds are commonly used only in prisons, hospitals, barracks, schools and convents, though found 'even in private houses' in England. In France only the poorer classes, he says, are beginning to adopt this inelegant material in the home. The mattress of the metal bed of the 1850's lay on stout metal laths that were slightly springy, but resilience still depended on the super-imposed feather-bed, which mankind seems to have mistrusted throughout its history, and to have used with a rather guilty enjoyment.

237

'Half-tester bedstead in iron or brass',
1855

Facing page: *Coil-spring mattress;
a British patent of 1865. Wire mattress with adjustable tension, 1890.
Three mattresses by Heal, 1896*

Da Vinci objected to 'lying upon the spoils of other dead creatures',
and it is surprising that he did not invent a spring mattress. John
Locke even held that 'being buried every night in feathers melts and
dissolves the body'. Hair was used from about 1650; moss was tried
in 1770 and was said to repel mice. (Pet hamsters still sometimes
establish stores of food that decay in the inaccessible coils of modern
mattresses.) In the seventeenth century the new art of carding wool,
instead of merely beating it, afforded a much springier filling. In
1781 came a great contribution to comfortable repose: the box-
shaped hair-mattress that replaced the shapeless sack of straw. The
lit de canne of 1785 had a woven base, like a cane-seated chair, instead of webbing. *Encyclopaedia Britannica* of 1823 defines 'Bed' as

a convenience for stretching and composing the body on, for ease, rest,
or sleep, consisting generally of feathers enclosed in a ticken case . . .

and remarks that

most of the peasants about Manchester lie on chaff at present, as do
likewise the common people all over Scotland.

Daily Wants of 1840 recommends beech leaves for the mattress—
'they remain both sweet and elastic for years'. Pine shavings were
advised in America in the 1880's, and incidentally relieved bronchial
troubles. Lady Barker found in an Irish hotel a mattress stuffed with
seaweed, in which she suspected 'many curious specimens of marine
zoology had been entombed by mistake'. None of these provided
the answer, and despite its reputation as unhealthy, the feather-bed
survived until the spring mattress became really durable. British
patents for springs date back to the eighteenth century, but the spiral

238

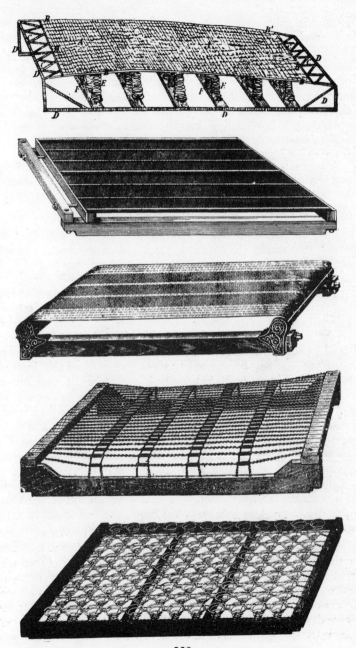

239

spring does not seem to have been used in furniture until 1826, and then only in a seat for use on shipboard to counteract seasickness. The difficulty was to keep the springs in place; they tended to turn over on their sides when compressed, until the invention of the conical spring allowed the coils to nest together flat. The metallurgy was imperfect, and the sudden escape of a broken spring could be painful. The woven wire mattress avoided this problem, and it could be wonderfully soft when new. but it tended to sag in time. It was evidently a novelty in 1870:

... strange as it may appear, it can be used as an excellent sleeping arrangement with only a folded blanket above the wire. The surface ... is in fact as sensitive as water, yielding to every pressure and resuming its shape as soon as it is removed.

To cure the sag, by taking it up from time to time, a method was devised that recalls the old 'bed-twitch' for corded beds. The wire mattress had a heavy wooden frame to which only one end of it was fixed. The other end was fixed to a wooden cross-member sliding within the frame. When a stout screw was turned by means of a 'bed-key', this moved the cross-member and took up at least the lengthwise sag—after some years, nothing could quite get rid of the central furrow. Alternatively, one end of the mesh was fixed to a roller, on which it could be tightened with a tommy-bar, and held by a ratchet. About the 'eighties there came countless permutations and combinations of wire mesh, chain-link, vertical coil-springs in compression, and marginal coil-springs in tension. Many such an heirloom is still in use as a mere support to a modern mattress; others may be seen rusting in hotel outhouses, or embodied in chicken-runs and fences together with old bed-ends, or submerged in country brooks—how is it, that a man too lazy to bury his unwanted bedmongery, is willing to carry it to a beauty-spot a mile from human habitation?

Coil-springs are now kept neatly under control by packing each in a separate fabric cylinder. The next development is the foam-rubber mattress. One lone voice has been raised in objection to this inexpensive luxury—that of Dr. Stopes; it is 'pernicious', she says, because rubber is an insulator, and cuts you off from electric currents of the earth with which you should be in contact. Some may accept her reasoning—those, for example, who dangle little chains from their motor-cars, in contact with the road, to prevent car-sickness; one notices, though, that when the end links break unobserved, and contact ceases, they seem to enjoy undiminished protection.

240

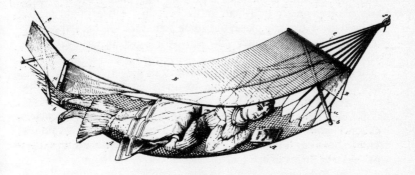

44

Beds Blown and Slung

THE inflated air-bed, like so many other inventions, has over and over again been hailed as new. The bunch of parallel sausages on which the present generation camps, sun-bathes, or floats in helpless panic out to sea, stems from John Clark's patent of 1813 for 'inflated beds, pillows and cushions' of rubberised fabric. This patent is ten years older than the one that put Macintosh's name into the dictionary. The idea need not depend on rubber, and goes still further back. 'Oilskin' air-beds, made of skins stuck together—not the later 'oilskins' of impregnated silk—were advertised in France in 1770. In 1610, in Ben Jonson's play *The Alchemist*, Sir Epicure Mammon declares 'I will have all my beds blown up, not stuffed'. Jonson may well have had in mind the portable bed, intended for the weary or watchful hunter, described only four years earlier in a book about the chase by one Du Fouilloux:

. . . a bed filled with air, which can be made thus: skins must be sewn together in the form of a rectangular mattress; the joints must be made as carefully as those of a sack; then, when it is well stitched up all round, a little valve must be fitted in one corner, as for a sack or for bagpipes, which will shut automatically when the air has been put in; then it must be filled with air by means of a pump or with a good bellows like those goldsmiths use.

241

Even then the idea was more than a century old, for Louis XI had a *lit de vent* of leather in 1478. This too was blown up with bellows—essentially the same accessory that is sold with the air-bed of today. Heliogabalus, we are told, had an air-bed. In what far night of the past, and in what stony place, did some benighted vintner happen by chance on the blissful couch afforded by a bunch of air-filled wine-skins?

The hammock, too, is an old device. For a tropical night, what more cool and airy support could be imagined than 'a lot of holes held together by string'? Though the definition was coined for the net, it fits the hammock. A kind of hammock was used in the trenches by French troops of the fifteenth century. The true network hammock seems to have come in as a novelty from Brazil, where the aboriginals wove it from strips of bark of the *hamack* tree. Columbus saw it in 1492, and Raleigh noted that in the Caribbean the natives 'lay in hammocks, which we call Brazil beds'. Gonzalvo Ferdinando de Oviedes described it in his *Summarie and generall Historie of the Indies*:

In the Gulfe of Uraba where the Rio Grande enters the Sea, are many Palme trees in the middest of the River growing neere together, on the tops whereof are houses made—in which many Inhabitants dwell together and have their beds tyed to the lower parts of the said Palme trees. These beds they call Hamacas, being coverlets of Cotton of good thread and well woven, of two or three braces long, but narrower, with cordes at the ends. The cordes are of Cotton, of Henequen or Cabuya, this the courser thread, that the finer and able to cut Iron; made of the leaf of a certaine Herbe.

The hammock was often rediscovered and was attributed to many lands: to Louis XIII it was his *lit à la chinoise*, despite the fact that this hammock, of green cord, was given to him by Prince Maurice of Nassau who had been Governor of Brazil. Evelyn in 1647, visiting the eccentric Thomas Bushell, noted a 'grot' where the owner lay in a hammock 'like an Indian'. By 1777, one is advertised as a *hamac de l'Inde*, and another soon after as coming from Spain. Hammocks had been used in French ships from the early seventeenth century, and they appear among the stores for both merchant and royal navies as *branles à la matelotte*, *branle* meaning also 'a shaking or teasing motion'; the feminine ending to *matelotte* brings to mind that the morning summons 'show a leg!' is said to derive from the custom of allowing women to board and sleep in newly arrived ships; a female leg showed that the occupant of the hammock was not one of the crew, and might rest from her labours.

Until recent times, naval officers were allotted empty cabins which they had to furnish out of their own pockets. My Lord the Earl of Sandwich, First General in Restoration days, had a fine 'bed-chamber' in the flagship, complete with a new chimney; his secretary Mr. Pepys' cabin was 'little, but very convenient, having one window to the sea and another to the deck, and a good bed'. Unfortunately the deck above needed caulking, and not only was his bed soaked when it rained, but

about three in the morning the people began to wash the deck, and the water came pouring into my mouth, which waked me, and I was fain to rise and get on my gown and sleep leaning on my table.

The furnishings of Charles II's yacht, the *Royal Escape*, so named because he had fled in her from England ten years before, and now luxuriously refitted, included 4 quilted beds, 2 small feather-beds, 6 feather-pillows, 6 coverlet quilts, 6 pairs of white blankets, 4 pewter candlesticks and 2 pewter chamber-pots.

Passengers in the early days likewise had to bring their own beds and linen. The fare in an Indiaman to Bombay or Calcutta in the early nineteenth century was about £100, and this provided only a tiny empty cubicle. Emigrants in Yankee and Australian packets fared far worse, when even the Liverpool–New York run might stretch to sixty days, and especially in bad weather, when water might get below and swamp the bedding. Rules for emigrant passengers were laid down in 1848, not by the shipping companies, but by the Emigration Commissioners, in the passengers' interest:

Every passenger to rise at 7 a.m. unless otherwise permitted by the surgeon.

Passengers to be in their beds by 10 p.m.

The passengers when dressed, to roll up their beds, to sweep the decks, including the space under the bottom of berths, and to throw the dirt overboard.

Breakfast not to commence until this is done.

The occupant of every berth to see that his own berth is well brushed out.

The beds to be well shaken and aired on the decks and the bottom boards, if not fixtures, to be removed and dry scrubbed and taken on deck at least twice a week.

The companies were eventually made to provide the bedding, but as soon as the inspector had gone ashore and the ship sailed, the best of this was quite likely to be taken away again.

The term 'state-room' does not come in until the days of the

Mississippi stern-wheelers, which had very roomy, though communal sleeping-quarters. The so-called state-room allotted to Charles Dickens, sailing to America in the mail steam-packet *Britannia* in 1842, did not come up to his great expectations:

That this state-room had been specially engaged for 'Charles Dickens, Esquire, and Lady', was rendered sufficiently clear even to my scared intellect by a very small manuscript, announcing the fact, which was pinned on a very flat quilt, covering a very thin mattress, spread like a surgical plaster on a most inaccessible shelf. But that this was the state-room concerning which Charles Dickens, Esquire, and Lady, had held daily and nightly conferences for at least four months preceding: that this could by any possibility be that small snug chamber of the imagination, which Charles Dickens, Esquire, with the spirit of prophecy strong upon him, had always foretold would contain at least one little sofa, and which his lady, with a modest yet most magnificent sense of its limited dimensions, had from the first opined would not hold more than two enormous portmanteaus in some odd corner out of sight (portmanteaus which could now no more be got in at the door, not to say stowed away, than a giraffe could be persuaded or forced into a flower-pot): that this utterly impracticable, thoroughly hopeless, and profoundly preposterous box, had the remotest reference to, or connexion with, those chaste and pretty, not to say

Charles Dickens' 'State-room' in S.S. Britannia, *1842*

244

gorgeous little bowers, sketched by a masterly hand, in the highly varnished lithographic plan hanging up in the agent's counting-house in the city of London . . . I do verily believe that, deducting the two berths, one above the other, than which nothing smaller for sleeping in was ever made except coffins, it was no bigger than one of those hackney cabriolets which have their door behind, and shoot their fares out, like sacks of coals, upon the pavement.

Dickens fared little better on a canal boat between Harrisburg and Pittsburg:

I have mentioned my having been in some uncertainty and doubt, at first, relative to the sleeping arrangements on board this boat. I remained in the same vague state of mind until ten o'clock or thereabouts, when going below, I found suspended on either side of the cabin, three long tiers of hanging bookshelves, designed apparently for volumes of the small octavo size. Looking with greater attention at these contrivances (wondering to find such literary preparations in such a place), I descried on each shelf a sort of microscopic sheet and blanket; then I began dimly to comprehend that the passengers were the library, and that they were to be arranged, edge-wise, on these shelves, till morning.

Lots were drawn for these bunks. Down the centre of the cabin was a red curtain forming a 'sexual division'.

I found it [the bunk], on after-measurement, just the width of an ordinary sheet of Bath post letter-paper; and I was at first in some uncertainty as to the best means of getting into it. But the shelf being a bottom one, I finally determined on lying upon the floor, rolling gently in, stopping immediately I touched the mattress, and remaining for the night with that side uppermost, whatever it might be. Luckily, I came upon my back at exactly the right moment. I was much alarmed on looking upward, to see, by the shape of his half-yard of sacking (which his weight had bent into an exceedingly tight bag), that there was a very heavy gentleman above me, whom the slender cords seemed quite incapable of holding; and I could not help reflecting upon the grief of my wife and family in the event of his coming down in the night.
. . . One of two remarkable circumstances is indisputably a fact, with reference to that class of society who travel in these boats. Either they carry their restlessness to such a pitch that they never sleep at all; or they expectorate in dreams, which would be a remarkable mingling of the real and ideal.

All of which makes a hammock sound comparatively comfortable, given some acquired skill in its use. The raw Navy recruit sometimes misunderstands his instructions in the tricky art of so varying the

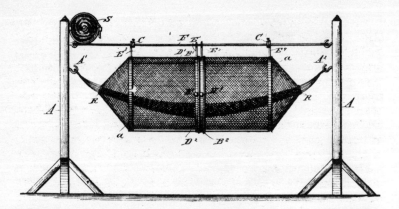

Hammock combined with mosquito net, 1885. The cylindrical net is carried on hoops which slide apart to admit the occupant

lengths of the shroud-lines at the ends of his hammock that it will lie concave; if he gets their order reversed, it lies convex, and at once ejects him, to the joy of his messmates. Even if it is rightly rigged, it is not difficult for the inexperienced to fall out. Failing this, they can always amuse themselves by cutting his lanyard while he sleeps, dropping him head or feet first according to their taste in fun. Captain Marryat's hero Frank Mildmay, exasperated by the repetition of this joke, not only retaliates in kind, but first puts a shot-case underneath his tormentor's hammock to receive his head, and has the satisfaction of putting him into hospital for a fortnight. My Lords of the Admiralty, a somewhat conservative body, seem reluctant that the bunk should supersede the hammock, which is still in use at sea and ashore. During the late war, a squad of 'bell-bottoms' was marched into a commandeered hotel furnished with shining brass bedsteads. Delighted with the change, they made up their beds—only to be ordered by an outraged Petty Officer to un-make them, and to sling their hammocks in shipshape fashion, each one just above a bedstead.

In two ways the hammock has proved a life-saver. With plenty of them to hand, a damage-control party may effect a temporary seal over a shell-hole below the water-line. Thrown overboard from a sinking ship, a hammock can trap enough air to support a man, like Queequeg in his coffin, till rescue comes.

246

To mid-Victorians it was unthinkable that a lady—though fully clad—should be seen recumbent out of doors, but in the emancipated 'eighties, when ladies in bloomers began to bicycle, hammocks multiplied in English gardens. Safe enough under the well-balanced hips of ancient mariners, they revealed two dangers for the landlubber, who could fall out of a taut hammock, or be ensnared like a wild beast in a slack one. Hence many inventions designed to hold the net at a proper tension, as well as others to provide end supports in treeless gardens, and overhead protection against the elements; one has a cylindrical mosquito net carried on hoops which slide apart to admit the occupant. Perhaps the last word in hammocks is the 'Hammock Tricycle' of 1883, which is inverted when the traveller has pedalled to his night-stop, the hammock slung inside it between the wheels, and a waterproof cover spread over all to 'convert the vehicle into a sleeping apartment'.

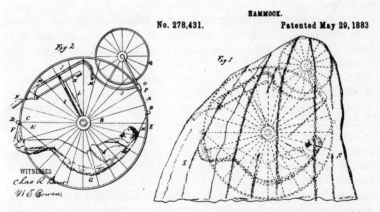

HAMMOCK.

No. 278,431.   Patented May 29, 1883

Hammock combined with tricycle, 1883. 'A waterproof cover spread over the whole allows one to convert the vehicle into a sleeping apartment'

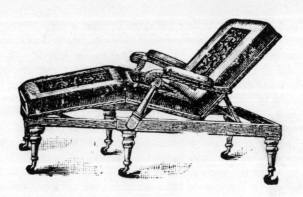

45

Whimsical Chayres

ABOOK could be written about the countless means devised to make beds to fold up for transport, or to be put out of sight; beds to tilt the occupant into a variety of positions; multi-purpose beds to serve also as chairs or tables or baths; beds combined with bookcases or even with pianos. To no other item of furniture have so many nuts, bolts, hinges, levers, springs and handles been devoted.

The first patent in the field of 'invalid beds' is British Patent No. 16 of 1620 for 'A Backframe or Back-screene for Bedridden Invalids ... for the Ease and Reliefe of such sick Persons ... as are troubled with Heate on their Backes through continuing lying on their Beddes.' In 1664 Evelyn describes 'a chayre to sleepe in with the leggs stretcht out', which can 'draw out longer or shorter', and also 'a whimsical chayre, which folded into so many varieties as to turn into a bed, a bolster, a table, or a couch'. Thereafter, 'mechanical beds', that tilt or change their shape, multiply rapidly. Dr. de Lostalot-Bachoué, in a treatise recommending how to live actively to the age of eighty, recommends a bed sloping steeply from head to foot. He admits that this posture has no real advantage for ordinary sleep, but points out that to be accustomed to it will be invaluable, if one becomes bedridden —presumably when over eighty. Another bed, by means of various springs and rods, can be so tilted about that it can somehow be made without waking the patient, and is recommended as particularly useful when the odd surgical operation is to be carried out in the home. Yet another is a four-poster with a most complicated mechanism of cables, a winch, gears and a retarding flywheel, to raise or tilt the mattress. The 'Sofa or Machine for the Care of Invalids' covered by British Patent No. 3744 of 1813, with a mattress made in three sections that can be moved to various angles by worms and gears, shows the same predilection for doing things the hard way. As for

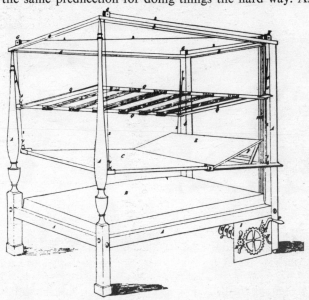

English 'Invalid Bed', 1794, raised by a complicated mechanism. Below: 'Sofa or Machine for the Care of Invalids', 1813. The mattress, made in three sections, is moved to various angles by a system of winches, worms and gears

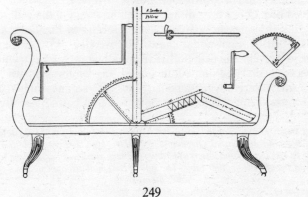

the French 'Surgical Chair Bed' of 1828, the works are so complicated that the patent specification fills ten pages. The American
'Variety-Couch' of 1838 (which has nothing to do with the conditions
of employment of variety artistes) adds a provision for suspending it
by rods from the ceiling, should this seem an advantage. Thomas
Webster's 'Invalid Couch' of 1840 has a simpler mechanism than
most, but it can hardly be classed as a thing of beauty.

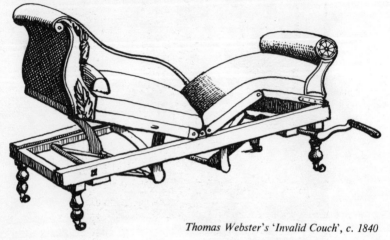

Thomas Webster's 'Invalid Couch', c. 1840

Early among the beds designed to fold up against the wall is Jacob
Schuebler's 'Newly-invented French Bed' of about 1750. At about
the same date, M. Dufresne comes out with a thing that, starting
apparently as a mere sideboard, unfolds to reveal a bookcase, a
writing-desk, and a wardrobe, and is finally transformed into a
canopied bed. Other beds disappear behind doors in the wall, or into
projecting dummy cupboards. Oliver Goldsmith mentions a piece
that is a bed by night and a chest-of-drawers by day. Gadgets were
added to prevent the bed-clothes from falling into a heap when the
bed was closed. The Pompadour's *lit en baignoire* was a bath hidden
in a couch. A Paris advertisement of 1781 offers a fine walnut cabinet,
with bronze fittings, concealing both bed and bath. That inventive

Facing page, above: *Jacob Schuebler's 'Collapsible Bed', c. 1750.* Below: *the
'Table-Bedstead' or 'Grand Ottoman', 1849. The table is converted into a bed by
folding up two leaves, and unscrewing and removing the lower parts of the legs. The
third leaf then forms another table. The side of the small ottoman slides up to reveal
toilet utensils*

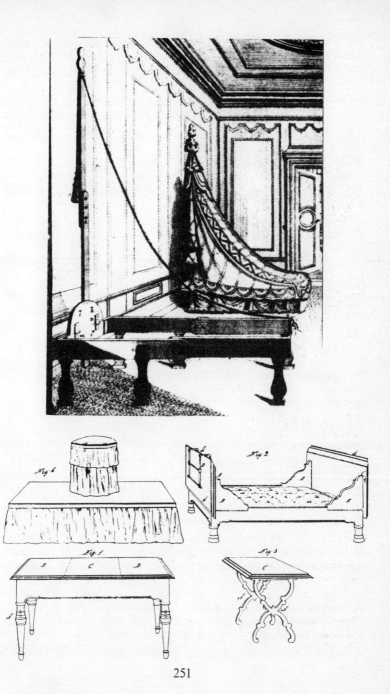

architect and President of the United States, Thomas Jefferson, chose for some reason to put his bed in a passageway between his study and his dressing-room, which it completely blocked, but he contrived means of hauling it up to the ceiling by ropes during the day. An inventor of 1849 states:

I have invented the Table-Bedstead or Grand Ottoman with its small ottoman, so as to include a dining table and other different useful articles.

When the middle leaf of the table is removed, folding legs hinged to it turn it into an occasional table. The lower parts of the main table-legs are removed, and the end leaves are folded upright to become bed-ends. The separate small ottoman converts into a wash-stand and holds toilet utensils. At the Great Exhibition of 1851, Mr. T. Starkey of Farthingoe shows 'a table, convertible into a bedstead, wardrobe, suite of drawers, spongebath, etc.'

Folding beds were much in demand for the cramped 'bed-sitters' of the lower-middle class. In Dickens' *Old Curiosity Shop*, Dick Swiveller, lodging in the neighbourhood of Drury Lane, has a bed concealed in a dummy bookcase. Not only does he hope that his visitors think that a bedroom adjoins; he tries to deceive himself:

. . . he firmly believed this secret convenience to be a bookcase and nothing more . . . closed his eyes to the bed, resolutely denied the existence of the blankets, and spurned the bolster from his thoughts. No word of its real use, no hint of its nightly service, no allusion to its peculiar properties, had ever passed between him and his most intimate friends.

Another good market was found among the pioneers in America going west. Their folding beds were not luxuriously finished; most of them have the solid 'cottage' quality of the 'Wardrobe Bed' of 1859, which 'possesses the combined advantage of a secretary, wardrobe and toilet accommodations' but would hardly have pleased Sheraton. Far more combined advantages were possessed by the 'Piano Bed' of 1866:

The convertible piano has been designed principally for the benefit of hotels, boarding-schools, etc., containing apartments which are used for parlors, etc., in day-time and yet required for sleeping-rooms at night.

A huge drawer can be pulled out from the piano frame, at floor-level, and contains a bed. Bed-clothes, a wash-bowl, a pitcher, towels, a chest-of-drawers, and a writing-flap, are revealed in turn. 'It has been found by actual use that this addition to a pianoforte does not in the least impair its qualities as a musical instrument.' (The author offers no apology for repeating this item from his previous book *Clean and Decent*. It is clearly eligible for both books, and should he write a book on pianos, he reserves the right to use it a third time.)

The 'Bed Lounge' of 1872 offers a conversion more likely to be of practical use: a sofa which becomes a twin bed. The mechanism is sound and simple; the pivoting of the lower inverted mattress enables the twin bed to be produced with one movement. The basic difficulty of the convertible sofa-bed is that a width really adequate for a bed makes the sofa too wide to sit on in comfort. Sheraton

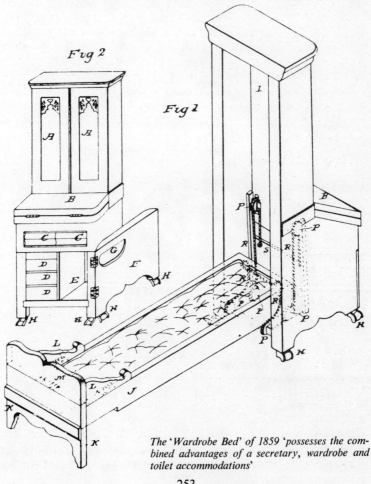

The 'Wardrobe Bed' of 1859 'possesses the combined advantages of a secretary, wardrobe and toilet accommodations'

253

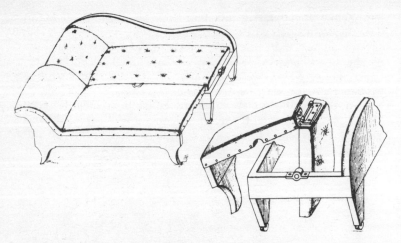

'Bed Lounge', 1822. The pivoting of the lower inverted mattress enables a twin bed to be produced with one movement

Sheraton's 'Camp Bedstead', 1803. An original solution to the problem of converting a narrow sofa into a wide bed

had offered an original solution to this difficulty in his T-shaped 'Camp Bedstead', in which the sofa was the head of the T, and its short additional upright formed the bed; though he did complicate matters by adding an elaborate 'tent'.

The 'Parlor Bed' of 1891 is merely the old wardrobe bed, but it is noteworthy for its weighty Jacobean style; one wonders why the lady shown in this expensive setting cannot run to a guest-bedroom.

American 'Parlor Bed', 1891

Inventors have been equally prolific in the field of portable folding beds for travellers, successors to the old *lits de camp*. They are specially numerous in the late eighteenth century. M. Charles invents one complete with canopy, bedding, folding stool and table, that stows in one sack, and can, he claims, be erected in two minutes. M. Tranoi's iron bed is 'without screws, bolts or hooks' but takes six minutes. Another has no component more than 3 ft. long, and goes into a portmanteau. Meanwhile many *'malles à lit'* or bed-trunks are advertised. The nobility continued to travel with their beds until the Revolution, and some of these great structures, even when dismantled, made awkward loads of which we hear as hazards to the pedestrian in narrow streets.

Visitors to the army museum at the *Invalides* may see the folding iron camp-bed on which Napoleon died—though one Major Rétif has

As a Bedstead.

'Iron Folding Chair Bedstead. Prices—Best quality, with Stout Brass Front Legs, Cushions stuffed with Wool, covered in Cretonne . . . £2.2.0. Ditto, Cheaper quality, Plain Legs . . . £1.5.0'

As a Chair.

—READING IN THE GARDEN.
SUMMER ENJOYMENT.

*'Rain me sweet odours on the air,
And wheel me up my Indian chair,
And spread some book not overwise,
Flat out before my sleepy eyes.'*
(O. W. Holmes)

The *'Triclinium'*:
left, *open for use;*
right, *folded for travelling*

256

THE PRINCE'S CHAIR

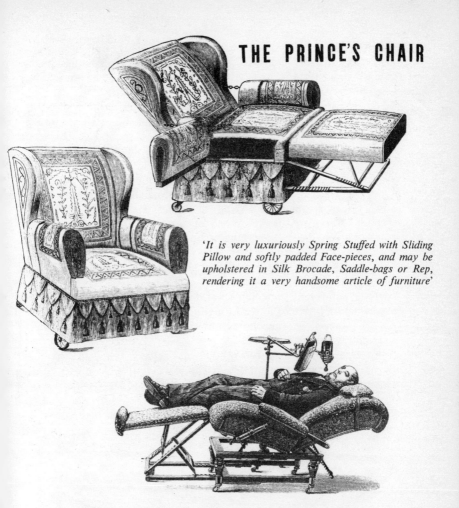

'*It is very luxuriously Spring Stuffed with Sliding Pillow and softly padded Face-pieces, and may be upholstered in Silk Brocade, Saddle-bags or Rep, rendering it a very handsome article of furniture*'

'*The Carlton Treble-Action Chair and Couch Combined. Superior quality in Walnut or Mahogany, luxuriously Spring stuffed all hair, with a German spring edge and deep top stuffing, upholstered in Rep or Tapestry. Velvet with plush borders, and Saddle-bags or Silk Brocade, extra.*'

Also the 'Literary Machine' for easy reading

*HOME COMFORTS
from the catalogue of
John Carter, 1897.*

sought a court ruling that his identical example is the authentic relic. The court, further confused by a claim that Napoleon had twin camp-beds at St. Helena, and perhaps believing that he may have died on both, has refused a decision. Wellington's camp-bed at Stratfield Saye is better authenticated. An American camp-bed of the Civil War is contrived by connecting two camp-stools 'by means of rods between which is extended a piece of sacking'. 'Graves's Combined Camp-Chest, Lounge, Table Etc.' folds to a cube of just over 2 ft., but as well as bed and table it offers two chairs, washing gear, cooking and table utensils, and a cooking stove.

An engineer has been defined as 'one who can do for a pound what any fool can do for five'. Taking the pound as a unit of weight, the standard 'service issue' camp-bed of the British forces is not the work of an engineer. Something very like the 1929 model illustrated, with its thirty-two stout oaken legs, weighing some 20 lb., was still being issued with 'Camp Kit, Officer's' in the 1940's; even to aircrew who had to fly about the world with it. Compare its metal counterpart the 'Safari Bed', in which equal strength and far greater resilience are achieved with two jointed longitudinals and four one-piece legs, all of light steel rod, the whole rolling up into a slender parcel 30 ins. long and weighing 8 lb.

An even simpler engineering solution has been found for the old problem of tilting the invalid bed. The work of all that former complex machinery is done by a few broad straps across the patient, and by two metal hoops welded to the sides of the bed. Given a healthy volunteer occupant, and rolled along the corridors at high speed, it offers a new sport to bored medicals.

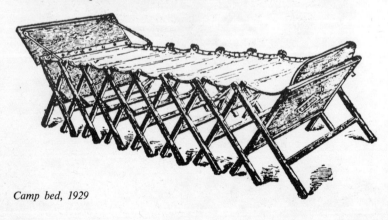

Camp bed, 1929

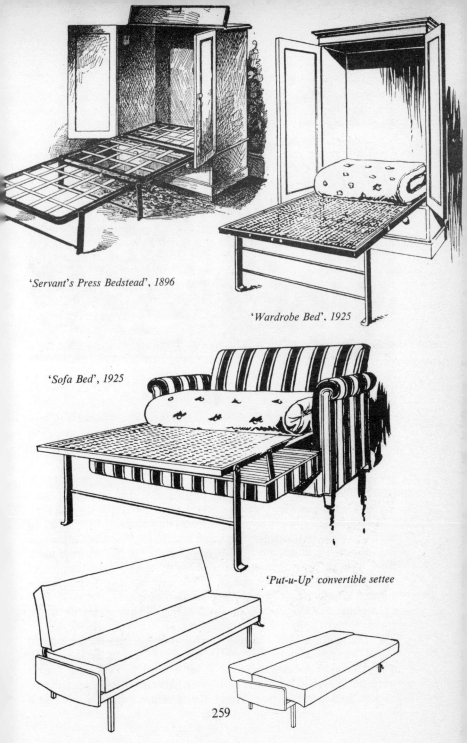

'Servant's Press Bedstead', 1896

'Wardrobe Bed', 1925

'Sofa Bed', 1925

'Put-u-Up' convertible settee

259

46

Traveller's Rest

THE first travelling bed was the man-powered, enclosed litter, with carrying-handles for porters. An arrangement of multiple handles, used in ancient China, enabled no less than sixteen porters to share the load and increased the pace; to each end of the two projecting main beams, an H-shaped extension for four men was attached by its crossbar. When horses were used, there were shafts at front and rear of the litter, and it was important that their gaits should be matched. The new habit of London prostitutes, who conduct their profession in motor-cars, recalls that an edict of the Emperor Domitian forbade the like use of double litters, which Havard calls '*alcôves ambulantes*'.

Cardinal Richelieu, bedridden in his old age but determined to travel, was not content with a mere litter. He went in his actual bed, a monumental structure worthy of his eminence. Two stout beams were put under it, with sets of leather harness whereby it could be carried by six strong men. Amid a vast retinue, and followed at a respectful distance by the gaping peasantry, the great bed went swaying up hill and down dale, on and off shipboard, and into towns whose gates might be too small, so that their walls, and perhaps a house or two, had to be demolished by masons who went ahead. When the guest-chamber for the night was on an upper floor, its window was enlarged, and a massive timber ramp was built up to the opening. Woe betide the human gimbals if they failed throughout to keep the Cardinal on an even keel. A difficult master to serve, Richelieu, and perhaps not always a welcome guest.

For an important personage or an invalid, a bed could be made up in a sufficiently roomy coach. Hobbes, the philosopher, during his last illness at the age of 91, was a dependent of the Duke of Devonshire, and

... my Lord being to remove from Chatsworth to Hardwyck, Mr. Hobbes would not be left behind; and therefore with a fetherbed laid into the Coach, upon which he lay warme clad, he was conveyed safely. . . .

though he did, alas, die soon after 'for want of the Fuell of Life'.

Mr. Pepys slept in a coach with a party of four:

... a frolic, being mighty merry, took us, and there we would sleep all night in the coach in the Isle of Dogs: so we did, there being now with us my Lady Scott; and with great pleasure drew up the glasses, and slept till daylight. . . .

but they cannot have awoken fully refreshed, for upon their morning arrival at Sir G. Carteret's, they all went to bed. A hammock was sometimes slung inside a coach; it was known in France as a *strapontin*, which still applies to the folding extra seat in a taxi-cab. It would be put fore-and-aft or athwartships according to whether the pitching or the rolling of the vehicle was worse. The height of cosy coach-sleep was reached in the field-carriage used by Napoleon in the campaign of 1815. A model of compactness, it held a light bedstead of steel. Even *le petit caporal* was too tall to lie full length in the carriage, so his feet rested inside a little box projecting in front. Thus he slumbered as he was jolted along the dreadful roads of Europe, until Waterloo, where the carriage was among the loot, ending its days in the great fire at Madame Tussaud's exhibition in London.

The first proposal for a railway 'sleeper' dates from the earliest days of the railways, when a 'coach' still meant one of the row of traditional horse-drawn-coach-type bodies that were mounted on a four-wheel truck. The idea was put forward by Lieutenant le Count of the London and Birmingham Railway, that the mail trains should include 'bed carriages':

The centre coach carries four persons inside. The first coach is built as a coupee, carrying only two persons, and the hinder part will carry either four persons sitting or two lying down. The fares, of course, correspond with the accommodation. In the bed carriage it would be double, every person occupying the usual seats of two. The carriage is divided into two parts longitudinally, so that each person lying down has half the carriage to himself; but, if two persons take this half, their fare should be lowered in proportion. The bed is made by placing a third cushion fixed to a board, which slides in between the two opposite seats, filling up the place where the legs of the passengers were. A door then lifts up at the back of the carriage, from the seat upwards, and fastens to the roof. This door opens into a boot which is fixed behind the mail, and into this opening go the feet of the person, the total length being about 6 ft. 4 in. A stuffed hair pillow is also provided.

We do not see why those who choose to pay for it could not yet have more accommodation, namely, the luxury of undressing, and going really to bed, instead of lying down without taking off their clothes, the difference in comfort between the two being so very great. All that is necessary for this purpose is to have a box containing two blankets, a pair of sheets, pillow-case, a night-cap, which could be easily stowed in the boot, and when emptied and hung up, to the roof, would form a receptacle for passengers' clothes . . . In fact, carriages could easily be constructed with bed places on each side like the cribs in sailing packets, and would doubtless pay well.

The Lieutenant had put his finger on the mechanical and financial problems that were to exercise railway engineers and directors for the next half-century, but he met no response. In England, the comparatively short rail distances offered less incentive to providing such comforts than in America, where as early as 1836 a rudimentary sleeping-car was improvised for the Cumberland Valley Railroad of Pennsylvania, although the night journey concerned, from Harrisburg to Chambersburg, took only a few hours. An ordinary day-coach was divided into four compartments, in each of which three bunks were built against one side wall. At the rear of the coach were offered the luxuries of wash-basin, water-can and towel, though there were no bed-clothes; passengers lay fully dressed on mattresses, wrapped in their overcoats or shawls. Other lines soon followed suit. Heat came from box stoves, and light from candles.

On British trains, the first form of bed offered was made by laying an extra cushion on a stretcher bridging the foot-space, as suggested by Lieutenant le Count; such was the provision in Queen Adelaide's private carriage on the London and Birmingham Railway in 1838.

Sleeping car on the Baltimore & Ohio Railroad, 1847

Known as 'the twin sticks', it survived into the 'nineties; its hire was a perquisite of the guard.

On the Erie Railroad, although its whole length could be covered in three hours, two sleeping-cars were put into service in 1843. These 'Diamond Cars' were so-called from the shape of their windows, dictated (like the 'cottage casements' of the Wellington bomber aircraft about a century later) by their diagonal frame construction. Thanks to the 6-ft. rail gauge, they were 11 ft. wide, and had six single seats on each side, in pairs back-to-back. At bedtime, a bar was slid from under a seat on the aisle side and fixed to the opposite seat. Seat cushions were laid on this bar, and rested also on a rail at the wall. The back cushions then replaced the seat cushions. This provided beds for only half the passenger capacity, and robbed the bedless even of their seats. These sleeping-cars cannot have been very comfortable or popular, for they were soon relegated to use on sidings by track-labourers.

The 'Templar night-cap for railroad, 6s. 6d. to 18s. 6d.' advertised in 1844, seems to have been before its time, for few passengers then had any opportunity to undress. No lady would travel alone at night, but by 1847, ladies travelling on the Baltimore and Ohio Railroad were offered a sleeping-car

. . . divided into several apartments or sleeping rooms each holding six beds, or rather couches, placed in three tiers along the sides. Three perpendicular straps guarantee the sleepers from falling.

The floor was of bare boards, the 'couches' were narrow wooden bunks without bedding, and the need for the perpendicular straps indicates the riding qualities of the cars; according to the illustration, no straps are provided for the topmost ladies, who need them most.

The first U.S. Patent in this field, in 1854, contrives two double beds from four seats, by hinging two seat-backs to form a low 'upper berth' as well as bridging the foot-space to form a 'lower berth' rather cramped for headroom. Four seats have at last provided four beds—of a sort. This is the basic problem: to transform *all* the seats into beds. Few passengers could afford to enjoy, and few companies therefore to provide, sleeping-cars devoted to that purpose alone, a profitless load in the daytime; but if a day-car is made convertible, a horizontal passenger must take up at least twice as much floor-space as a seated one, and the beds must somehow be stacked one above the other. By the 1850's as many as five berths were being superimposed, so that

. . . in the topmost berth, the passenger lay so close to the ceiling that he could not sit upright, and in the lowest, so close to the floor that he could look out on the soles of passing feet.

(How simple if, to this stacking of human beings, one could apply the happy solution found by the Chinese for shipping live pigs, which are dosed with opium, packed in airy wicker baskets, and piled in a ship's hold to lie in happy hog-slumber until their arrival. Not that airlines today stint the alcohol; and drugs may soon be easing the pains of prolonged space-travel.)

Soon there were countless raising, tilting, hinging, swivelling, 'reclining and self-adjustable' seats, but none survived long trial. The solution that was to stand for a century came in 1856 in Theodore T. Woodruff's two patents, the 'Seat and Couch for Railway Cars' and the 'Improvement in Railroad Car Seats and Couches', the essence of which lay in the folding of the upper berth between the wall and the ceiling.

In the democratic U.S.A. there was one travel class only—except of course for negroes and immigrants—and no luxury either by day or by night, until George M. Pullman entered the field. In 1858 he built his first sleeping-cars for the Bloomington–Chicago run on the Chicago and Alton Railroad, by remodelling two ordinary daycoaches. These were 44 ft. long mounted on four-wheel bogies, with

264

flat roofs like box-cars, little over 6 ft. high, with windows just over 1 ft. square. Into each, Pullman got ten sleeping-car sections, besides a linen-locker and two washrooms. Heated by box stoves and lit by oil lamps, they were upholstered in plush. The upper berths followed Woodruff's arrangement, and when closed, served to store the bedding. These cars cost about $1,000 each. There was no 'porter'; the brakeman made up the beds.

A Pullman conductor of 1859 describes a different type of car, with four upper and four lower berths. The backs of the seats hinged, and to make up the lower berth, the seat-back was dropped until it was level with the seat itself. The upper berths were suspended from the ceiling by ropes and pulleys, held against the ceiling by a catch during the day, and hung about half-way down at night. This seems to be the 'Hoisted Railroad Bed' found in a patent of 1858, except for the substitution of iron rods for the bulky wooden corner-posts of the patent drawing. Curtains all round each berth gave reasonable privacy. A mattress and a blanket were provided, but no sheets. The lighting was by candles, and a 'toilet room' held a tin wash-basin and a can of water. This conductor tells how he had to train the passengers to the unfamiliar habit of taking their boots off at bedtime. At first, he says, business was very poor, because people were used to sitting up all night, and did not see much point in trying

Night travel in an American 'day-coach' in the 'sixties

'Car Seat and Couch', 1854. One of the first American sleeping car patents. Beds, resembling tables, are obtained by folding over the seats and seat-backs

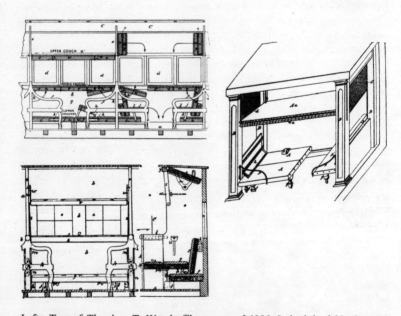

Left: *Two of Theodore T. Woodruff's patents of 1856. In both he folds the seats down to floor level. In one he dissects the upper berths; in the other he swings them up into the angle between the roof and the wall, an idea taken over by Pullman.* Right: *'Hoisted Railroad Bed', 1858. 'The upper bed is neatly fitted into the roof of the car, and when out of use is drawn up into its place. The bed is easily drawn down by the loop with pillow and blanket upon it, ready for use by two passengers'*

to sleep in a train. *Harper's Weekly* in that year jests upon this new subject:

CONVENIENCE OF THE NEW SLEEPING CARS

(*Timid Old Gent, who takes a berth in the Sleeping Car, listens.*)
BRAKEMAN: 'Jim, do you think the Millcreek Bridge safe tonight?'
CONDUCTOR: 'If Joe cracks on the steam, I guess we'll get the Engine and Tender over all right. I'm going forward!'

Progress was delayed by the Civil War until 1865, when Pullman's palatial *Pioneer* sleeping-car came into service. 'Its beauty and the artistic character of its furnishing were unprecedented', and 'it provided the comfort of a good hotel'. Fully equipped, it cost over $20,000. Mounted on bogies, it was 2 ft. 6 ins. higher and 1 ft. wider than any existing car; indeed, it was too big for any existing railroad, but one after another they raised their platform roofs and widened their bridges to suit it. The loading gauge of American railroads still follows the standard set by the *Pioneer*, the only increase since being in length. The lower berths were seats folded down to floor level, and the upper berths folded flush with the ceiling. A newspaper notes with approval the absence of 'mattresses or dingy curtains' by day, the beauty of the window-curtains 'looped in heavy folds', the 'French plate mirrors suspended from the walls', the 'several beautiful chandeliers, with exquisitely ground shades' hanging from a ceiling 'painted with chaste and elaborate design upon a delicately tinted azure ground', the black walnut woodwork and the rich Brussels carpeting. Public reaction was tested by putting the new cars, at $2 extra per night, on trains with the old ones at $1.50, which thereafter ran almost empty, and were scrapped. The *Pioneer* made its first journey in the funeral train of the murdered President Abraham Lincoln.

RAILWAY FOLDING LEG REST.

For connecting the seats of a railway carriage. With the aid of a Railway Rug a comfortable bed may be arranged for long journeys. **Price 10/6.**

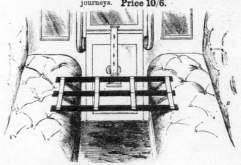

Known as 'the twin sticks', the railway leg-rest survived into the 'nineties. Its hire was a perquisite of the guard

267

In 1867 on the Great Western Railway of Canada, on which, we are told, 'a speed of forty miles an hour was often maintained for considerable periods', came the first 'hotel car', *The President*, a sleeping-car with a kitchen at one end, and tables set up by day.

The first really luxurious private sleeping-car was that embodied in the *Train Impérial* built by the Paris-Orleans company for Napoleon III in 1857, its interiors designed by none less than Viollet-le-Duc.

'Train Impérial', *presented to Napoleon III by the* Chemin de Fer de l'Est, *1855*

Powdered flunkeys served the Emperor and Empress as they lay in real beds in curtained alcoves. Queen Victoria never had a 'Royal Train', but she had several 'Royal Saloons'. Her first, built by the Great Western in 1840 for the old broad gauge (7 ft.) was not a 'sleeper', but it did have the first British railway lavatory; the South Eastern Railway's Royal Saloon of 1850 had a 'patent convenience' hidden in a sofa. By 1861 the London & North Western had provided her with a bed, and her sleeper of 1869 on this line had a sitting-room and a bedroom, with a lavatory between. So fond was she of this, that she would not allow the Company to replace it; beginning as two six-wheelers with bellows between, it was rebuilt as one long twelve-wheeler in the 'nineties, and it still survives as a museum piece. William I of Germany had three saloons—a day saloon, a study and dressing-room, and a bedroom, but with military rigour he confined himself to a simple camp-bed. A Russian sleeping-car built by the Alexandrovsky works in 1867 even had an observation compartment built above the roof, anticipating the 'vista-dome' of present American practice. In 1875 the train belonging to 'the late Emperor of the French', which had nine coaches 'communicating with each other by tastefully decorated bridges', was bought by the Czar, re-fitted, redecorated, and enlarged to fifteen saloons, running on ninety wheels, with eight sleeping-cars, including a boudoir for the Czarina and a nursery for the royal children.

The American railroad magnates had some splendid private cars;

their memory is perpetuated in *The Gold Coast*, a palace on wheels fitted up and furnished in 'Old Federal style' by Lucius Beebe and Charles Clegg, with a real fire-place in the saloon, and a Louis XV bed in the sleeping-chamber; in this, these lovers of good living have dwelt royally, on a siding at Carson City, while writing railroad history.

Britain, with its shorter and faster runs, lagged behind in the matter of sleeping-cars, but important travellers could contrive to be comfortable. In *Home Life with Herbert Spencer* we find that great philosopher arriving for a railway journey complete with carrying-chair, hammock, rugs, air-cushion, and endless paraphernalia, including his current manuscript safely tied to his waist with string. Mr. Spencer had been 'taught by experience that by travelling in a hammock when going a long journey he avoided the evil consequences which usually followed the shaking of the train'. When the rite of slinging the hammock drew a crowd, he would have the blinds drawn; then, as the train drew out, he would bend down graciously from the hammock to thank the officials—four of them were needed—'You have done very well. Good-bye.'

Night travel on the C.P.R., in 1888, involves a form of apartheid: *Scots sit on the left, Irish on the right*

269

Sleeping Car—going to Bed.

Pullman sleepers were imported from America by the Midland Railway in 1874 (see also facing page)

The first British sleeper was built by the North British works at Cowlairs in 1873. It had two three-berth compartments with three longitudinal berths in each, as well as a servants' and a luggage compartment. As in the French *lits-salon*, the seat-back was tipped over the seat to reveal a bed on the seat-back. Passengers had to bring their own bedding, and pay a supplement of 10s. over the first-class fare. A few weeks later, the London & North Western had a sleeping-saloon running in the Special Scotch Mail. It was entered through the centre compartment, which had two reversible sofas and a movable table. Each end compartment had one reversible sofa, and a Pullman-type 'section' with two armchairs drawing forward to form a lower berth, and an upper berth slung from the roof. In the same year it was announced that England was soon to be offered the joys of Pullman travel: the Midland had ordered eighteen Pullman cars, to make up two day and two night trains. The first two pairs of these stood at St. Pancras for some weeks before running, to be inspected by the wondering natives. An American visitor remarked that

270

These are the first sleeping cars in use in this country. . . . but there is no difficulty in getting a berth. They are exclusively patronised by Americans. An Englishman has a horror of being pitched into eternity in his underclothes . . . and they don't know who this Pullman is.

Bedding was provided, but it was still found necessary to print on the backs of the tickets a warning that passengers must not retire with their boots on. Meanwhile Colonel Mann, an American would-be rival to Pullman, had improvised for the Great Northern perhaps the most uncomfortable sleeping-car in history. In each of the two four-berth compartments, each passenger has one wall; they lie at right-angles, with another man's face or feet alongside each pillow. Three of the four beds embody a tip-up seat hinged to a door, one of these the lavatory door. Every time a passenger or a ticket-collector enters, or uses the lavatory, a bed must be vacated, folded and re-arranged. Mann's 'Boudoir Cars' between Vienna and Munich, much better designed, were the first public sleeping-cars on the Continent. One of his cars on the London, Chatham & Dover line had a 'Honeymoon Compartment'—but without a bed; it is a fairly short line.

Private - Room

271

Pullman cars were generally lit by Argand lamps burning paraffin, which like gas could be dangerous in an accident. It is difficult now to determine exactly what did happen on the November night of 1882 when the wooden Pullman sleeper *Enterprise* caught fire near Hunslet, Leeds, on the Midland Railway. There seems to have been a general wish to protect the reputation of the one fatal casualty, who was not only a respected doctor, but a first-class passenger. It does seem, though, that Dr. Arthur was very drunk; the conductor had not only administered soda-water, but had removed a cigar from his mouth as he lay in his richly appointed berth. According to the wood engravings in *The Graphic*, the *Enterprise* certainly made an impressive pyre.

By this time private sleepers were so common that at the carriage works at Wolverton might be seen

. . . whole stacks of mattresses, and whole piles of the neat little brass bedsteads that belong to the furnishing of night saloons . . .

Even if every bed were booked, for each passenger something over a ton of dead weight had to be hauled, the actual average being probably nearer 4 tons.

Long before that noble title '*Compagnie Générale des Wagons-lits et des Grands Express Européens*' had been lettered in gold on the (fortunately lengthy) coaches of the Continent, the prototype of the first-class sleeper of today, with side-corridor, single-berth compartments, and entrance by end vestibules, had appeared on the East coast Scotch expresses—this was in 1894. English travellers began to complain of the communal sleeping-cars of American railroads. Thus, Dr. Muirhead in 1898:

Few things provided for a class well able to pay for comfort are more uncomfortable and indecent than the arrangements for ladies on board the sleeping cars. Their dressing accommodation is of the most limited description; their berths are not segregated at one end of the car, but are scattered above and below those of the male passengers; it is considered *tolerable* that they should lie with the legs of a strange, disrobing man dangling within a foot of their noses.

(Sixty years later, a Hollywood film-producer would consider this not merely *tolerable*, but great fun, and a fine subject for a romp.) In 1922, H. W. Nevinson was making similar criticisms of

. . . long trains where one smokes in a lavatory, and sleeps at night upon a shelf screened with heavy green curtains and heated with stifling air, while over your head or under your back the baby yells, and the mother tosses moaning . . .

Queen Victoria's two coaches for Continental travel, in the 'nineties, contained a drawing-room, a dressing-room in Japanese style with much bamboo, and a bedroom with two beds, the larger for the Queen. Beyond was 'a sort of luggage room' where the maids slept on sofas. 'The bedding is the Queen's own,' we are assured, 'and she takes it away on leaving the train.' In Queen Alexandra's bedroom on the Royal Train of the London & North Western, the bed was 'tented'. King George V inherited it. King Edward VII's saloon, built by the East coast companies in 1908, was in advance of its time in that it had an early form of air-conditioning.

Third-class sleepers, long established in Russia and in Scandinavia, reached Britain in 1928. At first, except on the Great Western, they were convertible day-coaches with folding upper berths; there was still some mixing of the sexes, and undressing tended to be furtive and incomplete. By the 1930's unconvertible third-class sleepers were in service. The current layout puts upper and lower berths on each side of a central aisle. The British first-class sleeper has not changed basically since 1900, though its style changes with fashion, subject to a lag of a decade or two, and to its private cell are added such minor luxuries as air-flow and temperature under the passenger's control, a collapsible wash-stand, a desk, a thermos bottle, a 'dental faucet', and a 'shoe servidor' whereby shoes can be taken for cleaning

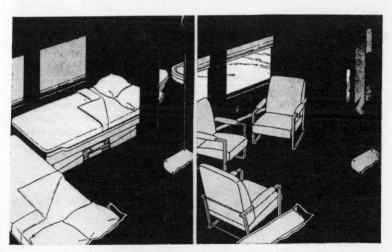

Pullman 'Master Room', convertible for day or night use, 1939

273

and returned by unseen hands. The second-class sleeper of today (third class having vanished in our equalising society), with upper and lower berths, only two to a compartment, compares well with the Continental six-berth '*couchette*', rather reminiscent of a family vault. Thanks to the train ferry, you can now sleep all the way from London to Paris.

The tale of luxuries on wheels may well include an unpublished passage by the hand of a railway authority who will prefer to remain anonymous:

I used sometimes to go north by the old 7.40 p.m. Euston to Inverness, which stopped at Bletchley to make an Oxford connection. When it stopped one summer evening, two expensive-looking ladies of London alighted from one Inverness sleeper without luggage and disappeared down the platform. One of my friends on the L.M.S. said this was quite common. They returned to London by a late train while their clients went on to Scotland. A first-class single berth might be close, but it was also cosy!

This recalls Jessica Mitford's account of a naughty establishment in Paris, where those addicted to fellow-travellers, but having no other cause for a journey, could hire a convincing replica of a Pullman sleeper, complete with synthetic vibrations, sound-effects, and painted scenery moving past the windows.

A tail-piece to our chapter is provided by the *Daily Telegraph*'s account of proceedings at Clerkenwell magistrate's court in April 1961, against a bricklayer and a plumber's mate:

P.C. Cecil Wackett said: 'These two men were lying full length, taking up four seats each, on a Circle line train. They went round and round the Circle for four hours before I finally got them off the train at King's Cross.

'They were told once at Aldgate station to get off the train after a porter had noticed them still snoozing away as the train visited the station twice in succession as it made its way round the Circle. They told him to blow off.

'When I questioned them they said they had been up all night and wanted to sleep. They had with them a ticket bought at Piccadilly at 6.20 a.m. today and it was 10.10 a.m. when I woke them at King's Cross.'

Mr. Powell said: 'It sounds like a case of Weary Willie and Tired Tim. They seem to like trains.'

(*Our book, as noted on page 112, got off the train of historical sequence at Waterloo; having completed our diversionary circuit, we now resume an orderly chronology.*)

John Leech, Punch, *c. 1850*

47

The Holy of Holies

I N Victorian England, according to the social historians, a new
and prosperous middle class is emerging—indeed, predominat-
ing. It is with good reason that we visualise the Victorian
bedroom as being in a middle-class household. The nobility and
gentry (politically and artistically conservative) are still bedded much
as of old, because they will neither put 'modern' furniture into an
older architectural setting, nor lightly gut an interior by Adam or
Kent to conform with current fashion. They are not interested in the
new machine-made replicas of Art; they have inherited the real thing,
which they need not yet start selling to America. It is the successful
manufacturer (politically a liberal, artistically a savage, and content
to derive his Art as well as his income from the factory) who has the
new 'mansion' and the big money to spend inside it. The lower orders,
when they can refurnish at all, probably have older second-hand
pieces—such as might nowadays be fairly good Georgian antiques.
The middle-class bedroom therefore is the type of the time.

275

SERVANTGALISM.—No. VI.

Lady. "WISH TO LEAVE? WHY, I THOUGHT, THOMPSON, YOU WERE VERY COMFORTABLE WITH ME!"

Thompson (who is extremely refined). "HOH YES, MAM' I DON'T FIND NO FAULT WITH YOU, MAM—NOR YET WITH MASTER—OUT THE TRUTH HIS, MAM—THE HOTHER SERVANTS IS SO 'ORRID VULGAR, AND HIGNORANT, AND SPEAKS SO HUNGRAMMATICAL, THAT I REELY CANNOT LIVE IN THE SAME 'OUSE WITH 'EM—AND I SHOULD LIKE TO GO THIS DAY MONTH, IF SO BE HAS IT WON'T ILLCONVENIENCE YOU!"

John Leech, Punch, *1853*

The 'Victorian style' does not accede with Victoria in 1837. The bedrooms pictured by Phiz in Dickens' works, and by Leech in *Punch*, until about 1850, are still what we would call 'Regency'. The stuffiness, the over-elaboration, the phoney mediaevalism, the machine-made Art in substitute materials, all the bobbles and aspidistras and anti-macassars that have aroused so much laughter until lately (but are now being sought anew in the antique shops)—these stem from the Great Exhibition of 1851, the Paris Exhibition of 1855, the South Kensington Exhibition of 1862. As late as 1878 there are still die-hards who favour some 'Regency' restraint, and have to be reproved by an apostle of the 'modern' fashion:

I am always longing to overlay a little of the modish primness of the distant days we are now copying, with something of this busy nineteenth century's tokens of a love of art and literature . . .

says Lady Barker. Mr. von Falke in *Art in the House*, in 1879, is even more smugly confident in the rightness of current taste:

. . . from the early part of the present century, until the impetus given to Art by the great Exhibition had had time to take effect, the general taste in

276

furnishing houses of all but a very few persons, was at about its worst . . . It cannot be doubted that the efforts made in our day to diffuse aesthetic knowledge and promote sound taste will be rated in future histories of the latter half of the nineteenth century as one of its most striking features.

The High Victorian style thereafter endures so long, percolating down to the lower class levels, that much of the expensive Victoriana that now adds quaint charm to commuters' cottages was discarded only yesterday.

But when we arrive with our notebook at the Victorian bedroom door, we may find it locked. We know what the furnishings are; we have the catalogues; but we can only guess what goes on among them. A taboo has fallen. No longer do *pater* and *mater* lie cheerfully before all in the *lectus genialis*. Queen Victoria is never seen again in her dressing-gown, after that historic morning at Kensington Palace in 1837. No wedding-guests escort Mr. and Mrs. Gladstone with flowers and laughter into their bridal chamber. *Fun in Bed* will not be conceivable as a book title for another century yet. The novelists and biographers stay discreetly on the ground floor; even Lytton Strachey seldom penetrates upstairs. Until the 'nineties, furniture manufacturers no more dare to illustrate a complete bedroom, even unoccupied, than to illustrate a lavatory. Strange, that this sex-taboo should have ruled at the very time when the gospel of *production* applied as much in the home as in the factory. As the author of *The Victorian Tragedy* remarks,

. . . one wonders, sometimes, how beings so apparently devoid of fleshly passion as the heroes and heroines of most Victorian novels could ever have affected the transition from courtship to parenthood. It has been asserted that the Brownings—two of the greatest lovers, in all conscience, that ever lived—never saw each other naked. Evidence on such a point must be hard to collect, and the statement itself may conceivably have originated in a deduction from an article of Victorian faith, that the Holy of Holies is as proper within as without.

When one does piece together the picture of the Holy of Holies, the first impression is that it is rather dark and stuffy. At least half of the light from the window is trapped by the curtains even when they are open, and at the first hint of direct sunlight they are closed completely, or the blind is drawn. Behind them, the glass is so festooned with *guipure vitrage* ('lace curtains' to those of commoner speech; costing from 10½d. a yard) as to suggest that somebody's underwear has been hung up to dry. No good housewife has less than two pairs of lace curtains for every window; the most curious of neighbours will

277

catch no glimpse of life within. The windows of the nursery and the sick-room in particular should, by 9 or 10 a.m., be

. . . shut up rigorously, darkening those on which the sun would beat, *out-side* the glass—by means of blinds or outer shutters—until the evening.

To keep the window in the least open overnight is 'a risk—nay, a certainty—of illness to some very young children, to many old people, and to nearly all invalids'. (Of these invalids there are plenty; nobody stays quite well for very long, and every household seems to have its Brer Tarrypin 'lounjun 'roun en suffer'n'. Writers on domestic arts always devote a chapter to the sick-room. Surgical operations are performed in the home, and child-bearing, in the best bedroom, as a matter of course.) Dr. Squire allows that a healthy person's window may be partly open on *summer* nights; Mrs. Gladstone will have it opened only on rising; *The Handbook of the Toilet* holds that ventilation will be sufficient if the 'register' of the fire-place is left open in *warm* weather. Lacking this device, the flue can be blocked up with a bag of straw (there are records of alarming occasions when its presence was forgotten and the fire lit), and the doorway can be sealed up with strips of lint. The fear of sunlight probably meant no more than that of fading the aniline-dyed curtains and carpet ('and before you let the sun in, mind it wipes its shoes', says Mrs. Ogmore-Pritchard in *Under Milk Wood*), but it is harder to find a basis for the fear of fresh air, and the especial terror of 'night air'. The swampy vapours of the Maremma may well have been thought poisonous, before men learned of the connection between mosquitoes and malaria; but even London air does not become corrupt because darkness falls. Plumbing standards were such that there might indeed be a vent from a soil-pipe just below the window, but air drawn from inside the house would be no purer. Perhaps such risks were subconsciously invented to give some zest to a home life that could hardly be described as exciting. With most outdoor activities barred to ladies, and most indoor ones left to a plentiful staff, there was little left for wives and daughters but reading and embroidery. Their boredom may have been relieved by the flavour of danger brought into the daily round by the warnings of every doctor and domestic adviser: against chills and fevers borne by poisonous winds, the 'exchange of emanations' between unsealed bedrooms, diseases arising from over-heavy bed-clothes, shock from cold beds, enervation from warm ones, malformation due to high pillows, septic changes in the paste used by the paper-hanger, walls that 'attract and retain objectionable atoms', 'delirious fancies' induced by patterned papers, poisoning from green wallpaper or from flowers,

278

'giddiness and malaise' from gas lighting, 'the evil that may spring from imperfectly dried feathers', the 'pernicious gas' that lies like a lake two feet deep over every bedroom floor, even 'ornamental plaster liable to give way and fall down at any moment' on to the bed; not to mention the moral evil awaiting young persons who did not sleep with their hands folded on their chests as if in prayer.

The bedroom is large—its size partly dictated by the builder's preference for brick partitions exactly corresponding with those of the reception floor below. Its shape, maybe only a simple rectangle, is not immediately apparent, it is so completely dominated by its furniture. It is significant that we can no longer identify any cabinet-makers. In the previous century, these had ranked almost as artists; now, names disappear as the machine takes over. Its output is all too plentiful, but the bedroom chattels, even if new, are so miscellaneous that no formal relation between any two items seems to be intended. There is no more sense of space than in an over-stocked antique shop. It is difficult to move about without knocking things over, though the mistress of the house must do so in a crinoline. The great 'French' double bed is of brass, from Birmingham, where the output of brass beds in 1849 was a mere 400 a week, but rose soon after the Exhibition to some 5,000. It is probably a half-tester, with lace curtains elaborately festooned and gathered and ribboned; a high proportion of fires in the home at this period is recorded as due to candles near bed-curtains. The feather-mattresses are piled so high that bed-steps are still needed, and so soft that to lie down is 'like dropping into light dough'. On either side of the bed, a night-table conceals a chamber-pot, perhaps supplemented by a 'commode', though this convenience may be concealed within the bed-steps. At the foot of the bed is a day-couch, its leather stuffed with horsehair, its railway-waiting-room severity relieved by cushions and antimacassars gay with crewel-work in Berlin wool and beads. The wardrobe is so enormous that a later generation may cut it into two or even three. The dressing-table is so draped with frilly muslin over 'batiste' that its structure can only be guessed at (there is an example in Tenniel's illustration for *Alice in Wonderland*, showing the lobster brushing his hair—strictly according to the text he should be *sugaring* his hair, but we cannot give time to the matter). The wash-stand, with a marble top, is either mahogany or walnut, or perhaps one of Mr. Bray's 'wash-stands of *papier-maché*, japanned and ornamented with gold mouldings'. It carries flowered bowls and jugs, china soap-dishes and sponge-bowls, tooth-glasses and water bottles on brackets; below is a china slop-pail and perhaps a china foot-bath. There is no bathroom; the bath is a portable one, but it may be kept permanently

The bedroom furniture of 1878 has at least a certain massive respectability

280

in the dressing-room, or in a recess or curtained corner in the bed-room itself. Every gallon of water, cold or hot, for washing or bathing, is carried up from the basement, and back again. Running water in the bedroom, or even on the upper floor at all, is still a rare luxury until the 'seventies.

The marble of the mantelpiece, with the texture and colour of brawn, is almost hidden behind its 'mantel-drape' of embroidery and ball-fringe. There is an ormolu clock, but no alarm-clock; this vulgar object belongs in the servant's room; it is significant that an alarm-clock shown at the Great Exhibition is called a 'servants' regulator'. Even the bell-handles flanking the fire-place are beribboned. (These may survive to puzzle the great-grandchildren: 'Mummy, what are bells *for*?') The 'whatnots', the occasional tables of bamboo or of *papier-maché* inlaid with mother-of-pearl, and the Gothic fret-work brackets, hold anything and everything from a Bible to 'a pin-cushion in the form of a harp'. The pattern of the wallpaper is bold, but hardly one full repeat can be seen between the pictures and photographs in frames of every shape, size and material: perhaps 'yellowing dickybird-watching pictures of the dead', though no truly refined lady will undress in a bedroom where a gentleman's portrait hangs—the strictest of them, it is said, would allow books by male and female authors to adjoin on the shelves in the living-rooms, but not in the bedrooms. No object of any decorative value—and few objects are not—is likely to be stored away out of sight. It is to be hoped that the life of the occupants is more harmonious than their surroundings, for this would hardly be a room in which to have an angry spouse start throwing things.

The daily dusting involves moving pin-trays, hair-tidies, button-hooks, ring-stands, vases, ferns, statuettes, albums and pomatum-pots; and amid this hoop-la the housemaid has to carry out her bed-making. Fortunately she has ample guidance, printed so that she may absorb it during her half-day free in seven. The Rev. J. P. Faun-thorpe's *Readings in Necessary Knowledge for Girls and Young Women* is judged by *The Saturday Review* to be a useful prize in any Sunday school, and particularly suitable as a present to a young ser-vant. Passing reluctantly over the chapters headed 'Necessity for Clothing' and 'Importance of Needlework and Knitting', we come to 'A Week's Work in a Well-Regulated House':

First, what do we mean by a well-regulated house? The word regulated comes to our language from the Latin *regulo*, which signifies to rule or direct, and *regulus* in the same tongue means a king or chieftain. Therefore we see that whenever anything has to be regulated or ruled, it requires some competent person to take the direction and management of it. . . .

281

Now all of you girls hope to become women, but then you must not forget that you will have to bear many responsibilities, and to fulfil numerous duties of which you are now ignorant. . . .

Numerous indeed the duties were, and even better detailed in Lady Darling's *Simple Rules for the Guidance of Persons in Humble Life, More Particularly for Young Girls Going Out to Service*:

As soon as the family are settled at breakfast, she should go through all the chambers, opening the windows and stripping the beds; this should be done in a neat manner (and by all means with clean hands and a clean apron), not suffering the bed clothes to drag on the floor, or turning them head to feet, or inside outwards; to secure this when clean sheets are put on, let the right side of the under sheet be uppermost, and the mark at the right hand corner at the head of the bed; let the right side of the upper sheet be placed inwards, and the mark at the left hand corner, at the head of the bed.

(One suspects that the mistress may have had to repeat the latter part of that sentence slowly before the Person in Humble Life quite grasped it.)

In stripping, place two chairs at the foot of the bed, and remove each article by itself, smoothly and carefully doubled, and they will always come right. Feather beds must be thoroughly well shaken, and turned daily; and mattresses should be turned once a-week. Having stripped and shaken all the beds, they may be left to air, and settle while the housemaid empties all the slops, and scalds the different vessels, wiping them dry with cloths kept for the purpose; then go round again, making up the beds in the same order in which they were stripped; fold the curtains, lay them across the head and foot of the bed, unless they be looped up; draw the flue from under the bed with a long broom, or in hot weather with a damp mop; dust every article of furniture in the same manner as in the parlour, and last of all fill all the ewers and water bottles with soft and spring water, as may be ordered.

Better still, 'maids being what they are', let the mistress ensure that the airing of the bed is not skimped, by herself taking everything off it each morning, dotting the pillows about on chairs, hanging the bed-clothes around the room, and even hauling the mattress daily over to the window. At intervals the feather-bedding must be emptied into a porous bag, beaten to extract the dust and restore the springiness, and replaced in ticking newly waxed to keep the feathers from coming through. Why give the maid more than half a day off in seven? Even if she has time for more relaxation, she will lack the energy to enjoy it. She is unlikely to give notice; it is an employers' market: in

282

1851 agriculture (with 1,790,000 employed) was the only trade class that outnumbered domestic service (with 1,039,000).

The cluttering-up of the bedroom seems to have been a purely British habit, as evidence the comments of a French visitor, Hippolyte Taine, in the 'sixties. He is staying at what he calls a 'cottage', but as the owner keeps three or four horses, two carriages, six indoor servants and a gardener, we may call it a week-end house.

Not an article in the house but it bears witness to a studied and even meticulous taste . . . In my bedroom the table is of rare wood; on it, a square of marble, on the marble a round mat of woven rushes, all this to carry an ornamental water carafe capped with a drinking glass. One does not simply put a book down on the table, there is a little rack on it especially placed to hold books. You are not provided simply with a candlestick and candle which you blow out when you want to sleep. The candle is in a wide lamp-glass equipped with an automatic extinguisher. There are other even more striking details, and one has to stop and think for a moment before grasping the use of them. Sometimes all this apparatus seems rather a nuisance; it is taking too much trouble merely to be comfortable.

As you travel south through France and Italy, he adds, life becomes less encumbered with 'inconvenient conveniences'.

An Englishwoman, he tells us,

. . . does not dress to please her husband, does not know how to make herself attractive, and has not the gift of being *coquette* and *piquante* in the privacy of her own home.

This was certainly true of her night-wear, though it is unlikely that Taine ever saw it. The authors of *The History of Underclothes* offer a good reason for its forbidding aspect:

The fact that (respectable) women began to wear 'attractive' nightwear only after the introduction, in the early eighties of last century, of the practice of birth-control, has an obvious implication. In the days of unlimited birth-rate the feminine nightdress was markedly unappealing: perhaps a calculated discretion.

The night-dress in Leech's drawing of 1850 is certainly not much more appealing than its wearer. A lady's night-cap fitted her head like a baby's bonnet, sometimes frilled to frame the face, and tied under the chin. Prices of 1851 include:

Longcloth nightdress, 2*s*. 6*d*.
Nightcaps, 6*s*. to 10*s*. a dozen.
Longcloth frilled nightdresses, plain 3*s*. 6*d*., richly trimmed, 7*s*. 6*d*.

283

But the last of these items would be thought rather daring. Not until the 'seventies do we find nighties 'as much trimmed down the back of the bodice as the front' or with the 'Watteau pleat'.

The Englishwoman's Domestic Magazine of 1866 reveals that young ladies were not only laced tightly into stays to attain 'the fascinating undulations that Art affords to nature', but had to sleep in them. At one boarding school where stays were compulsory, they were sealed up by the mistress on Monday morning, and removed only on Saturday for one hour 'for the purpose of ablution'. A mother remarked that sleeping in stays 'carried no hardship beyond an occasional fainting fit'.

Men's night-shirts increased to a more decent length, and could further be kept under control by tying the hem to the ankles with elastic. Most men still wore night-caps; the 'Officer's Kit and Equipment in the Field', as per *Army Circular* dated 1st December 1877, includes:

1 Map of the Country
Sword
Pistol
1 Woollen Nightcap

*Jaeger nightgown of
the 1880's*

and this last item was also obligatory for the 'Autumn Manoeuvres'. Martial fibre seems to have softened since the day when Wellington had remarked

In Spain I shaved myself over-night, and usually slept five or six hours; sometimes, indeed, only three or four, and sometimes only two. In India I never undressed; it is not the custom there; and for many years in the Peninsula I undressed very seldom; never for the first four years.

But it is time to move further down the social scale.

284

48

The Seamy Side

To learn how 'the other half' slept—to explore the couches of The Great Unwashed—we can find no better guide than Henry Mayhew. Between 1846 and 1860 he toured the prisons of London. A generation earlier, Rowlandson and Pugin had illustrated, in 'The Pass-Room at Bridewell', 'beds' formed of rows of planks set on edge on the floor, fixed by angle-irons at the ends; each sty was filled with loose straw. Mayhew could record some improvement. He did find the prisons crowded, for it was all too easy to get oneself 'inside'. At the House of Correction in Tothill Fields, partly a juvenile prison, a 16-year-old was in for a month for *'going into Kensington Gardens to sleep'* when his father had refused to keep him. A 10-year-old was in for *'spinning a top'*, and an 8-year-old was doing fourteen days, with a flogging, for *'stealing 6 plums from an orchard'*. Two thirds of these young criminals slept in separate cells measuring 8 ft. by 6 ft. The agreed minimum cubic capacity for a sleeper, actually being provided in the New Model Prison at Pentonville ('an admirably contrived hive made of iron', says Taine), was 900 cu. ft. These cells gave 432 cu. ft. There was no means of warming or lighting. The rest of the boys slept in a dormitory, fifty of them on iron bedsteads most of which, according to the dimensions of the room, must have touched; and a further thirty-seven on mattresses on the floor. With 350 cu. ft. each (about a

285

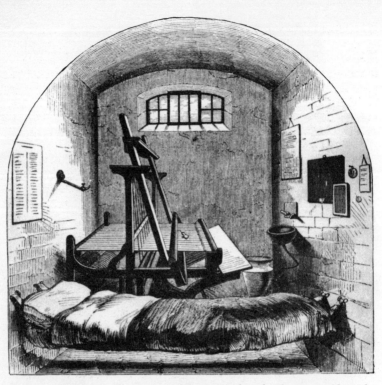

Separate cell in Pentonville Prison, with hammock slung for sleeping, and loom for day-work, 1850

7-ft. cube) they were locked up here, with two officers to watch the eighty-seven, from 6 p.m. till 6.30 a.m., with no occupation whatever save whispered mutual instruction in crime. Adult prisoners, under the dreadful 'silent system', however well-behaved, were separately confined for twelve hours a day, and might not speak a word to a fellow-prisoner throughout the twenty-four. The separate cell usually had a hammock, slung at night across the width of the cell from hooks in the walls. At the House of Correction in Coldbath Fields the hammock was of coconut fibre, 'brown and bending as a strip of mahogany veneer'. It had one advantage over the bed: one of the stout brass rings by which it was slung, if detached, made an excellent knuckle-duster for felling a warder; or one could tie the ring to a short rope and get a proper swing at him.

In the old Coldbath Fields prison, built in 1794, the cells had only 502 cu. ft., and in the new prison, even less. Hearing that the men prefer the cells in summer, but the dormitory in winter, Mayhew

286

asks about the heating system, and learns that there is none. He sees no gas or other lighting in the cells, but it is explained that none is needed, because when it is dark the prisoners go to bed. In winter, therefore, they pass twelve hours alone in complete darkness. If a prisoner is taken ill, he has no means of attracting attention. Let it be hoped that he is so worn out by a day of 'grinding the wind' on the treadmill—in which useless labour he may have climbed over a mile vertically in the day—that he sleeps soundly and careless of comfort on his *lit de justice*.

The dormitories are at least sociable, if silent. There are five of these, with from 82 to 101 'beds' in each. They are ventilated—by a hole in the wall near roof level—and lit by gas; prisoners may read selected improving works such as *Self Help* until 10 o'clock. There are lavatories at each end, 'made out of slate'. Every inch of space is used. Four stout iron tubes, resting on supports a foot from the floor, run along the entire length of the room at 6-ft. intervals. From these tubes hammocks are slung in three rows, forming one great sea of canvas, leaving only a 5-ft. passage at one side along which the warders patrol.

The sides of the hammocks curl round the prisoners' forms, so that they look like so many mummies ranged along three deep . . . So silent was the room, it seemed like an immense deadhouse—as if we had entered some huge morgue, where some hundred corpses were laid out on the floor before us.

But being so closely packed, they perhaps whispered faintly of nights.

Dormitory at Coldbath Fields Prison, 1850

287

In the notorious Newgate Prison, conditions seem to have been better, despite the gruesome tales told when it was pulled down in 1904 to make way for the present 'Old Bailey'. (The demolition of a prison is a good occasion to publicise its defects, thus diverting attention from evils that continue elsewhere.) A visitor in 1827 reported that 'a most exemplary cleanliness reigns throughout', and although seven or eight shared a room, each was allowed a mattress, two blankets, and coals for a fire. Mayhew found them sleeping in comparatively tolerable three-tier bunks.

At Millbank Prison, in some of the dormitories, instead of a hammock or bunk, the prisoner enjoyed 'an iron framework, resting at the head and foot on two large stone supports'; in others, a flat wooden board which served both as a bedstead and as a work-table for tailoring. Those under correction at Wandsworth in 1846 were sleeping four to a cell, on mattresses on the floor, one lying crossways, and the other three sharing a space 3 ft. 9 in. wide, under the same covering. The Female Convict Prison at Brixton had a decorative feature that anticipates the modern taste for differing walls: although the new cells were smaller than the old, they had 'not nearly so jail-like a look about them; for the sides of these are built of corrugated iron'.

Separate sleeping-cell in one of the new wings of the Female Convict Prison at Brixton, 1850

288

In spite of miseries enough to determine the released prisoner never again to sleep on a prison bed, it must not be supposed that the joys of freedom necessarily involved better sleeping conditions. The system of *useless* prison labour might well have been designed to determine him never to work again, and few old lags would rise above the level of the rookery or the common lodging-house. According to Mayhew, perhaps one-tenth of the 'low lodging-houses' might offer a family a separate room, but the general rule was to let out 'beds' by the night. The usual charge was 2*d.*, but a small child might be admitted for 1*d.* The windows had rather more paper, or other substitutes, than glass: 'the windows there, sir, are not to let the light in, but to keep the cold out'. A resident in a lodging-house near Drury Lane assured Mayhew that 'you could study the stars, if you were so minded, through the holes left by the slates having been blown off'. He had slept in rooms holding thirty where twelve would have been a proper number, and their breaths rose 'in one foul, choking steam of stench'; it was a matter of routine to collect a handful of bugs from the bed-clothes and crush them under the candlestick. Not only did two or three share a bed none too large for one, but between and partly under the beds were other bodies on the floor. In the better establishments such a 'shake-down' would be a thin palliasse; in the worst, a bundle of rags; loose straw, we are told, was used only in the country. At busy times, many slept in the kitchen, men and women huddled together ('where indecencies are common enough') with nothing but their clothes between them and the stone or brick floor. This saved the lodger 1*d.*, and enabled one landlord to house as many as 200. Another landlord did provide real beds, for when the Small Pox Hospital at King's Cross was pulled down, he bought enough for four lodging-houses, which cost him only £20 because nobody else would bid for this infected furniture. Rather better was a dockland lodging-house where eighty-four bunks were fitted in, each 1 ft. 10 in. wide, with low partitions between them, each having a raised 'grating' holding a straw mattress. 'The coverings are a leather or a rug, but leathers are generally preferred'— the luxury of these comparatively bugless leathers cost 2*d.* a night. After the scare of the cholera epidemics, many houses took to washing the rugs and blankets from time to time. In 1844 in the rookery of St. Giles, the charge was as high as 4*d.* a night in the upper rooms and 3*d.* in the cellars, though after six nights the seventh was free. There were advantages here to justify the price: this area abounded in courts, back-yards with low walls, and connected cellars, affording easy escape to any resident sought by the 'officers of justice'. Some houses had escape routes from the upper sleeping quarters, from one back window to the next, by way of rows of spike nails in the outside wall; one row to step on, another above to hold.

Common lodging-houses were licensed as such after Shaftesbury's Lodging House Bill was forced through Parliament in 1851. Good results were not immediate; in a licensed lodging-house Mayhew counted about ninety persons sleeping in three rooms. But one of the more respectable houses now offered iron bedsteads with flock-mattresses, two sheets, blanket, coverlet and pillow, for 3*d*. a night. The rooms were ventilated by a flue, and other advantages included religious services and tracts supplied by the rector of Christ Church, and water-closets. Mayhew could now say that there were only about thirty 'filthy receptacles' of the worst class in London; on these he records the comments of two inmates:

When a man's lost caste in society, he may as well go thé whole hog, bristles and all, and a low lodging-house is the entire pig.

Why, in course, sir . . . you *must* get half-drunk, or your money for your bed is wasted. There's so much rest owing to you, after a hard day; and bugs and bad air'll prevent its being paid, if you don't lay in some stock of beer, or liquor of some sort, to sleep on. It's a duty you owes yourself . . .

Beds were to let for other purposes than sleep; thus, according to Taine:

Throughout the day, in the Strand and Haymarket, a large number of shops and more or less respectable-looking houses display this notice: 'Beds to Let.' At evening, in the same places and elsewhere, numerous figures are to be seen entering and leaving, figures which have the bearing, the look, the gravity which is peculiarly English.

Other reformers following in Mayhew's footsteps were exposing some frightful slum bedrooms. Charles Kingsley, in a tailor's sweat-shop, found the tailor, his wife, his sister-in-law, four children and six men, all living in two rooms, of which the *larger* was 10 ft. by 8 ft. Turn-up beds enabled the room to serve as a workshop during the day. The six men slept, three in a bed, in the smaller room. The attention of the Queen herself was drawn to such evils: when an earnest clergyman from the East End told her of seven persons sleeping in one bed, she made a memorable comment: 'Had I been one of them I would have slept on the floor.' One of the first practical examples of housing improvement was 'Prince Albert's Model Dwelling' of 1851: four flats in a block, with living-room, scullery, water-closet, and three bedrooms whose 'external ventilation' was thought worth mention. One bedroom was of 100 sq. ft., and two of 50 sq. ft. Each flat cost about £450, and could be let at 3s. 6d. or 4s. a week, though this rent was within the means only of a mechanic in good and regular work.

Middle-class flats, common for centuries on the Continent, did not appear in London until the 'fifties, the pioneer block being in Ashley Gardens, Westminster. Gradually losing its association with the working-class tenement, the flat became acceptable at higher income-levels, and Londoners grew inured to the odd experience of living and sleeping on the same floor.

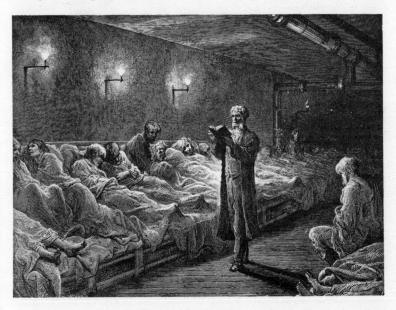

Night Refuge in Smithfield, 1872

'*The superintendent is a mild, but firm, intelligent and discerning man. He distributes the regulation lump of bread to the guests, and they pass on, by way of the bath—rigorously enforced for obvious reasons—to the dormitories set out like barracks, and warmed with a stove, which is always the centre of attraction. Here, when all are in bed, a Bible-reader reads, comforting, let us hope, many of the aching heads. The women and children have a ward apart. . . . some have cast themselves to rest under the leather coverings and, with inexpressible weariness, are in the land of dreams. I have paced these dormitories early and late, and have been with strong men who have burst into tears, as their eyes have fallen upon the rows of sleeping mothers . . . young and old are here—houseless, and with babes to carry forth to-morrow into the east wind and sleet. This story is told by the coughs that crackle like a distant running fire of musketry—all over the establishment.*'

(B. Jerrold)

291

The Charité *Hospital, Paris*

49

The Dying House

THERE is an old connection between the prison and the hospital, especially evident in France with its *hospices-prison*. The idea that crime is a disease, and disease a crime occurred before *Erewhon*. Typhus was known equally as 'gaol fever' and as 'hospital fever', and was contracted inside the hospital more often than it was brought in to be nursed. The first hospitals were founded, by healthy persons, more to protect themselves by isolating the sick than in much hope of curing them. The crowded hospital was regarded as a dying-house that the wise would refuse to enter. Bedfellows were associated regardless of their diseases, and a trio might comprise one ill, one dying, and one dead. Only in quite recent times has every patient been able to expect a bed to himself. At the notorious *Hôtel-Dieu* in Paris, there were four or five to a bed in 1625, and although a legacy was then earmarked for the provision of single iron beds,

292

conditions had grown worse a century later. 1,219 beds served at least 3,000 persons when the death-rate happily kept pace with a current epidemic; up to 6,000 when it did not. Most of the beds held six or eight, thanks to a double-decker arrangement. Above, half of the sad company slept; below, the others awaited their turn. Another attempt to provide single beds—this time by the benefaction of Mme Pompadour—seems also to have failed, for by 1787 the practice was to put two or three at the head of a bed, while between their faces were two or three pairs of reciprocal feet.

At the Manchester Infirmary (founded in 1752, and 'Royal' from 1830) life was a little better, and death a little easier, with never more than two to a bed; most of the beds had the hygienically doubtful advantage of curtains. Under regulations of 1771, every new admission had clean sheets, to be changed every three weeks, and two might not share a bed 'except that there is no spare bed in the house'.

In Paris under the Commune of 1792, wounded 'comrades' enjoyed the special favour of separate beds, at the expense of the politically unsound who therefore had to lie in sixes. An ingenious architect contrived—and the authorities rejected—a '*lit tournant*' in which, he claimed, up to twelve patients could lie, isolated by curtains, radiating in a circle with feet inmost, like soldiers in a bell-tent. In 1793 at the *Conciergerie*, a prison-hospital, an inspector found forty-five men sharing ten *grabats* (crude low single beds); fourteen sharing four; thirty-eight dying in nine; in three cells, eighty-five men sharing sixteen *paillasses*; fifty-four women sharing nineteen. When a patient was so lucky as to die, his face was covered with the blanket shared by his companions, who had to await the regulation hour for the removal of the corpse. (Even this was not overcrowding by the standards of English workhouses: in the Shoreditch parish workhouse, thirty-nine children were sharing three beds.)

The rule of 'one patient, one bed' was again imposed—and again had to be relaxed—at Manchester in the 1840's. There was trouble over bed-linen being burned by patients smoking in the ward, and a 'No Smoking' rule came in. One of the students caused trouble, too, according to the Minute Book of 1818:

In consequence of the accident by fire which has taken place in Mr. Midgley's apartment it was resolved unanimously:

1st. That Mr. Midgley shall not be permitted to have the use of a candle on going to bed for three months from this time.
2nd. That the House Apothecary by himself or his deputy before he retires to rest, visit the apartment of all the apprentices to be assured that all their candles be extinguished.

3rd. That if any apprentice be hereafter found to have been reading in bed by candlelight, he shall never again be permitted during the whole of his apprenticeship to have the use of a candle at bedtime.

As the meaning of cross-infection dawned on the doctors, and with the coming of antiseptics, a higher proportion of patients made a brief stay and departed alive; overcrowding diminished; at 'Bart's' by 1866 the beds were being spaced 5 yards apart. By 1900 the hospital ward had become high, light, airy, clean, aseptic, and even more depressing.

Much of the ritual surrounding the hospital bed seems designed more for the discipline of the nurse than for the comfort of the patient. In newer and in smaller hospitals patients are becoming human beings, but as with British public schools and regiments, the more famous the establishment, the harsher the regime. In the Eton and Guards kind of hospital, the patient must watch his step. The hospital bed has become higher, and as it is on wheels, it has to be coaxed into stillness like a mettlesome horse before he can mount. The wheels, to please the Matron if for no other reason, must at all times be dressed in exact alignment. If doctors' feet or wardmaids' brooms upset their symmetry, staff-nurses, in terror of the sisters, are ready to jerk up the bed and kick them straight again. The patient may drop his book, but the bed is so high that he cannot pick it up without a risk of falling out. Continent and incontinent alike must squirm on a fragrant rubber strip covered by a coarse twill draw-sheet. These incompatible textures battle to escape each other, so that the patient soon lies as on a newly furrowed field. The draw-sheet, of infinite length, is from time to time tweaked from under him and fed away somewhere between the mattress and the springs. Though he may like his bed-clothes loose about him, and his pillow conveniently askew, he finds himself and his bed reconstructed, as one unit, by every passing nightingale; his pillow pounded and set cold and straight; the corners of his blanket folded by a sleight-of-hand known only to nurses, into 'envelope corners' (a good envelope corner rates at least one mark in a 'practical'). Once more his covers

'*Invalid's Bedstead and Patent Mattress*', 1897

294

constrict him into immobility. Thus strait-jacketed, he is a credit to
the ward.

The hospital bed is one in which normal sleep is forbidden. At
an hour when he would normally be dining, the patient may get a
sleeping-draught. 'Wake up and take your sleeping-draught' is a
Punch joke of 1906, but well authenticated before and since. Thereafter, the night-sister's torch may rouse him to answer the kindly
query, whether he is sleeping well. He may not hear the giggles of
the probationers with the late-night 'housemen', but at dawn, a
tooth-mug will be thrust under his nose, with perhaps worse exhor-
tations to untimely bodily activity. He may accept an unwelcome
wash for the sake of a welcome but inseparable cup of tea. If he
knows how to read his chart unobserved, he can be surprised to
learn that his nights have been good and his progress excellent.

Beds from the catalogue of the Army & Navy Co-operative Society, 1880

50

To be had of Gorringe

Y about 1880, though the middle-aged and obese Prince of
Wales had still over twenty years to wait for his brief throne,
the 'Edwardian' period in art and manners may be said to
have begun. The 'Arts and Crafts' movement was under way;
William Morris, finding that he could not furnish his new house
decently from the existing catalogues, had founded the firm of Morris,
Marshall, Faulkner & Co. in 1862, offering well-designed furniture,
wallpapers and fabrics, with a supposedly 'Old English' flavour. An
artist as famous as Ford Madox Brown was not above designing a
cheap bedroom suite for Morris—who by the way designed no furniture himself. The virtues of hand-made things and honest materials
began to be preached. But good results are not apparent in the catalogues directed at the middle incomes; these do reflect the new ideas,
but all of them at once, as mere additions to the old favourites: Gothic,
Jacobean and Louis XV rub shoulders with *art nouveau* and
Japanese and even Moorish, in rooms as busy as before. Furniture
manufacturers note the reaction against machine-made stuff, and so
turn over their machines to the quantity-production of 'hand-made'
stuff. They become 'exhibition-minded', and like Academy painters,
they vie in showing unusual and outsize works that do not sit happily
in the average home. The aspidistra still occupies its brass pot on a

bamboo stand, even in the bedroom, though as a concession to the new taste a portfolio of etchings is leaned against it with studied carelessness.

At the same time many writers—most of them ladies of title, or at least with surnames redolent of class—are setting out to reform the hygiene as well as the aesthetics of the bedroom, though their ideas do not seem very daring now in either field. The voice of the Ladies' Sanitary Association is heard in the land. The fear of fresh air is just perceptibly moderated. 'It is only too easy to shock some people, and at the risk of shocking many of my readers at the outset' —begins Lady Barker in *The Bedroom and Boudoir* of 1878, and we wonder what is to come—but she declares only that 'very few bedrooms are so built and furnished as to remain thoroughly *sweet*, fresh and airy all through the night'. She recommends 'Tobin's Tube', which is 4 in. square and brings that much air from outside to a high point in the room, but she will not accept the risk of opening the window overnight. Some prefer 'O'Brien's Bed-Ventilating Tube', which feeds air right into the bed—but presumably only while it is unoccupied. There is also 'Dr. Arnott's Improved Ventilating Valve', in plain or ornamental form, a hole in the wall such as the Borough Surveyor will insist upon a generation or two later, when builders tire of spending money on unused bedroom fire-places, and no other ventilation remains save the closed window. Fug-lovers will then paste over these statutory ventilators with paper, as soon as the inspector has departed, and stew happily in their own carbon dioxide.

Lady Barker prefers the new wire-spring mattress to the 'old frowsty feather bed', which nevertheless long survives her day. On the aesthetic side, she describes an 'essentially modern' bedroom: the wallpaper is of trellis and Noisette roses; the same roses recur in the border of the carpet and in the chintzes. The door-handles and the tiles of the fire-place have been painted 'by the skilful fingers of the owner'—with Noisette roses. The quilt, and the cover of the writing-table, have been embroidered—with Noisette roses. For good measure, the window looks out on to a spreading bush of *real* Noisette roses. Let nobody suggest that a connecting decorative theme has not been consistently maintained. She favours 'Japanese curtains' of paper if they are hung only on the wall, but not as window-curtains, because they crackle and rustle and have a tiresome way of bursting into flame.

As long as a woman possesses a pair of hands and her work-basket, a little hammer and a few tintacks, it is hard if she need live in a room which is actually ugly.

Such a woman can, for example, easily construct a spare bed for a visitor, by means of two 'bullock trunks' set 3 ft. apart, and provided with eyelets into which a piece of sacking is pinned.

Now I cannot endure to possess anything of any kind which had better be kept out of sight wrapped carefully away under lock and key. My idea of enjoying ownership is for my possession to be of such a nature that I can see it or use it every day.

No bedroom, she says, can look really comfortable without a trivet and a kettle; a brass kettle for preference, 'as squat and fat and shining as it is possible to procure'. She also finds in the bedroom 'a delightful corner for a piano'; the tidying-up process has not yet got very far.

Charles Eastlake, architect and furniture-designer, is another reformer whose words rouse hopes that his illustrated deeds do not fulfil. He replaces feminine fripperies by a certain masculine massiveness, but his cabinet-maker carves yards of 'Old English' ornament in place of the ousted millinery. Like the older school, he is still on the hopeless quest for a high moral tone in furniture. The truth of his repeated claim that his is simple and practical may be judged from his drawings: his bed-canopy is framed on projecting spears, the spears are hung on chains, the chains from a ceiling-beam so conveniently placed that it would be unwise to consider moving the bed to another room. Some idea of Eastlake's colour-schemes may be gained from his dictum that iron bedsteads are best painted in Venetian red, chocolate or sage green.

Mrs. Panton, in *From Kitchen to Garret* in 1888, instructs an imaginary and rather unlikeable newly married couple 'Edwin' and 'Angelina' in every detail of home-making. The bedroom must have a 'real' dado, either of cretonne or of Indian matting—the only objections to these dados are 'expense, and possible culture of dirt and creeping things'. The walls should be painted terra-cotta ('the pink shade, not the brown') and the ceiling covered with a diaper-patterned terra-cotta paper; the mantelpiece and woodwork painted to match; the doors panelled with terra-cotta chintz, and given new brass handles and finger-plates in place of the 'hideous' china ones. As for pictures,

. . . they should be chosen carefully, either for their beauty or for the lesson they teach. Having a positive horror of gambling, horse-racing, or betting in any shape or form myself, I cannot regard any house satisfactorily furnished without autotypes of my father's pictures of 'The Road to Ruin'. These admirable pictures have pointed a moral over and over again in my house, and will, I hope, point many another; for the children are always ready to look at them and make out for themselves the dismal o'er-true

298

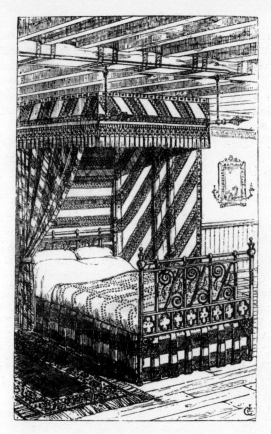

Iron bedstead by Eastlake, 1878

tale. If, however, these pictures should be objected to, I should advise autotypes of some of Sir Joshua's lovely child-pictures, Leader's 'At Evening Time It Shall Be Light', 'Chill October', any of the etchings after Burton Barber's amusing dog-pictures, and those equally entertaining fox-terrier sketches of Mr. Yates Carrington, Waller's 'The Day of Reckoning' . . . in years to come the walls will doubtless be decorated with photographs of the children at different stages; but Angelina's wedding photographs will be useful at first. . . .

If Angelina cannot afford pictures in any way, she can, no doubt, afford brackets. These are very cheap indeed in carved wood (which can be painted to match the room), would hold a scrap of blue and white china, and can be made even more decorative if surrounded by a 'trophy' or artistic arrangement of the ever-useful Japanese fans, one of which should be covered with silk and plush, and made into a bed-pocket for handkerchief, watch, or keys. . . .

The mantelpiece should have a full flounce of blue and white Lahore cretonne, used also for covering the eiderdown, its colour being repeated in the tiles of the wash-stand. In one window is a big 'box ottoman' covered with 'odds and ends of cretonnes properly frilled', with a big square frilled pillow, and a large 'drapery' of gold thread tapestry of the same pattern as for the toilet-covers, the table-cloths, and the runners on the two cupboard-tables. These last are of deal, painted, and panelled with Japanese leather paper; the handles, locks and hinges must be of brass. Each needs a fern in a pot, and one may 'dot books and photographs about them just as one would on a table'. Pretty brass rings, sewn on flat straps of plush or serge worked in some conventional design, are 'the nicest bell-pulls possible'.

A narrow strip of looking-glass about a foot wide, and enclosed in a painted deal frame, makes a pretty bedroom shelf; this can be supplemented by fans, brackets, and the ever-useful cheap and pretty chinas to be had of Gorringe.

(How perfectly those few words 'to be had of Gorringe' sum up the old relationship between the lady and the shopkeeper.) The wardrobes are painted, one terra-cotta, the other a lovely colour that we hope the foreman painter understood and knocked up promptly: 'not bluer than "hedge-sparrow egg" or greener than "electric turquoise".' These wardrobes, like the doors, have the Japanese leather panels and brass fittings. As well as the ottoman, Angelina must have a sofa ready for the seemingly inevitable periods of convalescence, protected by a screen. Mrs. Panton will not allow the wooden bedstead—'a detestable thing'—she has in mind what she delicately calls 'certain small animals'. She recommends a chain-mattress, with a hair-mattress on top, and she only reluctantly allows a feather-bed. She objects to bed-curtains as being stuffy, but advises for those who do not like the bare appearance of an uncurtained bed, a 'draped alcove'. We learn that the preference in bedrooms for ferns and aspidistras, rather than flowering plants, is based more on hygiene than on aesthetics:

If the toilet-table is chosen with brackets, cut and scented flowers should never be allowed there. A few ferns and immortelles look nice, especially the pretty pink everlastings one can buy in the summer, but scented flowers are bad for a bedroom, though I much recommend a growing plant or two; they look nice, and are very healthy; but no flowers here even; a fern, a small palm, or the ubiquitous aspidistra being all to be preferred, because the leaves give out a healthy atmosphere, and are therefore useful as well as ornamental, while strongly scented blossoms poison the air and render it unfit for a sleeper to breathe.

300

. . . While we are on the subject of beds, I may mention that a matchbox, the boxes of Bryant and May's, painted with enamel paint, and embellished with a tiny picture, nailed to the wall just above one's head, is an excellent thing.

And finally, if the scent of cooking should penetrate to the bedroom, Angelina has only to burn one or two of the joss-sticks sold at the Baker Street Bazaar at 6d. a packet—'these make your room at once like an Eastern palace'.

We now begin to hear of 'the servant problem'. The maid is no longer content to serve for a lifetime in the household to which it has pleased God to call her, or to sleep in the kitchen and keep her box in the back kitchen like Mrs. Carlyle's maid, who had been patient enough not only to endure but to count the 200 bugs in her bed. She is becoming 'tiresome' and has to be pampered. But Mrs. Panton, when she advises about the maid's bedroom, never quite reconciles her wish to be kind, with the poor creature's obvious inability to appreciate or look after anything better than was offered in her parents' slum. 'After all,' she reminds us, 'maids are but mortal,' and the routine of the maid's life is rather dull, despite 'the joy of her morning gossip with the tradesmen, and her few hours on Sunday'; she suggests that we sometimes give the girl a cheerful account of our visit to the theatre. Her servants' bedrooms are rather different from her own:

. . . the floor should be bare of all covering, and should simply have dhurries laid down by each bed, and by the washing-stands &c. These wash splendidly, and always keep clean and nice, while the curtains at the window should be some cheap cretonne that would wash nicely, and draw and undraw easily, or else they will soon be rendered too shabby for use.

Each servant should have a separate bed, if possible, and that bed should be as comfortable as can be, without being unduly luxurious. . . . No valances or curtains of any kind should be allowed, neither should their own boxes be kept in their rooms. One can give them locks and keys to their chests of drawers and wardrobes; but if their boxes are retained in the room, they cannot refrain somehow from hoarding all sorts of rubbish in them.

I should like myself to give each maid a really pretty room, but at present they are a little hopeless on this subject—as witness the smashed china and battered furniture that greets our alarmed sight at the inspection that should take place at least twice a year—but, alas! it is impossible. No sooner is the room put nice than something happens to destroy its beauty; and I really believe servants only feel happy if their rooms are allowed in some measure to resemble the homes of their youth, and to be merely places where they lie down to sleep as heavily as they can.

But Mrs. Panton shows a kindly respect for the servant's personal dignity when she advises that all her sheets, pillows, blankets and other portable property should be marked with 'her name'; that is, *Cook*, *Housemaid* or *Parlourmaid*; this makes her individually responsible for its care.

Clearly the servants' room, with or without joss-sticks, is unlike Angelina's Eastern palace. A catalogue of 1895 gives a 'Complete Estimate for Furnishing in a Substantial and Artistic Manner for £150, a Flat of Eight Rooms', from which the difference between the Best Bedroom and the Servant's Room can be judged to a penny:

BEST BEDROOM

	£	s.	d.
1 'Woodberry' Carpet, 10 ft. 6 in. by 7 ft. 6 in.	1	10	0
1 Black Kerb Fender and Fire Irons		14	6
1 Bamboo Cornice Pole, complete		3	9
1 Pair Art Serge Curtains		10	6

The 'Camberley' Bedroom Suite, No. 12
    5 ft. 6 in. Wardrobe,
    4 ft. Toilet Table,
    4 ft. Washstand,
    3 Cane-Seated Chairs,
    Pedestal Cupboard,
    Towel Horse,

	£	s.	d.
In White Enamel, finished in a superior manner, complete for	15	15	0
1 Toilet Set, No. 610		9	9
1 5 ft. Black and Brass French Bedstead ⎫			
1 5 ft. Woven Wire Spring Mattress ⎬	5	12	0
1 5 ft. Wool Mattress ⎪			
1 Bolster and 2 Pillows ⎭			
	£24	**15**	**6**

SERVANT'S BEDROOM

1 3 ft. 6 in. Maple Chest of Drawers
1 Japanned Washstand
1 American Birch Toilet Glass
1 Cane-Seated Chair
1 3 ft. Iron Bedstead, with Woven Wire Mattress attached
1 3 ft. Wool Mattress

	£	s.	d.
1 3 ft. Wool Bolster and 1 Feather pillow, complete for	4	0	0
Set of Crockery		3	0
Square of Carpet		10	0
	£4	**13**	**0**

A 'do-it-yourself' urge swept through the homes of the 'nineties, though confined largely to the needle and the paint-brush. With the remarkable enamel advertised here, it seems unnecessary to wear overalls or to protect the carpet, and the bed can be enamelled without removing the bedclothes

Whatever the multiple required to adjust such figures to present-day values, even the 'good Baronial effect' mentioned in the catalogue was not expensive in Curtain Road, E.C., and however low the wages in the furniture factory, one suspects, at the price, the workmanship of the suites in 'basswood stained Chippendale mahogany or green', the durability of the '*carton-pierre* enrichments', and the authenticity of the 'XVI Century Bokhara Plushes for Draperies' at 3*s.* 11*d.* a yard. At prices ranging from £4 15*s.* to £31 10*s.* for a complete bedroom suite, one could choose between 'the grace of Sheraton and Chippendale, the luxurious dignity of the Empire period, the charm and convenience of modern art', not to mention 'Arabian Furniture, Decorations and Curios Manufactured at Damascus and Cairo' and bedrooms in 'The Cairene and Moucharabeyh Style'. On one and the same page we find 'Electric Lighting a Specialty' and 'Stained Glass Windows and Doors to any Design'. The impeccable taste of it all is vouched for not only by our Mrs. Panton of *The Gentlewoman*, but by Miss Charlotte Robinson of *The Queen* ('Home Art Decorator to Her Majesty'), Mrs. C. Talbot Coke of *Hearth and Home*, and Mrs. Conyers Morrell of *The Lady's Pictorial*.

Vacillating between their crusades for Health and for Art—a synthesis which perhaps only an ancient Greek could have attained in full—the Edwardians never quite reconciled the two causes, for

764   766

THE "CHESHAM" BEDROOM SUITE, No.

As above, consisting of a handsome 5-ft. recessed Wardrobe, fitted with drawer and jewel drawers, large glass attached; Washstand, with rouge royal marble-top,

Copper Sconces

Arm Chair, upholstered in tapestry, £2 10s. 0d.; Writing Table (Sconces extra), £

—perfect curtain mater

From a catalogue of 1895

304

769

770

IGATED MAHOGANY, OR STAINED GREEN.

rved panels and bevelled plate, copper handles; 4-ft. Toilet Table, with cupboard
 shelves; three cane-seat Chairs; Towel Horse; Pedestal Cupboard.
stand, extra. **Complete for £33 10s. 0d.**

 in canvas, ready for covering, £4 10s. 0d.; Tyrolese Muslin and Guipure Vitrage
rom 10½d. per yard.

their supposedly most healthy devices are their least artistic, and their most artistic are somewhat unhygienic. The opposites are nicely illustrated in their night-wear. The rule of 'wool next the skin' was much encouraged by Dr. Jaeger, whose rather gruesome goon-suit of 1885 leaves absolutely nothing exposed to the night air but the hands and face. A bride of the 'eighties writes to her mamma that she is spending the honeymoon making 'him' nice long night-gowns to replace his night-shirts, 'so that I shan't be able to see any of him'. But it is Health for the men, and Art for the women, who by the 1890's can have 'delightfully cosy winter night-gowns of cream and pink flannel trimmed with lace and ribbons', and others of pink nun's-veiling with gathered waists, puffed shoulder sleeves, and lavish trimmings of baby-ribbons. The more emancipated woman can sport 'the Combination Night-gown or Lady's Pyjama', which is made as combinations, has frills at the knees and wrists, with a high collar, and requires 4½ yards of calico or flannel. *The Lady's Realm* in 1903 advises on a trousseau:

Two or three dozen nightdresses are not too many . . . Americans and other ultra-smart folk are very fond of black silk or gauze nightgowns; but I do not think they should have a place in bridal trousseaux; I confess to a predilection for the purest white.

Elinor Glyn's heroine Evangeline, of 1906, wears a semi-transparent nightdress, but it evokes an elder's comment that 'no nice woman wants things to look becoming in bed!' An actor wearing pyjamas on the stage in the same year shocked many London theatregoers.

Left: *'Complete Sleeping Suit' by Jaeger, 1885*

Above: *Pyjamas by Jaeger, 1899*

Right: *Pyjamas by Peter Robinson, 1902*

306

HANDSOME MODEL NIGHTGOWN, *open and trimmed down front with lace and insertions of a new pattern patent lace. Pretty sleeve, transparent at wrist, finished with ribbons to tie at waist. Copied in nainsook and patent lace from 3½ guineas. Also made in good washing silk from £4. 18s. 6d. A large variety of all descriptions of Nightgowns always in stock, trimmed lace or embroidery. Price varying from 8|11, 12|9, 14|9, 18|9, 21|9, 31|9, 35|9, up to 8½ guineas. (Advertisement in* The Queen, *1896)*

51

Palace Pains

To be an overnight guest of Queen Victoria or King Edward was not to enjoy the palace luxuries of the fairy-tales. To stay at Windsor, Buckingham Palace or even Sandringham was something of an ordeal. In the old Queen's time, any gentleman craving a cigar would have to slink to his bedroom, and even there, smoke up the chimney to disperse the incriminating aroma. The grim tenor of palace life was seldom relieved by such little tricks as that played by Prince Alfred, the Queen's second son, upon the shy and inexperienced Alexandra, 'terribly frightened' at her first stay there; he taught her that it was polite to ask the Queen every afternoon, 'Have you enjoyed your forty winks?' There would be a good fire in one's bedroom, but no bath or lavatory within fair walking distance, and only newspaper was provided in the latter apartment. Nobody might go to bed, or even sit, until the monarch had retired. In Queen Victoria's time this relief came blessedly early. A Lady-in-Waiting in 1840 noted that the Queen, however sleepy, would not directly command Albert to leave his chess and come to bed, but would send the message 'Tell Lord Alfred to let the Prince know that it is 11 o'clock; tell him the Prince should *merely* be told the hour. The Prince *wishes* to be told, I know. He does not see the clock.' But at Sandringham, King Edward would play baccarat until 4 or 5 a.m., and all the men of the party had to stay up whether they played or not. They arranged to sleep in relays in the billiard room, tipping a footman to warn them when the baccarat was over. One night, when Queen Alexandra had gone to bed, the King walked round counting heads, and found one short. General Sir Dighton Probyn, aged 75, had not felt well and had risked retiring. On the King's orders he was awakened, and made to dress and return.

Sir Frederick Ponsonby, rare as a loyal lifetime courtier with a sense of humour, tells of an unhappy night passed at Windsor by the Baron D'Estournelles de Constant. Staying up late talking, he rashly said that he knew his way to his room, and refused the guidance of a page. He started well, going up the stone staircase and quite correctly through the 300-ft. length of St. George's Hall. At the end, on each side of the throne, were two doors, indistinguishable from the panelling, but one of them open—the wrong one. After long wanderings he found himself in the chapel, then in the vestry, which was clearly wrong. He found his way back to St. George's Hall and tried other exits, without success. After a long search he decided to return to the billiard room and start again, but he never found it, and met nobody. At 2 a.m. he gave up, collected some rugs and mats from the floor, and made himself as comfortable as he could on a sofa in the State Gallery. There a housemaid found him in the morning, and brought a policeman who did not believe his story until guarantors had been found.

Nobody knows exactly how many rooms there are in Buckingham Palace (which is not so new throughout as its façade); the figure is agreed to be about 600, but so many rooms are cupboard-size that some surveyors list them as cupboards, others as servants' bedrooms. In the early days of Queen Victoria's reign, the footmen and such slept ten or twelve to a room, and in the latest, the laundrymaids still slept four to a bed. This palace was the scene of another nocturnal nonsense: Colonel John Clerk, Equerry to Princess Beatrice, was temporarily given a grand guest-bedroom. A foreign monarch arrived with an unexpectedly large suite, and the Master of the Household, short of rooms, sent a message to Clerk asking him to move to a smaller one. Unfortunately the message never reached him, and returning at about 1 a.m. he breezed into 'his' room and threw his top-hat on the bed. A lady awoke with a piercing yell, and as the unhappy colonel fled, his top-hat, which had landed on a royal stomach, was hurled after him.

The beds in which King Edward slept at the Hotel Weimar, during his annual 'cure' at Marienbad, proved profitable to the management. Each year they and the other furniture hallowed by the royal contact were sold at a generous profit, and renewed.

Any Edwardian country house worthy of the name would have at least eleven spare bedrooms, so that a visiting team of gentlemen cricketers could be accommodated; but there, too, luxury and discomfort still mingled. Lutyens was arguing in vain that every bedroom should have a bathroom—at least two of his big houses (Crooksbury and Munstead Wood) were built with no bathroom at all.

Bed in enamel and gold by Majorelle of Paris, c. 1870

52

Delicious Depravity

THE tradition of the courtesan and her glamorous setting survived the French Revolution, and the sundry upsets of the following century. Her sisters of more democratic days ploughed back profits into the business, still furnishing shrines worthy of the triumphs of Venus. The celebrated La Païva set up in Paris in 1841, with such distinguished supporters as Delacroix, Saint-Beuve and Taine. Her first salon was merely borrowed, but Count Henckel von Donnersmark provided funds for a palace in the *Champs-Elysées* that was ten years in building. Known as the *Hotel Païva*, its cost has been calculated to equal a year's wages for 3,000 workmen. Gautier declared it 'fit for a sultana out of *The Thousand and One Nights*'. For the onyx staircase, the playwright

310

Emile Augier proposed an inscription, adapted from Racine, 'Vice, like Virtue, has its steps'. The state bed alone was said to have cost 100,000 gold francs, a tidy sum in two senses. (The *Hotel Païva* is now tenanted, and rather differently conducted, by the Travellers' Club.) Later came Cora Pearl, who had talents above her acting, bathed in champagne, and deserved though she never received an official 'Royal Appointment' to H.M. King Edward VII. Cora is generally agreed to have been the model for Zola's Nana. We know that he used to sit unobtrusively in her dressing-room taking notes. His description of Nana's last and most luxurious bed seems to tally with the picture of one made by the great *ébeniste* M. Majorelle:

Nana meditated a bed such as had never before existed; it was to be a throne, an altar, whither Paris was to come in order to adore her sovereign nudity. It was to be all in gold and silver beaten-work—it should suggest a great piece of jewellery with its golden roses climbing on a trellis-work of silver. On the head-board a band of Loves should peep forth laughing from amid the flowers, as though they were watching the voluptuous dalliance within the shadow of the bed-curtains . . . Labordette showed her two designs for the foot-board, one of which reproduced the pattern on the sides, whilst the other, a subject by itself, represented Night wrapt in her veil, and discovered by a faun in all her splendid nudity. He added that, if she chose this last subject, the goldsmiths intended making Night in her own likeness. This idea, the taste of which was rather daring, made her grow white with pleasure, and she pictured herself as a silver statuette symbolic of the warm voluptuous delights of darkness.

Sarah Bernhardt—though her professional and her private reputations are both on a rather different level from Cora's—slept and held court in a less expensive but more fantastic setting. In her studio in the *Boulevard Pereire*, amid brass lamps and palms and ferns, the couch was heaped with a mountain of cushions, and its silk canopy fringed with dying flowers. The pelts of polar bear, beaver, tiger and jaguar overflowed on to the floor, and up the walls among the moose-heads. The total effect as photographed suggests a bomb-incident in the zoo. George Moore, in his Paris days, sought a like atmosphere in his apartment in the *Rue de la Tour des Dames*, with its altar, Buddhist temple, statue of Apollo, bust of Shelley, church candlesticks, and burning incense; he shared his bedroom with a Persian cat, and a python that made a monthly meal of live guinea-pigs. His fellow-tenant Marshall had simpler tastes, and was content to fill his rooms with flowers and sleep beneath a tree of gardenias in full bloom. Delicious depravity, if one's sense of the ridiculous was not too strong.

When the owner, an Indian maharajah, lay on this silver bed, music emerged, in time to which the ladies automatically waved their fans and fly-whisks

An Indian maharajah went one better with his Paris-made bed, weighing over a ton, guarded not by the traditional four angels, but by four realistic life-size nudes. His weight on the bed triggered off a musical box, and set the arms of the figures in motion, so that two fanned his face, and two whisked the flies from about his feet.

In England the professional beauties lay in rather more restrained settings, though Lily Langtry's bedroom by no means suggests that of, say, a hockey-captain. When The Jersey Lily visited her native island, she discovered under the frills of her dressing-table two little girls hiding to watch the rites of the toilet. One of these was Elinor Glyn. Another famous London beauty, Mrs. Bovill, had already admitted little Elinor to these mysteries, and thus were sparks fanned in the smouldering imagination of that high-priestess of bedroom glamour, the authoress of *Three Weeks*, published in 1907 with an impact that puts *Lolita* by comparison in a class with *Pollyanna*. A generation of housewives and flappers learned how to loll before the hearth on a tiger skin, flower in mouth, or to improvise a love-couch of rose-petals.

312

'Boudoir moderne', *c. 1880*

Would you rather sin
With Elinor Glyn
On a tiger skin,
Or would you prefer
To err with her
On some other kind of fur?

Her protector Lord Curzon seems to have preferred—and in fact provided—the tiger skin. But the *fin-de-siècle* had passed, and the exotic bedroom was on the way out; the wrong background for the boyish 'flapper'. Notions of glamour changed between 1914 and 1918. When *Three Weeks* was filmed in 1923, and the hero Paul was to have played the final love-scene in pyjamas, the censor would have none of this, and in the approved version the queen tiptoed away from the fruitful couch of rose-petals, leaving him asleep but still wearing full tails and white waistcoat. In the state of Ohio, the censor turned down an early Mickey Mouse cartoon solely because Clara Cow, reclining on the grass, was reading *Three Weeks*. In her real-life bedrooms, though she did sew hundreds of those inevitable roses on and around her bed, Elinor did not always achieve the atmosphere of her fictional ones; she had a knack of getting into farcical situations overnight. In Anthony Glyn's biography, we find her benighted in a shack in Mexico and sharing one double bed and one child's cot with Charlie Chaplin, his wife Lita Grey, and a company of bugs: no bed of roses there. In a muddle over hotel reservations at Naples, five persons share a room: Elinor and her maid have a single brass bed, a Mr. Van Allen another, Elinor's husband Clayton a sofa, and Mr. Van Allen's valet a chair.

Williams was appalled at the presumption of sharing a bed with her mistress and slept on the very edge. Clayton and Mr. Van Allen undressed with difficulty behind a small screen; the valet did not even unfasten his collar. It was a disturbed night. The valet sat bolt upright on a small gilt chair, his mouth wide open, snoring hard, while his master occasionally shouted at him. At intervals Williams fell out of bed. The lamplight poured into the room through the Venetian blinds and when Elinor sat up in bed to get a breath of air, she noticed Mr. Van Allen propped on one elbow, staring at her, murmuring, 'God! what a form!' Whenever she woke up during the night, he was still sitting gazing at her, muttering passionately to himself.

'Old fool!' said Clayton the next day, who was not amused by the breakdown in his travelling arrangements, 'bothering about women when we were all so tired.'

53

The American Renaissance

'I WANT to see your reproductive furniture,' says the customer in a *New Yorker* joke. In the early years of the present century, a New Yorker was unlikely to see much else. To start thinking up new designs seemed like sawing sawdust. The mechanically inventive urge of 1850–90 had flagged, and the only aesthetic urge following the Chicago World Fair of 1893 was a mere influx of 'European taste', with good old Louis XV well to the fore. Elinor Glyn has reported on the Vanderbilt residence (one nearly called it a house) at Hyde Park, with its knee-breeched and periwigged footmen and its Charles Laughton butler; many of its antiques were genuine. Each bedroom, she says, had at least two Louis XV suites. The curtains, pillow-cases and sheets were fringed with real Venetian lace. Elinor's jerry-pot (or rather *pot-de-chambre*) had a lace cover, and in her water-closet (Louis XV?) the chain had a big blue satin bow on it. Mrs. Vanderbilt's own bedroom had the royal balustrade separating the state bed from the vulgar:

'I suppose,' murmured Elinor reminiscently, 'that only Princes of the Blood are allowed behind the balustrade.'
'Elinor!' said Mrs. Vanderbilt, deeply shocked. 'You must not say such things in America.'

Elsie de Wolfe, in *The House in Good Taste*, records the achievements of the prosperous, progressive and peaceful year of 1916:

315

I know of nothing more significant than the awakening of men and women throughout our country to the desire to improve their houses. Call it what you will—awakening, development, American Renaissance— it is a most startling and promising condition of affairs.

It is no longer possible, even to people of only faintly aesthetic tastes, to buy chairs merely to sit upon or a clock merely that it should tell the time. Home-makers are determined to have their houses, outside and in, correct according to the best standards . . . the standards that have come to us from those exceedingly rational people, our ancestors.

She makes it clear that the American home is *the woman's* home, and that it is the woman's personality that must be expressed in it:

Men are forever guests in our homes, no matter how much happiness they may find there . . . Therefore, you must select for your architect a man who isn't too determined to have *his* way. It is a fearful mistake to leave the entire planning of your home to a man whose social experience may be limited . . . I once heard a certain Boston architect say that he taught his clients to be ladies and gentlemen. He couldn't, you know.

Miss de Wolfe obviously can; but when she comes down to the details of the American Renaissance bedroom, scholarship gives way to a line of whimsy that Blondel would hardly have taken with Louis XV. 'Quaint', 'amusing', 'odd', 'adorable', and 'wee' are not Renaissance adjectives. Nor would Marot have evolved the design of an adorable boudoir from a single quaint lamp-jar, or built a bedroom around a wee rug; nor could he have sought the initial inspiration in 'a pair of appliques made from two old Chinese sprays of metal flowers' with electric light bulbs fitted. Again she rather shirks her duty to history, when she comes to the *chaise-longue*. This, she agrees, is essential in bedroom or boudoir—'it serves so many purposes'—but in any other room it would be 'a violation of good taste, because the suggestion of intimacy is too evident'. More delicate, this, than Mrs. Pat Campbell's robust heart-cry, 'O for the deep, deep peace of the double bed, after the hurly-burly of the *chaise-longue!*'—not to mention Elsa Lanchester's

> There are so many ways
> On this very *longue chaise*.

She is asked to advise on a Christmas gift for a wife who has everything already:

And so I suggested a *couvre-pieds* for her *chaise-longue*. Now I am telling you of the *couvre-pieds* because I know all women love exquisite things, and surely nothing could be more delicious than my *couvre-pieds*.

316

By 1916, Louis XVI has succeeded to the American throne, though Miss de Wolfe is never pedantic about period; she admits Adam to the Colony Club of New York:

The furniture was carefully planned, as may be seen by the little urns on the bedposts, quite in the manner of the Brothers Adam . . .

and her own bedroom is Elizabethan, faintly marred by ye olde radiator. Her boudoir rightly expresses her personality best of all:

The aquarium . . . is the home of the most gorgeous fan-tailed goldfish. There are water plants in the box, too, and funny little Chinese temples and dwarf trees. I love to house my little people happily—my dogs and my birds and my fish. Wee Toi, my little Chinese dog, has a little house all his own, an old Chinese lacquer box with a canopy top and little gold bells. It was once the shrine of some little Chinese god, I suppose, but Wee Toi is very happy in it, and you can see that it was meant for him in the beginning. It sits by the fireplace and gives the room an air of real hominess. I was so pleased with the aquarium and the Chinese lacquer bed for Wee Toi that I devised a birdcage to go with them, a square cage with gilt wires, with a black lacquer pointed canopy top, with little gilt bells at the pointed eaves. The cage is fixed to a shallow lacquer tray, and is the nicest place you can imagine for a whistling bullfinch to live in. I suppose I could have a Persian cat on a gorgeous cushion to complete the place, but I can't admit cats into the room. I plan gorgeous cushions for *other* people's 'little people', when they happen to be cats.

She is tolerably satisfied with her results in Miss Anne Morgan's Louis XVI boudoir:

I suppose there isn't a more charming room in New York . . . it is radiant with colour and individuality, as rare rugs are radiant, as jewels are radiant . . . Above the day bed there is a portrait of a lady, hung by wires covered with shirred blue ribbons, and this blue is again used in an old porcelain lamp jar on the bedside table. The whole room might have been inspired by the lady of the portrait, so essentially is it the room of a fastidious woman.

Most of her bedrooms for the Colony Club have open fire-places; the walls of the Bird Room are patterned with marvellous blue and green birds of paradise and paroquets, and it has black lacquer furniture; one adorable room is for a young girl, with the *chaise-longue*, the window-hangings, the bedspread, the stool-cushion, the dressing-table frills, all in the same chintz, and the electric lights 'cleverly made into candlesticks which are painted to match the chintz'. Then there is Miss Morgan's Louis XVI *Lit de Repos*, Miss Crocker's Louis XVI

'Artistic Corner Wardrobe, as presented to and graciously accepted by H.I.M. the Empress Frederick of Germany', 1895

Bed, Mrs. Frederick Havemeyer's Chinoiserie Chintz Bed, and Mrs. Payne Whitney's Green Feather Chintz Bed; the American male seems to accept the matriarchy, and never to buy himself a bed worth mention. 'We are getting more sensible about our bedrooms.' The 'dreadful epidemic' of vulgar brass beds is over ('the glitter of brass appeals to the untrained eye') likewise the 'spasmodic outbreak' of silverplated beds, and the 'mistaken vogue' of walnut. Other woods are permissible, and so is *white*-painted iron. Chintz is emphatically *in*—acres of it. And

Nothing so nice has happened in a long time as the revival of painted furniture, and the application of quaint designs to modern beds and chairs and chests. You may find inspiration in a length of chintz, in an old fan, in a faded print—anywhere!

Meanwhile, Britishers were carping less at the American hotel, as Dickens had carped, and as Dr. James Fullarton carped still in 1898, finding it *significant* that in the printed signal codes for bedroom bells, he never found an instance where 'the harmless necessary bath' could be ordered with fewer than nine rings, whereas a cocktail might often be obtained with three or four. His mirror he found 'large enough for a Brobdingnagian', but his wash-basin 'little larger than a sugar-bowl'.

The furniture of your bedroom would not have disgraced the Tuileries in their palmiest days, but, alas, you are parboiled by a diabolic *chevaux-de-frise* [*sic*] of steam pipes, which refuse to be turned off, and insist on accompanying your troubled slumbers by an intermittent series of bubbles, squeaks and hisses.

But hardy Britishers were growing used to the oddity of a bedroom warmed in winter. By 1912, Arnold Bennett (whose concept of heaven must surely have resembled a divinely run hotel) could admire in America

... the calm orderliness of the bedroom floors, the adequacy of wardrobes and lamps, the reckless profusion of clean linen, that charming notice one finds under one's door in the morning. 'You were called at seven-thirty, *and answered.*'

In fairness, let us append another of those 'contrasts too obvious for the purposes of art' already directed at the Old Country: the rules of the Buckthorn Inn, New York City, quoted by Richardson Wright in 1927. The charge was 8 cents a night, or 12 cents with supper; not more than five were permitted to sleep in one bed, and boots were to be removed before retiring. Or the sign on a rooming-house in Alabama, quoted by Reginald Reynolds with a tantalising lack of further explanation:

Beds, per night, 15 cents.
Safe beds, per night, 25 cents.

319

54

Good Beds for Single Men

THE comfort of the prison bed, under George V, depended on 'marks' earned by good conduct and industry. For the first month every newcomer (except females, youths under 16 and men over 60) slept on a plank-bed, with bedding but no mattress. At the second stage the mattress was allowed twice a week, but not until the fourth was it allowed every night. The solitary system had not yet given way to the overcrowding of the 1960's (when vast numbers sleep three to a cell) and officials seemed more worried by the 'evils of association' than by the madness and suicide rates.

Outside, W. H. Davies the poet-tramp could quote, like Mayhew, a beggar relying on the alcoholic anodyne to dull the miseries of the common lodging-house:

I go in for straight begging, without showing anything in my hand . . . I never fail to get the sixteen farthings for my feather, I get all the scrand I can eat; and I seldom lie down at night but what I am skimished . . .

feather being bed, *scrand* being food, and *skimished* being half-drunk. Davies, some time in the early 1900's, tries a lodging-house in the Blackfriars Road:

He then showed me into a room where there were a number of beds, and, pointing to one, said—'You are number forty-five,' when he left the room. Many of the beds already contained sleepers. I sat down on the edge of mine, wondering if there would be any disturbance in the night, whether any of these men would take a fancy to my clothes, or in the dark were likely to rummage their contents. The man in the next bed coughed, and then, turning towards me, said gently—'The beds are good, I admit, but that is about all you can say for this house' . . . 'If I hadn't been drunk last night and got chucked out of Rowton's, I wouldn't, on any account, be here.'

Taking the fact that Rowton House has chucked out a drunk as a strong recommendation of it, Davies moves there the next day, pays 6d. a night, and stays for two years. Then, to economise, he moves to the *Ark*, a Salvation Army lodging-house in Southwark Street, at 2s. a week:

I am very sorry that I have nothing to say in its favour . . . whether, in case of a surprise visit from its inspectors, beds were removed in the day: what I do know from experience is this, that it was with difficulty that a man could find room between the beds to undress. A row of 15 or 20 beds would be so close together that they might as well be called one bed. Men were breathing and coughing in each other's faces and the stench of such a number of men in one room was abominable. I was fortunate in having a bed next to the wall, to which I could turn my face and escape the breath of the man in the next bed.

Nor has George Orwell much to say in favour of Salvation Army lodgings a generation later, about 1930. The charge is now 8d. a night. At 10 o'clock an officer marches round the hall blowing a whistle, at which all the 200 occupants stand up, and flock off obediently to bed under supervision.

The dormitory was a great attic like a barrack room, with 60 or 70 beds in it. They were clean and tolerably comfortable, but very narrow and very close together, so that one breathed straight into one's neighbour's face. Two officers slept in the room, to see that there was no smoking and no talking after lights-out. Paddy and I had scarcely a wink of sleep, for there was a man near us who had some nervous trouble, shell-shock perhaps, which made him cry out 'Pip!' at irregular intervals. You never knew when it was coming, and it was a sure preventer of sleep . . . At 7 another whistle blew, and the officers went round shaking those who did not get up at once . . . In some of them there is even a compulsory religious service once or twice a week, which the lodgers must attend or leave the house. That fact is that the Salvation Army are so in the habit of thinking themselves a charitable body that they cannot even run a lodging-house without making it stink of charity.

In 1889 there had been 988 common lodging-houses in London, taking nearly 34,000 people. In 1931 this number had fallen to about

321

15,000, but an L.C.C. survey shows that there were still 1,897 men and 182 women virtually homeless:

Spending the night in the streets	60 men	18 women
In shelters and homes not licensed as common lodging-houses	1,057 men	137 women
In the crypt of St. Martin's-in-the-Fields church	88 men	12 women
In L.C.C. casual wards and hostels	674 men	15 women

Orwell lists the alternatives open to one who cannot afford at least 7*d.* for a bed in London, and his friend Paddy adds colourful comments; first upon the art of sleeping on the Embankment:

De whole t'ing wid de Embankment is gettin' to sleep early. You got to be on your bench by 8 o'clock, because dere ain't too many benches and sometimes dey're all taken. And you got to try to get to sleep at once. 'Tis too cold to sleep much after 12 o'clock, an' de police turns you off at 4 in de mornin'. It ain't easy to sleep, dough, wid dem bloody trams flyin' past your head all de time, an' dem sky-signs across de river flickin' on an' off in your eyes. De cold's cruel. Dem as sleeps dere generally wraps demselves up in newspaper, but it don't do much good. You'd be bloody lucky if you got t'ree hours sleep.

According to the law, you might sit down for the night, but the police had to move you on if they saw you asleep; the Embankment and one or two odd corners were agreed exceptions. The stated object was to prevent people dying of exposure, but it is not clear why sleepers on the Embankment should be immune from this risk, and if a man is liable to die of exposure in his sleep, he is as likely to die stumbling around the streets half awake.

Next up the scale came the 'Twopenny Leanover', a device at least old enough to have been pictured in Paris by Daumier in 1840. (There, it still cost only a *sou* in 1930.) The sleepers sit in a row on a bench, leaning on a rope stretched in front of them. At 5 in the morning a character humorously known as 'the valet' cuts the rope.

Next came 'The Coffin' at 4*d.* a night, a wooden box with a tarpaulin covering, which was cold, and had the further disadvantage that the bugs, being boxed in, could not escape.

Those who could run to 7*d.* could use a common lodging-house. Paddy did not recommend them:

Dese lodgin'-houses is full o' thieves. In some houses dere's nothin' safe but to sleep wid all yer clo'es on. I seen 'em steal a wooden leg off a cripple before now. Once I see a man—14 stone he was—come into a lodgin'-house wid four pound ten. He puts it under his mattress. 'Now,' he says, 'any ——

dat touches dat money does it over my body,' he says. But dey done him all de same. In de mornin' he woke up on de floor. Four fellers had took his mattress by de corners an' lifted him off as light as a feather. He never saw his four pound ten again.

Having few expenses beyond the rent, and taking from £5 to £10 a night, with no bad debts, the lodging-house business should have been profitable. At one in Pennyfields, where 'the sheets were not more than a week from the wash, which was an improvement', the charge was 9d. for beds 4 ft. apart, 1s. for beds 6 ft. apart; terms, cash down by 7 in the evening, or get out.

For a shilling, one could sleep in a house in Waterloo Road with a sign 'Good Beds for Single Men', but there were eight of these good beds in a room 15 ft. square and 8 ft. high.

In the morning I was woken by a dim impression of some large brown thing coming towards me. I opened my eyes and saw that it was one of the sailor's feet, sticking out of bed close to my face . . . it was, however, as I found later, a fairly representative lodging-house.

At the Rowton Houses the same shilling would buy a private cubicle, with the use of excellent bathrooms, and a half-a-crown allowed the luxury of a Rowton 'special'.

323

For the real tramp, when the weather made open-air nests untenable, there was the casual ward, or 'spike', provided under the Vagrancy Act of 1824, which laid down that any person sleeping out without visible means of support was a rogue and a vagabond, or on a second conviction, an incorrigible rogue. The tramp has to keep moving, for he is not allowed to enter any one spike, or any two London spikes, more than once in a month. Tobacco may be confiscated at the gate, and if caught smoking he may be turned out. Orwell describes his own first visit:

The spike consisted simply of a bathroom and lavatory, and, for the rest, long double rows of stone cells, perhaps 100 cells in all . . . a smell of soft soap, Jeyes' fluid and latrines—a cold, discouraging, prisonish smell . . . our coats, which we were allowed to keep, to serve as pillows . . . [the cell for two] measured 8 ft. by 5 ft. by 8 ft. high, was made of stone, and had a tiny barred window high up in the wall and a spyhole in the door, just like a cell in a prison. In it were six blankets, a chamber-pot, a hot water pipe, and nothing else whatever. Then, with a shock of surprise, I realised what it was, and exclaimed:

'But I say, damn it, where are the beds?'

'*Beds?*' said the other man, surprised. 'There aren't no beds! What yer expect? This is one of them spikes where you sleeps on the floor. Christ! Ain't you got used to that yet?'

The Chelsea spike was reputed the best in England; it was said that the blankets there were 'more like prison'.

Again moving on one generation, we find that the lodging-house population of London has fallen by about half since Orwell's time. In 1960 there were about twenty-five common lodging-houses, providing about 8,000 beds, of which 500 were for women. The Salvation Army manages most of them, the L.C.C. others, and private enterprise a few. (The Rowton hostels now provide cubicles, and are not registered as common lodging-houses.) Merfyn Turner, former warden of a hostel and the author of *Forgotten Men*, calls them 'artificial and abnormal congregations of the community's misfits'. His report suggests that we have not outgrown the Victorian aim of merely 'alleviating conditions'. He quotes a house in the Midlands where 300 men sleep in surroundings 'reminiscent of Newgate and the debtors' prisons'. But would-be reformers still have to admit that we can hardly rehabilitate by force the stubborn eccentric who demands only the cheapest possible 'kip', and no questions asked. After all, the bachelor clubman of Piccadilly, and the shaggy tramp sleeping in the sun in the park opposite, have only the same desire— 'to attain the advantages of the associated life without the cares of housekeeping'.

324

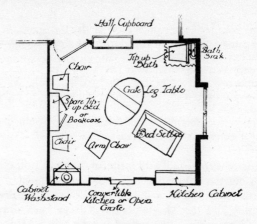

*How to live, cook, dine, bath and sleep in a room 12
feet square, 1924*

55

Blueprints for Bedrooms

IT seems to be the rule in England, at and below the lower-middle class level, that whatever the size of the family, it must fit into a three-bedroom dwelling. This has been so for a century or more, and conditions have improved because families are smaller, rather than because more bedrooms are being provided. In a family with four children, from the time when the youngest is about 2 years old and no longer sleeps with its parents, there must be two to a room, and if one sex predominates, three in one room. This continues until the eldest is about 20. In the Housing Act of 1935 the number of persons per dwelling is limited to

1 room	2 persons
2 rooms	3 persons
3 rooms	5 persons
4 rooms	$7\frac{1}{2}$ persons
5 rooms	10 persons

a child under 10 being half a person. But the Act does not specify how many may sleep in one room; it might legally contain five boys or five girls. The standards are still too low, and in many a slum are not attained. A latter-day Mayhew reports in *The Observer* (27/11/60) on six in a bed:

325

A coal fire licks round a pan of stew in the tiny grate. It is the only cheerful thing about the dark little room on the ground floor of 153, Field Street, in the heart of Liverpool slumdom.

A large lumpy bed takes up most of the floor space. There at night sleep Mrs. Caroline Syers, a plump seventy-two, her pale daughter, Mrs. Margaret Rowan, thirty-two, and *her* four children, aged eight, four, two and eleven months.

Mrs. Syers, who suffers badly from rheumatism, would spend the day in bed too if it weren't for the children.

An author of 1916 could still write of 'a small house of eight or ten rooms', but the era of the 'bed-sitter' had begun. In 1919 Lady Diana Manners could give a dinner party ('Winston, Beaverbrook, Nellie Romilly and the Montagus') in a large back drawing-room overlooking Green Park, that served as a bed-sitter. This unsatisfactory way of living stems from several causes: the emancipation of women, the overcrowding of cities, and a reluctant surrender to the impossibility of running a tall and narrow middle-class town house without servants, whereas to let it out as 'furnished rooms' is a paying proposition. In the mediaeval 'chamber', the bed had ample room to share with the trestle-table, the fireside bench, the aumbry and the chest. Now, it must share far less space not only with the furniture of bedroom and living-room combined, but often with that of a kitchen, scullery, larder, laundry and box-room; any residual space being given to gas and electric meters, and to a selection from the landlady's art treasures, nicely graded in quality according to the number of flights up. Like Dick Swiveller's, the inmate's first thought is to disguise the bed, so that in most bed-sitters it is never properly aired from one washing-day to the next. Sauce bottles tend to get on to the dressing-table, and hair-grips into the tea-cups. The rent of the room would have leased the whole house in its heyday. It is hard to understand why so few landlords find it profitable, below about five guineas a week in London today, to provide the bed-sitter with simple new built-in furniture, long since available, to ameliorate this caravan-like existence.

Even in a one-family house or flat, the bedroom tends to become a bed-sitter. A junior seeking privacy for a guest, for homework, for hobbies, for pop discs, no longer has the choice between living-room, dining-room, morning-room and day-nursery, offered in the larger houses a generation or two ago. Parents, too, need privacy. As Lewis Mumford has said in *The Culture of Cities*:

The cloister in both its public and private form is a constant element in the life of men in cities. Without formal opportunities for isolation and

326

contemplation, opportunities that require enclosed space, free from prying eyes and extraneous stimuli and secular interruptions, even the most externalised and extraverted life must eventually suffer. The home without such cells is but a barracks . . . To-day, the degradation of the inner life is symbolized by the fact that the only place sacred from interruption is the private toilet.

Until lately, the bedroom was unfit for such secondary uses for half the year, because it was unheated. Now, centrally or convection-heated, it can if compactly planned and furnished make a pleasant and very personal retreat, perhaps with a divan-bed, folding-bed, or bunk. Better still, where one medium-sized and one small room adjoin, the old arrangement can be reversed, and the smaller room be given solely to the bed, while the larger serves as a dressing-room and retreat. But even in a newly built house, where a neat little den can be planned in advance for every junior, a trouble arises that bedevils every family dwelling: the family expands, then shrinks again, but the home remains inflexible. One can perhaps add to it, but one cannot subtract. Father's carpentering tools are banished from his roomy upstairs workshop to the garage, to make way for a night-nursery. After the second or third child arrives, the aunt who comes to stay (and only relations can be subjected to the ordeal now) has to doss down in the living-room. But when after some twenty years the birds leave the nest, a middle-aged couple is left with unwanted bedrooms. Solutions have been sought through the use of prefabricated house-sections, or in the 'Scope' house in which the structure is completed, but only the ground floor need at first be divided into rooms and equipped, and the upper floor is left a shell until wanted— the saving, however, is quoted as only £300 in £4,000. The problem may be insoluble, except in terrace-houses or flats that might be planned, like hotel suites, for flexibility, the expanding family taking over bedrooms from the shrinking family next door. This might indeed involve some embarrassing enquiries between neighbours, as to their intentions in family planning, but officials who would gladly take over such a task are plentiful today.

By the 1930's America had taken the lead in domestic planning. A bedroom was no longer a blank rectangle on a blueprint into which furniture had to be fitted later. Taking the habits and needs of the occupant as a starting-point, and separating the functions of sleeping, clothes-storage, dressing and toilet, a logical furniture plan followed, and the walls were built around it. In a plan by Robert L. Weed, the ancillary units are grouped about a central sleeping unit, which thus becomes a clear uncluttered area, needing only a minimum of wall space, with one end given to a large bow window. The dressing-table

Lits nouveaux, *1900. The design above, the author explains, was made 'not from any desire for the austerely plain, but rather from a feeling that line, colour, and texture, together with sound construction, are far more to be desired than stuck-on mouldings and misapplied ornament. The ornament is introduced with restraint, and is of such a character as to obtain its fullest value in the general scheme. It is not plastered on with the relentless hand of one who feels that he has behind him the infinite resources of the carving machine, but is rather suggestive of the craftsman who, pleased with an honest piece of work, out of mere exuberance, adds just a touch of richness, as a proud mother sends away her child to her first party with a happy kiss'.*

328

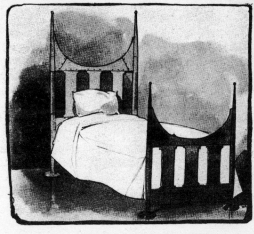

(Facing page, below): *'The wood is stained green, and the enrichments are in gesso work. It will be noticed in all these designs that simplicity is the prevailing note . . . arrived at by a process of severe self-restraint . . . one never tires of beautiful form any more than one tires of a statue from the Parthenon.'*

The bed above 'is even simpler still. It has a certain quaintness, though somewhat severe.' Of the room below, 'Who would not covet such an apartment and such furniture? And what a place for day dreams . . . This is just the chamber in which to read the finishing chapters of a thrilling romance by the light of the latticed panes from the bayed window that faces the West'.

need no longer obstruct the view down into the garden, nor its mirror block the light. Tooth-brushing and gargling need not intrude on a spouse's dreams. A competition-winning small house by J. and N. Fletcher has a central 'mechanical core' linking two blocks, one for living and one for sleeping, treated almost like separate houses. In climates like that of California the use of the roof-deck need not be limited to sun-bathing; it can carry a pleasant outdoor sleeping unit.

The bed itself becomes fully electrified; to its lighting and telephones (long since fitted) are added built-in radio, television, bed-temperature controls, coffeelator, and an extra loudspeaker wired to a microphone above junior's cot. Nothing is lacking to comfort, save perhaps quiet.

Meanwhile a major change has come over the American hotel room. The 'sleeping industry' of the U.S.A. is no mean business; more than $2\frac{1}{2}$ million bedrooms will be 'renting' this very night. Los Angeles alone could cope quite easily with the entire population of the American colonies of 1670. You can still rent a palatial penthouse suite at the Beverley-Hilton at $1 per sq. ft.—one five-year lease at $125,000 has just run out. But the normal room has shrunk. A hotel does not merely sell beds for the night; it has to provide other facilities that may account for 70% of the cost, and show little return. Nearly all the income has to be drawn from 'room rent'. Therefore, since luxuries below always increase, more but smaller rooms are needed. Though smaller, the room must serve for living as well as sleeping— it is no longer enough to design a mattress with edges that can be sat on, and supplement it with one chair. Hence the convertible sitting-sleeping-room, a new weapon in the war with the competing motel. It is well lit, with the long dimension on the window side. Convertible furniture makes it, in the morning, a comfortable if compact apartment, fit for entertaining in—subject in many hotels to the moral safeguard of the rule, that after 5 p.m. all room doors must be left ajar.

English hotel bedrooms, even within a given A.A. classification, now vary more than ever: in a north-country industrial town your room may be large enough to lodge a cricket team, but in a brand-new hotel in Mayfair, you may have to sit on the bed if you offer your guest the chair. The A.A. Handbook will help, if you trouble to learn the code, and know the vital differences between 'CH,HC,pb' and 'ch,hc,(A)'. You can of course stipulate the bedroom you want by the telegraph code; thus DIROH means four rooms with two beds each; ABEC is one room with three beds; TRANQ (more patently) means a very quiet room.

Art nouveau *bed from the Paris Exhibition, 1900*

56

Quintessential Comfort

BY 1900, Ambrose Heal and a few other honest designers had begun to experiment with 'modern' furniture—he won his first international award in that year with a bedroom suite—but their sanity was still rated eccentric. *Art nouveau* was at its zenith, and infected the British bedroom in a brief but violent epidemic. The aim of its disciples sounded reasonable enough—to jettison outworn traditions and to derive new forms from nature—but the results range from light fantasy to nightmare. The brass bedstead went out, for *art nouveau* demanded wood; preferably a softwood in which its coiling tendrils could more easily be cut. This would be enamelled white, or stained in a green appropriate to its vegetable forms, and contrasting nicely with beaten copper trimmings. Losing trade to the cabinet-maker, or rather to his successor the woodworking machinist, the tubewright retaliated with metal beds made with square-sectioned members and square cappings, painted to look like wood. 'At the present time it is easy to obtain bedsteads of artistic character in either wood or metal,' says the author of *The Art and Craft of Home-making* (significant title) in 1913—but by their fruits shall ye know them. Wood wins the day, and the best brass bedstead, some of its knobs a little askew by now, is demoted to a daughter's bedroom; her bed goes to a younger brother; his to the

331

housemaid; the time-scale of domestic taste runs vertically up the house. *Art nouveau*, too, soon goes upstairs; it hardly survives World War I, save for a rare residual influence. In the bedrooms of the 1920's and 1930's, superficial *décor* keeps pace with passing fashions, but no basically new ideas emerge. The furniture plan is the same. The *style moderne* of the Paris Exhibition of 1925, with its blossomy decorative trimmings applied over faintly classical bones, has brief repercussions, as in the 'Gayladye' bedroom furniture of Cohen and Sons, with its multi-coloured *millefiore* inlays. The 'Jazz', 'Modernistic' or 'Futuristic' vogue brings bed-heads and mirror-tops chopped into steps, and kaleidoscopic fabric patterns hardly conducive to rest. Pevsner's survey of shops in 1933 shows 'Jazz' furniture still forming 90% of the stock and display, but this too is mercifully dead before the Nazis—who disapprove of it as decadent—start the next interruption of the peaceful arts.

Architects were taking over furniture design in the 1930's, and for the first time since the eighteenth century, a room and its contents might be a unified whole. The 'Interior Decorator' lost prestige as a designer of furniture. '*Nous ne croyons pas à l'art decoratif*,' said Le Corbusier. Architects of the calibre of Aalto, Behrens, Breuer, Gropius, Rietveld and Van der Rohe were not above designing bedrooms in detail. The general run of architects have not been so successful in this. They do it all on the drawing-board, and spend too little time in the workshop. Their way of designing furniture like buildings, with a structural frame hidden by a skin of plywood, is unsound by a craftsman's standards. There are too many vulnerable edges and surfaces, too much pale veneer protected only by sprayed cellulose *on* the wood instead of polish *in* the wood; cellulose that, starting with a treacly gloss, can end crazed and shabby.

Exhibition-mindedness—the search for press-worthy novelty, the sales-point for the new season's model—has bedevilled design ever since 1851. The Exhibition of Art and Industry of 1935, the most important British effort of its kind since then, was housed in the august premises of the Royal Academy, and its committee boasted such names as Sir Edwin Lutyens, Frank Pick, Sir John Reith, Stanley Baldwin and the Archbishop of Canterbury; no stunt-merchants these; but the competition-winning bedroom was a circular one with a revolving bed. This can hardly have forwarded the cause of sound design in the average English home.

There was a brief vogue for 'off-white', producing some chilly bedrooms, with bedsteads in pale pickled oak, and polar bedspreads; one bedroom with fur walls. The clinical flavour of steel tube furniture did not please for long, nor did the hard glitter of the chromium-

332

1918   1918   1924

1927   1929   1939

The Empire style nightdress of 1909–18 gave way in the war years to shapeless 'jumper-pyjamas' in which women looked like schoolboys; the Edwardian 'boudoir-cap' revived awhile in the 1920's. By the 1930's the habit of pottering about the house in pyjamas was ending the association of nightwear with naughtiness

333

plated bed consort well with soft decorative covers. Tube was more successful in conjunction with the severer upholstery of Aalto's folding-sofa, its back-rest hinging to any angle, and when fully lowered, merging with the seat to form a reasonably wide bed.

Heal's, at The Sign of the Four Poster, still avoided the trend towards furniture designed by salesmen, and Bowman's, the pioneers of unit furniture, were showing what pleasant things could be done on a modest purse, catering more for the bed-sitter than for the luxury show-place. In the locust years, under the Utility Furniture Scheme of 1942 to 1949, it was illegal to manufacture a bed in Britain without a licence, even with pre-war stock materials, and with Purchase Tax at anything up to $66\frac{2}{3}\%$, any broken-down old bed that could somehow be transported to the auction rooms was worth its weight in Spam or dehydrated potato. Manufacturers whose works had been put to making aircraft perhaps learned from aircraft designers to 'simplicate and add lightness'—partly also because of the rising cost of materials, post-war furniture was simpler and lighter. The customer began to be thought of as a user as well as a buyer, as when in 1949 the Furniture Development Council was set up, to promote scientific research, improve design, test performance, and fix standards of quality. The Design Centre and the British Standards Institution continue this good work. Under these purging influences, most beds are now mere rectangular fabric-covered solids, perhaps with a headboard in a light wood or at most with rather over-luscious padding. They may not look particularly interesting, and despite simplicity and mass-production they do seem rather expensive; but certainly they are comfortable, as none ever before. In this respect, indeed, our beds and bedding were perfected only last year, as they will be newly perfected this year, and again next; this annual improvement on perfection is evident in the advertisements:

'Quintessential comfort' . . . 'A standard of comfort never before achieved' . . . 'Something that's going to change bedrooms for ever' . . . beds that 'almost make themselves' . . . 'the so-sweet-to-wake-up-to bedroom suite' . . . 'sleep on a bed of roses' . . . 'thrill to the touch' . . . 'as soft and deep as a dream' . . . sheets of 'silken smoothness' . . . dual-purpose sheets 'fleecy on one side for winter warmth and smooth on the other for summer coolness' . . . translucent sheets . . . sheets [cunning touch!] that 'look so marvellous on your line' . . . blankets of 'whispering softness' . . . 'twice as warm without the weight' . . . bedspreads 'that wash, drip dry and wear for ever' . . . 'heavenly beauty plus down-to-earth quality that *won't let* these bedspreads wear out' . . . 'cloud-soft, sink-into pillows for those who like to feel treasured' . . .

Anthropometrical research having shown that there are more tall men about these days, beds are to be 3 ins. longer, or 4 ins. if the gangling Swedes have their way. The Council of Industrial Design recommends 6 ft. 6 ins. by 3 ft. (single) and 4 ft. 6 in. (double). Some will think these widths mean, for time-lapse films of sleepers, which condense a night's rest into one hilarious minute on the screen, show that we seldom lie still for more than a few minutes at a time; the most relaxed of us, thus speeded up, tosses and turns like a landed fish.

The *monobedders* today are defeating the *polybedders*: an American survey shows that before the war, only 25% of the beds bought there were twins; in 1950, 68% were. The Director of the Family Relations Institute has said sternly that

This movement towards twin beds must stop. It was started by furniture dealers who make twice as much money selling two beds instead of one. The change from a double bed to twin beds is often the prelude to a divorce.

His argument seems to proceed by rather faulty logic, from the correct premises 'the sale of twin beds is rising' and 'the divorce rate is rising'. Might he not equally have concluded that the incompatibility which leads to divorce, leads also to the preference for twin beds? The fact that twin beds are easier to move and make has some bearing on the question, and bed-making is no small matter, for according to the United States Department of Agriculture, the average housewife walks four miles and spends twenty-five hours each year making one bed. (Send not to ask, what this has to do with the Department of Agriculture, whose pedometer would seem more aptly employed on a gardener making a flower-bed.) A popular compromise is a pair of twin beds, sharing one headboard, that open apart for making, or for quarrelling. For incompatible bedfellows there are 'Jack Spratt' beds, half soft, half firm; and double electric blankets with separate controls; even a double bed with a centre-board that can be raised by the unsociable or the coy, reminiscent of the sword of chastity laid of old between knight and lady. There are twin beds set head-to-tail for verbal intercourse. But to the compatible who may seek a 'His and Hers Room', at once masculine and feminine, Bebe Daniels in that fount of bed-lore *The News of the World* offers little hope: 'Believe me, there is no such room. So no matter how loud your man hollers, this room *must* be feminine.' For vacillating bedfellows, there are double mattresses that can be halved by unzipping; for those who live where bedding is dear but current cheap, or for exhibitionists, an electrically heated bed that needs no covers at all. Heralded as new is a divan with a built-in heater, whose advertiser gives no credit to its first inventor, Sheraton. For lovers of the past, there is still a divan with 'Queen Anne headboard and cabriole feet in a luxurious Regency cover'; another in a choice of 'Modern or Queen Anne', with legs available in Queen Anne or Tapered'; and

> . . . for gracious living, the Louis suite . . . a favourite with those people who prefer their furniture to be out of the ordinary. Distinction is the keynote with this suite, which is available in the delicate pastel shades of Ivory, Lilac, Pink Carnation and Mist Green.

The 'Louis Suite', 1960

A leading manufacturer is rather letting his side down, when he cheerfully and publicly states that 45% of the population is colourblind, and 90% form-blind. There may well be a feeling in Tottenham Court Road that such remarks are best left to the Director of the Design Centre, if they need be made at all. A fair percentage of the population, moreover, would seem to be comfort-blind, according to the President of the National Bedding Federation, who declares the British 'mean about their beds':

> Although we place luxurious sleeping equipment at everybody's disposal, many people are still today sleeping, or trying to sleep, on beds and mattresses in the last stages of senile decay.

Why people continue to defy sleep on lumpy, bumpy mattresses is a mystery to me. The same people probably have fine television sets and wonderful refrigerators. But they put their own well-being so low down on their personal priority lists that they economise on their sleep equipment and struggle on with mattresses fit only for the rubbish dump.

In support of which he quotes statistics showing that the average man spends £73 a year on smoking, and only 12s. 6d. a year on his bed. Were these allocations reversed, and men content to sleep soft on fifty-five cigarettes a year, even the poorest classes (teachers, librarians, even clergymen), and certainly the new and prosperous middle class which, according to the social historians, is now emerging, could take for granted a standard of comfort unknown a while since to the most sybaritic of monarchs. Nor should we sneer at comfort, for as Aldous Huxley has said, it is justified because it facilitates thought, while discomfort handicaps thought; but it must not be regarded as an end in itself—

One day, perhaps, the earth will have been turned into one vast feather-bed, with man's body dozing on top of it and his mind underneath, like Desdemona, smothered.

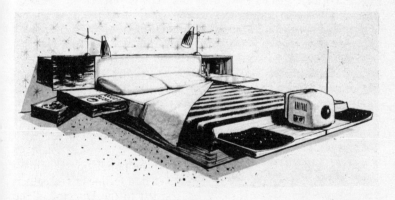

This mink-covered creation by Slumberland, shown at the Furniture Exhibition of 1959, priced at £2,500, and assumed by most visitors to be a publicity stunt, found several buyers

337

57

Bedtime in Space

The problem in a satellite
Is where to put the cat at night

according to an inspired advertisement copywriter; but in their first
thoughts about space-travel, even the experts foresaw no bedtime
problems for the spaceman; indeed, they assumed that in his
'weightless' condition he would enjoy a bodily relaxation even more
complete than that of a swimmer dozing afloat in a warm sea. But
second thoughts, based on experiments, suggested otherwise. Although Gagarin, on his pioneer circuits, startled the observers by
not merely sleeping, but oversleeping, he was tightly tucked in, and
in his tiny cabin escaped some of the troubles awaiting the crew of
a large ship, who cannot stay strait-jacketed for days on end. For
the first brief stage of their journey, the rocket-powered ascent,
lasting only a few minutes, they will lie pressed down by acceleration
forces; and strapped down, but only so that when the rocket thrust
ceases, they will not be flung away by the sudden release of their
mattress springs. The ship is now coasting, without power, at some
five miles a second, in utter silence. Unstrapping himself, the crewman
begins to feel a gap between himself and the mattress; he is now completely weightless. Turning to his tasks, he moves with caution, for
any sudden movement may throw him across the cabin. His senses
of direction, balance and touch have gone awry. He must learn,
like a deep-sea diver, to keep his unruly limbs in their proper positions.
There is no 'up' or 'down', but the crew do their best to keep sociably
upright in relation to each other. To tap a man on the shoulder

is to set him rotating. They learn to drink without choking, or letting their blob of vodka (or Coca-Cola) escape and float around.

By the end of the first day, if still sane, they are getting the hang of things, but at bedtime fresh troubles start. It is generally agreed that the spaceman will be so pre-conditioned by his terrestrial habits, as to be unable to relax and sleep without some simulation of the feel of a normal bed—without some pressure against the mattress to give the sense of lying *down*. Straps like Gagarin's may provide this, but would grow uncomfortable; or perhaps a hinged bed like a 'hot dog' in which the man is the sausage, kept closed by light springs. Possibly he will wear pyjamas with a metal in their weave, and adhere to his bed by virtue of a magnetic mattress. Another suggestion is a 'centrifuge bed' to which he can retire from time to time. But with or without such 'kinesthetic stimulations', it is doubted whether he will enjoy much sleep in this weird bedchamber. The pattern of day and night has gone; the sun and earth shine in a black sky, and he must accustom himself to an artificial wake-sleep cycle. His least movement may still give rise to confusing sensations. Dr. A. E. Slater points out that his 'otoliths', which normally tell him his position or movement in three planes, may signal simultaneously to his brain that he is upright, lying on his left side, and lying on his right. Though he may learn to master these sensations while he is awake, they may bedevil his subconscious mind and make for eerie nightmares. He may have to be drugged, or even put into suspended animation or 'frozen sleep' for most of the trip.

A fan may be needed to prevent his exhaled breath from lingering around his nose and suffocating him. Unless he is strapped to his bed, the jet-propulsion effect of his breathing may start him sliding to and fro, until he is awakened by bumping his head on the wall. On this suggestion, Dr. Slater comments:

Presumably he would then execute a manoeuvre equivalent to that of turning over in bed, and settle down again (if you can call it 'down') for another forty winks before being rudely awakened once more by contact with the opposite wall.

But we have still not quite reached the final solution of this pressing problem, because the jet from the sleeper's nostrils does not pass through his centre of gravity, but is directed obliquely forwards and 'downwards'. So his body would actually rotate slowly round some point in space behind and beyond his feet, and its path would not be a circle but an ever-widening spiral. The poor fellow would still fail to enjoy an uninterrupted night's sleep, and it is a nice mathematical problem to work out his point of first contact, complete with Estimated Time of Arrival.

However, not to worry: any sensible space-sleeper would strap himself in his bunk to ensure a good night's rest.

339

Weightlessness has been produced artificially, for periods of about half a minute, by flying a jet aircraft on a parabolic course. The reports of the subjects vary—some were very unhappy, others not; one said, 'Actually, I've never been so bloody comfortable in all my life. . . .' Dr. von Beckh included in such tests one directed to the problem of waking from sleep in a weightless condition. An experienced pilot was kept awake for forty-eight hours beforehand:

Twenty-five minutes after take-off the subject fell asleep, leaning against the right side of the cockpit. A string was fixed on his left wrist, which the pilot could pull to awaken him. The pilot avoided any rough maneuvers. The aircraft was then flown in a zero-g trajectory and the subject was awakened.

His first impressions upon awakening were that his arms and legs 'were floating away from him' so that he felt a desperate need to pull them back toward his body to maintain some sort of normal posture. He tried to hold on to the canopy and some part of the cockpit. He could not orient himself. He is a pilot of over 500 jet hours and never felt such a pronounced disorientation before.

There are two further remedies for disorientation, but neither will be available in the cramped quarters of the smaller early space-ships. The crew will not enjoy them until they transfer in mid-space to a large permanent satellite. The first is artificial gravity produced by rotating the cabin, so that 'outwards' from the axis becomes 'down'. Dr. von Braun has designed a satellite like a huge car-tyre, 250 ft. across, which by rotating once in every 12·3 seconds produces an earth-like gravity. In this the spaceman could lie normally in a normal bed, with his 'posture sense' restored, watching the earth reel past the windows. The second remedy, designed to ease his psychological troubles, is to emphasise the artificial 'up' and 'down' by introducing as many normal directional features as possible—certainly a conventional 'floor' and 'ceiling', and perhaps deliberately homely furniture. The space-captain's cabin may even one day contain a 'brass' bedstead of anodised aluminium.

Mars is comparatively near, and has been described as 'a rather promising and attractive goal', but the round trip is estimated to take 2 years and 8 months, and some far longer journeys are envisaged. The time must arrive when the captain's wife will come aboard, though the crew may make do with a wife in every satellite. In a weightless ship, where the lightest caress will send the lady spinning, the double bed offers further problems so delicate, that even the most detached of space-scientists treats them with a reserve which we must imitate.

340

58

Envoi

'BUT the quincunx of heaven runs low, and 'tis time to close the five ports of knowledge. We are unwilling to spin out our awaking thoughts into the phantasms of sleep, which often continueth precogitations; making cables of cobwebs, and wildernesses of handsome groves. Beside Hippocrates hath spoke so little, and the oneirocritical masters have left such frigid interpretations from plants, that there is little encouragement to dream of Paradise itself. Nor will the sweetest delight of gardens afford much comfort in sleep; wherein the dulness of that sense shakes hands with delectable odours; and though in the bed of Cleopatra, can hardly with any delight raise up the ghost of a rose.

'Night, which Pagan theology could make the daughter of Chaos, affords no advantage to the description of order; although no lower than that mass can we derive its genealogy. All things began in order, so shall they end, and so shall they begin again; according to the ordainer of order and mystical mathematicks of the city of heaven.

'Though Somnus in Homer be sent to rouse up Agamemnon, I find no such effects in these drowsy approaches of sleep. To keep our eyes open longer, were but to act our Antipodes. The huntsmen are up in America, and they are already past their first sleep in Persia. But who can be drowsy at that hour which freed us from everlasting sleep? or have slumbering thoughts at that time, when sleep itself must end, and, as some conjecture, all shall awake again?'

Sir Thomas Browne, *The Garden of Cyrus*, 1658.

BIBLIOGRAPHY

ACWORTH, W. M. *The Railways of England* (Murray; London, 1889).

ANTONGINI, T. *D'Annunzio* (Heinemann; London, 1938).

AUBREY, J. *Brief Lives* (DICK, O. L., Ed.; Secker & Warburg; London, 1958).

BAYNE-POWELL, R. *Travellers in Eighteenth Century England* (Murray; London, 1951).

BEHREND, G. The First British Sleeping Cars (article in *The Railway World*, February 1961).

BOSWELL, J. *The Life of Samuel Johnson, LL.D.* and *A Journal of a Tour to the Hebrides* (FITZGERALD, P., Ed.; Swan Sonnenschein; London, 1910).

Boswell's London Journal, 1762–1763 (POTTLE, F. A., Ed.; Heinemann; London, 1950).

BROOME, M. A. (Lady BARKER) *The Bedroom and Boudoir* (Macmillan; London, 1878).

BURKE, T. *The English Inn* (Longmans, Green; London, 1930).

BURNEY, F. See D'ARBLAY.

BYRNE, M. ST. C. *Elizabethan Life in Town and Country* (Methuen; London, 1946).

CABANÈS, A. *Les Indiscrétions de l'Histoire* (Michel; Paris, 1907).

Mœurs Intimes du Passé (Michel; Paris, 1908).

CARCOPINO, J. *Daily Life in Ancient Rome* (Pelican; London, 1956).

CARTER, H. and MACE, A. C. *The Tomb of Tutankhamen* (Cassell; London, 1933).

CASANOVA. *My Life and Adventures* (MACHEN, A., Transl.; Joiner & Steele; London, 1932).

CELLINI, B. *Memoirs of Benvenuto Cellini* (Everyman, Dent; London, 1907).

CHEYNE, G. *An Essay on Health and Long Life* (Strahan; London, 1724).

CHIPPENDALE, T. *The Gentleman and Cabinet Maker's Director* (London, 1754).

COWLES, F. *The Case of Salvador Dali* (Heinemann; London, 1959).

CROSSLEY, F. H. *The English Abbey* (Batsford; London, 1935).

CROUCH, J. and BUTLER, E. *The Apartments of the House* (Unicorn; London, 1900).

CUNNINGTON, C. W. and P. *The History of Underclothes* (Joseph; London, 1951).

D'ARBLAY, F. (BURNEY, F.) *Diary and Letters* (BARRETT, C., Ed.; Macmillan; London, 1927).

DAVIES, W. H. *The Autobiography of a Super-Tramp* (Cape; London, 1905).

DAVIS, F. *A Picture History of Furniture* (Hulton; London, 1958).

342

DEFOE, D. *Tour Through the Whole Island of Great Britain, 1724–6* (Davies; London, 1927).

DE LA MARE, W. *Behold This Dreamer* (Faber & Faber; London, 1939). *Early One Morning* (Faber & Faber; London, 1935).

DELONEY, T. *The Novels of Thomas Deloney* (LAWLIS, M. E., Ed.; Indiana University Press; Bloomington, 1961).

DE WOLFE, E. *The House in Good Taste* (Century; New York, 1916).

DICKENS, C. *All The Year Round*, Vol. X (1863). *American Notes* (1842) (Oxford University Press; 1957).

DORÉ, G. and JERROLD, B. *London* (Grant; London, 1872).

DUKES, C. *Health at School* (Rivington, Percival; London, 1894).

DUTTON, R. *The English Country House* (Batsford; London, 1935). *The English Interior* (Batsford; London, 1948).

EARLE, A. M. *Colonial Days in Old New York* (Nutt; London, 1896). *Stage Coach and Tavern Days* (Macmillan; New York, 1905).

EASTLAKE, C. L. *Hints on Household Taste* (Longmans, Green; London, 1878).

EDWARDS, R. and JOURDAIN, M. *Georgian Cabinet Makers* (Country Life; London, 1955).

ELLIS, C. H. *The Beauty of Old Trains* (Allen & Unwin; London, 1952). *Picture History of Railways* (Hulton; London, 1956).
The Development of Railway Engineering (Chap. XV, Vol. IV, of *A History of Technology*; Oxford University Press, 1956).

ERMAN, A. *Life in Ancient Egypt* (Macmillan; London, 1894).

EVELYN, J. *The Diary of John Evelyn* (DOBSON, A., Ed.; Macmillan; London, 1906).

FALKE, J. VON. *Art in the House* (Prang; Boston, Massachusetts, 1879).

FIENNES, C. *The Journeys of Celia Fiennes* (MORRIS, C., Ed.; Cresset Press; London, 1947).

FOURNIER, E. *Le Vieux Neuf* (Dentu; Paris, 1859).

FRAZER, Sir J. G. *The Golden Bough* (Abridged; Macmillan; London, 1954).

FUCHS, E. *Illustrierte Sittengeschichte* (Langen; Munich, 1909).

GEORGE, D. (Ed.) *A Book of Anecdotes* (Hulton; London, 1957).

GEORGE, D. M. *England in Transition* (Pelican; London, 1931).

GIEDION, S. *Mechanisation Takes Command* (Oxford University Press; New York, 1948).

GLYN, A. *Elinor Glyn* (Hutchinson; London, 1955).

GRAY, C. and M. *The Bed* (Nicholson & Watson; London, 1946).

GREGORY, E. W. *The Art and Craft of Home-Making* (Murby; London, 1925).

HABER, H. *Man in Space* (Sidgwick & Jackson; London, 1953).

HANRAHAN, J. S., and BUSHNELL, D. *Space Biology* (Thames & Hudson; London, 1960).

HARLING, R. *Home: A Victorian Vignette* (Constable; London, 1938).

HARPER, C. G. *The Old Inns of Old England* (Chapman & Hall; London, 1906).

HAVARD, H. *Dictionnaire de l'Ameublement* (Paris, 1890–4).

HEPPLEWHITE, G. *Cabinet Maker's and Upholsterer's Guide* (London, 1787).

HERODOTUS. *The History of Herodotus* (RAWLINSON, G., Transl.; Dent; London, 1910).

HOLLIS, C. *Eton* (Hollis & Carter; London, 1960).

HOMER. *The Odyssey* (LAWRENCE, T. E., Transl.; Milford; London, 1935).

HUSBAND, J. *The Story of the Pullman Car* (McClurg; Chicago, 1917).

JAMES, M. R. *Ghost Stories of an Antiquary* (Penguin; London, 1937).

JAPP, A. H. *Industrial Curiosities* (Marshall Japp; London, 1880).

JOEL, D. *The Adventure of British Furniture* (Benn; London, 1953).

KEVERNE, R. *Tales of Old Inns* (Collins; London, 1949).

LEWINSOHN, R. *A History of Sexual Customs* (MAYCE, A., Transl.; Longmans, Green; London, 1958).

LITCHFIELD, F. *Illustrated History of Furniture* (Truslove & Shirley; London, 1892).

LLOYD, H. A. *Some Outstanding Clocks . . . 1250–1950* (Hill; London, 1958).

LLOYD, N. *A History of the English House* (Architectural Press; London, 1930).

MACQUOID, P. and EDWARDS, C. H. R. *The Dictionary of English Furniture* (Country Life; London, 1954).

MARX, G. *Beds* (Farrar & Rinehart; New York, 1930).

MAYHEW, H. *Criminal Prisons of London* (Griffin, Bohn; London, 1862).

MIREAUX, E. *Daily Life in the Time of Homer* (Allen & Unwin; London, 1959).

MORGAN, K. R. How to Make the Round Table Square: article in *Horizon*, May 1960.

MORGAN, R. B. *Readings in Social History* (Cambridge University Press, 1923).

MORSE, F. C. *Furniture of the Olden Time* (Macmillan; New York, 1903).

NEVINS, A. *America Through British Eyes* (Oxford University Press; New York, 1948).

NUTTING, W. *Furniture Treasury* (Macmillan; New York, 1949).

O'DEA, W. T. *The Social History of Lighting* (Routledge & Kegan Paul; London, 1958).

ODOM, W. M. *A History of Italian Furniture* (Doubleday, Page; New York, 1919).

ORMSBEE, T. H. *The Story of American Furniture* (Macmillan; New York, 1946).

ORWELL, G. *Down and Out in Paris and London* (Gollancz; London, 1933).

OWENS, P. *Bed and Sometimes Breakfast* (Sylvan Press; London, 1944).

PANTON, J. E. *From Kitchen to Garret* (Ward & Downey; London, 1888).

PENDLETON, J. *Our Railways* (Cassell; London, 1894).

PEPYS, S. *The Diary of Samuel Pepys* (BRIGHT, M., Ed.; Everyman; London, 1953).

POLLEN, J. H. *Furniture Ancient and Modern* (S. Kensington Museum; London, 1875).

PONSONBY, F. *Recollections of Three Reigns* (Eyre & Spottiswoode; London, 1951).

POWER, E. *Mediaeval People* (Pelican; London, 1954).

PÜCKLER-MUSKAU, H. L. H. F., VON. *Tour in England, Ireland and France, 1828–9* (Wilson; London, 1832).

PUGIN, A. W. *Pugin's Gothic Furniture* (Ackermann; London, 1835).

QUENNELL, P. *Mayhew's London* (Pilot Press; London, 1949).

RADFORD, E. and M. A. *Encyclopaedia of Superstitions* (Rider; 1947).

RENDLE, W. *The Inns of Old Southwark* (Longmans, Green; London, 1888).

REYNOLDS, R. *Beds* (Deutsch; London, 1952).

ROE, F. G. *Victorian Furniture* (Phoenix; London, 1952).

ROUSSEAU, J. J. *Confessions* (unexpurgated; no imprint; no date).

SACKVILLE-WEST, E. *And So To Bed* (Phoenix; London, 1947).

SALZMAN, L. F. *Building in England* (Oxford University Press; 1952).
England in Tudor Times (Batsford; London, 1926).
English Life in the Middle Ages (Oxford University Press; 1926).

SAMPSON, H. *A History of Advertising* (Chatto & Windus; London, 1874).

SHEARER, T. *Designs for Household Furniture* (London, 1788).

SHERATON, T. *The Cabinet Dictionary* (London, 1803).

SHORTER, A. W. *Everyday Life in Ancient Egypt* (Sampson, Low, Marston; London, 1932).

SINGER, HOLMYARD, HALL and WILLIAMS (Eds.) *A History of Technology* (Oxford University Press; 1956).

SITWELL, E. *The English Eccentrics* (Faber & Faber; London, 1933).

STANLEY, A. (Ed.) *The Bedside Book* (Gollancz; London, 1932).

STENTON, D. M. *English Society in the Early Middle Ages* (Penguin; London, 1951).

STOPES, M. C. *Sleep* (Chatto & Windus; London, 1956).

STRANGE, T. A. *English Furniture, Decoration, Woodwork and Allied Arts* (Strange; London, undated, *c.* 1890).

SUMMERSON, J. *Architecture in Britain, 1538–1830* (Penguin; London, 1953).

TAINE, H. *Notes sur l'Angleterre* (Paris, 1872).

TREVELYAN, G. M. *English Social History* (Longmans, Green; London, 1944).

TURNER, E. S. *A History of Courting* (Joseph; London, 1954).

TURNER, M. *Forgotten Men* (National Council of Social Service; London, 1960).

'TWO'. *Home Life with Herbert Spencer* (Simpkin, Marshall; London, 1906).

VIOLLET-LE-DUC, E. E. *Dictionnaire Raisonné du Mobilier Français* (Morel; Paris, 1871).

WALN, N. *The House of Exile* (Cresset Press; London, 1933).

WALPOLE, H. *Horace Walpole's Correspondence* (LEWIS, W. S., Ed.; Oxford University Press; 1937).

WARD-JACKSON, P. *English Furniture Designs* (H.M.S.O.; London, 1958).

WARE, I. *A Complete Body of Architecture* (London, 1756).

WELLS, R. B. D. *Good Health, and How to Secure It* (Vickers; 1885).

WHITTICK, A. *The Small House: Today and Tomorrow* (Hill; London, 1957).

WILSON, J. D. *Life in Shakespeare's England* (Cambridge University Press; 1911).

WRIGHT, T. *A History of Domestic Manners and Sentiments in England During the Middle Ages* (Chapman & Hall; London, 1862).

YOUNG, G. M. (Ed.) *Early Victorian England* (Oxford University Press; 1934).

ACKNOWLEDGEMENTS

I am grateful to T. W. Bagshawe (for sundry material), to C. Hamilton Ellis (for correcting and amplifying the chapter on railway sleeping-cars), to Walter Ison (for reading the MS. and for sound advice), to Cyril Nortcliffe (for hospitality and guidance at the Oates Library at Selborne), and to Dr. A. E. Slater (for checking the chapter on space-travel—which nevertheless becomes daily more out-of-date).

Of the sources listed in the Bibliography, five must be acknowledged further, having been especially valuable: Fuchs' *Illustrierte Sittengeschichte*, Giedion's *Mechanisation Takes Command*, the Grays' anthology *The Bed*, Havard's *Dictionnaire de l'Ameublement*, and Wright's *History of Domestic Manners*.

The historian of the bedroom ought not to evade what Sheraton delicately calls 'the accidental occasions of the night', but the 'commode' and its many variants, like the dressing-table and the bath (often in the bedroom, and sometimes even combined with the bed), have been treated very briefly; they were fully covered in my previous book *Clean and Decent*.

The sources of illustrations are acknowledged on pages 347–51.

ILLUSTRATIONS

(Illustrations are not numbered, but are identified by their page-numbers. Sources included in the Bibliography are identified here by the authors' surnames only, in capitals. All drawings so described have been made for this book.)

iii, Mediaeval half-tester and hutch. (WRIGHT, from MS. Latin Bible, Bibl. Nat., Paris, 6829.) v, Adjustable couch and 'Literary Machine'. (Catalogue of John Carter, London, 1897.) vii, Engraving, '*Am Rande des Bettes*.' (FUCHS.) 1, Egyptian bed, Dynasty XVIII. (Drawing from photograph, Bettman Archive, *Metropolitan Museum of Arts*, N.Y.) 2, Details of a Dynasty I bed, *c.* 2000 B.C. (SINGER.) 3, Bedchamber of Queen Hetep-Heres, *c.* 2690 B.C. (SINGER.) 5(*a*), Bed from Tutankhamen's tomb, *c.* 1350 B.C. (Drawing from photograph, CARTER & MACE.) (*b*) Detail of ivory foot-panel: the god Bes. (Source as above.) (*c*) Head-rest from tomb of Tutankhamen. (Source as above.) (*d*) Head-rest from tomb of Tutankhamen. (Source as above.) (*e*) Ivory head-rest of the Middle Kingdom. (Drawing from photograph, SHORTER, from Brit. Mus. 30727.) 6, King Ashur-bani-pal. (*Horizon*, May 1960, from Heuzey, L., *Recherches sur les Lits Antiques*, Paris, 1873.) 7, From ninth century MS. (VIOLLET-LE-DUC.) 8, Greek couch and table. (LITCHFIELD.) 9, Greek couch. (POLLEN, from Lenormant & De Witte.) 11, Roman bronze couch from bas-relief at Boscoreale, first century A.D. (LITCHFIELD.) 14, Tenth-century bed. (VIOLLET-LE-DUC, from MS. Bible, Imperial Library, Strasbourg.) 15, The litter of Solomon. (VIOLLET-LE-DUC, from twelfth-century MS. by Herrade de Landsberg, Imperial Library, Strasbourg.) 16, The death of Holofernes. (Source as 15.) 17, 'Bedsteads' from an Anglo-Saxon MS. of the eleventh century. (Drawing from photograph, POLLEN, from Brit. Mus., *Claudius*, B. iv. fol. 27.) 19(*a*) (WRIGHT, from MS. *Holy Grail*, Brit. Mus., MS. Addit. 10293.) (*b*) (WRIGHT, from Brit. Mus., Harl. MS. 603.) (*c*) (VIOLLET-LE-DUC, from *Les Miracles de Notre Dame*, Bibl. du Seminaire de Soissons.) (*d*) (Source as 19(*b*.)) (*e*) (WRIGHT, from MS. *Caedmon*.) 22, Sir Launcelot at the queen's window. (WRIGHT, from *Romance of the Holy Grail*, Brit. Mus., MS. Addit. 10292–4.) 23, Mediaeval half-tester and hutch. (WRIGHT, from MS. Latin Bible, Bibl. Nat., Paris, 6829.) 24, The Perche, fifteenth century. (FUCHS.) 30, Neolithic stone bed at Skara Brae, Orkney Islands. (Drawing from photograph, Central Office of Information.) 32, Bed with turned legs, from fourteenth-century English MS. (SINGER.) 33, (Source as 22.) 34, (WRIGHT, from Brit. Mus., MS. Cotton, *Nero*.) 35, Mediaeval half-tester and hutch. (Source as 23.) 36, (FUCHS, from fifteenth-century woodcut.) 39, Knight and lady in bedchamber, fourteenth century. (LITCHFIELD, from miniature in *Otho*, by Christine de Pisan.) 42, Durham Cathedral Priory (Benedictine): the dorter, now a library. (Drawing from photograph, CROSSLEY.) 44, A well-behaved monk. (*Horizon*, May 1960, from Von Spalart, *Tableau Historique des Costumes*, Paris, 1804.) 45, A less well-behaved monk.

(FUCHS, from woodcut, Basle, 1493.)   47, The birth of St. Edmund. (POLLEN, from MS. *Life of St. Edmund, c.* 1400.)   52, (WRIGHT, from fourteenth-century MS. *Romance of Meliadus*, Brit. Mus., MS. Addit. 12228.)   55, (HAVARD, from miniature from *Enseignemens d'Anne de France*, St. Petersburg.) 56, Charles VI of France (1380–1422) gives audience. (HAVARD, from contemporary miniature.)   59, Wax effigy of Henry IV on his *lit de parade*, 1610. (HAVARD, from contemporary engraving.) 60, The truckle-bed. (WRIGHT, from MS. romance *Le Comte d'Artois*.) 62, The Great Bed of Ware. (POLLEN.)   65, Early Renaissance bed at the Chateau of Pau . . . 1562. (HAVARD.)   66, French bed . . . sixteenth century. (HAVARD.)   69, The Great Bed of Ware. (*Victoria & Albert Museum.*)   70, (FUCHS, from German woodcut.)   73, Dutch bedchamber, early sixteenth century. (Detail, from HAVARD, from V. de Vriese.)   75, Late fourteenth-century inn. (WRIGHT, from MS. romance *Les Quatre Fils d'Aymon*, Bibl. Nat., Paris, 6970.)   77, Fifteenth-century inn. (WRIGHT, from MS. *Cent Nouvelles Nouvelles*, Hunterian Lib., Glasgow.)   79, Brothel scene. (FUCHS.)   83, The Bishop blesses the marriage bed. (FUCHS.)   85(*a*), Bed, *c.* 1600, from the Davanzati collection, Florence. (Drawing from photograph from ODOM.) (*b*) Bed, *c.* 1650, from the Salvadori collection, Venice. (Source as 85(*a*).)   87, The bed staff, 1631. (WRIGHT, from print by Abraham Bosse.)   91, A Lady of Quality, 1686. (FUCHS, from French engraving.)   93, Bedchamber of *c.* 1631. (Source as 87.)   97, *Chambre de Parade* by Daniel Marot, seventeenth century. (HAVARD.)   98, Bed by Daniel Marot. (HAVARD.) 101, 'Winter Bed' of Marie Antoinette at Fontainbleau. (HAVARD.) 103, Chaise Longue or Day-bed . . . 1680–1700. (Drawing from photograph, *Metropolitan Museum of Arts*, N.Y.)   105, *Lit à impériale*; *lit à la turque*; *lit à la romaine*; *lit à la Dauphine*; *lit d'ange*; *lit à la duchesse*; *lit à quenouilles*; *lit clos*; *lit en tombeau*. (HAVARD.)   106, State Bedchamber of Louis XIV (1643–1715) at Versailles. (HAVARD, from drawing by H. Toussaint.)   109, Alcove at the Palais-Royale, by Roubo fils. (HAVARD.)   110, Bedchamber in the Pompeiian manner by Percier and Fontaine. (HAVARD.)   111, Alcove of the Restoration period. (HAVARD.)   112, Bed of the Empire period. (HAVARD.)   113(*a*), Napoleon's state bed at Fontainbleau. (HAVARD.) (*b*) Napoleon's iron camp-bed. (*Horizon*, May 1960, from Hazen, C., *Modern Europe*; Holt, New York, 1917.)   114, (FUCHS.)   117, The death of Nero. (WRIGHT, from *Josephus*, Bibl. Nat., Paris 7015.)   119, *Lit à impériale*, late sixteenth century. (HAVARD.)   122, The bedroom in Chelsea where Turner died. . . . (ROE.)   124, 'King Charles' Bedroom' at the *Saracen's Head*, Southwell. (HARPER.)   131, Sixteenth-century bedchamber. (WRIGHT, from Aldegraver, 1553.)   132, Italian bedchamber, 1499. (GIEDION, from Colonna.)   135, Queen Anne's bed, Hampton Court. (STRANGE.) 138, State bedroom by Sir James Thornhill, *c.* 1720. (WARD-JACKSON.) 142, Lacquered and gilt bed from Badminton, probably by Chippendale, *c.* 1760. (*Victoria & Albert Museum.*)   145, State Bed by Chippendale, 1761. (CHIPPENDALE.)   146, English State Bed by Sheraton, 1803. (STRANGE.)   148, (FUCHS.)   150, Drawing by Robert Adam: A Bed for Osterley Park, 1755. (*Soane Museum.*)   153, A Gothic Bed. (PUGIN.) 154, Eighteenth or early nineteenth-century bed, New York State. (Drawing from photograph from NUTTING.)   157, Late seventeenth-century American folding bed. (Drawing from photograph, *Metropolitan Museum of Arts*, New York.) 158, American 'Sheraton' bed with ogee canopy frame, 1790–1800. (Drawing from photograph from NUTTING.) 159, Early American cradle. (Drawing from photograph from NUTTING.) 160, Candle-snuffers. (HAVARD, from Cats.) 162, The White Hart ınn, Southwark, in 1827. (RENDLE.) 165, (CUNNINGTON, from Rowlandson.) 167, Toilet or Dressing Table for a Lady, by Chippendale, 1762. (CHIPPENDALE.) 168, Cradle, late fifteenth century. (WRIGHT.) 170, Swaddling. (WRIGHT, from fourteenth-century MS.) 171(*a*), American wicker cradle, *c*. 1620. (Drawing from photograph from NUTTING.) (*b*) A '*Mayflower*' cradle—made mainly of American white oak. (Source as 171(*a*).) 173, Cradles: (*a*) Fourteenth century. (WRIGHT, from MS. *Caedmon*.) (*b*) Fifteenth century. (HAVARD.) (*c*) Elizabeth I. (*Illustrated London News*, 1858.) (*d*) Seventeenth century, beaten copper. (HAVARD.) (*e*) Henry IV of France, *b*. 1589, Chateau de Pay. (HAVARD.) (*f*) Venice, *c*. 1750, painted wood. (Drawing from photograph from ODOM.) (*g*) Roi de Rome, son of Napoleon I. (HAVARD.) 173, Cradles, continued: (*a*) fifteenth century, painted wood. (HAVARD.) (*b*) Sixteenth century. (HAVARD.) (*c*) Seventeenth century. (HAVARD.) (*d*) The 'Victoria Regia Cradle', 1851. (*e*) 'Berceaunette', whence 'bassinet'. (Advertisement by Mrs. Addley Bourne, 1878.) (*f*) Iron Cradle, 1890. (Catalogue of J. Longley & Co., Leeds, undated.) 175, Cradle made for Queen Victoria, 1850. (LITCHFIELD.) 177, Adjustable couch, 1898. (Advertisement of John Carter in *The Queen*.) 181, The Hygienic Dog Bed, 1938. (Drawing from photograph, advertisement in *Animal World*.) 185, A Perfect Invalid's Adjustable Couch. (Advertisement of A. Carter Ltd., *The Queen*, 1896.) 186, Adjustable couch and 'Literary Machine'. (Catalogue of John Carter, London, 1897.) 193, A Belgian invention. (Coppersmith, F. & Lynx, J. J., *Patent Applied For*; Press & Publicity, *c*. 1949.) 194, Van Gogh's bedroom at Arles. (*The Letters of Van Gogh*; Thames & Hudson, 1958.) 197, A candle-lighting alarm clock. (HAVARD.) 199, (FUCHS, from Gavarni, 1830.) 201, 'Summer Bed in Two Compartiments'. (SHERATON.) 203, Italian alarm clock, copper. (HAVARD.) 205, Wooden alarm clock, German, sixteenth century. (HAVARD.) 207(*a*), Clock recording Nuremberg hours, *c*. 1400. (Drawing from photograph from LLOYD, H. A.) (*b*) Monastic alarm clock, *c*. 1500. (Source as 207(*a*).) 209, 'The Burglar's Horror'. (Advertisement of Clarke Ltd., *Illustrated London News*, 1890.) 210(*a*), 'Nursery Lamp Food Warmer' and 'Night Light Watch Holder'. (Advertisement of Clarke Ltd., *The Queen*, 1896.) (*b*) 'Electric Night Clock'. (Advertisement, *The Queen*, 1896.) 212, Dormitory at Westminster. (Pugin, from *History of the Colleges of Winchester, Eton and Westminster, etc.*, Ackermann, 1816.) 216, Warming pan. (HAVARD.) 217, Chambermaid warming a bed. (HAVARD, from a painting by Freudenberg.) 220, Bed-wagon or *moine*, eighteenth century. (HAVARD.) 221, Belly-warmer, eighteenth century, at Bristol City Museum. (*Illustrated London News*.) 224, Bed by Du Cerceau. (HAVARD.) 226, Scandinavian bed. (*Horizon*, May 1960; Culver Service.) 229, Russian bed. (*Horizon*, May 1960.) 230, Bedstead in carved ebony, 1851. (LITCHFIELD.) 231, Teak bed of the Japanese imperial family. (*Horizon*, May 1960.) 233, Bedchamber of St. Jerome, by Dürer, 1511. (WRIGHT.) 235, Mediaeval cradle. (VIOLLET-LE-DUC.) 237, Iron bedstead, 1904. (Advertisement, *Strand Magazine*.) 238, 'Half-tester bedstead in iron or brass', 1855. (HARLING, from

Deane's Almanack.) 239, Spring mattresses: (*a*) British Patent 99, 12. Jan. 1865. (GIEDION.) (*b*) J. Longley Ltd., Leeds, 1890 (catalogue). (*c, d, e*) Heal & Son Ltd., 1896 (catalogue). 241, Hammock of 1893. (GIEDION; U.S. Patent 495532, 18 April 1893.) 244, Charles Dickens' 'State-room' in S.S. *Britannia*, 1842. (Redrawn from GIEDION.) 246, Hammock combined with mosquito net, 1885. (GIEDION; U.S. Patent 329763, 3 November 1885.) 247, Hammock combined with tricycle, 1883. (GIEDION; U.S. Patent 278431, 29 May 1883.) 248, 'Leveson's Patent Telescopic Couch'. (Advertisement of 1895.) 249(*a*), English invalid bed, 1794. (GIEDION; British Patent 2005, 7 Aug. 1794.) (*b*) 'Sofa or Machine for the Cure of Invalids', 1813. (GIEDION: British Patent 3744, 1 Nov. 1813.) 250, Thomas Websters 'Invalid Couch', *c.* 1840. (Redrawn from GIEDION.) 251(*a*), Jacob Schuebler's 'Newly-invented French Bed', *c.* 1730. (GIEDION, from *Neu inventierte franzoesische Feldbetten*, Nuremberg, 1730.) (*b*) 'Table-Bedstead', 1849. (GIEDION; U.S. Patent 6884, 20 Nov. 1849). 253, 'Wardrobe Bed', 1859. (GIEDION; U.S. Patent 23604, 12 April 1859.) 254(*a*), 'Bed Lounge', 1872. (GIEDION: U.S. Patent 127741.) (*b*) Sheraton's 'Camp Bedstead', 1803. (STRANGE.) 255, 'Parlor Bed', 1891. (GIEDION, from *Decorator & Furnisher*, New York, 1891.) 256–257, Home comforts from the catalogue of John Carter, 1897: 256(*a*), 'Iron Folding Chair Bedstead'. (*b*) 'Reading in the Garden'. (*c*) 'The Triclinium'. 257(*a*), 'The Prince's Chair'. (*b*) 'The Carlton Treble-Action. Chair and Couch Combined'. (*c*) 'The Triclinium', folded for travelling. 258, Camp bed, 1929. (Catalogue, Army & Navy Stores Ltd., 1929.) 259(*a*), 'Servant's Press Bedstead.' (Catalogue of Heal & Son Ltd., 1896). (*b*) Wardrobe bed, 1925. (GREGORY.) (*c*) Sofa bed, 1945. (GREGORY.) (*d*) 'Put-u-Up' convertible settee. (Greaves & Thomas.) 260, Sixteenth-century litter. (CABANÈS.) 263, Sleeping-car, Baltimore & Ohio R.R., 1847. (GIEDION, from *L'Illustration*, Paris, 1848.) 265, Night travel in an American 'day-coach' in the 'sixties. (ELLIS.) 266(*a*), (*b*), (*c*), (*d*), (GIEDION.) 267, 'Railway Folding Leg Rest'. (Catalogue of John Carter, London, 1897.) 268, '*Train Impérial*' presented to Napoleon III ... 1857. (GIEDION, from *L'Illustration*, Paris, 1857.) 269, Night travel on the C.P.R., 1888. (ELLIS.) 270, British Pullman sleeping-car, 1874. (*The Graphic*.) 271, Private room in British Pullman sleeping-car, 1874. (*The Graphic*.) 273, Pullman, 'Master Room' convertible for day and night use, 1939. (GIEDION.) 275, Detail from drawing by John Leech, *c.* 1850. (*Punch*.) 276, Drawing by John Leech, 1853. (*Punch*.) 280, Bedroom furniture of 1878. (BROOME.) 284, Jaeger nightgown, early 1880's. (CUNNINGTON.) 285, (DORÉ.) 286, Separate cell in Pentonville Prison, *c.* 1850. (MAYHEW.) 287, Dormitory at Coldbath Fields Prison, *c.* 1850. (MAYHEW.) 288, Separate sleeping-cell in one of the new wings of the female convict prison at Brixton, *c.* 1850. (MAYHEW.) 291, Night refuge in London, 1872. (DORÉ.) 292, The *Charité* Hospital, Paris. (HAVARD, from Abraham Bosse.) 294, 'Invalid's Bedstead and Patent Mattress', 1897. (Catalogue of John. Carter, London.) 295, Beds from a catalogue of 1880. (Army & Navy Co-operative Society.) 296, 'Nightgown in cambric, with frills and insertions of real Valenciennes lace', 1896. (Advertisement of Woolland Bros., Knightsbridge, in *The Queen*.) 299, Iron bedstead by Eastlake, 1878. (EASTLAKE.) 303, Redecorating the bedroom, 1896. (Advertisement from *The Queen*.) 304–5, 'The Chesham Suite', 1895. (Catalogue of W. Wallace & Co.,

London.) 307, 'Handsome Model Nightgown', 1896. (Advertisement from *The Queen*.) 306(*a*), Jaeger complete sleeping suit, 1885. (CUNNINGTON.) (*b*) Jaeger pyjamas, 1899. (CUNNINGTON.) (*c*) Pyjamas by Peter Robinson, 1902. (CUNNINGTON.) 308, A bed of Napoleon. (HAVARD.) 310, Bed by Majorelle, Paris, *c*. 1870. (HAVARD.) 312, The Paris-made bed of a maharajah. (*Horizon*; Kollar-Christophle.) 313, '*Boudoir Moderne*', by Penon of Paris, *c*. 1880. (HAVARD.) 315, (Advertisement, Booth and Fox.) 318, Artistic Corner Wardrobe, 1895. (Wm. Wallace & Co's catalogue.) 320, 'The Twopenny Leanover'. (Daumier.) 323, (Advertisement from *The Queen*.) 325, How to live in a single room, 1924. (GREGORY.) 328–9, Art Nouveau in the Bedroom, 1900. (CROUCH & BUTLER.) 331, Art Nouveau bed by Perol Frères, Paris Exhibition. 1900. (Drawing from photograph from JOEL.) 333, Ladies' nightwear, 1918–39. (All from CUNNINGTON except '1929' from advertisement, Army & Navy Stores.) 336, The 'Louis suite', 1960. (L. Marcus Ltd.) 337, The 'Slumberland' mink-covered £2,500 bed, 1959. (Slumberland.) 338, (Source as 237.) 341, (WRIGHT.)

INDEX

Aalto, A. 334
Abishag the Shunnamite 218
Abyssinia (nightwear in) 202
Accouchement, *see* Childbirth
Adam, John and Robert 143, 150–2
Addison 197
Adelaide, Queen (her private railway
  carriage) 262
Air-bed, -mattress 223, 241, 242
Alarms, alarm-clocks 197, 203–9, 211,
  281
'Alarum bedstead' 208
Albert, Prince Consort 228, 290, 308
Albret, Jeanne d' 65
Alcoves 108–11
Alençon, Duke of (woos Queen
  Elizabeth) 73
Alexander, Lord (his female valet) 130
Alexandra, Queen 273, 308
Alfred, King 18, 20
Alienor of Poitiers 40
Allen, Thomas (regains his watch) 204
All Hallows Eve 234
Amboise, Cardinal d' 61
America, North 154–9, 170, 245, 252,
  262–9, 272–3, 315–19, 327, 330, 335
Anglo-Saxon, *see* Saxons
Anne, Empress of Russia 190, 227
— of Brittany 58
— St. 58
Antarctic (sleeping-bags) 231
Antin, Duc d' 102
Antoinette, Marie 100
Arthur, King 37, 224
'Arthur's O'on' 224
Art nouveau 296, 331–2
Artois, Comte d' (his martial bedroom)
  227
Artois, Le Comte d' 60
Arundel Castle (chimney-sweep at) 183
— Earl of 48, 50
Ashur-bani-pal (Sardanapalus) 6
Assyria 6
Aston Hall (Long Gallery at) 64
Aubrey, John 72, 187–9, 235
Augier, Emile 310–11
Australian aboriginals 234
Avranches, Bishop of (his hot-water
  bottle) 220

Babel, Tower of 8
Bacon, Francis 79, 187, 219

Badminton 142–3
Balzac (on double beds) 200
Bancs-lits, banlits 103
Barbellion, W. N. P. 236
Barker, Lady 238, 276, 297
'Bart's' (St. Bartholomew's) Hospital
  294
Bassinoire 221
Baths, bathrooms 9, 10, 13, 20, 26, 37,
  74, 101, 136, 159, 250, 252, 279,
  308–9, 319
Bayard (shares his bed) 58
Beaumont, Duc de (nursed to death)
  171
Beaumont and Fletcher (share a bed)
  200
Beauty sleep (a myth) 198
Bec Abbey (schoolboys at) 213
Beckford, William 152
Beckh, Dr. von 340
Bedding ceremonies, *see* Bridal
  customs
Bedford, Duke of 144, 147
Bed-making 18, 25, 29, 53–4, 201, 220,
  236, 282, 335
Bed-pushing 184
Beds, *see* Air, Box, Camp, Celestial,
  Day, Death, Dog, Double, Field,
  Folding, Four-poster, Hospital, Hot-
  water, Ice, Invalid, Jack, Jack
  Spratt, Marriage, Parlor, Piano,
  Press, Revolving, Safari, Self-pro-
  pelled, Sleigh, Sofa, Spool, Stone,
  Summer, Tent, Truckle, Trussing,
  Twin, Under-eaves, Wardrobe,
  Wheel, Winter, *see also* Lit
Bed-sitting-rooms 252, 325–7, 334
Bed-staff 53–4, 87
Bed-twitch 126
Bed-wagon 220
Bed-wetting (by Dali) 229, (a cure) 233
Beebe, Lucius 269
Beerbohm, Max 178
Beethoven (improperly dressed) 178
Belly-warmer 221–2
Bennett, Arnold (on American hotels)
  319
Beowulf 20–1
Bernard, St. (central heating for) 217
Bernhardt, Sarah 311
Berry, Duchesse de 174
Berseil, bersouère (berceau) 170

352

355

357